New Stepping Stones 3

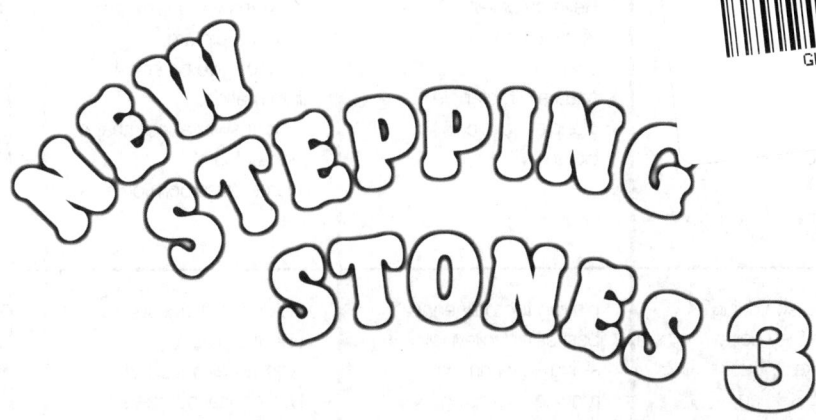

TEACHER'S GUIDE

Julie Ashworth   John Clark

Syllabus	2
Introduction	7
Lesson Notes	14
Resource File	164
Wordlist	179

LONGMAN

Syllabus

	Unit	Main Structures	Vocabulary	Main Communicative Functions	Tasks and Activities
Shape		What colour's ...? What's your name? How old are you? How many ... have you got? What's your favourite ...? Is this...? *Adjective + colour + noun*	*Revision of level 2 vocabulary* shapes square rectangle triangle circle clown	Ask/answer questions about a picture. Ask for/give personal information. Ask/answer about shapes and colours. Name classroom objects.	Revision quiz Game (I-spy) The Shape Game Action game Group survey Listening task Puzzles Workcards Make magic pictures
Spare Time	**1a**	What's he/she doing? What are they doing? Do you like ...? I like + VERB -ing I don't like + VERB -ing I'm/not good at ... Which car is *first*? The *red* one	playing football/tennis/ basketball/volleyball skiing swimming running jumping hopping first second third last win	Ask/answer questions about a picture. Ask/talk about sports. Use ordinal numbers to talk about races.	Group survey Listening task The Sports Game Action game Reading task Personal file
	1b	Can you/he/she...? I can/can't ... What can I/he/she do? Who can ...?	swim dance play the piano/guitar ride a horse/bike ski sing skip jump read write skate	Ask/talk about ability using **can**.	Listening tasks Personal survey Mime game Memory game Bingo Board game Class surveys Wordsearch
	1c	What are these? Where's this ... from? This ... is from ... Is this *English*? Are these *English*? No, it's/they're ... Do you collect ...?	*countries/nationalities* stamps coins autograph postcard badge	Talk about collecting things. Ask/say what country things are from. Ask/talk about nationalities.	Make a badge Writing Puzzle Listening task Personal file
	1d	What's he/she doing? What are they doing? He's/she's/they're +VERB -ing Are you +VERB -ing? I love/hate +VERB -ing Do you like +VERB -ing? Does he/she like +VERB -ing?	watching TV washing up cleaning having a bath sleeping eating drinking reading writing drawing painting doing homework	Ask/say what people are doing. Talk about everyday activities. Talk about what you like doing.	Action game Mime game Personal file Listening task Personal survey Group survey Song Story listening/reading
	1e	I/you/they like/don't like +VERB -ing He/she likes/doesn't like +VERB -ing Do you like +VERB -ing? Can you ...?	comic story hero magazine watch collect hobbies team	Talk about comics/magazines and spare time. Describe characters from fiction. Write a story.	Personal survey Personal file Stepping Stones game Tongue twister Write and illustrate a story Story listening/reading
	1f	*Revision of all structures from unit*	countries flag English the EU (European Union) gold star earthworm	Recognise and describe flags.	Board game Write and colour Supersnake Evaluation

Places

Unit	Main Structures	Vocabulary	Main Communicative Functions	Tasks and Activities
2a	Which town ...? Go ... Where's ...? In ... Where do(es) ... live? What's his/her/their ...? How do you spell ...?	cities/countries north south east west island mountain sea river postcard near Mr Mrs Miss Ms address telephone number	Follow/give directions around a map. Talk about famous monuments. Ask for/give addresses and telephone numbers.	Listening task Puzzle Class survey Writing Song Reading task Story listening/reading
2b	Where's ...? Is ... near ...? There is /are ... Which building ...? next to opposite between by near	museum cinema supermarket library church river cafe park hospital hotel station plan	Ask/answer questions about a picture. Talk/write about buildings/towns. Follow directions around a town plan.	Listening task Puzzle Personal file Reading task Pairwork
2c	Can I help you ? Have you got ...? How much ...? Where can I/you buy ...? I'd like ...	packet bag bar pound/pence newsagent's butcher's baker's chemist's newspaper soap medicine chicken toothpaste shopping list	Talk about shops/shopping. Order food in a restaurant. Ask about prices.	Role play Listening task Whole class game Board game Word categories Reading task Pairwork
2d	*Comparatives* bigger than faster than Find ...	van bus lorry motorbike wheels engine fetch burning pour on	Ask/answer questions about a picture. Write/talk about modes of transport. Carry out a traffic survey.	Personal file Song Listening task Word categories Crossword Quiz Traffic survey Story listening
2e	What does this sign mean? opposite near next to in	drive right/left-hand side danger roundabout traffic lights turn crossing working smoking library supermarket cafe hotel park church cinema museum	Talk about road signs. Write/talk about towns and cities. Read/answer questions about a story.	Workcard Personal file Tongue twister Story listening/reading Stepping Stones Game Personal survey Whole class games
2f	*Revision of all structures from unit*	town be careful! watch out! fast dangerous dirty too many wrong way	Talk about dangers in a town/city.	Board game Supersnake Make a flying Supersnake Evaluation

Syllabus

Opposites

Unit	Main Structures	Vocabulary	Main Communicative Functions	Tasks and Activities
3a	What's the opposite of ...? Are you ...? Have you got ...? Can you ...? Do you like ...?	opposite laugh cry stupid clever always never fat thin happy sad long short new old man woman boy girl	Listen to/say a poem. Compare pictures. Talk about likes and dislikes.	Poem Action game Crossword Make a word-wheel Pairwork Class survey Board game Puzzles Reading task
3b	When's your birthday? How old are you? Who's the *tallest*? Are you *taller* than ...? I'm *older* than ... I've got *longer* hair than ... Is ... *taller* than ...?	months of the year tall short long old young same different opposite first second third last	Compare pupils' heights and ages. Ask/answer about ages/dates of birth. Ask/answer questions about a calendar.	Workcards Class survey Reading task Listening task Personal survey Puzzle Speaking activities
3c	Which letters look the same? Which letters are upside down? Were you right?	bat ghost in front of behind backwards upside down	Ask/answer questions about where things are. Read/answer questions about a story. Find out about mirror images.	Workcards Puzzle Drawing puzzle Story listening/reading Role play Reading task
3d	Is he/she + VERB -ing? Is his/her *glass* empty/full? Has he/she got ...? What's your name? What's your address? Where are you from? How tall are you? How much do you weigh?	full empty light dark clean dirty thick thin hot cold passport nationality	Ask/answer questions about a picture. Find a 'secret' message. Ask for personal information.	Listening tasks Reading task Memory game Find the hidden numbers Game (I-spy)
3e	It looks like ... It's got/hasn't got ... Who is the ...? Who has got the ...? was/were	because ('cos)	Listen to/say a poem. Describe 'crazy' animals. Read/answer questions about a story. Ask/answer questions about your class.	Poem Personal file Tongue twister Story listening/reading Stepping Stones Game Personal surveyReading task Writing
3f	*Revision of all structures* Why did ... swim/ jump/climb ...? the longest... the tallest ... the highest ...	*Revision of story vocabulary*	Talk about 'crazy' animals. Design an advertisement.	Board game Supersnake Draw and write Evaluation

Time

Unit	Main Structures	Vocabulary	Main Communicative Functions	Tasks and Activities
4a	What's the time? ... o'clock quarter to/past ... half past ... What day is it today? What's the date today? was born	second minute hour day week month year leap year measure calendar(s) diary/ies add divide	Talk about measuring time. Ask about/tell the time.	Workcard Make a calendar Calendar game Listening task Reading task Action game Crossword Writing
4b	How long does it take to ...? It takes ... *Past simple* What time did ...? is/was eat/ate got went	ready, steady, go! tie count spell	Talk about how long things take. Listen, read and write about morning routines.	Tongue twister Workcard Personal survey Personal file Reading task Writing Puzzles Song Whole class game Pairwork
4c	*Past simple* What did ...do? Did he ...? Where were you ...? What was on? What time did you ...?	morning afternoon evening breakfast lunch dinner detective bank robber	Talk about daily routines. Ask/answer questions in the past tense.	Listening task Action game Story listening/reading Quiz Personal file Role play Game
4d	*Past simple* What does ... mean? When was ...? Where did ...? It takes/took ... I went ... I'm going to ...	past present future passport plane train boat bus tickets	Talk about objects from the past, present and future. Ask/answer questions about journey times.	Board game Quiz Puzzle Story listening/reading Reading task Writing
4e	*Past simple* Where did ...? Why ...? ate found saw bought went Because ...	please pass	Talk about important dates. Tell a story. Ask/answer about what you did last week.	Story game Group survey Tongue twister Groupwork Story listening/reading Personal survey Stepping Stones game
4f	*Revision of all structures from unit*	late lines	Talk about the importance of being punctual.	Board game Supersnake Make a Supersnake clock Evaluation

New Stepping Stones

is a four-year English course for young learners beginning English at primary level. The course is carefully constructed around a conceptual framework in which the tasks, activities and language points reflect the interests and development of young learners.

The key features of *New Stepping Stones* are as follows:

A syllabus geared to the child's development
The *New Stepping Stones* syllabus has been designed to meet the specific needs of young learners, providing four achievable years of English. The syllabus takes into account the cognitive development of children this age. The choice of themes therefore reflects children's developing awareness.

The syllabus also grades the tasks and activities in which children participate. This is related to a thorough coverage of appropriate structures, functions, words and pronunciation. All the language points are regularly revised and reviewed to ensure maximum progress for all learners.

Topic-based learning
Level 3 of *New Stepping Stones* is divided into four topics. Within each topic, the language items are carefully selected and graded. Pupils are presented with language which allows them to communicate in a genuinely meaningful way about each topic. The topic-based syllabus also offers maximum opportunity for project work.

Personalisation
Children get great motivation and satisfaction from talking and writing about themselves. *New Stepping Stones* offers many opportunities for pupils to do this in English.

Variety of learning styles
It is generally acknowledged that all children learn in slightly different ways. To accommodate this, *New Stepping Stones* exploits a wide range of tried and tested techniques and activities to allow all pupils to fulfil their maximum potential.

For example, in Year 1 of the course pupils acquire the vocabulary to identify members of their family in English. In Year 2 they go on to talk about their homes. Now, in Year 3, they take a wider perspective, looking at their town, learning the names of other countries, thinking about the past and the future ...

Teaches positive learning habits
One of the purposes of learning English at primary level is to provide positive motivation for future studies. This includes not only laying foundations in terms of language and enjoyment, but also developing positive learning habits in young learners.

New Stepping Stones teaches pupils organisational skills, the importance of co-operation, referencing skills, and the need to use language for real purposes. The Activity Book contains self-assessment activities to help pupils monitor their own learning.

Comprehensive coverage of skills
The syllabus in *New Stepping Stones* is carefully graded in order to ensure comprehensive coverage of all four skills. Within each lesson, pupils are engaged in listening, speaking, reading and writing in English, with listening and speaking having prime importance in the early levels of the course.

Interdisciplinary
The topics and activities in *New Stepping Stones* provide an interdisciplinary approach to language learning, enabling teachers to link the study of English with work in other areas of the curriculum.

Simple to use
The teaching notes to *New Stepping Stones* include a step-by-step guide to every activity in every lesson. Reproduction of pages from the Coursebook and the Activity Book alongside the teaching notes provides an immediate reference for teachers.

Pupils learn by doing
The activities in *New Stepping Stones* require the active participation of the pupils. There are games which practise the language through physical involvement, tasks which involve making things, and emphasis upon learning through concrete activities.

Learning is fun
New Stepping Stones is based on the belief that learning is most effective when it is fun and moreover that enjoyment provides motivation and encourages pupils to continue in their studies.

Introduction

ORGANISATION

Contents of the course

Level 3 of *New Stepping Stones* consists of:

Coursebook

64 lively, full-colour pages, featuring stories, cartoon strips, project tasks, games, songs and rhymes and numerous activities for presenting and practising the language.

Activity Book

80 pages providing practice in all the skills, with questionnaires, puzzles, games, tests and self-assessment activities to fully involve pupils in the learning process.

Reader

Each Activity Book comes complete with its own Reader. This is a pull-out colour booklet, containing four original stories and poems.

Teacher's Guide

A simple to use, lesson-by-lesson guide giving instructions for all activities. Reproductions of Coursebook and Activity Book pages greatly simplify preparation and classroom use, while the **Resource File** at the back of the book provides a wealth of additional ideas.

Cassettes

The cassettes feature both adults and children and provide a wide range of natural listening material including dialogues, songs, rhymes and listening tasks.

Objectives of the course

The main objectives of *New Stepping Stones* are as follows:
- To instil the idea that learning languages is enjoyable.
- To encourage pupils to want to go on learning English in secondary school.
- To enable pupils to talk and write about themselves.
- To lay the foundation for future study in terms of basic structures, lexis, language functions and basic study skills.
- To enable pupils to use English for a purpose and to regard English as a means of communicating real information.

Organisation of the course

New Stepping Stones Level 3 is made up of four topics:
SPARE TIME
PLACES
OPPOSITES
TIME

Pupils explore each topic in sufficient depth to enable them to talk and write about themselves, their family, their classmates and their possessions. Each topic contains an introductory story and six teaching units, ending in a final evaluation lesson.

There is also an introductory unit on 'Shape' providing revision of Levels 1 and 2. Each unit is divided into three lessons of approximately one hour, which together with story and evaluation lessons provides a total of 72 lessons. In the Resource File, further suggestions for projects and a wealth of other teaching ideas supplement the core material. There is constant revision throughout the course, four progress tests and four self-assessment sections.

Adaptability of the course

New Stepping Stones is designed to be as flexible as possible: the Coursebook and Activity Book are divided into units rather than lessons because the time available will vary from situation to situation, according to factors such as class size and age of pupils.

Simply work through the material in the order shown in the Lesson Notes. The topic-based structure and in-built revision make it possible to begin a lesson at any point. The extra ideas in the **Resource File** also give the teacher greater flexibility in managing time.

Organisation of the Coursebook and Activity Book

Each unit consists of two pages in the Coursebook and three pages in the Activity Book. The text of the introductory story or poem appears in the pull-out Reader in the middle of the Activity Book.

Key vocabulary and classroom language is given in wordlists at the back of the Coursebook.

Organisation of the Teacher's Guide

Each two-page spread is devoted to one lesson, i.e. approximately one hour's worth of material. There is a step-by-step guide giving detailed teaching instructions for each activity. Reproduced pages from both the Coursebook and the Activity Book allow teachers to see instantly which exercises are being referred to. Tapescripts and answers are also included.

The symbol // is used in some tapescripts. This is an indication that the teacher should either stop the tape temporarily or use the 'pause' button.

Resource File

The Resource File is at the back of the Teacher's Guide. It contains suggestions and ideas for extra games, activities and projects. Many of these activities can be used at any stage; others are more applicable to particular lessons. Suggestions as to when extra activities are appropriate appear in the syllabus box at the top of each page of Lesson Notes. The numbers of appropriate activities from the Resource File are given here.

Main Language Items			Resource File	Materials Needed
wanted	run/ran	pet	story	
bought	slept	rabbit	title	25
didn't ...		frog	Reader	Reader (see pull-out section of the Activity Book)
hop/hopped		bird		cassette/cassette player
jump/jumped		fish		
fly/flew		mouse		
swim/swam		cat		

These extra ideas will also be helpful in dealing with mixed-ability groups, since they include suggestions for reinforcement work and extension activities.

TEACHING PROCEDURES

The following notes deal with how to use *New Stepping Stones* in the classroom. Pupils are required to learn only a limited number of techniques, which can be applied to a wide range of activities in the Coursebook and the Activity Book. All variations upon these techniques are given in the Lesson Notes.

The activities in *New Stepping Stones* can be loosely divided into those which concentrate on one of the four skills (speaking, listening, reading and writing) and those which practise two or more skills simultaneously.

Speaking Activities

Pairwork

The **Pairwork** exercises provide much of the initial presentation and practice of new language, and range from very controlled exercises (i.e. drills in which both questions and answers are given) to freer exercises based on picture prompts.

For controlled exercises the following procedure is recommended, although as a first step it may be useful to demonstrate exercises with one pupil, or get more able pupils to show the rest of the class.

a Divide the class into pairs and give each pair question and answer roles. For suggestions on organising pupils into pairs, see **Classroom Management** on p. 12.
b Each pair uses only one book, placed between them, open at the appropriate page. The words should always be covered. Pupils must not read while listening.
c Pupils repeat after the tape. All pairs work simultaneously. P1 repeats the questions, pointing and referring to pictures as appropriate to contextualise the questions. This is important since for example 'What's this?' is meaningless unless it is clear what is being referred to. P2 answers.

As the course progresses, pupils can be encouraged to test themselves by trying to answer before the tape.

d Practise without the help of the tape. P1 now uses the words in his/her book as prompts to ask the questions.

NOTE – Simply reading the question aloud destroys natural rhythm and pronunciation, so encourage pupils to adopt a 'Look and Say' method here, i.e. pupils read the question silently before looking up at their partner and asking the question.

P2's book should remain on the table with the words covered. He or she answers the questions using the pictures as prompts, with help from P1 if required.

e Change roles and repeat step d.
f Practise until the whole exercise can be done using only the pictures as prompts. This stage will be reached gradually, as skill and confidence increase.
g During the practice phase, the teacher's task is to circulate and help the pupils where necessary. Praise and encourage natural speed and intonation, the use of 'Look and Say' techniques and co-operation between pupils, helping and checking, etc.

These procedures are goals to be worked towards. Pupils will take time to get used to working in pairs. Therefore during **Pairwork** it is important to keep a few points in mind:

Take your time ...

All pupils vary in ability: some will instantly grasp the technique while others may still be getting used to it in Topic 2.

Communication before correctness ...

Don't expect instant perfection. Communication is more important initially: correctness will come gradually.

Timing ...

Controlled **Pairwork** will usually take about fifteen minutes. Pupils will vary in terms of what they can achieve in this time. The more able pupils will be able to produce both questions and answers without the help of the words, while less able pupils should at least know key vocabulary items and question words.

Noise levels ...

Pupils working simultaneously in pairs will inevitably generate some noise. The sound of a class working is a healthy learning environment, but only tolerate noise that relates to the task in hand.

These techniques are invaluable in maximising the involvement of all pupils. Individual capabilities vary, but even less able pupils will be more active and involved in their own learning than if the teacher is asking all the questions. To begin with, **Pairwork** may be time-consuming, but a little initial patience in using the above techniques will be greatly rewarded.

In freer **Pairwork**, the basic practice procedures are the same from the teacher's point of view although the model questions and answers are not on the tape. Demonstrate by asking appropriate questions to the whole class until pupils understand the nature of the exercise and the language forms needed.

Groupwork: Questionnaires

Questionnaires provide pupils with a real purpose for communication and an opportunity to talk about themselves. Always demonstrate **Questionnaires** to the class first, so that pupils know exactly what they have to do. Quickly draw a grid on the blackboard. Select one or two pupils. Write their names on the grid. Then ask the questions to be practised and write each pupil's answers alongside their name.

Name	dog	cat	other	no pet
Alex				
Anna				

a Divide the class into groups of three or more, depending upon the nature of the questionnaire. Ensure that pupils are not always in the same groups, so that questionnaires are less predictable. For suggestions on the organisation of groups, see **Classroom Management** on p. 12.
b Then pupils complete their own questionnaires. Set a 5–10 minute time limit for the task.
c The teacher's task is to circulate, giving assistance if required. Ensure that pupils are using English and that they are asking questions and not simply copying each other's answers. Communication is more important than correctness here.
d When pupils have completed their questionnaires, ask the class questions about the information they have collected.

Workcards

A new activity type is introduced in *New Stepping Stones*: the **Workcard**. Most of the **Workcards** are in the Activity Book and they are clearly identifiable.

There are two types of **Workcard**: those which involve oral communication where pupils carry out an experiment and those which are based more on written communication. The tasks and simple experiments on the **Workcards** are drawn from different curricular areas, such as Maths, Science, Geography and Art. Attention is focused on the ways in which language is used to perform tasks in other subjects, rather than on the subject matter (e.g. language is used for hypothesising, agreeing/ disagreeing and describing processes). The tasks are designed so that pupils have to use language to communicate.

a Prepare any materials needed for the activity in advance.
b Pupils work in pairs, or alone in the case of some **Workcards**.
c Always demonstrate to the class how an experiment works before pupils begin. In the case of written work, provide examples where possible.
d In the case of experiments, set a time limit for the task.
e The teacher's task is to circulate, giving assistance if required. Ensure that pupils are using English and if necessary help them find the language they need to talk about the experiment. Communication is more important than accuracy.
f When pupils have completed the **Workcards**, round up the experiments by asking them to report their findings.

Role play

The **Role plays** in *New Stepping Stones* are based around pictures or sketches and require some degree of improvisation on the part of the pupils. They encourage the transfer of language to new and less predictable situations. Insist upon gestures, movement and the use of correct stress, intonation and tone of voice. The following points offer guidance on procedure:

a Set the scene by telling pupils to look at the pictures and then asking questions about who and what they can see.
b Play the dialogue on the tape, if relevant.
c Role plays usually involve two characters. All pairs work simultaneously. Pupils should be standing or sitting as appropriate to the situation.
d Pupils work out their dialogue together. Encourage them to use props where possible. The emphasis is on *playing a role*, so spontaneity and communication are more important than accurately 'reading' a prepared dialogue.
e Enthusiastic volunteers can act out the **Role play** in front of the class. Don't force reluctant pupils to perform publicly.

Tongue twisters

Pronunciation practice is integrated throughout the course. Poems and rhymes are used to develop good stress and intonation patterns. Alliteration is widely used to focus on individual sounds, for example 'Maureen's Morning', 'David's Day'.

Tongue twisters are included to provide good pronunciation practice in a fun way. The following procedure is recommended for practising **Tongue twisters**:

a Look at the picture and read the **Tongue twister** *slowly*.
b Check that pupils understand all the words in the **Tongue twister**. Briefly practise any new words in isolation.
c Divide the class into pairs, play the **Tongue twister** on the tape. Play it again while P1 in each pair repeats. Do this twice. Then P2 repeats.
d Pupils practise the **Tongue twister** in pairs. P1 says the **Tongue twister**. P2 listens and corrects. Change and repeat.
e Pupils gradually try to increase the speed at which they recite.
f The teacher circulates, giving assistance with pronunciation if required. Ensure that pupils recite the **Tongue twister** as a connected sentence and do not say it word by word.
g Volunteers can say the **Tongue twister** in front of the whole class. This can be organised as a race or competition, but restrict to volunteers only.

Listening activities

Presentation

The **Presentations** focus on the key language for each lesson and take a variety of forms: descriptive passages, action games, pictures, poems and discussions. They contextualise the language items to be practised and provide listening and reading practice. All the texts in the Coursebook and the Reader are recorded on the cassettes.

The **Presentation** phase of the lesson can also be used to go over homework exercises or briefly to revise material from the previous lesson.

Listening (Task)

These exercises provide a contrasting type of listening exercise to the **Presentation** activities. Rather than listening for general meaning pupils are now required to listen for specific detail and carry out a set task. The activities themselves vary and details of procedures are given in the Lesson Notes. All **Listening (Task)** exercises are on tape.

Reassure pupils that they do not have to understand all the words, but only listen for specific information.

Stories

Each of the four topic sections in *New Stepping Stones* opens with a story. All the stories are recorded on cassette, but it is much better to read them to the class yourself. You can hold pupils' attention more effectively than the cassette player by drawing attention to pictures as you read and animating the story with gestures and movements.

Always ask pupils some warm-up questions before you begin the story, e.g. what they think it might be about, what is going to happen, what their opinions about the topic are. The pictorial opening spread of each topic in the Coursebook (e.g. pp. 4–5) is designed to provide a springboard for such discussion.

Supersnake

The focus of the **Supersnake** strips is on reading and listening. Encourage pupils to read silently for themselves before they listen to the tape.

Reading activities

Reading (Task)

With the **Reading (Task)** exercises, pupils are directly involved in performing a task, this time based upon a written passage. Once again, the pupils do not have to understand all the words, but only that information which will enable them to complete the task.

Pupils should work individually. The ability of the group will dictate the amount of time each activity takes.

The **Resource File** provides suggestions for extra work for faster pupils.

Encourage pupils to compare their work when they have finished. Round off the activity by going over correct solutions on the blackboard.

Look and find

Some **Look and find** activities are based on questions asked orally by the teacher; suggestions for these appear in the **Lesson Notes**. Others are introduced by a series of written instructions. These instructions direct pupils to look at a picture and find specific things. Pupils can work in pairs and discuss where the things are to be found in each picture. These exercises are basically a form of guided discussion. The teacher's role is to circulate, encourage pupils to speak in English, and provide help, if required.

Stepping Stones Game

This is a simple sentence-making game. The object of the game is to make as many sentences as possible. Pupils work from left to right and select a word, or words, from each column. Each sentence must be a true statement or a correct description of an item in the Coursebook. Pupils may choose not to select a word from a column if they wish, but must still work across from left to right. One pupil from each pair should write their answers on a piece of paper. Demonstrate the game by constructing a similar grid on the blackboard and asking pupils to make sentences. Write these on the board.

Set a limit of ten minutes, then ask each pair how many sentences they have made. Check that all sentences are correct and appropriate to the picture. Correct any mistakes. Pupils must deduct incorrect sentences from their total. The pair with the most correct sentences are the winners. Pupils' answer sheets can be collected to assess progress.

Writing Activities

Puzzles

A variety of **Puzzles** and **Crosswords** provide valuable revision and reinforcement of vocabulary and structures in an enjoyable way.

Personal File

The **Personal File** gives pupils the opportunity to write about themselves. These exercises are always based upon a model. Pupils' attention should be drawn to these models before, during and after the exercise, to allow them to monitor their own work.

The **Personal File** involves pupils drawing and colouring pictures and then describing them. It is often helpful if the teacher provides a model on the blackboard first, giving personal information about herself as an example.

If pupils create their **Personal Files** on loose sheets, these can make excellent wall displays, providing motivation and the opportunity for follow-up work involving the whole class. Pupils derive satisfaction from seeing their own work displayed, despite differences of ability.

Other writing exercises

Most of the other writing exercises in *New Stepping Stones* are there to provide reinforcement of the spoken word. They can be used for homework, but always ensure that pupils understand what they are required to do. Begin the exercise as a whole-class activity, using the blackboard.

Freer writing exercises, in which pupils write questions or messages for their partners to answer, are an effective way of dealing with mixed-ability classes, since they ensure faster pupils always have something to do (see **Resource File**).

Integrated skills

Cut-outs

The cut-out material is located in the centre pull-out section of the Activity Book. The cut-out town pieces etc. are used with specific activities, e.g. 'Read and put the buildings on the town plan' on page 28 of the Activity Book, and provide an added element of physical manipulation in practising the language. Instructions for their use appear in the Lesson Notes.

Games

The games in *New Stepping Stones* provide variety in the presentation and practice of the language. Although they are there to be enjoyed, they all have a linguistic purpose. Games such as 'I-spy' are traditional children's games and introduce an element of cultural study. Encourage pupils to use English throughout.

Songs and poems

Many of the poems in *New Stepping Stones* are well known to British children, providing an important element of authenticity in the course.

They are activities for the whole class. Always use the pictures to clarify meaning and use actions wherever appropriate.

The **Lesson Notes** indicate when the song or poem is to be first presented, but once pupils know the tune and words they can be repeated in any lesson.

Other activities

All other activities in *New Stepping Stones* are fully explained in the **Lesson Notes**. These include board games, quizzes, 'Make' activities and surveys.

Evaluation

Although evaluation in *New Stepping Stones* is continuous, there is a teacher-administered test and a self-assessment activity at the end of each of the four topics.

Teacher-administered tests

The teacher-administered tests are to be found in Lesson 2 of Units 1F, 2F, 3F and 4F. They are useful in that they signal some stages in the learning process and allow both teacher and pupils to look back on what they have achieved up to that moment.

Some pupils are easily discouraged by their mistakes, so avoid using red ink to correct tests and try to focus on the improvement in their work rather that on their deficiencies. In this way, they will be able to appreciate the positive aspects of their school experience.

Test yourself

The self-assessment activities, which follow the teacher-administered tests in the Lesson Notes, help centre pupils' attention on what they have learned. The score which they must circle at the bottom of the page, gives them instant feedback on their performance.

Self-assessment is essential in that it allows pupils to become more aware of their own strengths and weaknesses. Point out to them that errors are a natural part of the learning process and remind them that you can be sure of avoiding mistakes only if you learn nothing.

Classroom management

The organisation of your classroom is very important. Always ensure pupils know exactly what they are doing before they start an activity. A demonstration is often more satisfactory than an explanation. Although this can be time-consuming with new activities, a little time spent before an activity can save a lot of time and effort later.

Organising pupils into pairs and groups is another important job for the teacher.

Pair pupils with the person sitting next to them, if possible. This can be done if pupils are sitting around tables:

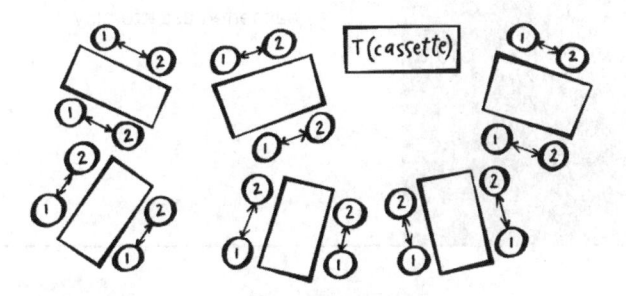

Or in rows:

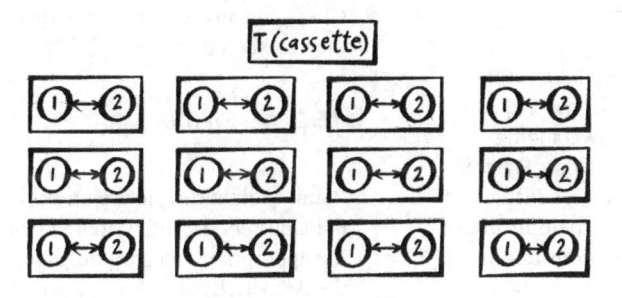

Pupils can always turn to work with the person behind them:

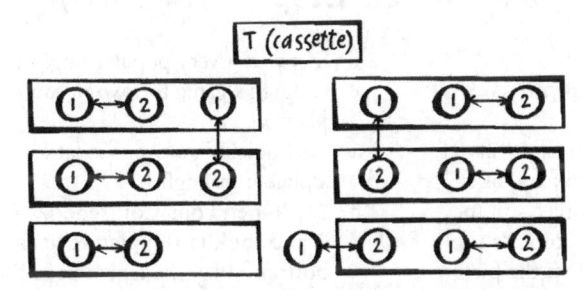

Give pupils roles. Since the questions and answers in *New Stepping Stones* are colour-coded, this can be used as a prompt when giving roles. Say to each pupil in turn '**You are blue. You are red.**' Next, ensure pupils understand the roles they have been given. Say '**Blue stand up!**' etc. Then write the first two questions on the blackboard in coloured chalk. Initially use these as prompts while pupils repeat. Pupils will quickly learn to get themselves into pairs, so this procedure can soon be abandoned.

For **Groupwork**, ensure that pupils are facing one another and not spread out in a line, making communication impossible.

Organisation of equipment is another important responsibility for the teacher. A list of items required for each lesson is given in the syllabus box in the Lesson Notes. Encourage pupils to be responsible for bringing their own coloured pencils etc., but try to have a class set available, to avoid time wasting.

It is probably a good idea for the teacher to look after the cut-outs if they are to be used most effectively. (See **Resource File** for ideas on the storage of cut-outs.)

Language in the classroom

Using English in the classroom is a very good way of both introducing and constantly recycling language. *New Stepping Stones* encourages this through the teacher's script, which is given in the Lesson Notes.

Extensive piloting has shown that *New Stepping Stones* can be used equally effectively with or without the mother tongue. The mother tongue may be useful for classroom management, although a demonstration is often an equally effective substitute. Use English wherever possible and encourage pupils to do the same. Pictures or actions can usually be used instead of translation to explain meaning. As pupils become familiar with English expressions and classroom language, such phrases should always be used.

Pupils need to become familiar with the following phrases as quickly as possible, if they are not already.

Give me …	Thank you.
Come here, please.	Listen.
Read.	Write.
Draw.	Colour.
Repeat.	Cover the words.
Good.	Well done.
Quiet.	Hands up.
You ask the questions.	You give the answers.
Get into pairs.	Get into groups.

KEY TO SYMBOLS

Coursebook and Activity Book

Listening material

Reader

Activity Book only

Writing to be done in exercise book or on a sheet of paper

Starter lesson 1

Main Language Items	Resource File	Materials Needed
What colour …? How many …? Is this …? What's this?	27 29 30	cassette/cassette player

Step 1 Discussion (L1)

a In their L1, tell pupils that in this new course they are going to talk about many interesting things. The first few lessons will deal with shapes, both around themselves and in nature.

b Ask them to think about the shapes of objects that they see every day and have a few volunteers draw them on the board: the sun, the full moon, a window, a box, etc.

c Ask them to call out the words in English for as many square, round and triangular objects as they can, and list them on the board.

Step 2 Quiz

a Say 'Open your Coursebook on page 2. Look at the picture.' Point to various objects and ask 'Is this … ?' and 'What's this?' to see if pupils can remember the English names.

b Divide the class into two teams. Play the first question on the tape, making sure you pause before the answer is given. The first pupil to raise their hand gets a chance to answer, and if correct, wins two points for their team. If the answer is wrong, the other team may answer the question for one point.

c Play the tape to confirm the correct answer.

d Do all the questions in the same way (See tapescript on page 178).

Step 3 Pairwork

a Elicit questions from pupils about the picture on page 2. Pupils may use any question forms they know, ranging from simple questions such as 'What's this?', to more complex ones such as 'How many clothes are there in the picture?'. Write the questions on the blackboard.

b Divide the class into pairs. Each pair uses one book and pupils ask and answer questions about the picture.

Step 4 Memory game

a Pupils remain in pairs (P1 and P2). P1 in each pair takes the book and asks P2 the colours of three objects in the picture by asking 'What colour's the *pencil*?' P2 does not look at the picture but answers from memory (or guesses). P2 gets a point for each correct answer.

b Then P2 takes the book and asks the questions.

Step 5 Look and find

The instructions ask pupils to look carefully at the picture at the top of page 2 in the Coursebook and find specific objects.

a Do the first with the whole class to demonstrate the exercise. Say '**Find four vegetables.**'

b Pupils then work in pairs and complete the other tasks.

c Check the answers and write them on the blackboard.

Step 6 Write

Pupils look at the picture on page 2 of the Coursebook and write the words in the appropriate category on page 2 of the Activity Book.

Step 7 Game (I-spy)

'I-spy' is a very popular English children's game for two or more players.

a First quickly go over the letters of the alphabet in English.

b Say '**Open your Coursebook on page 2 and look at the picture at the bottom.**' Play the tape. Pupils listen and read at the same time.

c Ask pupils if they have ever played a similar game. Then demonstrate the game. Say, for example, '**I spy with my little eye something beginning with "c"**', and explain to pupils that you are thinking of something in the picture at the top of page 2 which begins with 'c'. It could be, for example, 'cat', but don't tell the pupils! The pupils must look carefully at the picture and guess which the object is, saying the names of all the things in the picture that begin with 'c'. The first pupil to say 'cat' is the winner.

d Then divide the class into small groups or pairs to play the game themselves.

Shape

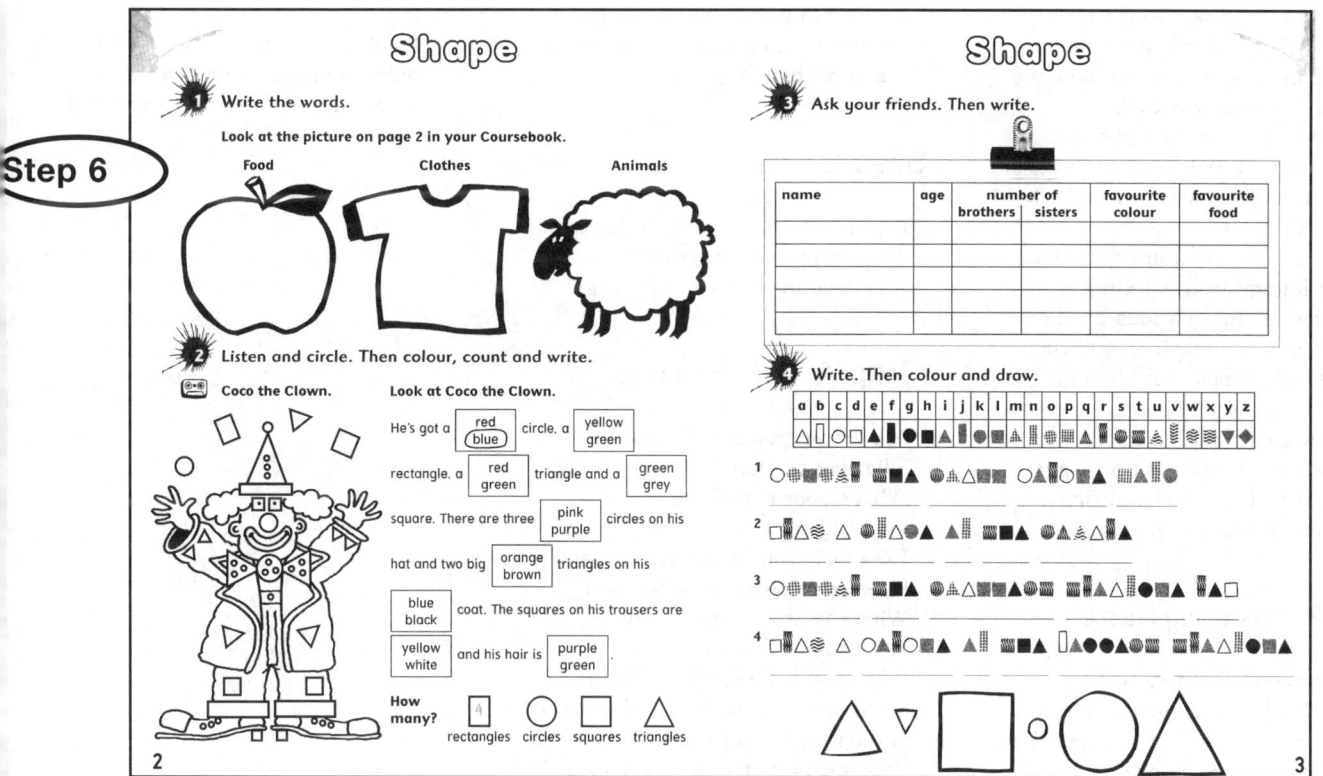

Look and find

1 Find four vegetables.
2 Find six animals.
3 Find two letters.
4 Find two toys.
5 Find four things beginning with 'p'.

I Spy

I spy with my little eye, something beginning with 'b'.
Er ... book?
Yes. Your turn.

Play Is this your shape?

The Shape Game

WORKCARD
1 Look at the black circle in the square.
2 Count to 30.
3 Look at a piece of white paper.
4 What colour are the triangles now?

What colour is the mouse?

Step 2
Step 3
Step 4
Step 5
Step 7

Shape

1 Write the words.

Look at the picture on page 2 in your Coursebook.

Food   Clothes   Animals

2 Listen and circle. Then colour, count and write.

Coco the Clown.   Look at Coco the Clown.

He's got a [red/blue] circle, a [yellow/green] rectangle, a [red/green] triangle and a [green/grey] square. There are three [pink/purple] circles on his hat and two big [orange/brown] triangles on his [blue/black] coat. The squares on his trousers are [yellow/white] and his hair is [purple/green].

How many? 4 rectangles   circles   squares   triangles

Shape

3 Ask your friends. Then write.

name	age	number of brothers	sisters	favourite colour	favourite food

4 Write. Then colour and draw.

a b c d e f g h i j k l m n o p q r s t u v w x y z

1
2
3
4

Step 6

15

Starter lesson 2

Main Language Items			Resource File	Materials Needed
What's your name?	*Shapes:*	clown		
How old are you?	square		5	flashcards (shapes)
How many… have you got?	circle		29	coloured pencils
What's your favourite …?	rectangle		30	cassette/cassette player
	triangle			

Step 1   Action game

a You will need to make four flashcards for this game: a square, a circle, a rectangle and a triangle. Display the cards around the classroom. Alternatively, draw the shapes well apart on the blackboard.

b Motion four pupils to come to the front. Use instructions such as '**Stand up! Walk! Stop!**'

c Say '**Point to a square.**' Demonstrate. Pupils copy. Then say '**Touch a triangle.**' Repeat similar instructions using all the shapes. Continue until the four pupils can carry out the instructions without your guidance.

d Repeat c with the whole class. You can revise other instructions such as '**Pick up …**', etc.

e Divide the class into teams. One player from each team stands up. Give an instruction: '**Point to a square.**' The first player to carry out the instruction correctly wins a point for his or her team. Then the second players in each team take their turn, and so on.

f The game will be more interesting if more flashcards are used, showing shapes in a variety of colours.

Step 2   Listening (Task)

a Say '**Open your Activity Book on page 2. Look at the picture of the clown.**' Point to one of the shapes. Ask pupils '**What shape is this?**'

b Then play the tape two or three times. Pupils circle the correct colours.

c Finally pupils colour the picture according to the instructions on the cassette.

Tapescript:
Look at Coco the Clown. He's got a blue circle, a yellow rectangle, a red triangle and a green square. There are three purple circles on his hat and two big brown triangles on his blue coat. The squares on his trousers are yellow and his hair is green.

Step 3   Puzzle

Pupils count the number of shapes in the clown picture and write the answers at the bottom of the page.

Step 4   Questionnaire

a Ask various pupils in the class the following questions:
What's your name?
How old are you?
How many brothers have you got?
How many sisters have you got?
What's your favourite colour?
What's your favourite food?

b When pupils are familiar with the question forms, ask them to look at the grid on page 3 of their Activity Books. Copy the grid onto the blackboard. Ask one pupil the questions again. Write his or her answers in the grid.

c Then all pupils work simultaneously, asking each other the questions and filling in their charts.

d Finish the exercise by asking pupils questions about other class members, i.e. '**How many brothers has *Maria* got?**'

Step 5   Puzzle

Pupils use the code to discover the hidden sentences and then colour the shapes and draw pictures accordingly.

Shape

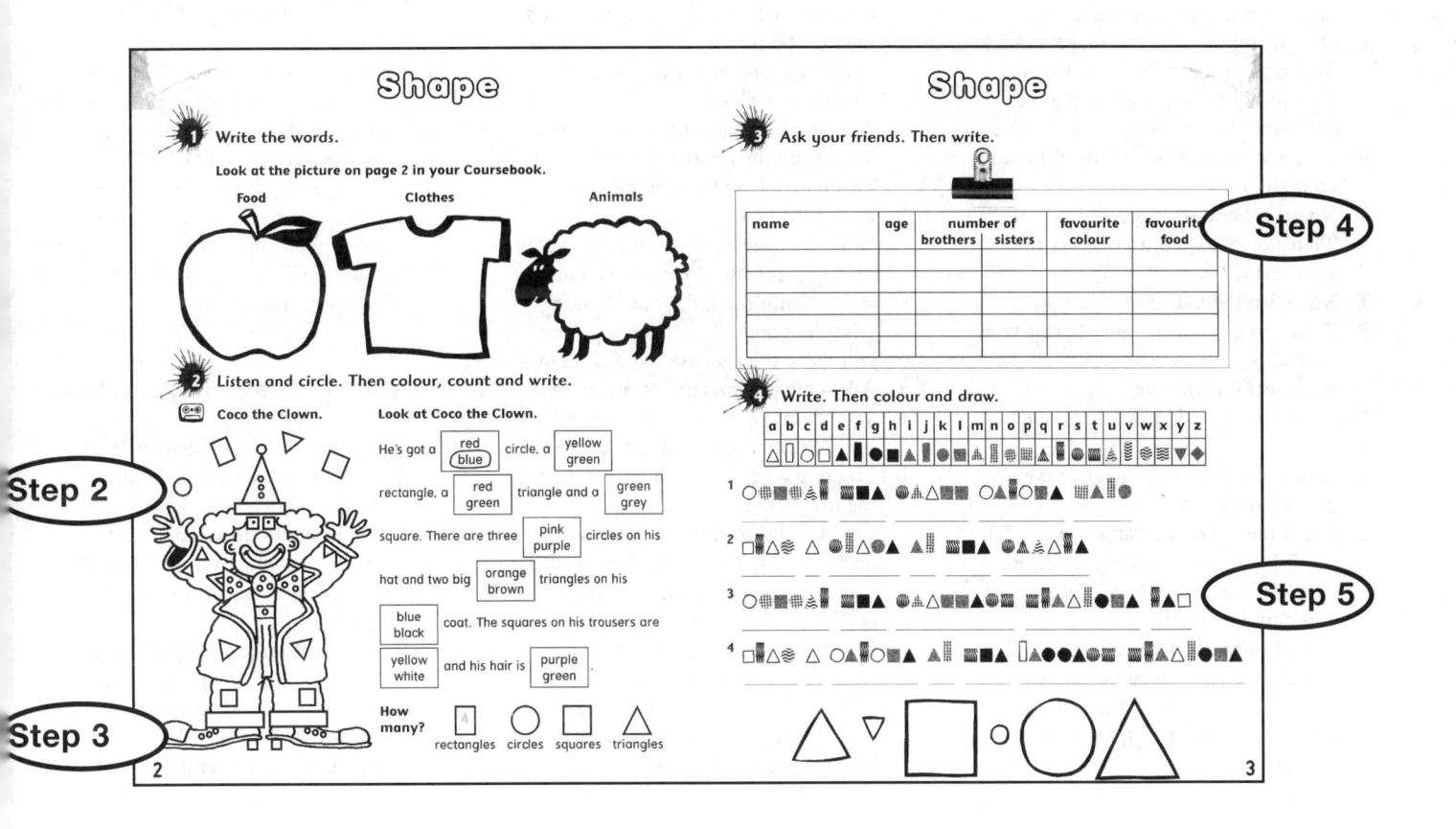

1 Write the words.

Look at the picture on page 2 in your Coursebook.

Food   Clothes   Animals

2 Listen and circle. Then colour, count and write.

Coco the Clown.

Look at Coco the Clown.

He's got a [red / **blue**] circle, a [yellow / green] rectangle, a [red / green] triangle and a [green / grey] square. There are three [pink / purple] circles on his hat and two big [orange / brown] triangles on his [blue / black] coat. The squares on his trousers are [yellow / white] and his hair is [purple / green].

How many? 4 rectangles ◯ circles ☐ squares △ triangles

Shape

3 Ask your friends. Then write.

name	age	number of brothers	sisters	favourite colour	favourite food

4 Write. Then colour and draw.

a b c d e f g h i j k l m n o p q r s t u v w x y z

Step 2
Step 3
Step 4
Step 5

Starter lesson 3

Main Language Items		Resource File	Materials Needed
Word order:	shape		
adjective – colour – noun	circle	3	coloured pencils
Is this your shape?	rectangle	56	coloured card (optional)
No, it isn't …	square	63	sheet of white paper
	triangle		

Step 1 The Shape Game

a Say '**Look at the Shape Game on page 3 in your Coursebook.**' Demonstrate the game as follows: Select one shape from the picture. Write a three-word description of the shape on a piece of paper (do not show it to anyone), e.g. **big red circle**.

b The aim of the game is to determine which shape has been selected but ask as few questions as possible.

c One pupil points to any shape and asks '**Is this your shape?**' If it is not, you must give a reason. For the big red circle, the dialogue may be as follows:

P: (Points to small green triangle) **Is this your shape?**
T: No, my shape isn't green.
P: (Points to small red triangle) **Is this your shape?**
T: No, it isn't small.
P: (Points to big red triangle) **Is this your shape?**
T: No, it isn't a triangle.
P: (Points to big red circle) **This one?**
T: Yes.

d Repeat the game until pupils have grasped the rules.

e Pupils then play the game in pairs, P1 and P2. P1 writes down a shape, P2 tries to identify the shape. Each pair uses only one book.

f To make the game more fun, a competitive element can be added by counting the number of questions pupils ask in order to guess their partner's shape.

Step 2 Reading (Task)

Steps 2–4 are based on 'after-image' illusions. An after-image is the appearance of coloured shapes on a white surface created by focusing the attention of the eye on a solid shape or picture for a short period of time. The illusion works best if the shape or picture is kept simple, and if there is a focus of attention for the eye. These exercises will generate discussion and involve the participation of all pupils. Encourage pupils to use English as much as possible.

You could also ask a few volunteers to investigate the reasons for this phenomenon and report back to the rest of the class.

Read the instructions in the **Workcard** on page 3 of the Coursebook aloud and perform the task yourself along with the pupils. The following hints will make the exercise more successful.

a Ask some preliminary questions before you begin, i.e. Point to the picture and ask, '**What colour is this triangle?**'

b Ensure pupils focus their attention on the black circle.

c Count aloud so they can practise the numbers. The longer you look at the picture the stronger the after-image will be.

d The bigger the white surface, the clearer the after-image. Therefore, if possible, pupils should look at a sheet of white paper. Sometimes blinking helps to focus the after-image.

e Ask pupils what colour the triangles and circles appear to be on the white paper. (They should have reversed!)

f Repeat the above procedure using the picture of the mouse. Ask pupils to predict what will happen to the mouse. (It should turn blue/green with a purple eye. There may be some disagreement here!)

Step 3 Reading (Task)

a Repeat the procedure of Step 2 with the black and white picture of the bird in the Activity Book (the tones should appear reversed).

b Pupils then colour the bird. They must use one colour only of their choice. (The brighter their colouring the better the illusion.) Ask pupils what colour after-image this creates.

Step 4 Make magic pictures

a Using the words and pictures in the Activity Book as a guide, pupils make their own after-image pictures.

b If the materials are available, cutting shapes out of coloured card provides a more effective way of creating after-image pictures.

c Encourage pupils to swap pictures with each other. Then ask pupils about each other's pictures, i.e. '**Maria, what colour is *Alex's* picture? And what colour is it on the white paper?**'

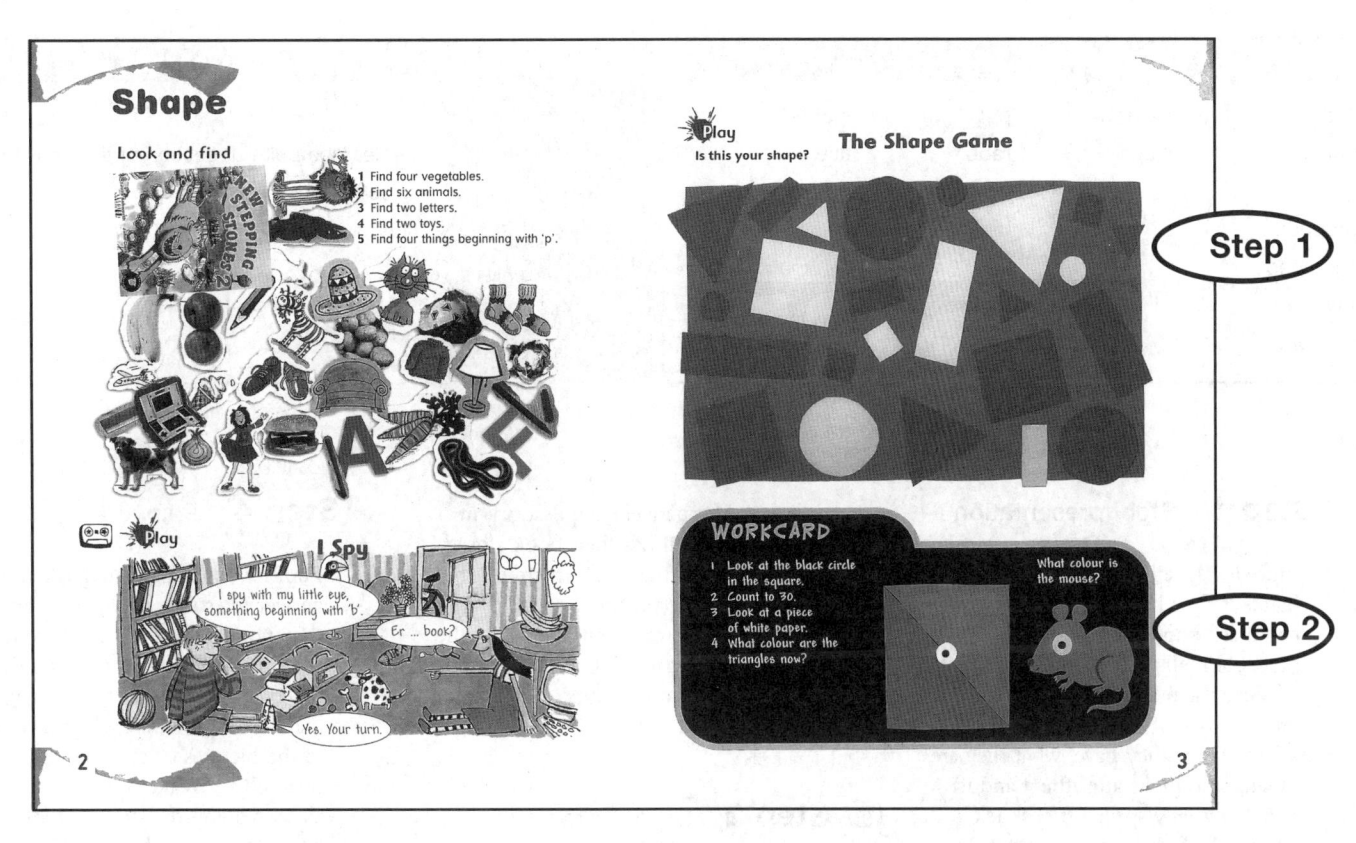

Shape

Look and find

1 Find four vegetables.
2 Find six animals.
3 Find two letters.
4 Find two toys.
5 Find four things beginning with 'p'.

Play — I Spy

I spy with my little eye, something beginning with 'b'.
Er ... book?
Yes. Your turn.

Play — Is this your shape?

The Shape Game

Step 1

WORKCARD

1 Look at the black circle in the square.
2 Count to 30.
3 Look at a piece of white paper.
4 What colour are the triangles now?

What colour is the mouse?

Step 2

Shape

Step 3

WORKCARD

A
1 Look at the bird's eye and count to thirty.
2 Quickly look at the white rectangle.
3 What colour is the bird now?

B
1 Colour the bird.
2 Look again.

Make — Magic Pictures

1 Draw a shape or a picture.
2 Colour your picture with two colours.
3 Put a small black circle in your picture.
4 Look. Count. What colour is your picture now?
5 Look at your friends' pictures.

You need: paper, coloured pencils

Step 4

Spare time 1A

1 Ask and answer. Then write.

Do you like tennis?

names sports	me	friend 1	friend 2	friend 3
tennis				

2 Write.

What are they doing?

Gary is swimming
Bill is playing
Kev
Julie
Suzy
Kate

Suzy, Bill, Kate, Julie, Kev, Gary

3 Listen and number the pictures.

Which sport?

19

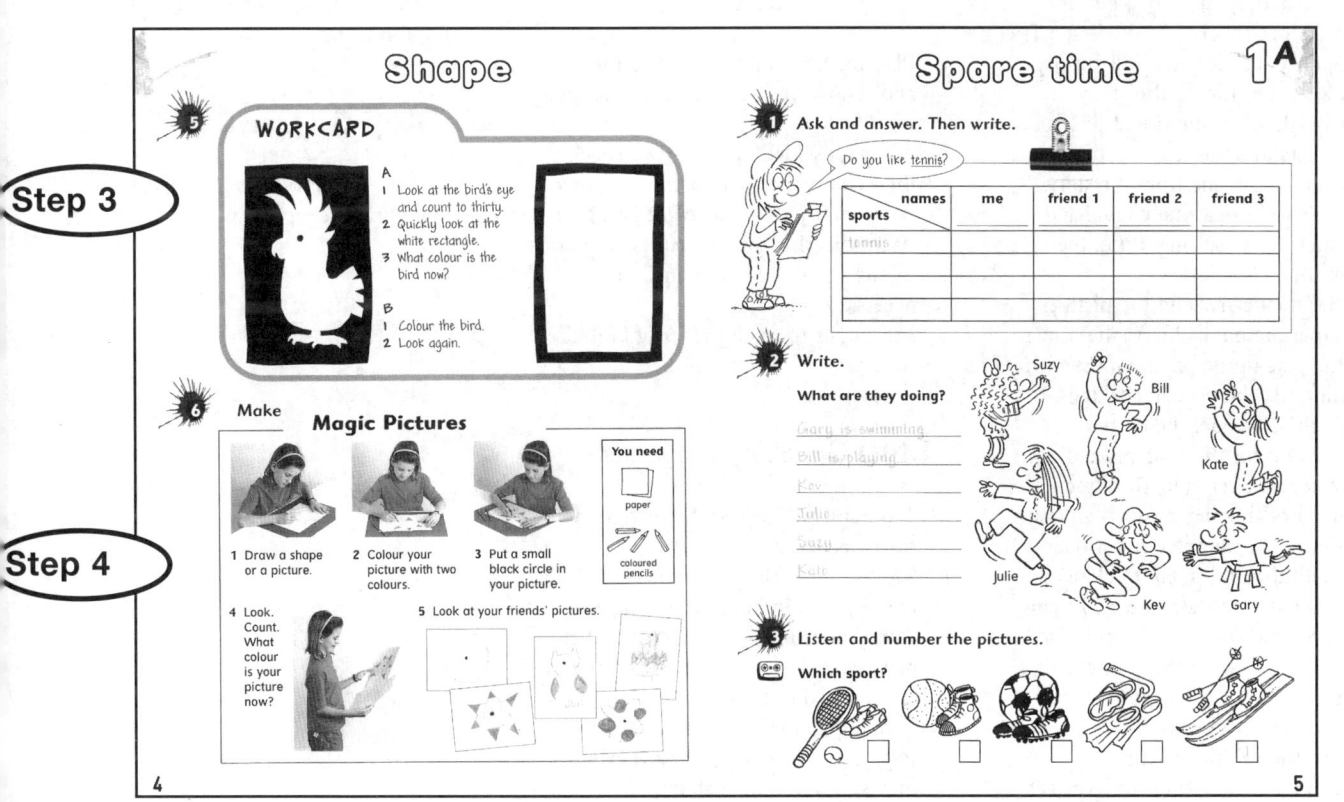

1 Story lesson

Main Language Items			Resource File	Materials Needed
wanted	run/ran	pet	story	
bought	slept	rabbit	title	25
didn't …		frog	Reader	Reader (see pull-out section of the Activity Book)
hop/hopped		bird		cassette/cassette player
jump/jumped		fish		
fly/flew		mouse		
swim/swam		cat		

Step 1 Story presentation

a In their L1, tell pupils to raise their hands if they have any pets. Or you could ask pupils in groups to brainstorm all the pets they can think of. Give them a time limit of two minutes. Ask several children what kinds of pets they have, what they are called, who looks after them and if they know any special tricks. Ask pupils where they can buy a pet. Elicit the words '**pet shop**'.

b Say '**Open your Coursebook on page 4. Look at the title of the story:** *Alice's Pet.*' Explain the title if pupils do not understand it and explain that the picture shows a scene from the story.

c Tell pupils to look at the picture and ask in their L1 what they think the story is about.

d Ask what they can see in the picture. Ensure that the pupils know the names of all the pets in the picture in English by pointing at the pets and asking '**What's this?**' Model the correct pronunciation for the students and ask them to repeat after you. To introduce an element of fun and competition ask pupils to look at the picture for one minute and then tell them to close their books. Divide the class into two teams and ask questions to each team in turn:
How many frogs are there in the picture?
What colour is the snake?
What are the rabbits eating?
Give each team one point for a correct answer. Alternatively, pupils work in pairs: one pupil has their book closed while their partner 'tests' them on the contents of the picture.

e Elicit what the different animals in the picture '**do**' by miming the verbs to the pupils. e.g. **a rabbit hops, a fish swims, a bird flies** etc.

Step 2 Story 'listen and read'

a Play the tape. Pupils listen to the story and follow in their Reader at the same time.

b Ask pupils some questions to check their comprehension of the story. e.g. '**How many pets did Alice buy?**' or '**Why did the animals run at the end of the story?**' Do this in L1 if necessary.

c Ask pupils to retell the story in their L1.

Step 3 Story vocabulary

a Tell pupils to look at the picture in their Reader again.

b Say '**Point to the** *frog*.' Check that all pupils are pointing to the correct animal and then repeat for the other pictures. Ask pupils to mime all the actions of the story.

c Give pupils the opportunity at this stage to ask you about any vocabulary they still don't understand.

Step 4 Pairwork

Pupils work in pairs and ask and answer questions about the story as they point to the relevant pictures. Alternatively, pupils try to tell the story by covering the words and using the pictures as prompts. Tell pupils to point to the pictures or to mime the story as they tell it. Weaker pupils may simply enjoy reading the story out loud in pairs. Monitor to help pupils with pronunciation.

Step 5 Storytelling

Read the story to pupils yourself or rewind the tape to play the story again.

1 Spare time

STORY

Alice's Pet

Step 1

1A Lesson 1

Main Language Items			Resource File	Materials Needed
What's he/she doing?	running	swimming	5	cassette/cassette player
What are they doing?	jumping	reading	39	
Do you like …?	hopping	skiing	41	
	playing football		41a	
	playing tennis			
	playing basketball			
	playing volleyball			

Step 1 Presentation

a Ask pupils to name some popular sports in their L1. Write them on the board. Next to each word, write its equivalent in English and pronounce it. Ask pupils to say how spelling and pronunciation differ. Say **'Open your Coursebook on page 6. Look at the picture.'**

b Ask some questions about the picture. For example, point to someone playing football and ask **'What's he doing?'** Say **'Playing football.'**

Step 2 Pairwork

a Say **'Look at the pictures at the bottom of page 6. Cover the words next to the pictures.'** Divide the class into pairs.

b Play the tape. Pupils repeat after the tape. P1 repeats the questions, P2 answers. Repeat five times, changing roles.

c Then pupils ask and answer the questions without the help of the tape. P1 asks the questions using the words in the book to help, P2 answers using only the pictures.

d Pupils change roles and repeat the procedure.

e Continue until pupils can ask and answer the questions without the help of the words.

Step 3 Questionnaire

a Ask various pupils about sports they like. Use the following question form **'Do you like … ?'** Supply the English names for other sports, if applicable.

b Copy the chart on page 5 of the Activity Book onto the blackboard. Select one pupil. Direct him or her to write the names of any three sports in the left-hand column of the chart and the names of three pupils along the top. Then he or she asks the three pupils **'Do you like tennis?'** etc., and records the answers using ticks and crosses.

c Then all pupils work in groups of four, first filling in the information about themselves, and then asking other group members similar questions and filling in the charts in their Activity Books.

d Finish the exercise by asking pupils questions about other class members, e.g. **'Does *Alex* like tennis?'**

Step 4 Write

Pupils must decide from the body positions what sports the characters are playing, and write a sentence describing each picture.

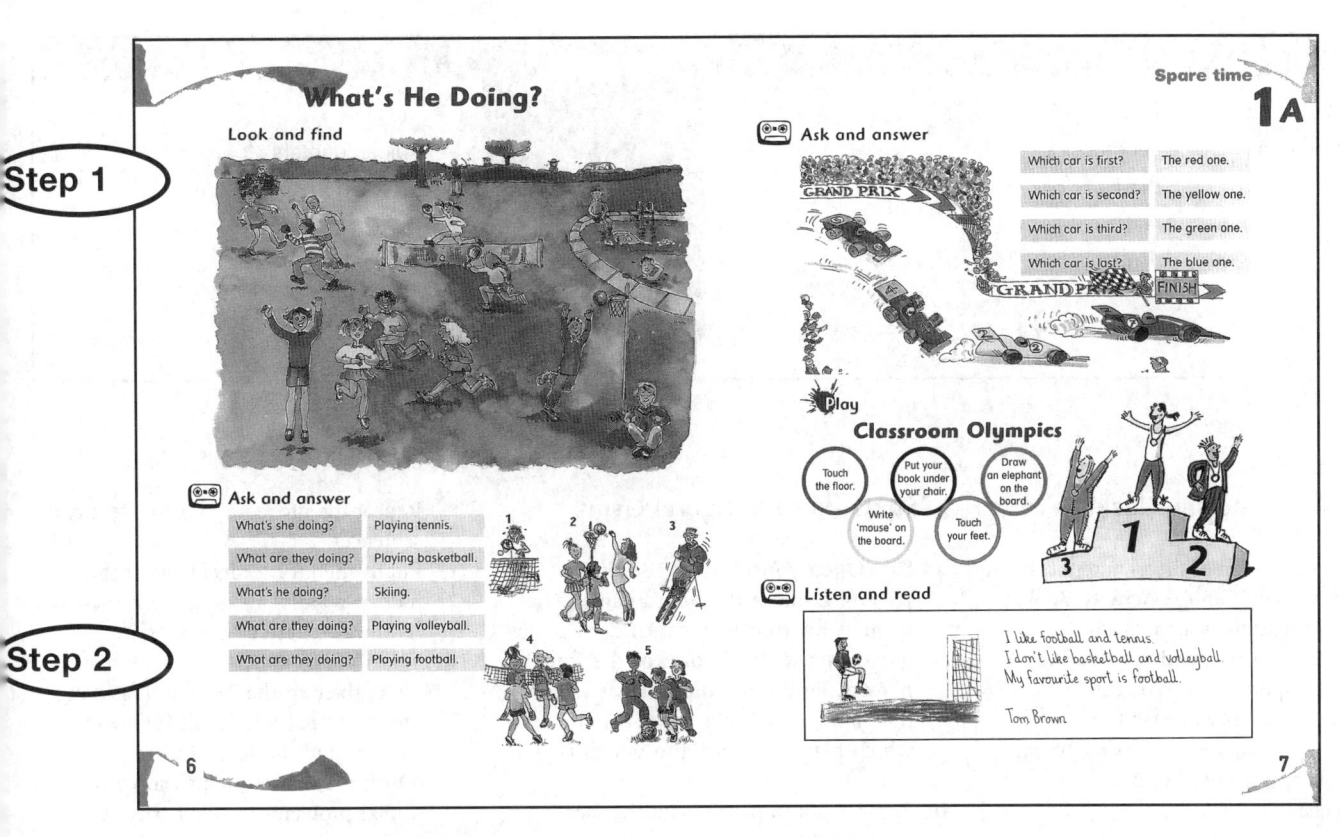

What's He Doing?

Step 1

Look and find

Ask and answer

What's she doing?	Playing tennis.
What are they doing?	Playing basketball.
What's he doing?	Skiing.
What are they doing?	Playing volleyball.
What are they doing?	Playing football.

Step 2

Spare time 1A

Ask and answer

Which car is first?	The red one.
Which car is second?	The yellow one.
Which car is third?	The green one.
Which car is last?	The blue one.

Play

Classroom Olympics
- Touch the floor.
- Put your book under your chair.
- Draw an elephant on the board.
- Write 'mouse' on the board.
- Touch your feet.

Listen and read

I like football and tennis.
I don't like basketball and volleyball.
My favourite sport is football.

Tom Brown

6 / 7

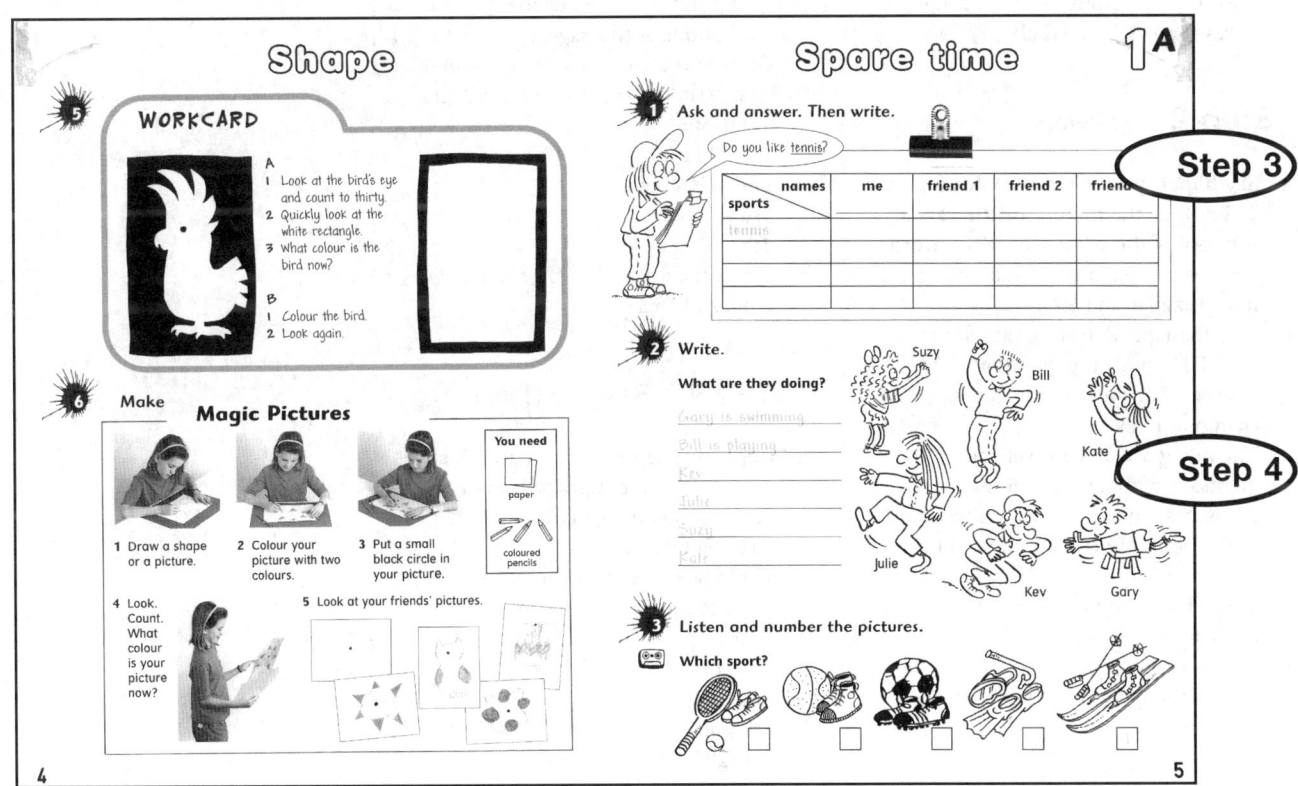

Shape

5 WORKCARD

A
1 Look at the bird's eye and count to thirty.
2 Quickly look at the white rectangle.
3 What colour is the bird now?

B
1 Colour the bird.
2 Look again.

6 Make Magic Pictures

You need: paper, coloured pencils

1 Draw a shape or a picture.
2 Colour your picture with two colours.
3 Put a small black circle in your picture.
4 Look. Count. What colour is your picture now?
5 Look at your friends' pictures.

Spare time 1A

1 Ask and answer. Then write.

Do you like tennis?

sports \ names	me	friend 1	friend 2	friend
tennis				

Step 3

2 Write.

What are they doing?

Gary is swimming
Bill is playing
Kev
Julie
Suzy
Kate

Suzy, Bill, Kate, Julie, Kev, Gary

Step 4

3 Listen and number the pictures.

Which sport?

□ □ □ □ □

4 / 5

23

1A Lesson 2

Main Language Items		Resource File	Materials Needed
Which car is first?	first	31	dice/counters
the red/yellow/green one	second	32	cassette/cassette player
	third	38a	
	last	76c	
	win		

Step 1 Listening (Task)

a   Ask pupils to look at the pictures at the bottom of page 5 in the Activity Book.
b   They will hear the sounds of five sports being played, and must decide what each sport is and write the appropriate number in each box.
c   Check pupils' answers by asking '**What is happening in number one?**'
   Answers:
   1 Skiing 2 Tennis 3 Swimming
   4 Football 5 Basketball

Step 2 Pairwork

a   Say 'Open your Coursebook on page 7. Look at the picture of the cars at the top of the page. Cover the words next to the picture.' Divide the class into pairs, P1 and P2.
b   Play the tape. Pupils repeat after the tape. P1 repeats the questions, P2 answers. They repeat four times, changing roles.
c   Then they ask and answer the questions without the help of the tape. P1 asks the questions using the words in the book to help, P2 answers using only the picture.
d   They change roles and repeat the procedure.
e   Continue until pupils can ask and answer the questions without the help of the words.

Step 3 The Sports Game

a   Say 'Open your Activity Book on page 6. Look at the board game. The game is for four players. Under the game are the dice scores of the four players. Find out which player wins the game, which player is second, which player is third and which is last.'
b   Pupils work in pairs, count the dice moves and then answer the questions at the bottom of the page.
c   Go over the answers with the whole class. Ask '**Who is the winner?**' etc.
   Solution:
   1st – Player 3
   2nd – Player 4
   3rd – Player 1
   4th – Player 2
d   Pupils then play the game in pairs or groups of four.

Step 4 Reading (Task)

a   Copy the shapes and letters at the top of page 7 of the Activity Book on to the blackboard. Write the following three sentences:
   The first letter is in the big triangle.
   The second letter is in the small circle.
   The third letter is in the big rectangle.
b   Ask pupils '**What letters are in the big triangle?**' Write the letters on the blackboard next to the question. Repeat the procedure for the next two sentences.
c   Pupils then try to decide what the hidden word is. Ask questions such as '**Is the first letter "n" or "c"?**'.
d   When pupils understand the task, direct them to the Reading (Task) at the top of page 7. Pupils follow the clues to find the second word.
e   (**Optional**) Faster pupils can write similar problems for their friends.

What's He Doing?

Look and find

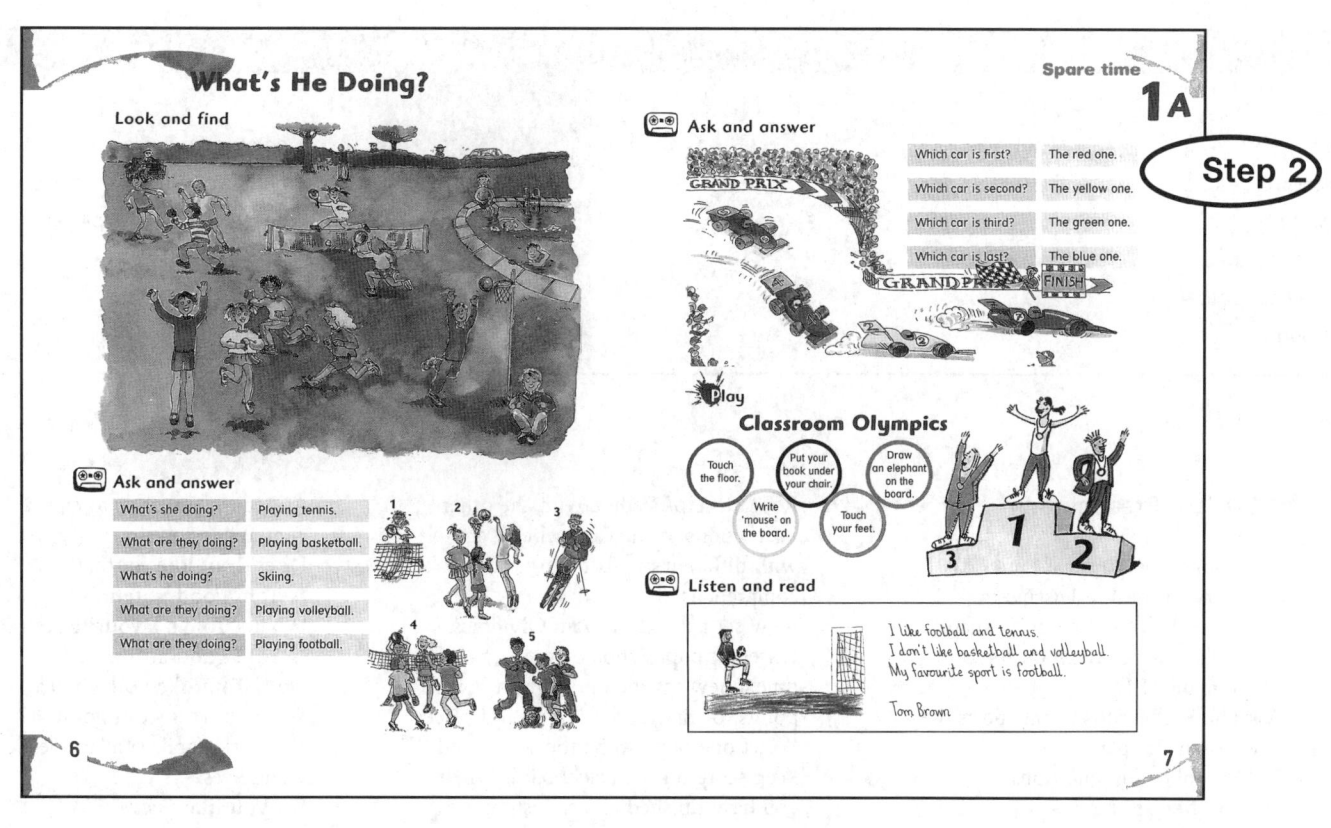

Ask and answer

What's she doing?	Playing tennis.
What are they doing?	Playing basketball.
What's he doing?	Skiing.
What are they doing?	Playing volleyball.
What are they doing?	Playing football.

Spare time 1A

Ask and answer

Which car is first?	The red one.
Which car is second?	The yellow one.
Which car is third?	The green one.
Which car is last?	The blue one.

Play

Classroom Olympics

- Touch the floor.
- Put your book under your chair.
- Draw an elephant on the board.
- Write 'mouse' on the board.
- Touch your feet.

Listen and read

I like football and tennis.
I don't like basketball and volleyball.
My favourite sport is football.

Tom Brown

1A Spare time

4 Play the game and write.

The Sports Game

- FINISH
- 28
- 27 Skiing is dangerous. Go back to twenty-four.
- 26
- 25
- 20
- 21 There is no water in the swimming pool. Go back to nineteen.
- 22
- 23
- 24
- 19
- 18
- 17 You don't like sport. Go back to thirteen.
- 16
- 15 You haven't got a football. Go back to twelve.
- 10 GOAL! Go to fourteen.
- 11
- 12
- 13
- 14
- 9
- 8
- 7 You can't swim. Go back to four.
- 6
- 5
- START HERE
- 1
- 2 You like tennis and basketball. Go to five.
- 3
- 4

Player 1 (Red)
Player 2 (Blue)
Player 3 (Yellow)
Player 4 (Green)

Who wins the game? Player ____
Who is second? Player ____
Who is third? Player ____
Who is last? Player ____

Spare time 1A

5 Write the letters and find the words.

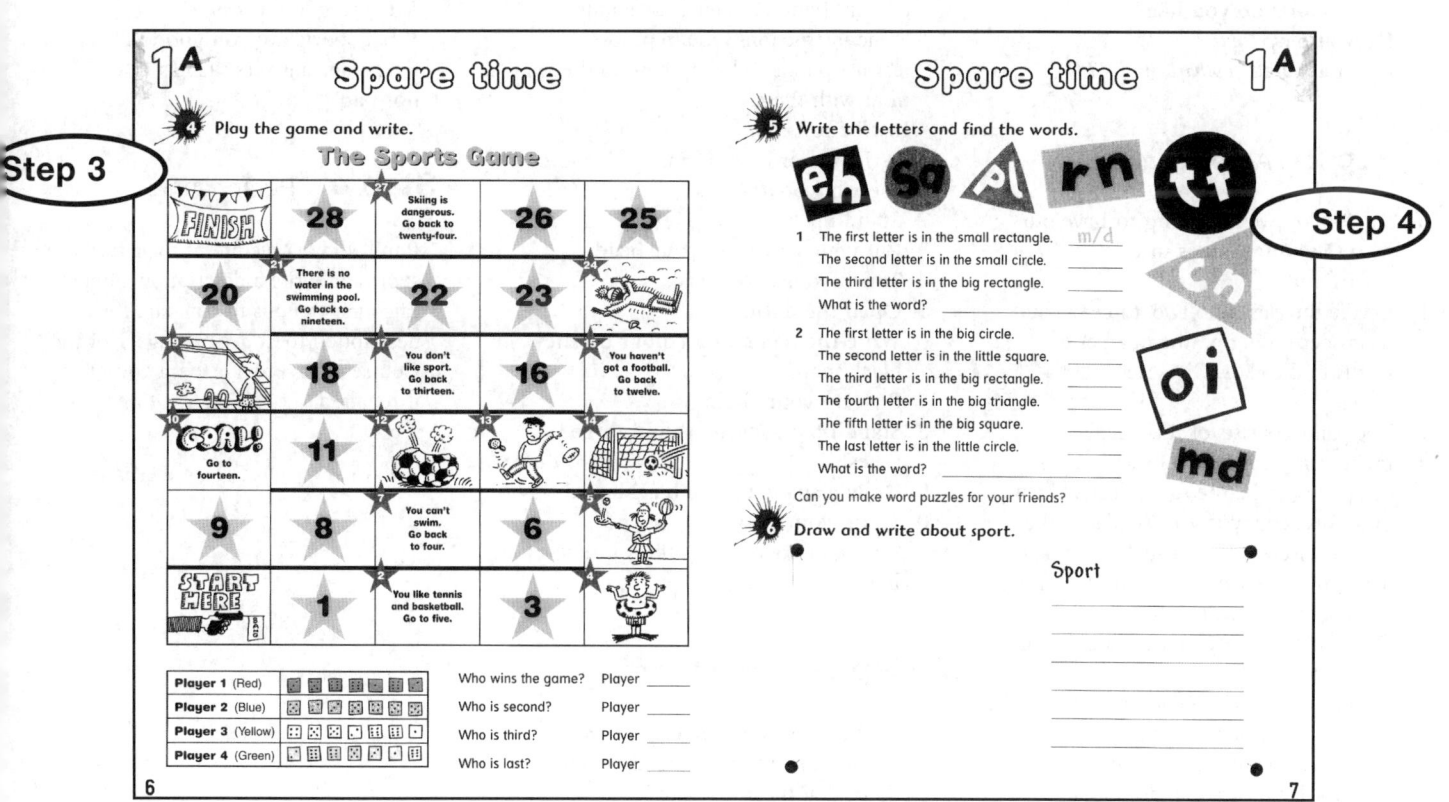

1. The first letter is in the small rectangle. m/d
   The second letter is in the small circle. ____
   The third letter is in the big rectangle. ____
   What is the word? ____

2. The first letter is in the big circle. ____
   The second letter is in the little square. ____
   The third letter is in the big rectangle. ____
   The fourth letter is in the big triangle. ____
   The fifth letter is in the big square. ____
   The last letter is in the little circle. ____
   What is the word? ____

Can you make word puzzles for your friends?

6 Draw and write about sport.

Sport

1A Lesson 3

Main Language Items		Resource File	Materials Needed
I like …	OK	4	coloured pencils
I watch …	not bad	10	paper for display (optional)
I play football/etc.		28	cassette/cassette player
I'm good at …		53	
I'm not good at ….			
I like playing football/etc.			
My favourite ….			

Step 1 Presentation

a Ask pupils why physical exercise is necessary for health. Discuss the consequences of not being in shape and make a list of them on the board in the pupils' L1.

b Ask pupils questions about sports they like, watch and play.
Use the following questions:
Do you like sport?
What sports do you like?
Do you play *tennis*?
Do you watch *football* on TV?

Step 2 Action game

a Say 'Today we are going to have our own Olympic Games in the classroom.'

b Divide the class into two, three or four teams depending on the number of pupils in the class. Give each team a colour.

c The game consists of the teacher giving simple instructions and pupils competing to be the first to carry them out. This activity is very similar to the previous Action Games in *New Stepping Stones*, the major difference being the competitive element.

d One pupil from each team should come to the front of the class. They need to be sitting on chairs. Give the first instruction: '**Touch the floor.**' Ask the class who was first, second, etc. Since this is a demonstration, do not award points at this stage.

e Repeat the procedure with the other instructions in the Coursebook and with different pupils to ensure comprehension.

f Now start the Classroom Olympics. Different pupils should compete each time a new instruction is given. Award points for first, second and third places. Select one pupil to be the scorer and keep score on the blackboard. When you have finished all the instructions, add up the total number of points. Some instructions require props; instruct pupils to bring these to the front with them.
Instructions:
1 **Write a word beginning with S on the blackboard.**
2 **Stand up.**
3 **Put your pencil on your head.**
4 **Touch your shoulders.**
5 **Open the door.**
6 **Write the name of a colour on the blackboard.**
7 **Pick up your chair.**
8 **Stand up and turn around three times.**
9 **Draw a snake on the blackboard.**
10 **Sit on your book.**
You can of course add others if time allows.

Step 3 Presentation

a Say '**Look at the drawing on page 7 in your Coursebook.**' Pupils listen and read at the same time.

b Ask some questions to check comprehension:
Does Tom like football?
Is Tom good at tennis?
What's Tom's favourite sport?
Is Tom good at football?
Does Tom like volleyball?
What sport is Tom good at?

c Then ask pupils similar questions about themselves:
Do you like *football*?
Are you good at *tennis*?
What sports are you good at?
Encourage answers such as **OK** and **not bad**.

Step 4 Personal file

Pupils draw a picture of their favourite sport and write a description alongside. Encourage pupils to compare their description to Tom's on page 7 of the Coursebook. Provide extra vocabulary if required.

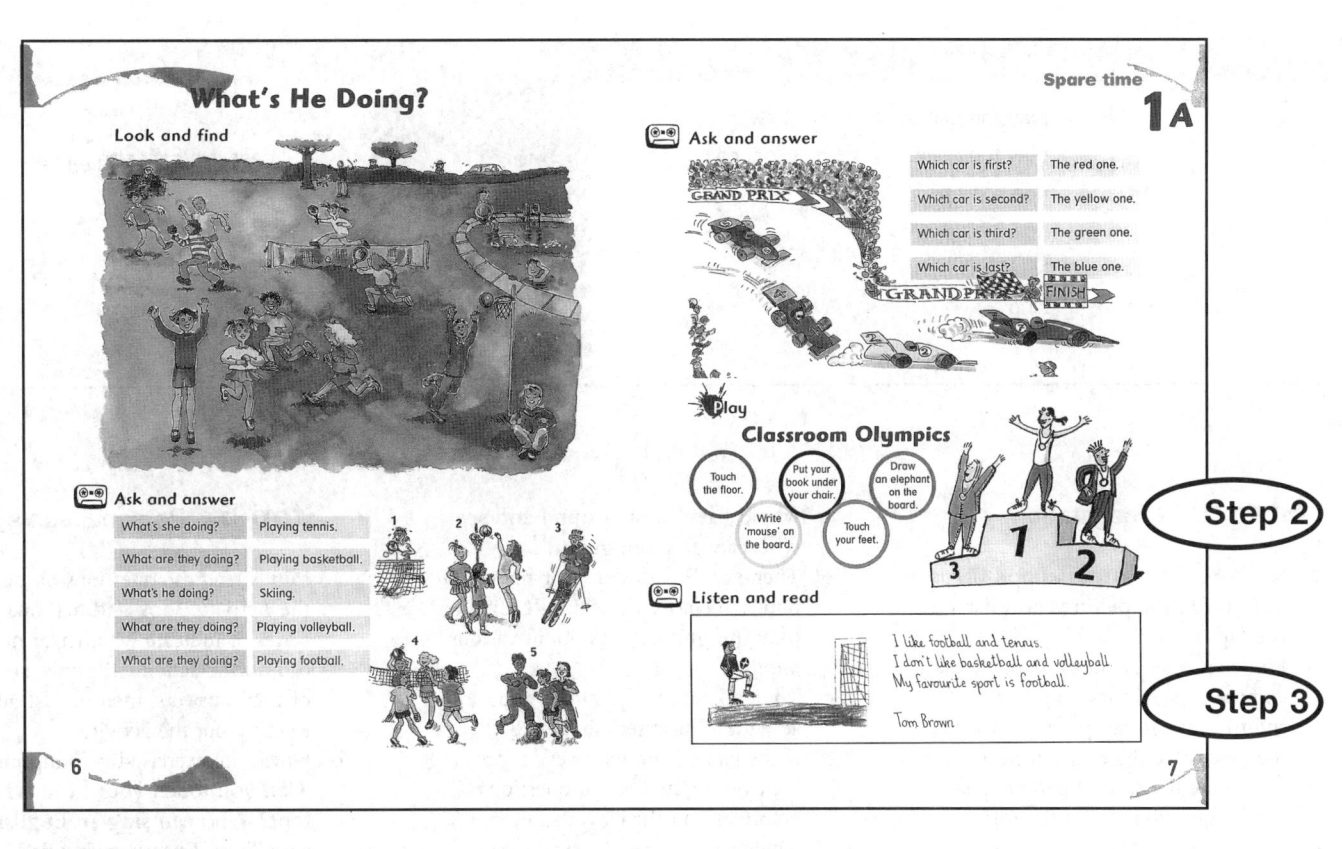

What's He Doing?

Look and find

Ask and answer

What's she doing?	Playing tennis.
What are they doing?	Playing basketball.
What's he doing?	Skiing.
What are they doing?	Playing volleyball.
What are they doing?	Playing football.

Spare time

1A

Ask and answer

Which car is first?	The red one.
Which car is second?	The yellow one.
Which car is third?	The green one.
Which car is last?	The blue one.

Play

Classroom Olympics

- Touch the floor.
- Put your book under your chair.
- Draw an elephant on the board.
- Write 'mouse' on the board.
- Touch your feet.

Step 2

Listen and read

I like football and tennis.
I don't like basketball and volleyball.
My favourite sport is football.

Tom Brown

Step 3

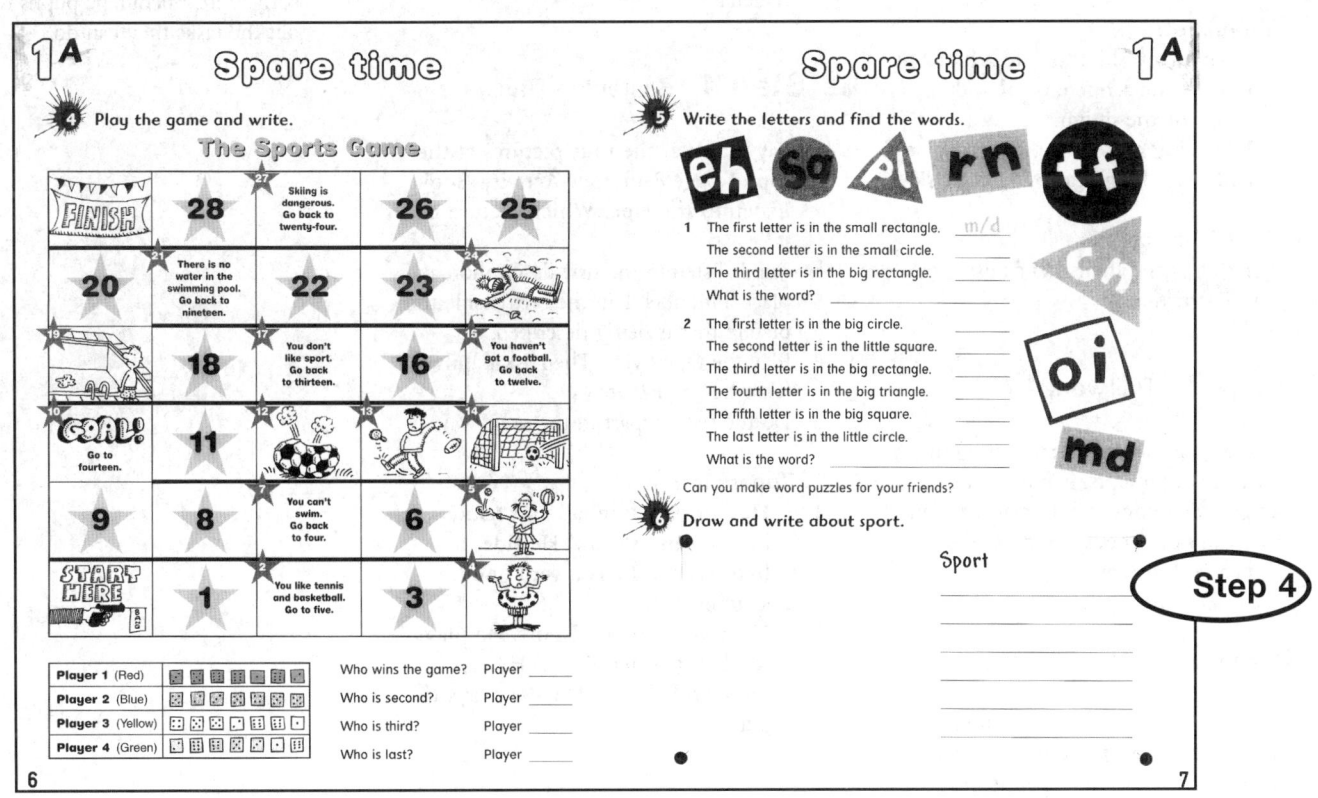

1A Spare time

4 Play the game and write.

The Sports Game

FINISH — 28 — Skiing is dangerous. Go back to twenty-four. — 26 — 25

20 — There is no water in the swimming pool. Go back to nineteen. — 22 — 23 — 24

19 — 18 — You don't like sport. Go back to thirteen. — 16 — You haven't got a football. Go back to twelve.

GOAL! Go to fourteen. — 11 — 12 — 13 — 14

9 — 8 — You can't swim. Go back to four. — 6 — 5

START HERE — 1 — You like tennis and basketball. Go to five. — 3 — 4

Player 1 (Red)
Player 2 (Blue)
Player 3 (Yellow)
Player 4 (Green)

Who wins the game? Player ____
Who is second? Player ____
Who is third? Player ____
Who is last? Player ____

Spare time 1A

5 Write the letters and find the words.

1 The first letter is in the small rectangle. m/d
  The second letter is in the small circle. ____
  The third letter is in the big rectangle. ____
  What is the word? ____

2 The first letter is in the big circle.
  The second letter is in the little square. ____
  The third letter is in the big rectangle. ____
  The fourth letter is in the big triangle. ____
  The fifth letter is in the big square. ____
  The last letter is in the little circle. ____
  What is the word? ____

Can you make word puzzles for your friends?

6 Draw and write about sport.

Sport

Step 4

27

1B Lesson 1

Main Language Items		Resource File	Materials Needed
Can you …?	play the piano	swim	
I can …	play the guitar	dance	31
Who can …?	ride a horse		39	cassette/cassette player
What can he/she do?	ride a bike		49a	
	ski		72	
	sing		73	

Step 1 Presentation

a Say 'Open your Coursebook on page 8. Look at the pictures and listen to the tape.'
b Play part one. Then ask pupils some comprehension questions: 'Can he swim?', 'What can he do?' etc. Play the tape more than once if necessary.
c Then play the second part and ask similar questions about the girl.

Tapescript:
1 I can swim, ski and ride a bike but I can't ride a horse or play the piano or the guitar.
2 I can sing and dance, ride a horse and play the guitar but I can't ski.

d Finally ask pupils to talk about themselves and their friends using the above structures.

Step 2 Pairwork

Divide the class into pairs. Using the pictures as prompts, pupils ask and answer questions about what they can and can't do. They should use the structure 'Can you … ?'

Step 3 Memory game

a Ask the whole class 'Who can play the guitar? Put up your hand if you can play the guitar.' Then tell the whole class 'Look around and see who can play the guitar.'
b Then say 'Put down your hands.' Test pupils' memory by asking 'Can *Alex* play the guitar?' Ask about various pupils.
c Then ask similar questions about other activities illustrated on page 8.
d If the game is proving very simple, increase the number of questions before asking the class if they can remember.

Step 4 Listening (Task)

a Say 'Look at the four pictures at the top of page 8 in your Activity Book. Listen to the tape. Which picture is it?'
b Pupils listen to the first description and place a number 1 in the box beside the picture that is being described.
c Play the tape twice. Then ask pupils 'Can he swim?' etc.
d Do the second part in the same way.

Tapescript:
1 He can play football and tennis but he can't ski. // He rides a bike // and he is a very good swimmer. //
2 He is very good at sport. He plays football and tennis. // He can swim and ski. // He also plays the piano.

Step 5 Personal survey

a Pupils read the questions on page 8 of the Activity Book and tick one of the boxes to indicate whether or not they can do the activity. If pupils are unsure of their answers, then they should try to carry out the activity.
b Finish the exercise by asking pupils 'Can you touch your head with your foot? Who can sing an English song?' etc. Encourage pupils to carry out the tasks they can do.

Step 1

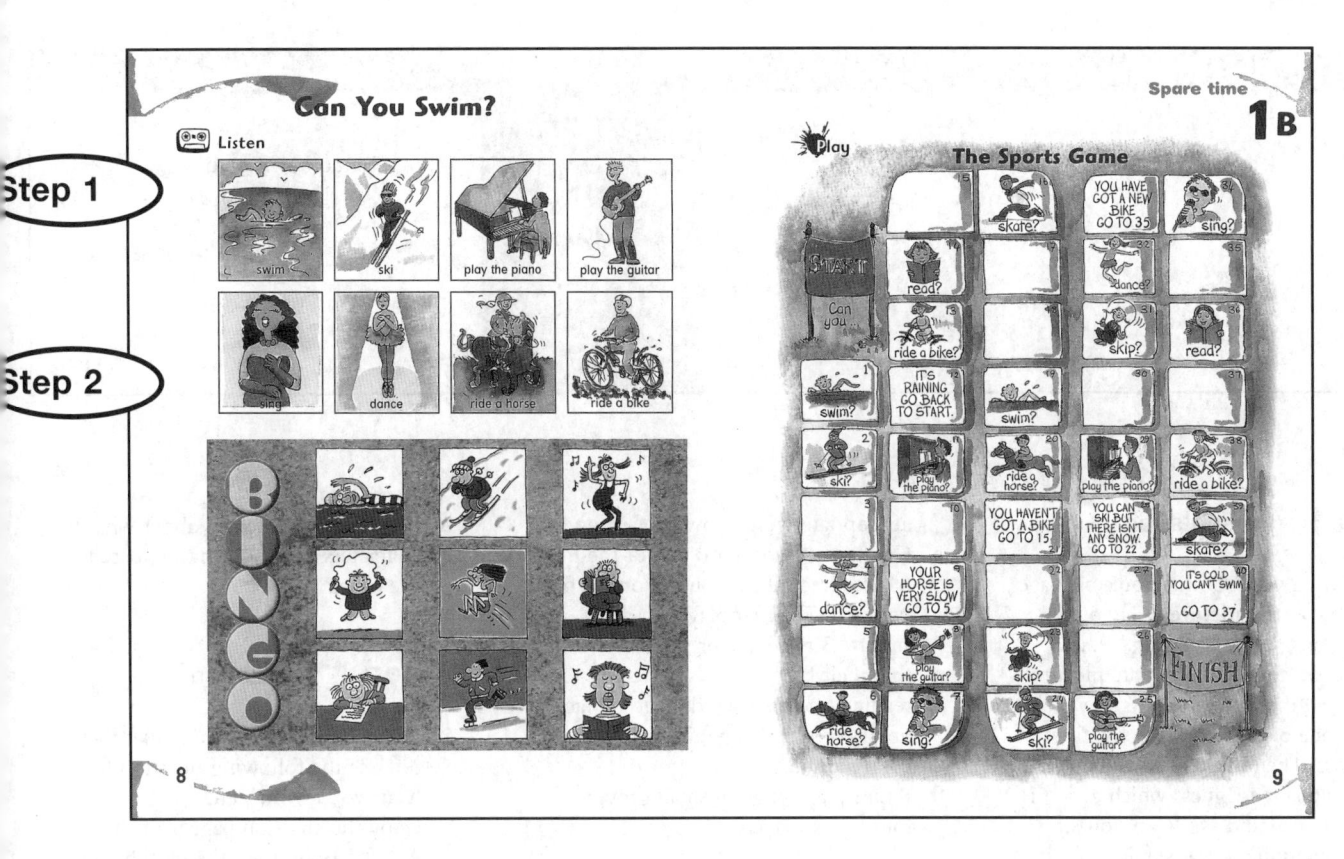

Can You Swim?

Listen

swim · ski · play the piano · play the guitar
sing · dance · ride a horse · ride a bike

BINGO

Spare time

Play

The Sports Game

Step 4

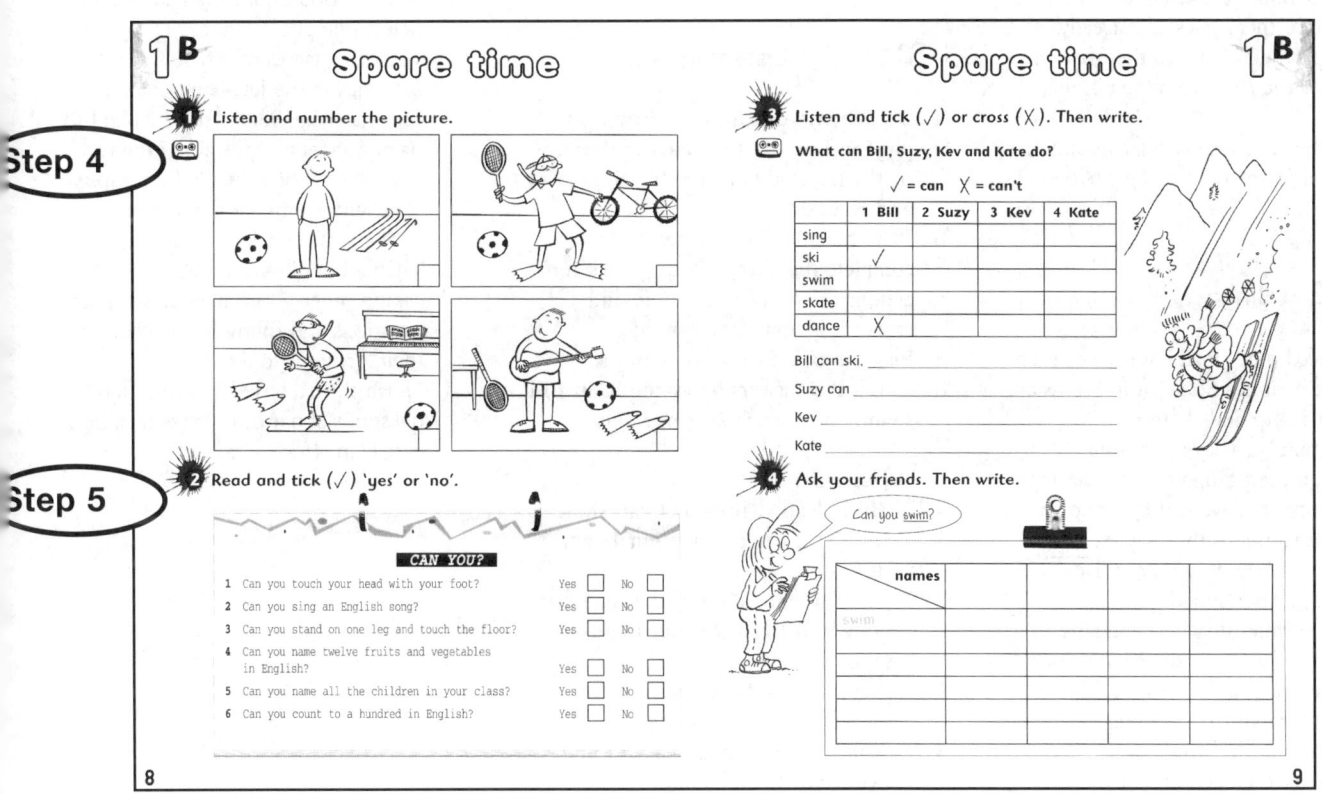

1B Spare time

1 Listen and number the picture.

2 Read and tick (✓) 'yes' or 'no'.

CAN YOU?

1 Can you touch your head with your foot? Yes ☐ No ☐
2 Can you sing an English song? Yes ☐ No ☐
3 Can you stand on one leg and touch the floor? Yes ☐ No ☐
4 Can you name twelve fruits and vegetables in English? Yes ☐ No ☐
5 Can you name all the children in your class? Yes ☐ No ☐
6 Can you count to a hundred in English? Yes ☐ No ☐

Spare time 1B

3 Listen and tick (✓) or cross (✗). Then write.

What can Bill, Suzy, Kev and Kate do?

✓ = can   ✗ = can't

	1 Bill	2 Suzy	3 Kev	4 Kate
sing				
ski	✓			
swim				
skate				
dance	✗			

Bill can ski. _____

Suzy can _____

Kev _____

Kate _____

4 Ask your friends. Then write.

Can you swim?

names				
swim				

29

1^B Lesson 2

Main Language Items	Resource File	Materials Needed
I can … What can I do? Can you …? Can he/she …?	5 28 31 49a	Bingo cover cards cassette/cassette player

Step 1 Presentation

a Say 'Open your Coursebook on page 8. Look at the pictures.' Say one of the actions, e.g. 'I can sing.' Pupils must point to the appropriate picture. Revise all the actions in this way.

b Mime one of the actions at the front of the class. Then ask pupils 'What can I do?' Pupils must guess which action is being mimed and ask 'Can you sing?' Pupils continue to ask similar questions until one of them guesses correctly. This pupil then comes to the front and mimes for the class. Continue in this way.

c Divide the class into two teams and award points to add a competitive element.

Step 2 Bingo

a Pupils need nine small cover cards each with one action written on it. Pre-teach the words **skip** and **skate**.

b Instruct pupils to cover any four squares on their bingo card by placing the appropriate cover card face down over the picture. In this way, each pupil's card should now have five different pictures showing.

c The bingo caller (teacher) will also need a set of word cards. Shuffle your cards. Lay them face down in front of you. Ask '**Are you ready?**' Select a card. Read out the word.

d Pupils cover each action that is called out, placing the cover card with the appropriate word showing face up.

e Continue calling until one of the pupils has covered all the squares on his or her card. The first player to do so shouts '**Bingo**'. He or she must confirm that their bingo card is correct by reading back the words that are face up. If correct, this pupil wins, if not, continue the game.

f Pupils play bingo in small groups of four to six players.

Step 3 Listening (Task)

a Say 'Open your Activity Book on page 9. Look at the chart at the top of the page. What can Bill, Suzy, Kev and Kate do?'

b Play the tape. Pupils listen and complete the chart, placing a tick for actions the characters can do and a cross for actions they can't do.

c Play the tape two or three times.

d Check the answers by asking 'Can Bill swim?' or 'Can Suzy sing?' etc.

Tapescript:

1 (Bill) I can swim and I can skate and ski. I can't dance but I can sing.

2 (Suzy) I can sing and dance. I can skate and I can ski, but I can't swim.

3 (Kev) I can't dance or sing, but I can swim, ski and skate.

4 (Kate) I can sing, dance, ski and swim, but I can't skate.

e Pupils write sentences about what the characters can and can't do, based on the chart.

Step 4 Questionnaire

a Ask various pupils about what they can do. Use the following question form: '**Can you swim?**', etc.

b Copy the chart on page 9 of the Activity Book onto the blackboard. Select one pupil. Direct him or her to write the names of any five sports or activities in the left-hand column of the chart (e.g. dance, ski, etc.) and the names of four pupils along the top. Then he or she asks the four pupils '**Can you swim?**' etc. and records their answers using ticks and crosses.

c Then all pupils work in groups of four, asking other group members similar questions and filling in the charts in their Activity Books.

d Finish the exercise by asking pupils questions about other class members, e.g. 'Can *Alex* swim?'.

Can You Swim?

Step 1 — Listen

swim | ski | play the piano | play the guitar
sing | dance | ride a horse | ride a bike

Step 2 — BINGO

Spare time 1B

Play — The Sports Game

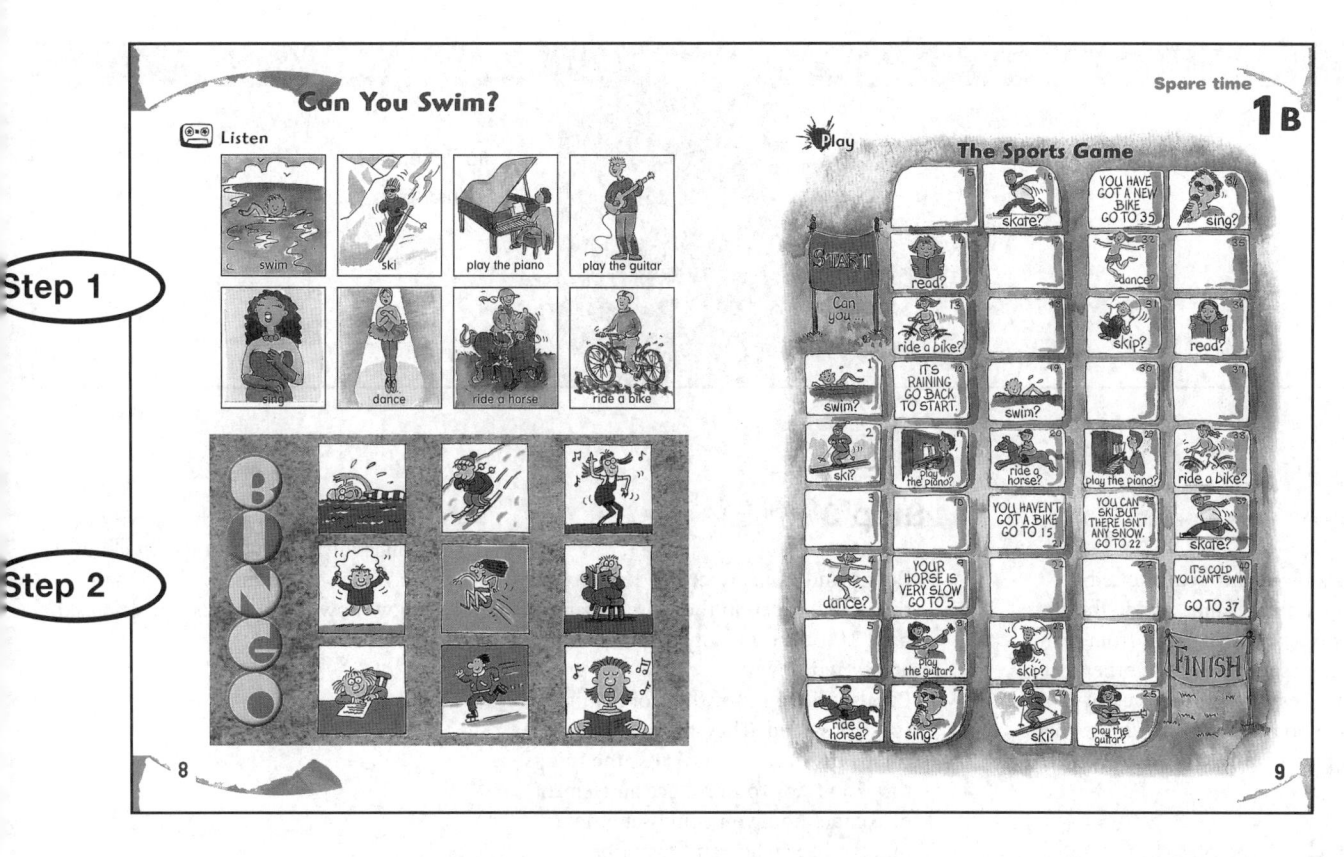

Spare time 1B

1 Listen and number the picture.

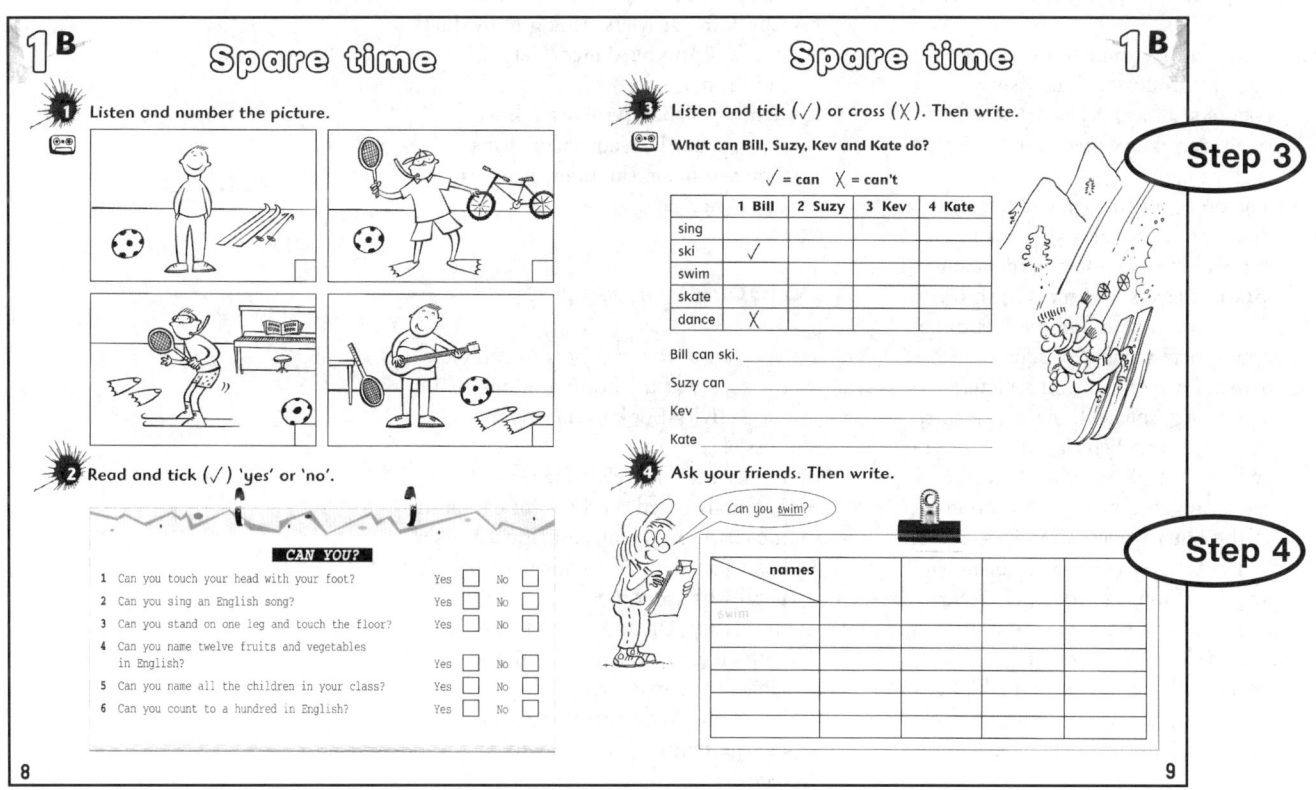

2 Read and tick (✓) 'yes' or 'no'.

CAN YOU?

1 Can you touch your head with your foot? Yes ☐ No ☐
2 Can you sing an English song? Yes ☐ No ☐
3 Can you stand on one leg and touch the floor? Yes ☐ No ☐
4 Can you name twelve fruits and vegetables in English? Yes ☐ No ☐
5 Can you name all the children in your class? Yes ☐ No ☐
6 Can you count to a hundred in English? Yes ☐ No ☐

3 Listen and tick (✓) or cross (✗). Then write.

What can Bill, Suzy, Kev and Kate do?

✓ = can   ✗ = can't

	1 Bill	2 Suzy	3 Kev	4 Kate
sing				
ski	✓			
swim				
skate				
dance	✗			

Bill can ski. _____
Suzy can _____
Kev _____
Kate _____

Step 3

4 Ask your friends. Then write.

Can you swim?

names				
swim				

Step 4

1B Lesson 3

Main Language Items	Resource File	Materials Needed
Can you ...?	5	dice/counters beans/coins

Step 1 Mime game

Quickly revise different sports by playing a mime game: divide the class into two teams. One pupil from each team mimes a sport to the other team. If they guess the sport correctly, they win one point. If they're wrong, they lose a point.

Step 2 The Sports Game

a This is a dice game to be played in pairs or groups of three, using counters, a dice, beans or coins and one Coursebook open at page 9 for each group.
b The object of the game is to collect as many beans or coins as possible.
c All players place their counters on 'Start'. Players take turns to throw the dice and move around the board the appropriate number of squares.
d When a player lands on a picture square, e.g. square 1 'swim', he or she must ask the other player(s) 'Can you swim?' The player who asked the question gets a bean or coin from each of the other players who answers 'Yes'.
e When a player lands on a square with an instruction, e.g. square 9 'Your horse is very slow. Go to 5', he or she must follow the instruction.
f When a player reaches 'Finish', the game ends. The player with the most beans or coins is the winner.

Step 3 Puzzle

a Pupils find as many of the 18 verbs as they can, hidden in the word square on page 10 of the Activity book, looking across and down.
b Pupils write a list of the words in the space provided. They then tick the things they can do and cross the things they can't do. To introduce an element of competition, you could set a time limit and see who can finish first.
c Check the answers, asking individual pupils 'Can you dance?', etc.
Solution:
Across – dance, write, stand, walk, sing, paint, fly, read, skate, drink
Down – swim, ski, draw, jump eat, run, point, sit

Step 4 Class survey

a The aim of this survey is to complete the survey at the bottom of page 10 in the Activity Book as quickly as possible.
b Pupils ask other class members questions based on the information in the chart, e.g. 'Can you ride a horse?' 'Can you dance?' Pupils must find one pupil who can do each of the tasks in the survey. The first pupil to finish with all answers correct is the winner.
c Finish the survey with the whole class by asking: **Who can** *ride a horse*? **Give me the name of a boy who can** *dance*? etc.
d You could follow up this activity by collecting all the information about the class and making a graph or chart to show how many pupils can skate, ski, swim etc.

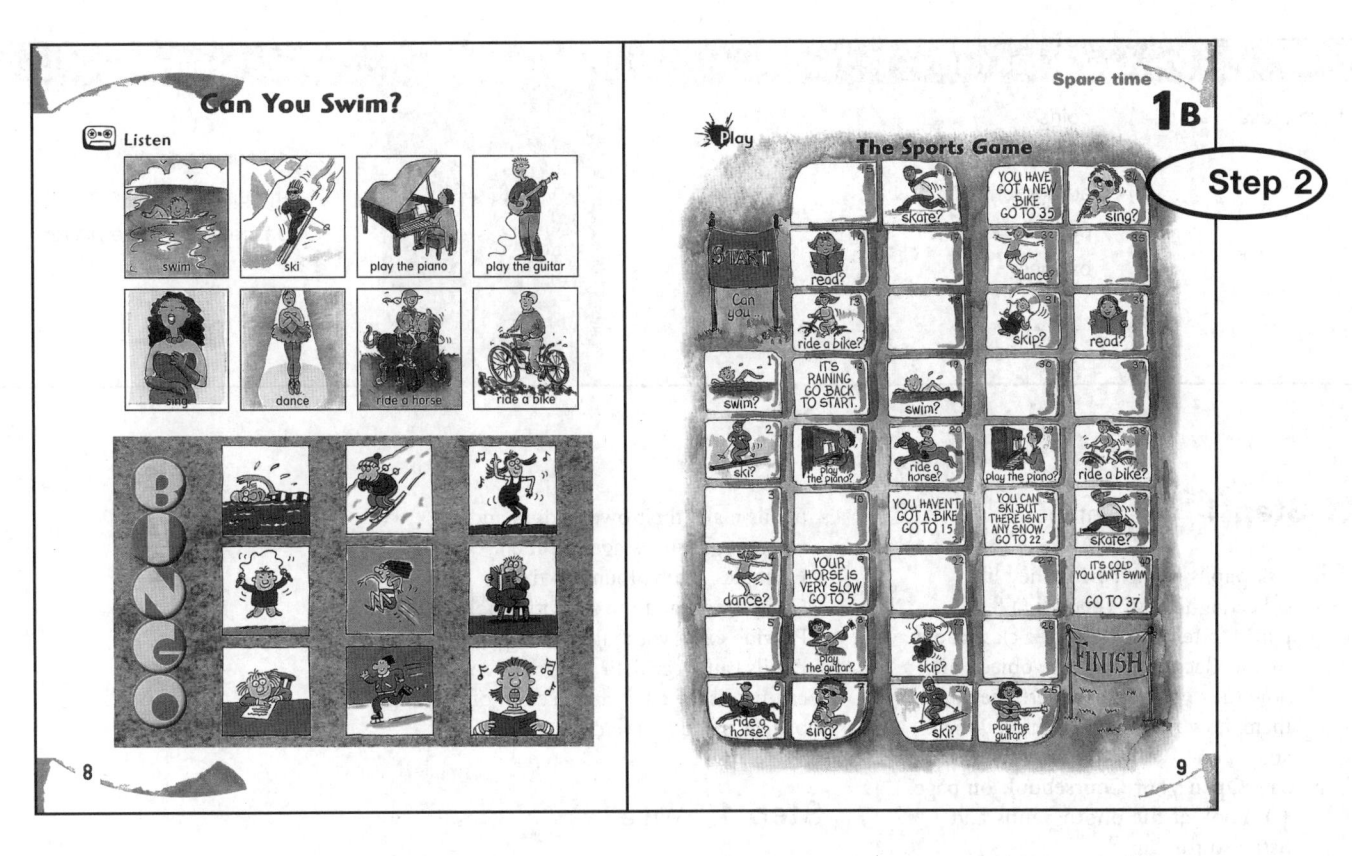

Can You Swim?

Listen

swim | ski | play the piano | play the guitar
sing | dance | ride a horse | ride a bike

BINGO

Spare time 1B

Play — The Sports Game

Step 2

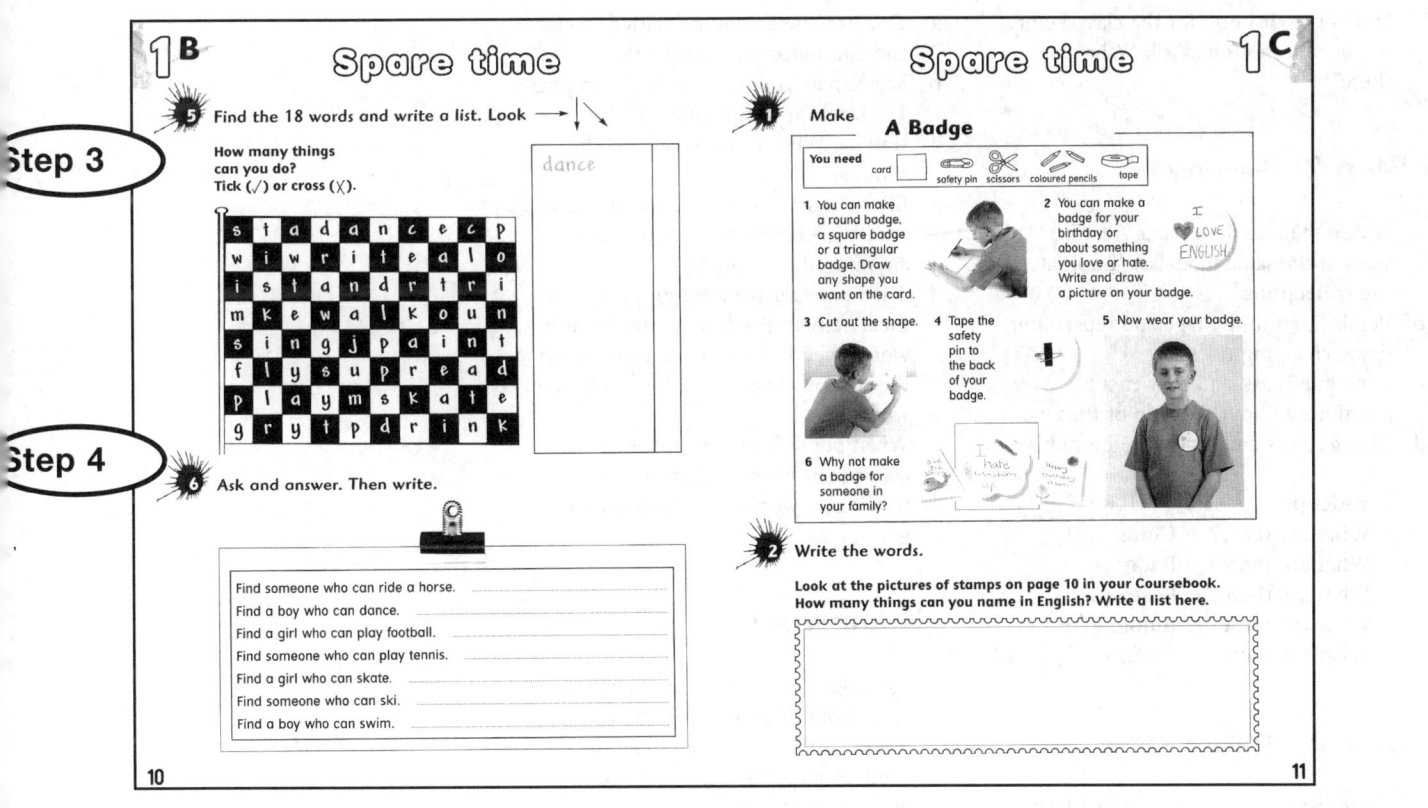

1B Spare time

5 Find the 18 words and write a list.

How many things can you do?
Tick (✓) or cross (✗).

s	t	a	d	a	n	c	e	c	p
w	i	w	r	i	t	e	a	l	o
i	s	t	a	n	d	r	t	r	i
m	k	e	w	a	l	k	o	u	n
s	i	n	g	j	p	a	i	n	t
f	l	y	s	u	p	r	e	a	d
p	l	a	y	m	s	k	a	t	e
g	r	y	t	p	d	r	i	n	k

dance

Step 3

6 Ask and answer. Then write.

Find someone who can ride a horse.
Find a boy who can dance.
Find a girl who can play football.
Find someone who can play tennis.
Find a girl who can skate.
Find someone who can ski.
Find a boy who can swim.

Step 4

Spare time 1C

1 Make — A Badge

You need: card, safety pin, scissors, coloured pencils, tape

1 You can make a round badge, a square badge or a triangular badge. Draw any shape you want on the card.

2 You can make a badge for your birthday or about something you love or hate. Write and draw a picture on your badge.

3 Cut out the shape.

4 Tape the safety pin to the back of your badge.

5 Now wear your badge.

6 Why not make a badge for someone in your family?

2 Write the words.

Look at the pictures of stamps on page 10 in your Coursebook.
How many things can you name in English? Write a list here.

33

1c Lesson 1

Main Language Items		Resource File	Materials Needed
What are these?	coins stamps autographs postcards badges	4 7 23	coloured pencils materials to make a badge cassette/cassette player

Step 1 Presentation

a Ask pupils in their L1 if they like collecting things. Then ask a few pupils to tell the rest of the class about their collections: what the objects are, how they got started, where they find them, how they store or display them, and so on.
b Say 'Open your Coursebook on page 10. Look at the photographs and listen to the tape.'
c Hold up your book for the class. Point to the collections and ask 'What are these?'

Step 2 Pairwork

a Divide the class into pairs. All pairs work at the same time. Say 'Look at the collections.'
b Pupils listen to the tape and repeat four times, changing roles.
c Then pupils ask and answer the questions without the help of the tape.
d Change roles and repeat the procedure.

Tapescript:
What are these? ~ Coins
What are these? ~ Badges
What are these? ~ Postcards
What are these? ~ Autographs
What are these? ~ Stamps

Step 3 Make a badge

a Using the words and pictures on page 11 of the Activity Book as a guide, pupils make their own badges and write English messages on them. Examples can be found in the Coursebook and the Activity Book. Provide extra vocabulary if required.
b Pupils can wear their badges or they can be displayed as a collection of badges made by the class.

Step 4 Write

a This exercise should be started in class and continued for homework.
b Say 'Open your Coursebook on page 10. Look at the pictures of the stamps. What can you see on the stamps?'
c Elicit the names of a few objects and ask, 'Which stamp is it on?' about anything they identify.
d Then pupils make a list on page 11 in their Activity Book of all the English words they know that are pictured on the stamps. (There are a lot of possible words!)
e When pupils have finished, they can count their words and then find out how many words their friends have got.

Homework

Ask pupils to collect a few stamps and coins from their own country or overseas. They will need them for the 'Collect and stick' activity on page 13 of the Activity Book.

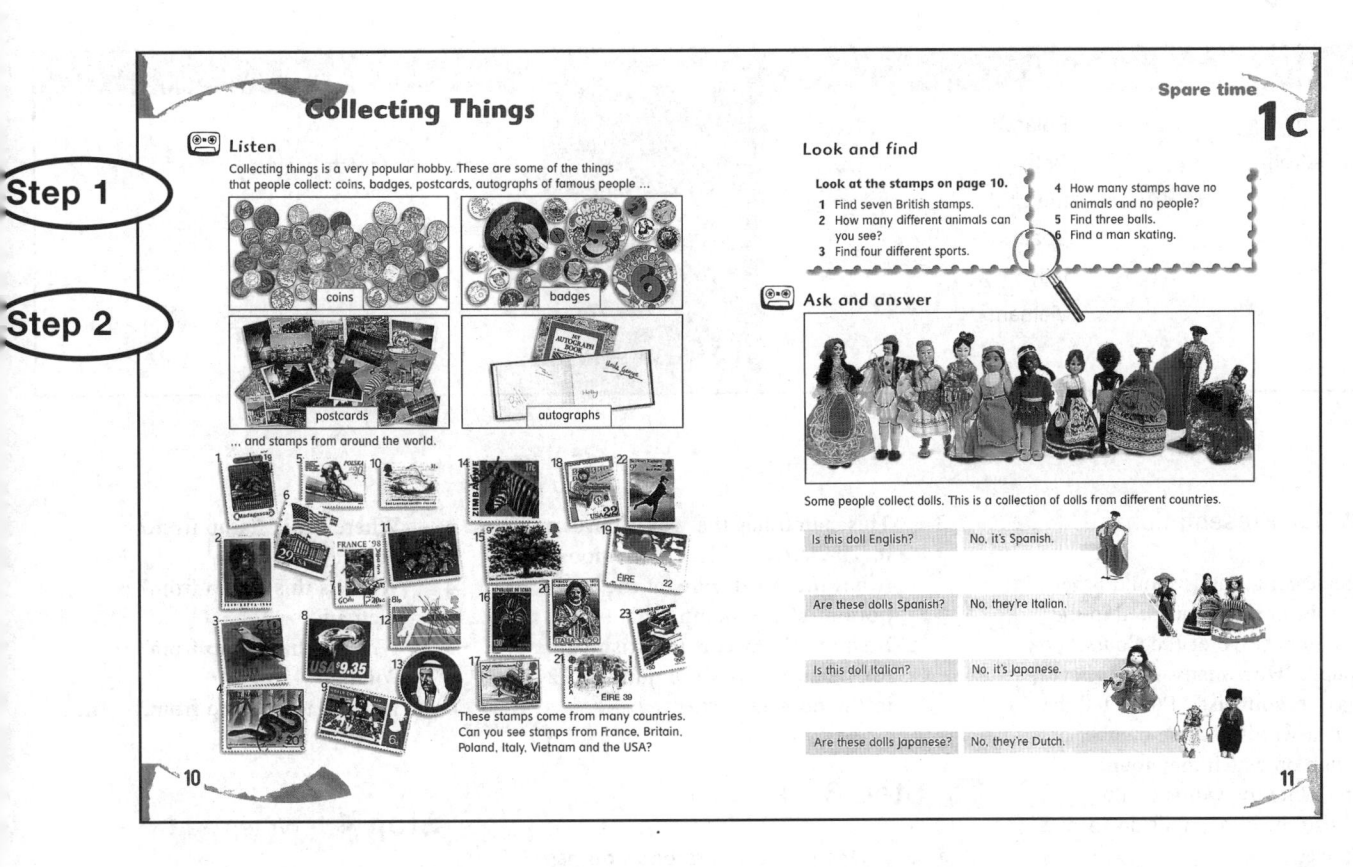

Collecting Things

Listen

Collecting things is a very popular hobby. These are some of the things that people collect: coins, badges, postcards, autographs of famous people ...

coins
badges
postcards
autographs

... and stamps from around the world.

These stamps come from many countries. Can you see stamps from France, Britain, Poland, Italy, Vietnam and the USA?

Spare time 1c

Look and find

Look at the stamps on page 10.
1. Find seven British stamps.
2. How many different animals can you see?
3. Find four different sports.
4. How many stamps have no animals and no people?
5. Find three balls.
6. Find a man skating.

Ask and answer

Some people collect dolls. This is a collection of dolls from different countries.

Is this doll English?	No, it's Spanish.
Are these dolls Spanish?	No, they're Italian.
Is this doll Italian?	No, it's Japanese.
Are these dolls Japanese?	No, they're Dutch.

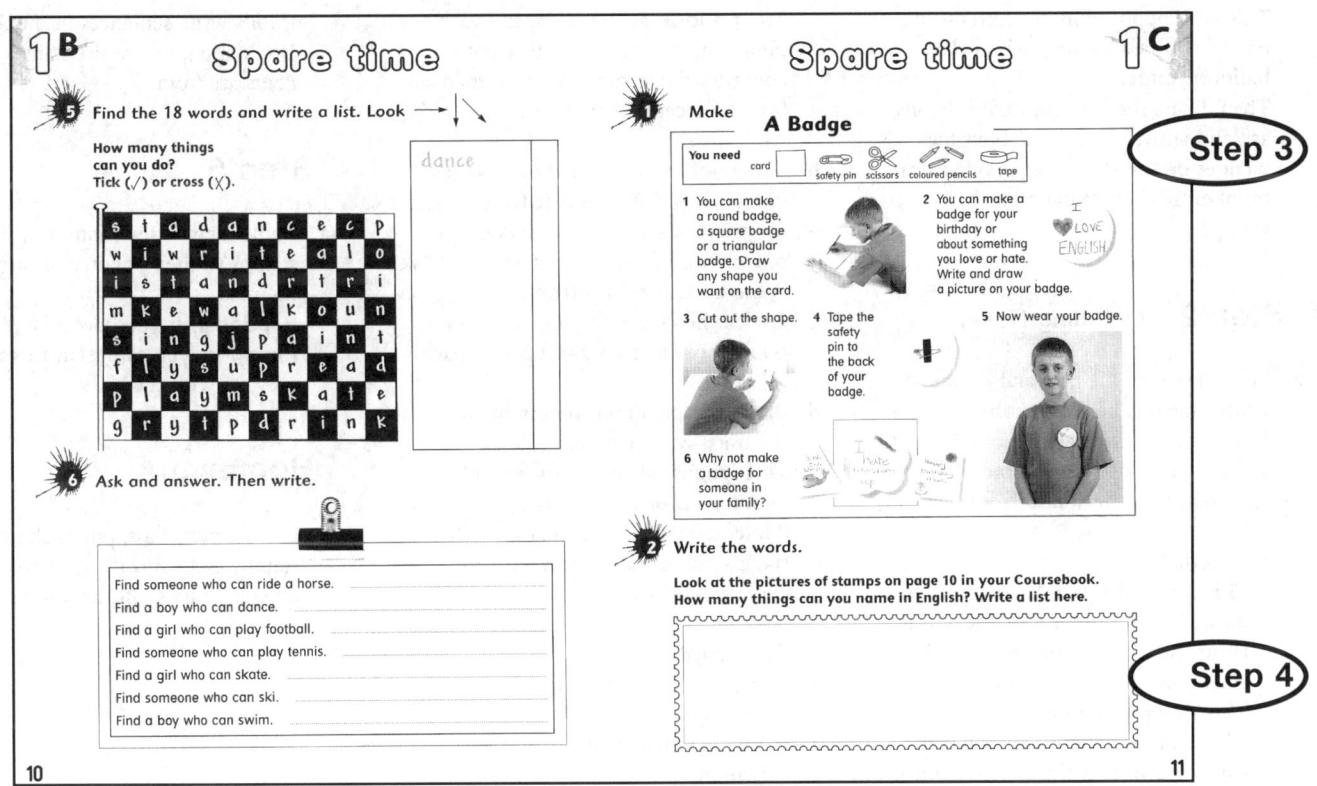

1B Spare time

5. Find the 18 words and write a list. Look ➡️↘️

How many things can you do?
Tick (✓) or cross (✗).

dance

6. Ask and answer. Then write.

Find someone who can ride a horse.
Find a boy who can dance.
Find a girl who can play football.
Find someone who can play tennis.
Find a girl who can skate.
Find someone who can ski.
Find a boy who can swim.

Spare time 1c

1. Make **A Badge**

You need: card, safety pin, scissors, coloured pencils, tape

1. You can make a round badge, a square badge or a triangular badge. Draw any shape you want on the card.
2. You can make a badge for your birthday or about something you love or hate. Write and draw a picture on your badge.
3. Cut out the shape.
4. Tape the safety pin to the back of your badge.
5. Now wear your badge.
6. Why not make a badge for someone in your family?

2. Write the words.

Look at the pictures of stamps on page 10 in your Coursebook. How many things can you name in English? Write a list here.

1c Lesson 2

Main Language Items		Resource File	Materials Needed
Where's this ... from?	Poland		
This stamp/coin is from ...	Britain	7	cassette/cassette player
	the USA	23	
	Spain	33	
	Italy	41b	
	Vietnam		

Step 1 Presentation

a For homework, pupils should have made a list of words pictured in the stamps on page 10 of the Coursebook.
b Ask pupils 'How many words have you got in your list?' Pupils tell the class their words and the number of the stamp on which they found each picture. Write the words on the blackboard or have pupils do so themselves.
This is an opportunity for introducing one or two new words such as **flag, balloon, spider**.
c Then divide the class into pairs. Pupils ask and answer questions about the pictures on the stamps, e.g. 'What's on number 14?' or 'What's on this stamp?'.

Step 2 Listening (Task)

a Pupils listen to the tape and decide which stamp is being described.
b Stop the tape after each description and ask the class 'Which stamp is it?' and 'Where is the stamp from?'.

Tapescript:
1 This stamp has the American flag on it. It has a picture of the White House where the President of the USA lives. It costs 29 cents.
2 This stamp has a picture of a man with a moustache on it. It has the word 'Kuwait' at the bottom and it isn't square: it's round.
3 This stamp has the word 'Love' on it. The letter 'O' is a red balloon. It has the word 'Eire' at the bottom of the stamp. This is an Irish word. 'Eire' is the Irish name for Ireland. It has the number 22 in the bottom corner.

Step 3 Pairwork

a Say 'Open your Coursebook on page 10 and look at the stamps.' Teach pupils the names of the different countries the stamps are from, then ask them to locate them one by one on the world map.
b Say 'Look at the first stamp. What can you see? Where is it from?' Hold up your book for the class. Point to one or two of the other stamps and ask 'Where's this stamp from?'.
c Divide the class into pairs. Only one book between each pair open at page 10.
d Play the tape. Pupils repeat answers in the usual way, changing roles.
e Then pupils ask and answer similar questions about all the stamps.
(Note: tell your pupils that only British stamps do not have the name of the country on them.)

Tapescript:
1 Where's this stamp from? ~ Madagascar.
2 Where's this stamp from? ~ Britain.
3 Where's this stamp from? ~ Poland.
4 Where's this stamp from? ~ Vietnam.
5 Where's this stamp from? ~ Poland.
6 Where's this stamp from? ~ the USA.

Step 4 Write

Pupils write sentences in the Activity Book about where the stamps and coins are from.

Step 5 Puzzle

a Pupils draw lines connecting the stamps to their country of origin on the map.
b (Optional) If you have a large map of the world, you can use it to go over the answers with the class.

Homework

For the next class, pupils should collect stamps and coins if they have not already done so in the last lesson.

Collecting Things

Spare time 1c

Listen
Collecting things is a very popular hobby. These are some of the things that people collect: coins, badges, postcards, autographs of famous people ...

coins   badges
postcards   autographs

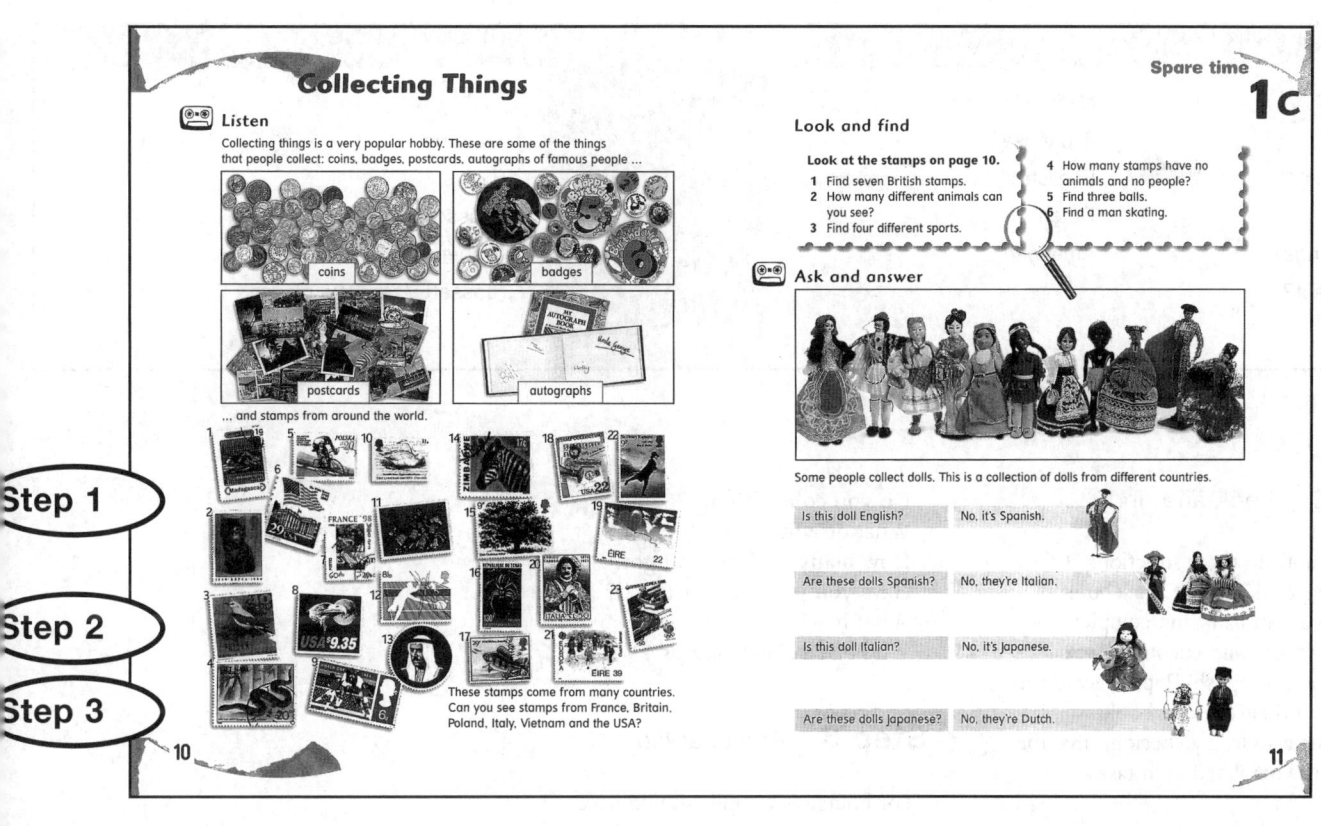

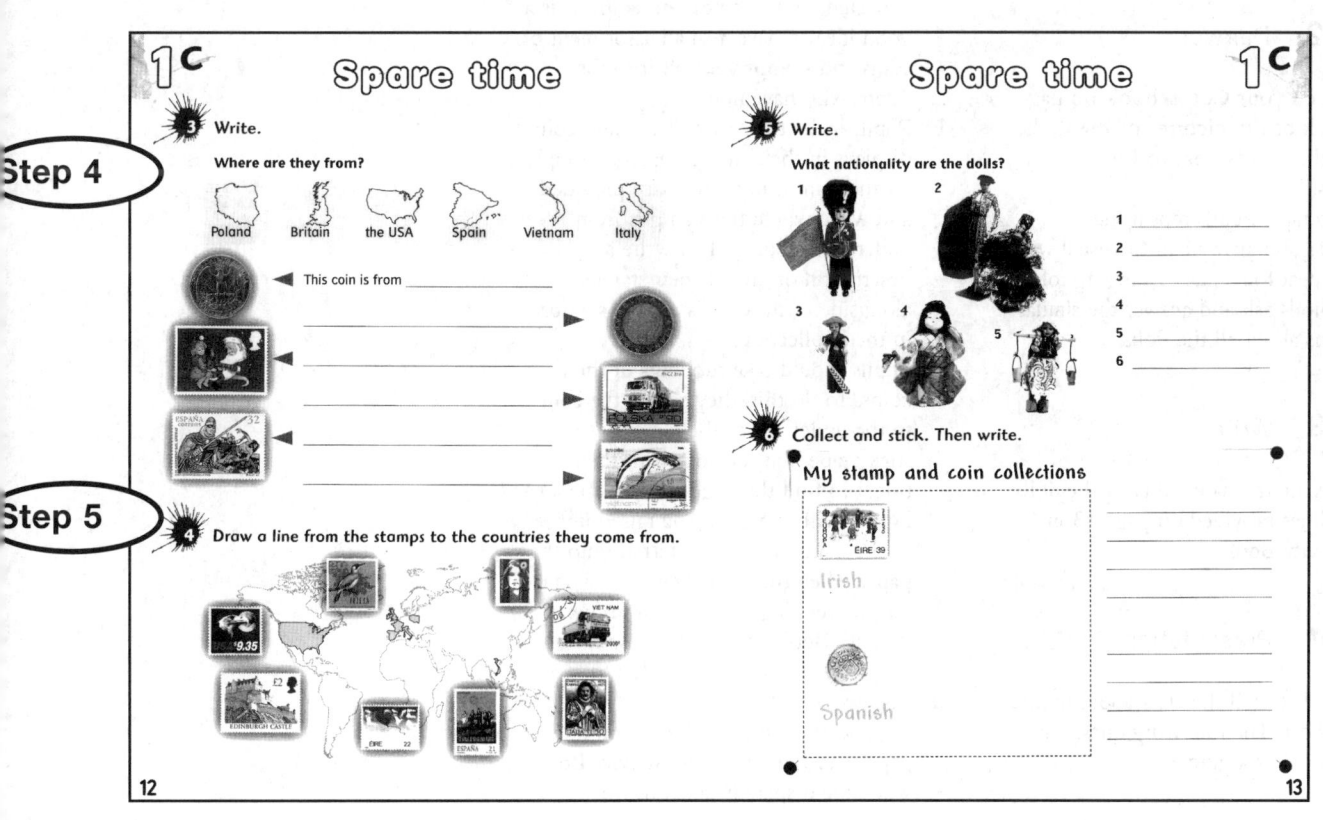

... and stamps from around the world.

These stamps come from many countries. Can you see stamps from France, Britain, Poland, Italy, Vietnam and the USA?

Look and find

Look at the stamps on page 10.
1. Find seven British stamps.
2. How many different animals can you see?
3. Find four different sports.
4. How many stamps have no animals and no people?
5. Find three balls.
6. Find a man skating.

Ask and answer

Some people collect dolls. This is a collection of dolls from different countries.

Is this doll English?	No, it's Spanish.
Are these dolls Spanish?	No, they're Italian.
Is this doll Italian?	No, it's Japanese.
Are these dolls Japanese?	No, they're Dutch.

10   11

1c Spare time

3 Write.

Where are they from?

Poland   Britain   the USA   Spain   Vietnam   Italy

This coin is from _____

_____

_____

_____

4 Draw a line from the stamps to the countries they come from.

Spare time 1c

5 Write.

What nationality are the dolls?

1 _____
2 _____
3 _____
4 _____
5 _____
6 _____

6 Collect and stick. Then write.

My stamp and coin collections

Irish

Spanish

12   13

37

1c Lesson 3

Main Language Items		Resource File	Materials Needed
Is this … English?	*Nationalities:*	4	stamps
No, it's …	Japanese	7	coins
Are these … English?	English		scissors/glue
No, they're …	Dutch		paper for display (optional)
Do you collect things?	American		cassette/cassette player
What do you collect?			

Step 1 Look and find

a Direct pupils to the instructions at the top of page 11 in the Coursebook.
b Pupils work in pairs and complete the tasks. Circulate and encourage discussion in English. Pupils record the answers in their exercise books.
c Finish the activity by checking that the pairs have completed each task.

Step 2 Pairwork

a Say 'Open your Coursebook on page 11. Look at the pictures of the dolls. Cover the words next to the pictures.'
b Play the tape. Pupils repeat the questions and answers in the usual way. They repeat four times, changing roles.
c Then pupils ask and answer the similar questions about all the dolls.

Step 3 Write

Pupils write the nationality of the dolls on the lines provided on page 13 in the Activity Book.

Step 4 Presentation

Ask pupils to tell the class about things they collect. The following questions can be used as a guide:

Do you collect things?
What do you collect?
How many … have you got?
Have you got a favourite … ?
What is it?
Who else collects *stamps*?

Step 5 Personal file

a For homework pupils should have collected a few stamps and coins. It is a good idea to have a small assortment of coins and stamps yourself for those pupils who have none.
b Pupils make their own stamp and coin displays in their Activity Books. Simply fix the stamps into the space provided and write where the stamp is from underneath. Pupils then write a description of one of their stamps alongside or make a list of the stamps in their collection.
c Pupils should take rubbings of their coins. To do this, they secure the coin to the underside of the paper with sticky tape, rub the coin with their finger to find the edge and rub the area lightly with a pencil. The raised image of the coin will be transferred onto the paper. Then they remove the coin, cut out the rubbings, stick them in their Activity Book and write a description alongside (see **Resource File** 65).
d This work makes an excellent wall display. The work can be put on loose paper and fixed into the Activity Book when the display is taken down.

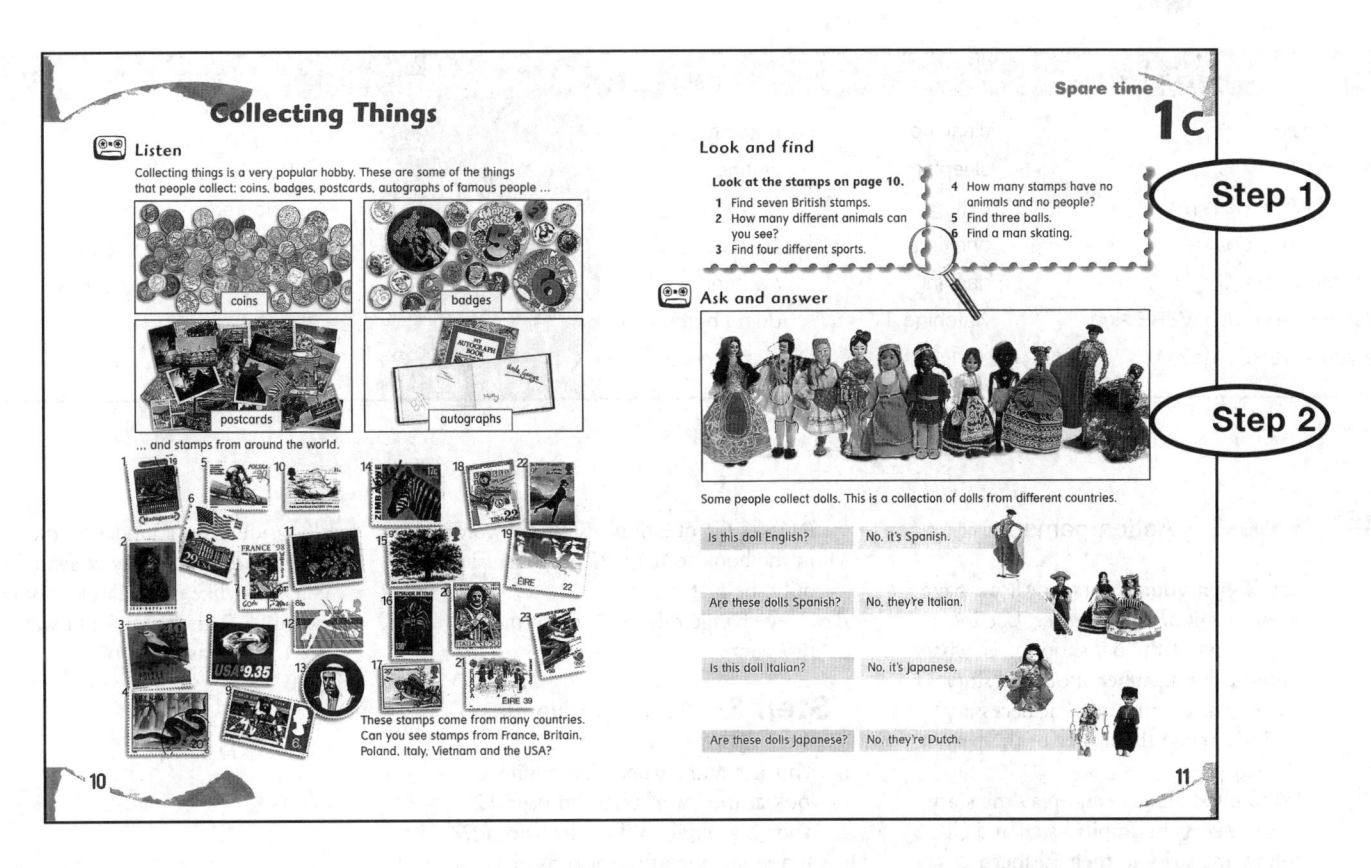

Collecting Things

Listen
Collecting things is a very popular hobby. These are some of the things that people collect: coins, badges, postcards, autographs of famous people ...

coins | badges
postcards | autographs

... and stamps from around the world.

These stamps come from many countries. Can you see stamps from France, Britain, Poland, Italy, Vietnam and the USA?

Spare time
1c

Look and find
Look at the stamps on page 10.
1. Find seven British stamps.
2. How many different animals can you see?
3. Find four different sports.
4. How many stamps have no animals and no people?
5. Find three balls.
6. Find a man skating.

Step 1

Ask and answer

Some people collect dolls. This is a collection of dolls from different countries.

Is this doll English?	No, it's Spanish.
Are these dolls Spanish?	No, they're Italian.
Is this doll Italian?	No, it's Japanese.
Are these dolls Japanese?	No, they're Dutch.

Step 2

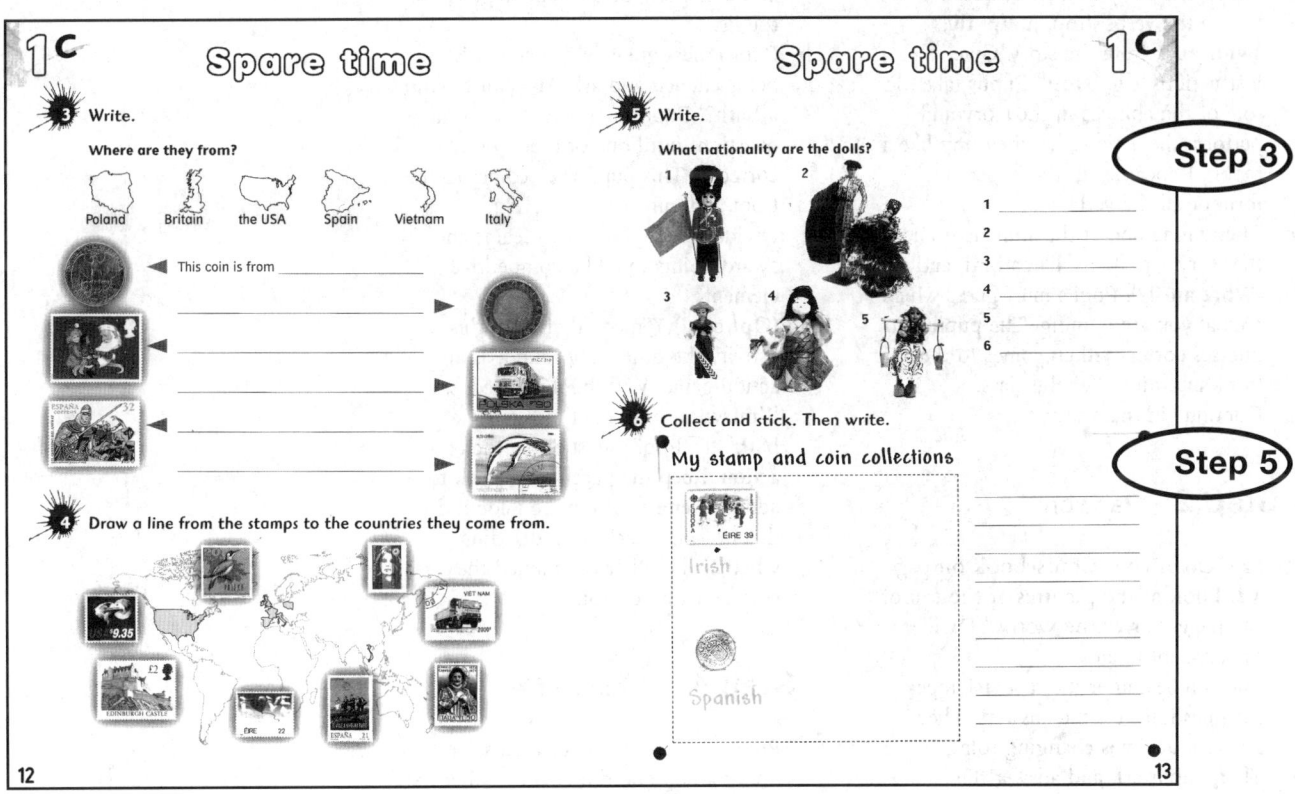

1c Spare time

3 Write.
Where are they from?

Poland | Britain | the USA | Spain | Vietnam | Italy

This coin is from _____

4 Draw a line from the stamps to the countries they come from.

Spare time 1c

5 Write.
What nationality are the dolls?

1 _____
2 _____
3 _____
4 _____
5 _____
6 _____

Step 3

6 Collect and stick. Then write.

My stamp and coin collections

Irish

Spanish

Step 5

1D Lesson 1

Main Language Items			Resource File	Materials Needed
Story revision	cleaning	reading	10	Reader
What am I?	sleeping	writing	31	coloured pencils
What's he/she doing?	eating	drawing		paper for display (optional)
What are they doing?	drinking	painting		cassette/cassette player
What am I doing?	dancing	swimming		
He's/she's/they're + VERB -ing	watching TV	doing homework		
Are you + VERB -ing?		washing up		

Step 1 Action game

a Say 'Open your Coursebook on page 4 and look at the picture.' Use the illustration of the pet shop to see what pupils can remember about the story *Alice's Pet*. Do this in L1 if necessary. Quickly revise the names of the pets in the story.

b Wind back the tape and play the story *Alice's Pet* again. Pupils listen and follow the story in their Readers.

c Revise the verbs: **hop, jump, fly, swim, run,** from the story. Give instructions, e.g. '**Hop!**' Pupils take the role of the animals in the story and perform the actions, i.e. they hop like a rabbit. Repeat using the imperative form of all the verbs.

d Then mime one of the animals from the story, e.g. flying like a bird, and ask '**What am I?**'. Pupils must guess which animal you are miming. The pupil who guesses correctly then comes to the front and mimes for the class.

e Continue in this way.

Step 2 Pairwork

a Say 'Open your Coursebook on page 12. Look at the pictures at the top of the page. Cover the words.' Divide the class into pairs.

b Pupils repeat after the tape. P1 repeats the questions, P2 the answers. They repeat four times changing roles.

c Then pupils ask and answer the questions without the help of the tape.

P1 asks the questions using the words in the book to help. P2 answers using only the pictures.

d They change roles and repeat the procedure.

Step 3 Game (whole class)

a This is a mime game. Tell pupils to look at the list of verbs on page 12. Then ask pupils '**What am I doing?**' and mime one of the actions given in the list.

b Pupils must guess which action is being mimed and ask '**Are you having a bath?**' Pupils continue to ask similar questions until one of them guesses correctly. This pupil then comes to the front and mimes for the class.

c Divide the class into two teams and award points to add a competitive element.

d **(Optional)** You could also try this activity the other way round, as an action game: With books closed, say '**I'm swimming**' or '**I'm having a bath**' etc. Pupils must mime the correct action. Keep the pace fairly quick to add an element of fun. You could do this in teams, each team deciding whether the other has mimed the correct action or not.

Step 4 Personal file

Pupils draw a picture of themselves doing a household task they either like or dislike and write a brief description alongside. Give a model on the blackboard writing about something you either like or don't like doing. For example: '**This is me. I am washing up. I hate washing up!**'

Step 2

Working and Playing

Ask and answer

What's he doing? — He's having a bath.
What's she doing? — She's doing her homework.
What's he doing? — He's washing up.
What are they doing? — They're watching TV.

Step 3

Play — What Am I Doing?

watching TV   sleeping   reading
washing up   eating   writing
cleaning   drinking   drawing
having a bath swimming   painting

Spare time 1D

Sing

This is the way...

This is the way I wash my face,
Wash my face, wash my face.
This is the way I wash my face,
At seven o'clock in the morning.

This is the way I clean my teeth,
Clean my teeth, clean my teeth.
This is the way I clean my teeth,
At seven o'clock in the morning.

This is the way I comb my hair,
Comb my hair, comb my hair.
This is the way I comb my hair,
At eight o'clock in the morning.

This is the way I go to school,
Go to school, go to school.
This is the way I go to school,
At nine o'clock in the morning.

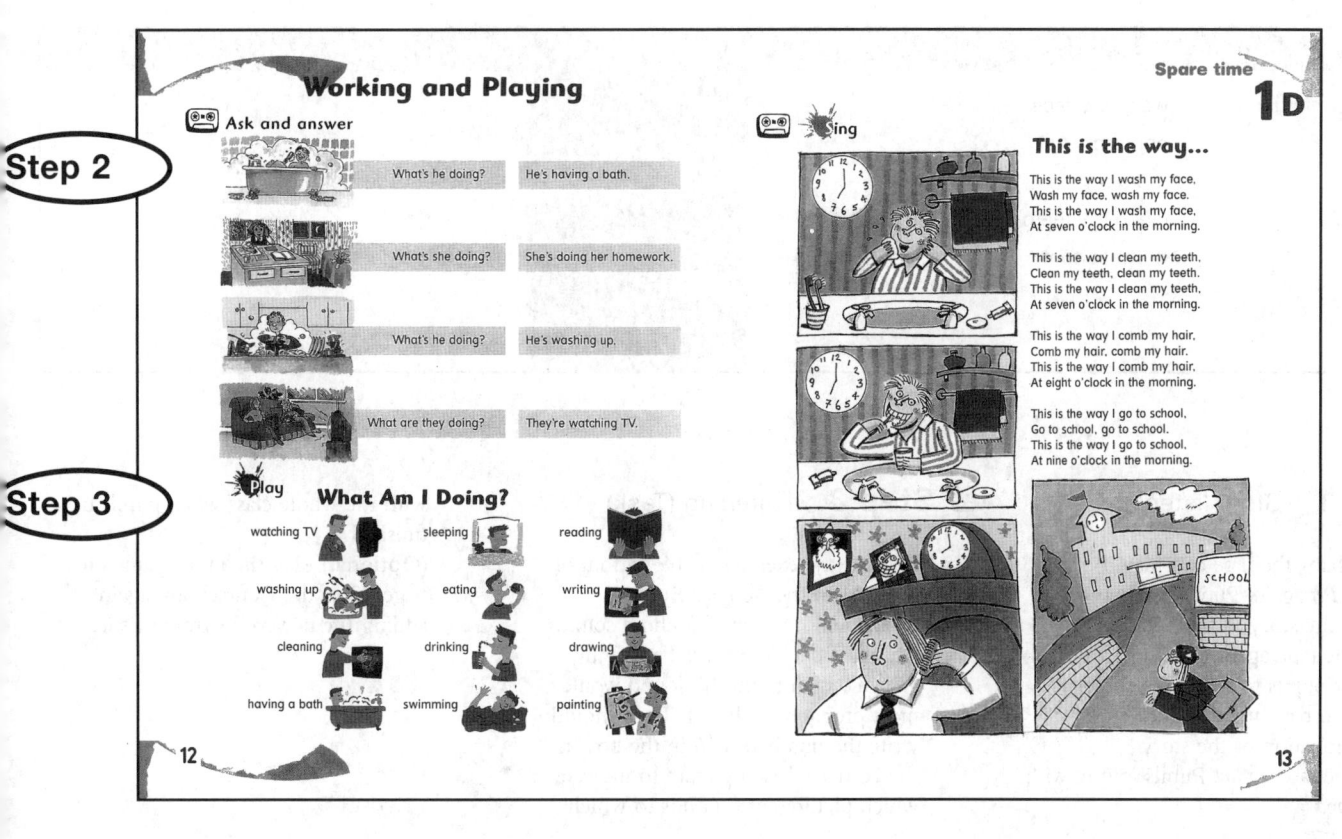

12 / 13

Step 4

1D Spare time

1. Draw and write.

What am I doing?
_____
_____
_____
_____
_____

2. Listen and number.

What are they doing?

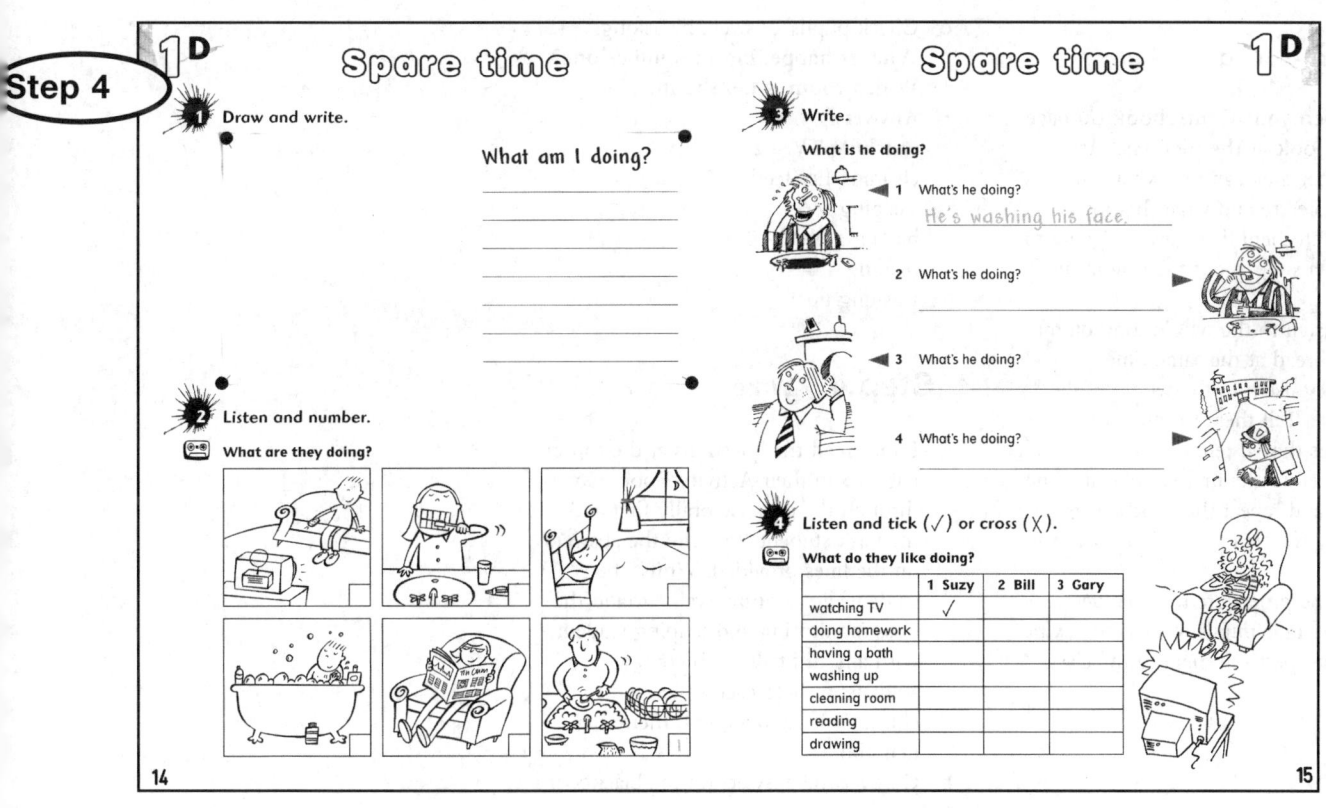

Spare time 1D

3. Write.

What is he doing?

1 What's he doing?
   He's washing his face.

2 What's he doing?
   _____

3 What's he doing?
   _____

4 What's he doing?
   _____

4. Listen and tick (✓) or cross (✗).

What do they like doing?

	1 Suzy	2 Bill	3 Gary
watching TV	✓		
doing homework			
having a bath			
washing up			
cleaning room			
reading			
drawing			

14 / 15

41

1D Lesson 2

Main Language Items		Resource File	Materials Needed
Present simple/continuous	wash my face	5	Reader
Story revision	comb my hair	31	cassette/cassette player
	morning	49a	
	clean my teeth		
	go to school		

Step 1 Story listening

a Wind back the tape and play the story *Alice's Pet* again. Pupils listen and follow the story in their Readers.

b Play the tape again, pausing after each line for pupils to repeat. Encourage pupils to pay attention to the rhythm and intonation of the story.

c Play the tape again. Pupils join in with the tape.

Step 2 Song

a Say 'Open your Coursebook on page 13 and look at the pictures.' Ask them what they can see, what time it is in each picture and what the boy is doing. Tell them that they are going to listen to a song about the boy in the picture.

b Pupils listen to the whole song on the tape and read at the same time.

c Then they listen to the whole of the first verse. Tell them to mime the actions as they listen.

d They listen to the first verse again, line by line, and repeat the words. Then they sing the first verse along with the tape.

e Repeat the procedure for each verse and encourage pupils to make up extra verses and perform them to the class.

Step 3 Listening (Task)

a Look at the exercise at the bottom of page 14 in the Activity Book.

b Pupils will hear six household sounds and must decide what is happening and in which room the sound would most probably be heard. They should write the numbers 1–6 in the box in the corner of each picture to indicate which picture corresponds to which sound.

c Check pupils' answers by asking:
What is happening in number one?
Which room is he/she in?
Answers:
watching TV – 2
cleaning her teeth – 5
sleeping – 6
having a bath – 3
reading – 4
washing up 1

Step 4 Write

a Pupils read the questions at the top of page 15 in their Activity Book. Go through the exercise orally first and then ask students to write the answers on the lines provided. Whilst the students are writing, walk around the class monitoring and helping students with any difficulties. Encourage students to help each other and to check their answers with their neighbour.

b Go over the answers on the blackboard with the whole class when pupils have finished.

c **(Optional)** Play the mime game on page 12 of the Coursebook again, adding the new verbs from this lesson.

Working and Playing

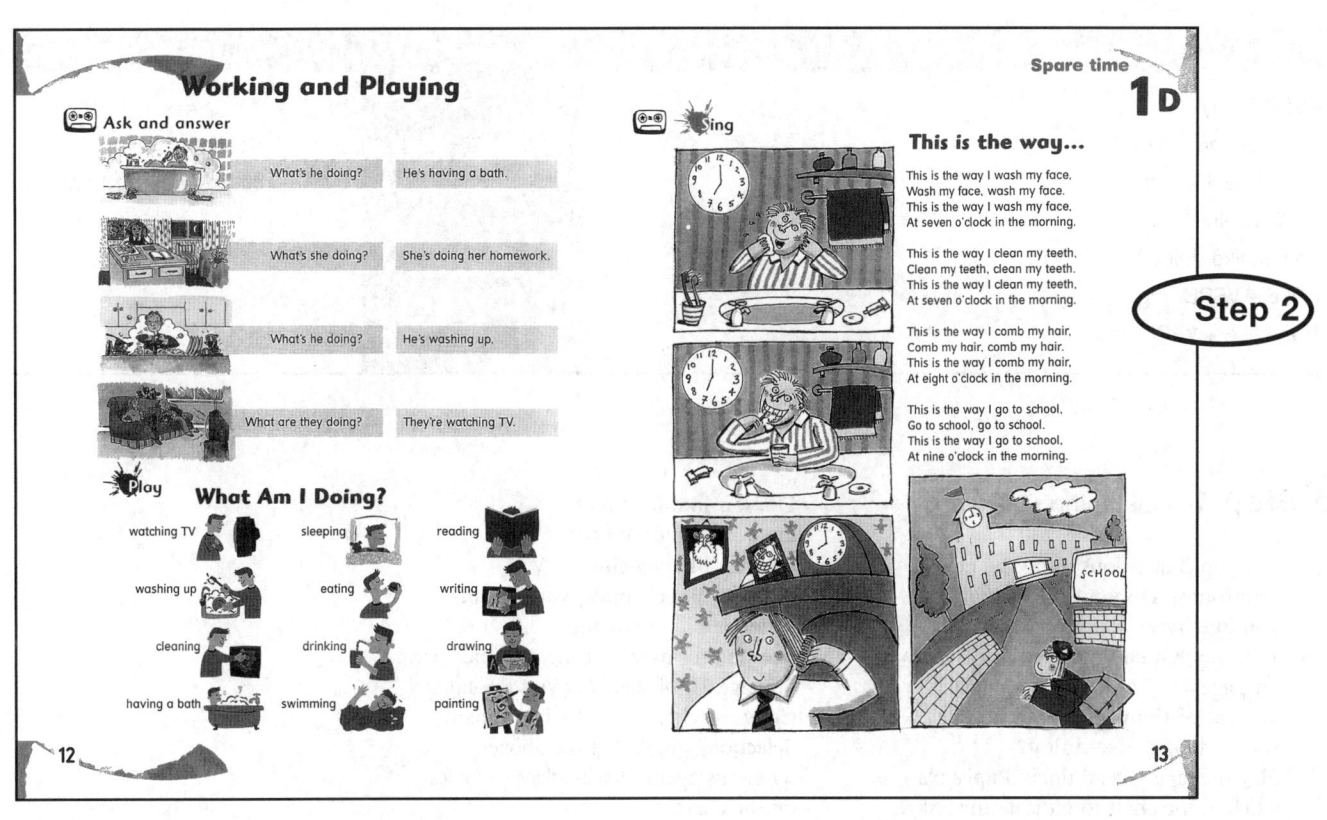

Ask and answer

What's he doing? — He's having a bath.
What's she doing? — She's doing her homework.
What's he doing? — He's washing up.
What are they doing? — They're watching TV.

Play — What Am I Doing?

watching TV, sleeping, reading
washing up, eating, writing
cleaning, drinking, drawing
having a bath, swimming, painting

12

Spare time 1D

Sing

This is the way...

This is the way I wash my face,
Wash my face, wash my face.
This is the way I wash my face,
At seven o'clock in the morning.

This is the way I clean my teeth,
Clean my teeth, clean my teeth.
This is the way I clean my teeth,
At seven o'clock in the morning.

This is the way I comb my hair,
Comb my hair, comb my hair.
This is the way I comb my hair,
At eight o'clock in the morning.

This is the way I go to school,
Go to school, go to school.
This is the way I go to school,
At nine o'clock in the morning.

13

1D **Spare time**

1 Draw and write.

What am I doing?

2 Listen and number.

What are they doing?

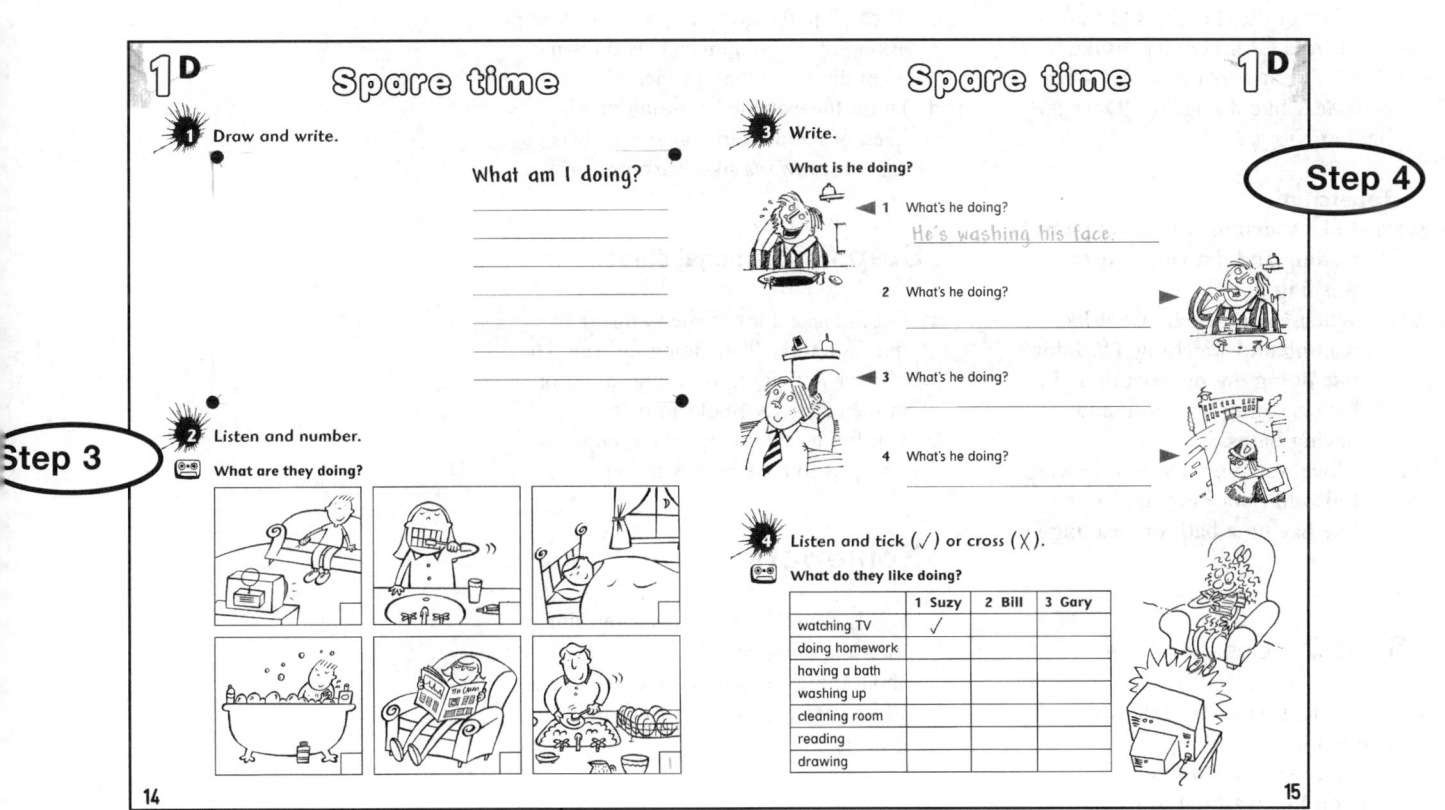

14

Spare time 1D

3 Write.

What is he doing?

1 What's he doing?
   He's washing his face.

2 What's he doing?

3 What's he doing?

4 What's he doing?

4 Listen and tick (✓) or cross (✗).

What do they like doing?

	1 Suzy	2 Bill	3 Gary
watching TV	✓		
doing homework			
having a bath			
washing up			
cleaning room			
reading			
drawing			

15

43

1^D Lesson 3

Main Language Items	Resource File	Materials Needed
I like + VERB -ing I love + VERB -ing I don't like + VERB -ing I hate + VERB -ing What do you like doing? Do you like + VERB -ing? Does *Marie* like + VERB -ing?	5 10 39	Reader cassette/cassette player

Step 1 Listening (Task)

a Ask pupils questions using the new verb forms: 'Do you like *reading*? Do you like *doing your homework*?' etc.

b Then say 'Open your Activity Book on page 15. Look at the chart at the bottom of the page. What do Suzy, Bill and Gary like doing?'

c Play the tape several times. Pupils place a tick in the chart to indicate the tasks that each of the characters like doing and a cross for those they dislike.

d Check the answers by asking 'What does *Suzy* like doing?' or 'Does *Bill* like *washing up*?'

Tapescript:

SUZY: I like watching TV, having a bath, reading and drawing. I hate washing up.

BILL: When I'm in the house, I like reading and watching TV. I don't like doing my homework and I hate cleaning my room and having baths.

GARY: I love watching TV and drawing. I also like washing up. I don't like having a bath or cleaning my room.

Step 2 Questionnaire

a Ask various pupils the following questions:
What do you like doing?
Do you like washing up?
Do you like reading?
Do you like drawing?
Do you like watching TV?
Do you like cleaning your room?

b When pupils are familiar with the question forms, direct them to the chart on page 16 of their Activity Book. Copy the chart onto the blackboard. Select one pupil. Ask the above questions again. Place ticks or crosses on the chart.

c Then all pupils work in groups of four asking other group members the same questions and filling in their charts.

d Finish the exercise by asking pupils questions about other class members, e.g. 'Does *Maria* like washing up?'

Step 3 Personal survey

a Pupils make a list of the things they like/don't like/hate doing on page 16 of their Activity Book using the verbs in their Activity Books to help.

b Finish the exercise by asking pupils 'Do you like *having a bath*?' etc.

Homework

Pupils write five sentences about things they like doing and five sentences about things they don't like doing, e.g: I like *playing football*. I don't like *dancing*.

Spare time — 1D

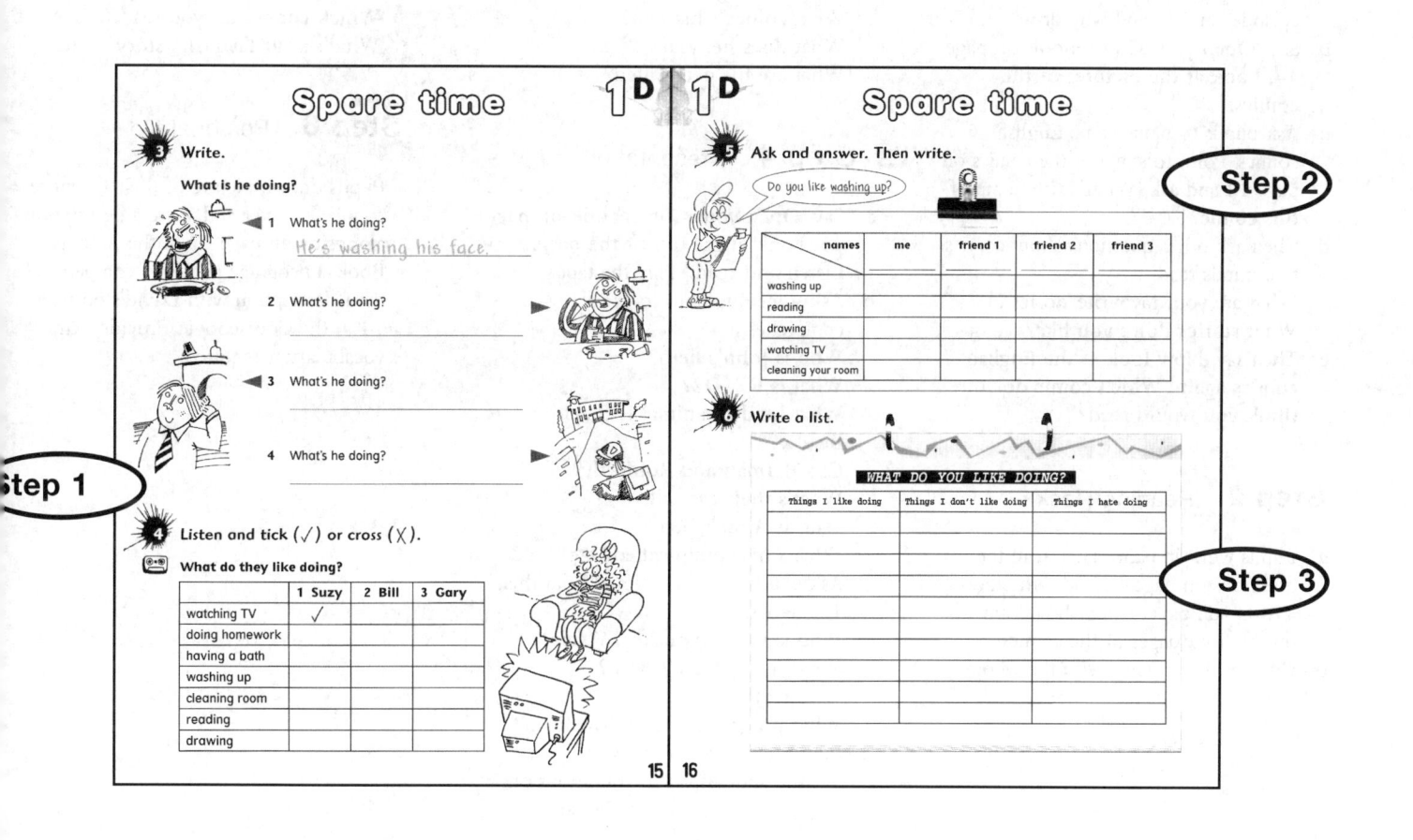

3 Write.

What is he doing?

1 What's he doing? He's washing his face.

2 What's he doing? _____

3 What's he doing? _____

4 What's he doing? _____

4 Listen and tick (✓) or cross (✗).

What do they like doing?

	1 Suzy	2 Bill	3 Gary
watching TV	✓		
doing homework			
having a bath			
washing up			
cleaning room			
reading			
drawing			

Step 1

1D Spare time

5 Ask and answer. Then write.

Do you like washing up?

names	me	friend 1	friend 2	friend 3
washing up				
reading				
drawing				
watching TV				
cleaning your room				

Step 2

6 Write a list.

WHAT DO YOU LIKE DOING?

Things I like doing	Things I don't like doing	Things I hate doing

Step 3

1E Lesson 1

Main Language Items		Resource File	Materials Needed
Which ... ?	comic	4	coloured pencils
How many ... can you see?	story	72	paper for display (optional)
He's/she's/it's called ...	hero	73	cassette/cassette player
	magazine		

Step 1 Presentation

a In their L1, ask pupils why they like comics, whether they read them regularly and where they get them from. Do they buy them, borrow them or swap them with their friends? Ask them to explain the difference between comic and TV characters. Which are more violent? Do they like the violent episodes on TV, and why or why not?

b Say 'Open your Coursebook on page 14. Look at the pictures of the comics.'

c Ask pupils to name some English comics. Point to some of the comics on page 14 and ask 'What's the name of this comic?'.

d Then ask other questions about comics that pupils read:
What are your favourite stories in ... ?
What stories don't you like?

e Then say 'Now look at the English comics again. Which comic do you think you would read?'

Step 2 Reading (Task)

a Pupils work in pairs. They read the questions on page 14 and write the answers on paper using the information on the front pages of the comics.

b Go over the answers with the whole class.

Step 3 Presentation

a Say 'Look at the drawing on page 14 in your Coursebook.' Pupils listen and read at the same time.

b Ask some questions to check comprehension:
What's David's favourite comic?
What's his favourite story?
Is Dennis a good boy?
What colour's his hair?
What does he wear?
What are his pets called?

Step 4 Presentation

a Say 'Open your Coursebook on page 15. Look at the top of the page. Listen and read.' Play the tape.

b Ask some questions to check comprehension:
Who is John's hero?
What is R2–D2?
What kind of animal is Black Beauty?
Can Batman and Robin fly?
What's their car called?
Who is Anna's hero?
What's his chimp called? etc.

c Ask pupils some questions about their TV heroes:
Who is your favourite TV star?
Have you got a TV hero?
Who is it?
What programme is he/she/it in?

d Pupils then work in pairs, read the passage and answer the questions on page 15 in their exercise books.

e Go over the answers with the whole class when pupils have finished.

Step 5 Personal survey

a Pupils answer the questions in the spaces provided at the top of page 17 in the Activity Book.

b Finish the exercise by asking pupils 'Which comics do you read?', 'What's your favourite story?', etc.

Step 6 Personal file

Pupils draw a picture of their favourite comic character and write a description alongside on page 17 in the Activity Book. Encourage pupils to compare their description with David's on page 14 in the Coursebook. Provide extra vocabulary if required.

Comics and Heroes

Look and find

In Britain there are many comics and magazines for children

Step 1

Step 2

1 Which magazine is about art?
2 Which comics have cartoons inside?
3 Which magazine costs 99p?
4 How many animals can you see?
5 Which magazine is about football?
6 Which magazines have puzzles in them?

Listen and read

Step 3

My favourite comic is The Beano! My favourite story is Dennis the Menace. Dennis is very bad. He's got black hair and wears a black and red jumper. He's got a black dog called Gnasher and a pet pig called Rasher.
David Lewis

Spare time

1E

Listen and read

Four British children talk about their favourite film and TV heroes.

John: My hero is R2–D2 in *Star Wars*. He's a robot. He's little and fat but very brave.

Paul: My heroes are Batman and Robin. They are very strong. They can't fly but they can climb up buildings. They've got a very fast car called the Batmobile.

Jane: My hero is Black Beauty. Black Beauty is a horse. He can run very fast and he is very beautiful.

Anna: Tarzan is my hero. He can climb trees and talk to the animals. He's got a pet chimp called Cheetah and he lives in a tree.

1 Who are Paul's heroes?
2 Where does Tarzan live?
3 Whose hero is a robot?
4 What kind of animal is Black Beauty?
5 What is Batman and Robin's car called?

Step 4

I	like	swimming
He	don't like	watching TV
She	likes	singing
	am	washing up
They	is	dancing
	are	reading

14

15

1D Spare time

5 Ask and answer. Then write.

Do you like washing up?

names	me	friend 1	friend 2	friend 3
washing up				
reading				
drawing				
watching TV				
cleaning your room				

6 Write a list.

WHAT DO YOU LIKE DOING?

Things I like doing	Things I don't like doing	Things I hate doing

Spare time 1E

1 Write.

1 Do you read comics?
2 Which comics do you read?
3 What's your favourite story?
4 What's your favourite TV programme?

Step 5

2 Draw and write.

My favourite comic or TV character

_____
_____
_____
_____
_____

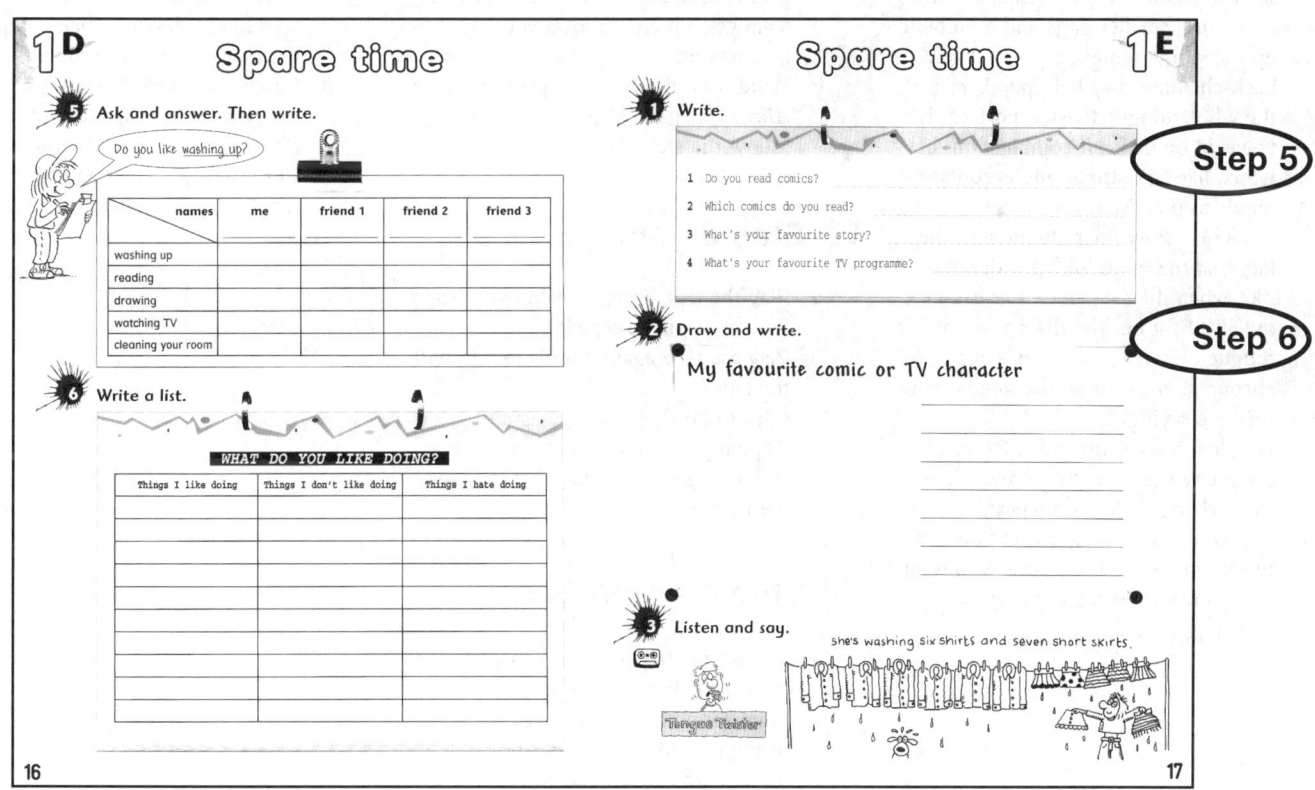

Step 6

3 Listen and say.

She's washing six shirts and seven short skirts.

Tongue Twister

16

17

47

1E Lesson 2

Main Language Items	Resource File	Materials Needed
Story revision	4 25 52	Reader cassette/cassette player paper for display (optional)

Step 1 Tongue twister

a Ask pupils if they know any tongue twisters in their L1. Encourage pupils to say them in front of the class. Tell pupils that they are going to listen to a tongue twister in English.

b Play the tape once so pupils can listen to the tongue twister. Play it twice more, with the class repeating.
Note: If the pupils find it difficult to say the whole tongue twister, break it down into smaller parts and then build up the whole sentence. Alternatively, back-chaining may help pupils to say the whole tongue twister more easily. Focus in on difficult combinations of words like '**six shirts**' and encourage pupils to practise saying them in isolation. Draw their attention to the fact that the 'x' in 'six', is reduced to a /k/ when the tongue twister is said quickly. Beat out the rhythm of the tongue twister for the pupils and encourage them to do the same when they are saying it.

c Divide the class into pairs. P1 says the tongue twister. P2 checks and corrects. They change roles and repeat.

d Pupils then try to say the tongue twister more quickly. Pupils who want to try in front of the class can be encouraged to do so.

Step 2 Story listening

a Before listening to the story of *Alice's Pet* again, play an action game by sticking some pictures of the various pets in the story around the classroom. These could be magazine pictures or drawings. Give pupils instructions such as '**Point to the rabbit**' or '**Run and touch an animal that hops.**' If you have a large class, do this as a team game – one pupil at a time from each team gets up and follows your instructions.

b Wind back the tape and play the story *Alice's Pet* again. Pupils listen and follow the story in their Readers.

Step 3 Story 'Join in'

a Play the tape again, pausing after each line for pupils to repeat.

b Play the tape again. Pupils join in with the tape.
(**Optional**) Play the tape again, stopping at various points in the story and asking pupils if they can tell you the next word or line.

Step 4 Write and draw

a Tell pupils they are going to write their own story. In pairs, ask pupils to brainstorm all the pets that they know in English. Make a list on the blackboard for students to use as a resource when they write their own story. Elicit from the pupils the actions that the various pets do e.g. **frog – jump** and the past form of each verb. Use this opportunity to give pupils any extra vocabulary they might want to know. Write any new vocabulary on the blackboard.

b Pupils fill in the spaces in the story in their Activity Book to make their own story. Walk round the class and help pupils as necessary.

c Divide the class into pairs. Pupils read their story to their partner.

d Pupils who want to read their story to the class can be encouraged to do so.

e (**Optional**) Pupils can write their stories out on paper and illustrate them for display or make a class book.

1 Spare time

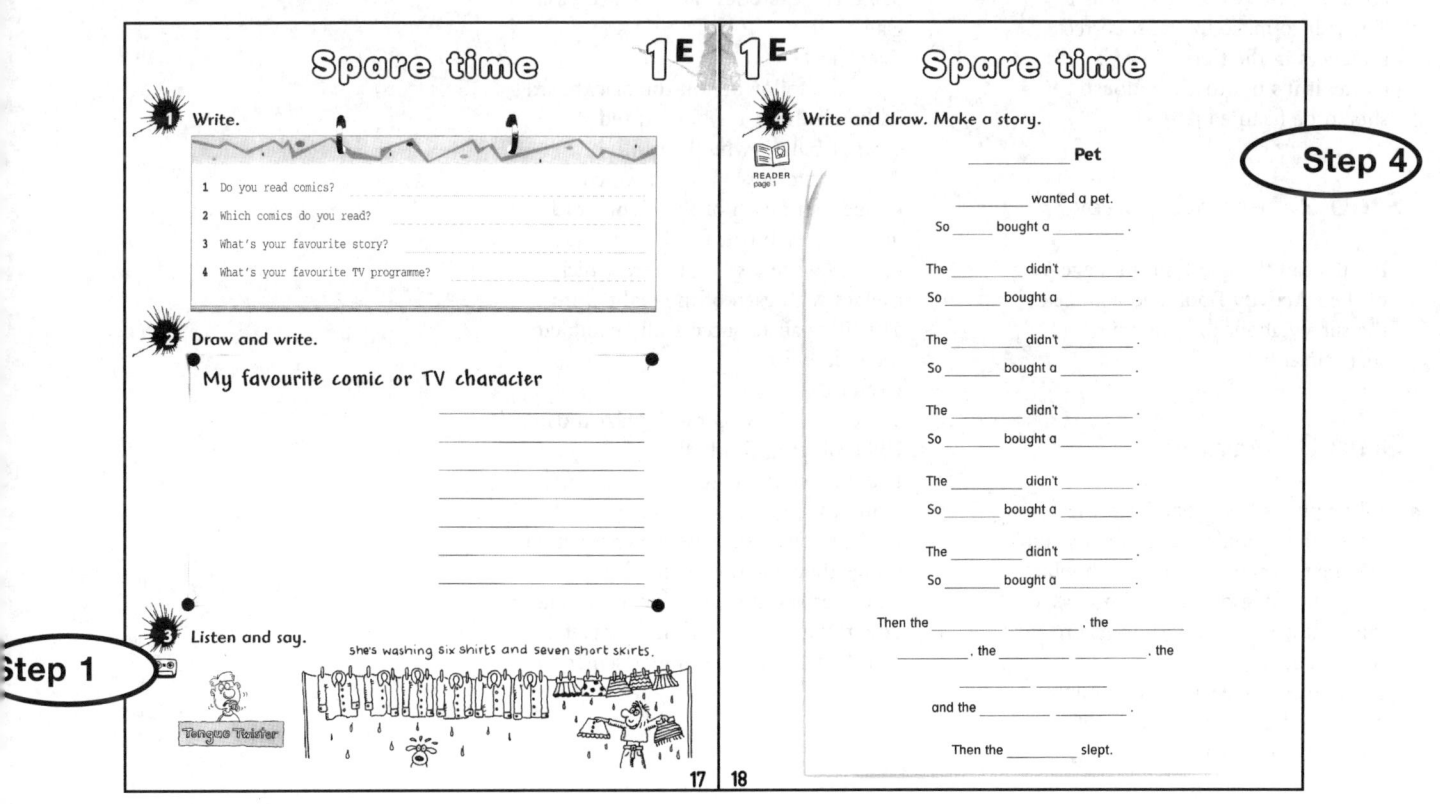

STORY
Alice's Pet

PET SHOP

Step 2

Step 3

Spare time 1E

1 Write.
1. Do you read comics? _____
2. Which comics do you read? _____
3. What's your favourite story? _____
4. What's your favourite TV programme? _____

2 Draw and write.
My favourite comic or TV character
_____
_____
_____
_____
_____

3 Listen and say.
She's washing six shirts and seven short skirts.

Step 1

1E Spare time

4 Write and draw. Make a story.

_____ Pet

_____ wanted a pet.
So _____ bought a _____ .

The _____ didn't _____ .
So _____ bought a _____ .

The _____ didn't _____ .
So _____ bought a _____ .

The _____ didn't _____ .
So _____ bought a _____ .

The _____ didn't _____ .
So _____ bought a _____ .

The _____ didn't _____ .
So _____ bought a _____ .

Then the _____ _____ , the _____
_____ , the _____ , the
_____ _____
and the _____ _____ .

Then the _____ slept.

Step 4

49

1E Lesson 3

Main Language Items		Resource File	Materials Needed
I/they like/don't like + VERB -ing	watch		
He/she likes/doesn't like + VERB -ing	collect	4	
Do you like + VERB -ing?	hobbies	5	
Present Continuous	team	10	
Can you … ?			
Are you good at …?			

Step 1 The Stepping Stones Game

a Divide the class into pairs. Pupils write as many sentences as they can in ten minutes from the words in the box. They work from left to right and take one word or pair of words from each column.

b The sentences must be both grammatically and factually correct about themselves or their friends.

c The pair to make the most correct sentences in the time allowed, wins. (Note: if it's not too late, **doesn't** should be featured.)

Step 2 Personal survey

Pupils read the questions on page 19 of their Activity Book and complete the survey about their hobbies and spare time.

Step 3 Pairwork

a When pupils have completed the survey they should work in pairs and ask their partners about their hobbies, using the questions in the book as a guide. It is not necessary to record each other's answers.

b Finish the exercise by asking pupils questions from the survey about themselves or their partners.

Step 4 Personal file

Using the information on page 19 as a guide, pupils write sentences about their hobbies in their exercise books.

Optional

These are round-up exercises to be done on paper. Pupils should work in pairs. The exercises can be played as games.

Exercise 1
Write the following on the blackboard:
a **blue** b **three** c **where** d **red**
e **can** f **ball** g **why** h **drink**.
Pupils write down a word which rhymes with each of the eight words given. As each pair finishes, instruct them to write a second word which rhymes with each of the eight words. The first pair to successfully complete the task, wins.

Exercise 2
Write the following on the blackboard:
I like playing football.
I don't like dancing.
Using the two sentences given as a guide, pupils write five sentences about things they like doing and five sentences about things they don't like doing. Pupils can work individually and then check each other's sentences.

Comics and Heroes

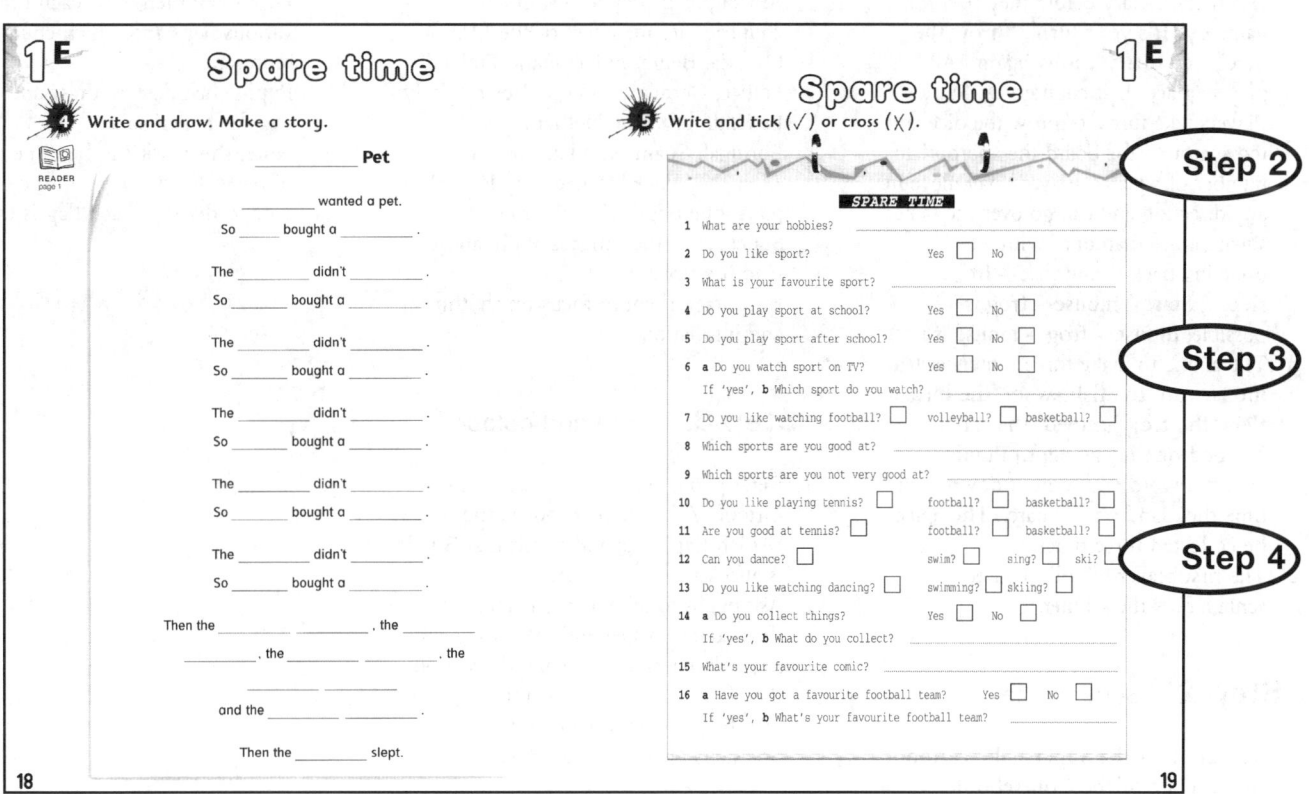

Look and find
In Britain there are many comics and magazines for children.

1 Which magazine is about art?
2 Which comics have cartoons inside?
3 Which magazine costs 99p?
4 How many animals can you see?
5 Which magazine is about football?
6 Which magazines have puzzles in them?

Listen and read

My favourite comic is The Beano! My favourite story is Dennis the Menace. Dennis is very bad. He's got black hair and wears a black and red jumper. He's got a black dog called Gnasher and a pet pig called Rasher.
David Lewis

Spare time — 1E

Listen and read

Four British children talk about their favourite film and TV heroes.

John: My hero is R2–D2 in *Star Wars*. He's a robot. He's little and fat but very brave.

Paul: My heroes are Batman and Robin. They are very strong. They can't fly but they can climb up buildings. They've got a very fast car called the Batmobile.

Jane: My hero is Black Beauty. Black Beauty is a horse. He can run very fast and he is very beautiful.

Anna: Tarzan is my hero. He can climb trees and talk to the animals. He's got a pet chimp called Cheetah and he lives in a tree.

1 Who are Paul's heroes?
2 Where does Tarzan live?
3 Whose hero is a robot?
4 What kind of animal is Black Beauty?
5 What is Batman and Robin's car called?

I / He / She / They — like / don't like / likes / am / is / are — swimming / watching TV / singing / washing up / dancing / reading

Step 1

1E Spare time

4 Write and draw. Make a story.

READER page 1

_____ Pet

_____ wanted a pet.
So _____ bought a _____ .

The _____ didn't _____ .
So _____ bought a _____ .

The _____ didn't _____ .
So _____ bought a _____ .

The _____ didn't _____ .
So _____ bought a _____ .

The _____ didn't _____ .
So _____ bought a _____ .

The _____ didn't _____ .
So _____ bought a _____ .

Then the _____ _____ , the _____
_____ , the _____ , the _____
and the _____ _____ .
Then the _____ slept.

Spare time 1E

5 Write and tick (✓) or cross (✗).

SPARE TIME

1 What are your hobbies? _____
2 Do you like sport? Yes ☐ No ☐
3 What is your favourite sport? _____
4 Do you play sport at school? Yes ☐ No ☐
5 Do you play sport after school? Yes ☐ No ☐
6 a Do you watch sport on TV? Yes ☐ No ☐
   If 'yes', b Which sport do you watch? _____
7 Do you like watching football? ☐ volleyball? ☐ basketball? ☐
8 Which sports are you good at? _____
9 Which sports are you not very good at? _____
10 Do you like playing tennis? ☐ football? ☐ basketball? ☐
11 Are you good at tennis? ☐ football? ☐ basketball? ☐
12 Can you dance? ☐ swim? ☐ sing? ☐ ski? ☐
13 Do you like watching dancing? ☐ swimming? ☐ skiing? ☐
14 a Do you collect things? Yes ☐ No ☐
   If 'yes', b What do you collect? _____
15 What's your favourite comic? _____
16 a Have you got a favourite football team? Yes ☐ No ☐
   If 'yes', b What's your favourite football team? _____

Step 2

Step 3

Step 4

1F Lesson 1

Main Language Items			Resource File	Materials Needed
Story revision	Japan	Greece		
flag	Spain	New Zealand	7	dice/counters
English	the UK		9	coloured pencils
the EU (European Union)	Australia		62	paper for display (optional)
gold	Italy			cassette/cassette player
star	France			
earthworm	the USA			

Step 1 Story game

a This is a dice game to be played in groups of four, using counters, a dice and one book for each group.

b Quickly revise the story *Alice's Pet*. Play the tape again or ask pupils to tell you the story.

c Say 'Open your Coursebook on page 16.' Tell pupils they are going to play *Alice's Pet* Game and give them some useful vocabulary before they start the game e.g 'It's your turn', 'throw the dice', 'my turn', 'throw again'. All players place their counters on **Start**. Players take turns to throw the dice and move around the board the appropriate number of squares. Players may move in any direction and can go over the same square more than once without doubling back (i.e. **mouse – frog – slept – Start – mouse – frog** is possible; **mouse – frog – mouse** is not).

d The aim is to make three sentences (**the mouse ran/the fish swam/the bird flew/the frog jumped/the rabbit hopped or the cat slept.**) Pupils collect a word and write it down each time they land on a square. 'The' must be collected three times.

e The first player to collect three sentences is the winner.

Step 2 Supersnake

a Say 'Look at the Supersnake cartoon on page 17 of the Coursebook.'

Remind the pupils of the characters in the Supersnake story. Ask what kind of animal Willy is (**a worm/earthworm**). Pupils then listen to the story and read at the same time.

b Ask pupils some comprehension questions to check their understanding of the story:
What's the EU?
What is on the EU flag?
What's Willy's EU?
Ask pupils if they know which countries are members of the EU. (Austria, Belgium, Denmark, Finland, France, Germany, Greece, Ireland, Italy, Luxembourg, The Netherlands, Portugal, Spain, Sweden, the UK)

c After they have listened, pupils work in pairs: one pupil takes the role of Supersnake, the other is Willy and they read the story.
Encourage them to focus on rhythm and intonation.

Step 3 Write and colour

a Refer pupils again to the Supersnake cartoon. Ask '**What colour is the British flag?**' Remind pupils that Britain is also known as the UK.
Ask pupils to tell you the colours of their country's flag and see if there are any volunteers to come and draw it on the blackboard. In L1, elicit from pupils why flags are important, and on what occasions flags are used or seen.

b Pupils write the names of the countries under the appropriate flag outlines and colour the flags on page 20 in the Activity Book. It may be useful to have some encyclopaedias or reference books at hand, so that the pupils can look up any flags they don't know. You could ask pupils to draw and colour some flags on sheets of paper and use them in a world map display (see **Resource File 7**).
Pupils can then 'test' each other on the various flags and which countries they represent.

c Pupils then design, draw and colour a flag for Supersnake.
Note: this work can be done on sheets of paper for display and the class can vote to decide which flag is the best.

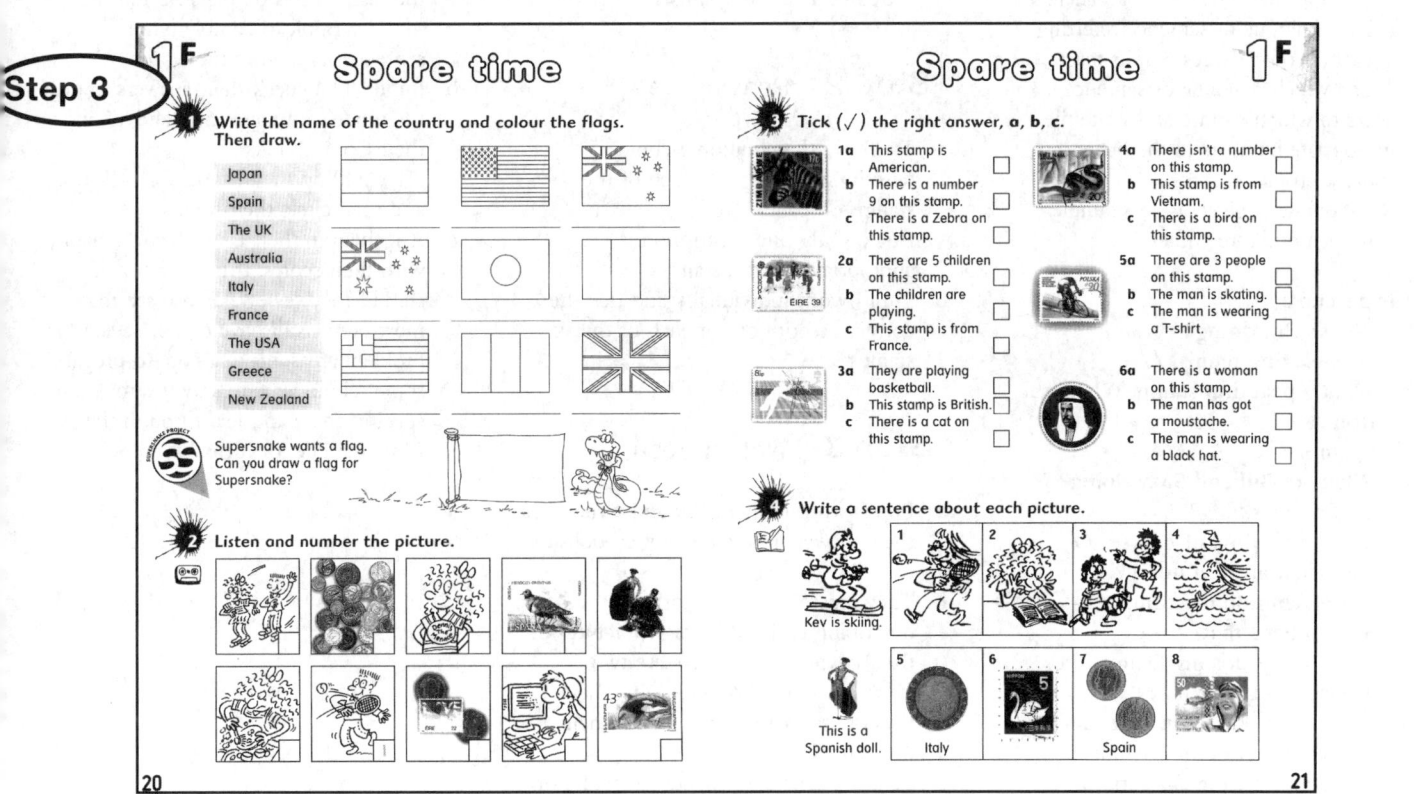

Step 1

The Mouse Ran

Alice's Pet Game

- rabbit — ran — the — swam — mouse
- jumped — the mouse ran ... — frog — the fish swam ... — flew
- bird — the — mouse — slept — rabbit — cat
- hopped — the bird flew ... — START — the frog jumped ... — the
- fish — jumped — cat — the — fish — hopped
- flew — the rabbit hopped ... — swam — the cat slept ... — bird
- the — slept — frog — the — ran

16

Step 2

Spare time 1F

SUPERSNAKE

What's that, Willy? — It's a flag.
Is it the British flag?
No. It's the EU flag.

No, Willy. This is the EU flag.
Look! A blue flag with twelve gold stars.
The EU is the European Union. It is ... blah ... blah ... blah ...

Yes! Yes! I know! But...
...this is my EU flag. The Earthworm Union! Look! A blue flag with twelve gold earthworms!

17

Step 3

1F Spare time

1 Write the name of the country and colour the flags. Then draw.

- Japan
- Spain
- The UK
- Australia
- Italy
- France
- The USA
- Greece
- New Zealand

Supersnake wants a flag. Can you draw a flag for Supersnake?

2 Listen and number the picture.

Spare time 1F

3 Tick (✓) the right answer, a, b, c.

1a This stamp is American.
b There is a number 9 on this stamp.
c There is a Zebra on this stamp.

2a There are 5 children on this stamp.
b The children are playing.
c This stamp is from France.

3a They are playing basketball.
b This stamp is British.
c There is a cat on this stamp.

4a There isn't a number on this stamp.
b This stamp is from Vietnam.
c There is a bird on this stamp.

5a There are 3 people on this stamp.
b The man is skating.
c The man is wearing a T-shirt.

6a There is a woman on this stamp.
b The man has got a moustache.
c The man is wearing a black hat.

4 Write a sentence about each picture.

1. Kev is skiing.
2.
3.
4.
5. This is a Spanish doll.
6. Italy
7. Spain
8.

20   21

53

1F Lesson 2 - Evaluation

Main Language Items	Resource File	Materials Needed
Round-up lesson (including tests) Revision of all structures		cassette/cassette player

This lesson contains a round-up of the material presented in the first topic of the book. It is intended as a testing lesson. However, if you do not want to test the pupils, the exercises are both useful and interesting in themselves.

Step 1 Listening (Test)

a Look at the pictures at the bottom of page 20 in the Activity Book. There is a short dialogue or sentence referring to each of the pictures. Pupils must decide which dialogue or sentence refers to which picture and write the appropriate numbers in the boxes under each picture.
b Number one is given as an example. Play each one three times.

Tapescript:
1 What's Bill doing?
  He's playing tennis. //
2 What a beautiful stamp. Where's it from?
  Spain. //
3 What are Bill and Suzy doing? Skating or skiing?
  They're skating, of course. //
4 Kev, what are you doing?
  I'm playing on my computer. //
5 Suzy, what's that?
  It's a badge. It's my Dennis the Menace badge. //
6 What can you see on that stamp?
  There's a picture of a whale. The stamp's from Bulgaria. //
7 Do you collect stamps?
  No, I collect coins. Look, here's some of my collection. //
8 Bill, do you know where Suzy is?
  Yes. She's in the kitchen. She's washing up. //
9 Here's your stamp! Look! It's between the two coins. //
10 Do you like my dolls?
  Yes, they're lovely. Where are they from?
  Spain. They're Spanish.

Step 2 Reading (Test)

a There are three multiple-choice descriptions alongside each of the stamps on page 21 of the Activity Book. Only one description is appropriate to each stamp.
b Pupils work individually and tick the correct description for each of the six stamps.

Step 3 Writing (Test)

a Pupils work individually and write their answers in their exercise books or on a sheet of paper.
b They must write one short sentence describing each of the eight pictures in the Activity Book. There are two examples in the book to help. They should use these as models for their own answers.
c Ensure pupils understand the nature of the test before beginning. Give further examples on the blackboard if necessary.
d If the exercise is being done as a test, then these should be collected in and marked by the teacher.

Step 4 Test yourself

a Pupils work individually and follow the instructions on page 22 in their Activity Book to complete the sentences and write the words.
b Pupils then check their answers against the models on pages 6, 7 and 12 in their Coursebooks.
c They add up their scores for each test and then circle their total score.
d Ask them in their L1 if they are happy with their scores. If not, what areas should they review? If you see that most pupils still have one or several problem areas, make a note to prepare some reinforcement activities for these specific areas, and leaf through the Resource File for ideas.

1F Spare time

Step 1

1 Write the name of the country and colour the flags. Then draw.

- Japan
- Spain
- The UK
- Australia
- Italy
- France
- The USA
- Greece
- New Zealand

Supersnake wants a flag. Can you draw a flag for Supersnake?

2 Listen and number the picture.

1F Spare time

Step 2

3 Tick (✓) the right answer, a, b, c.

1a This stamp is American.
b There is a number 9 on this stamp.
c There is a Zebra on this stamp.

2a There are 5 children on this stamp.
b The children are playing.
c This stamp is from France.

3a They are playing basketball.
b This stamp is British.
c There is a cat on this stamp.

4a There isn't a num... on this stamp.
b This stamp is from Vietnam.
c There is a bird on this stamp.

5a There are 3 people on this stamp.
b The man is skating.
c The man is wearing a T-shirt.

6a There is a woman on this stamp.
b The man has got a moustache.
c The man is wearing a black hat.

4 Write a sentence about each picture.

Step 3

1. Kev is skiing.
2.
3.
4.
5. This is a Spanish doll.
6. Italy
7.
8. Spain

1F Spare time

Step 4

5 Test yourself.

TEST 1 ★ Complete the sentences.

What's _____ doing?
Playing _____

What's _____ doing?

What are _____ doing?
Playing _____

What are _____ doing?
Playing _____

★ Check your answers on page 6 in your Coursebook.   SCORE /8

TEST 2 ★ Write the words.

★ Check your answers on page 7 in your Coursebook.   SCORE /3

TEST 3 ★ Write the words.

★ Check your answers on page 12 in your Coursebook.   SCORE /12

TOTAL /23

Circle your total score:
23 Excellent   22–21 Very good   20–15 Good
14–12 Quite good   11–0 Do it again!

2A Places

1 Listen and follow the directions.

Where's the treasure?

2 Read and follow the directions.

What is the treasure?

START HERE

I	Y	D	E	O	N
T	F	B	S	E	A
E	K	L	A	W	E
O	L	C	R	L	S
P	U	S	M	H	W
R	O	T	I	G	D

Go ...
south 5 ____   south 4 ____   south 2 ____
east 3 ____   west 2 ____   east 3 ____
north 2 ____   north 3 ____   south 4 ____
west 5 ____   east 5 ____   west 1 ____
north 1 ____   south 3 ____   north 4 ____
east 3 ____   west 1 ____

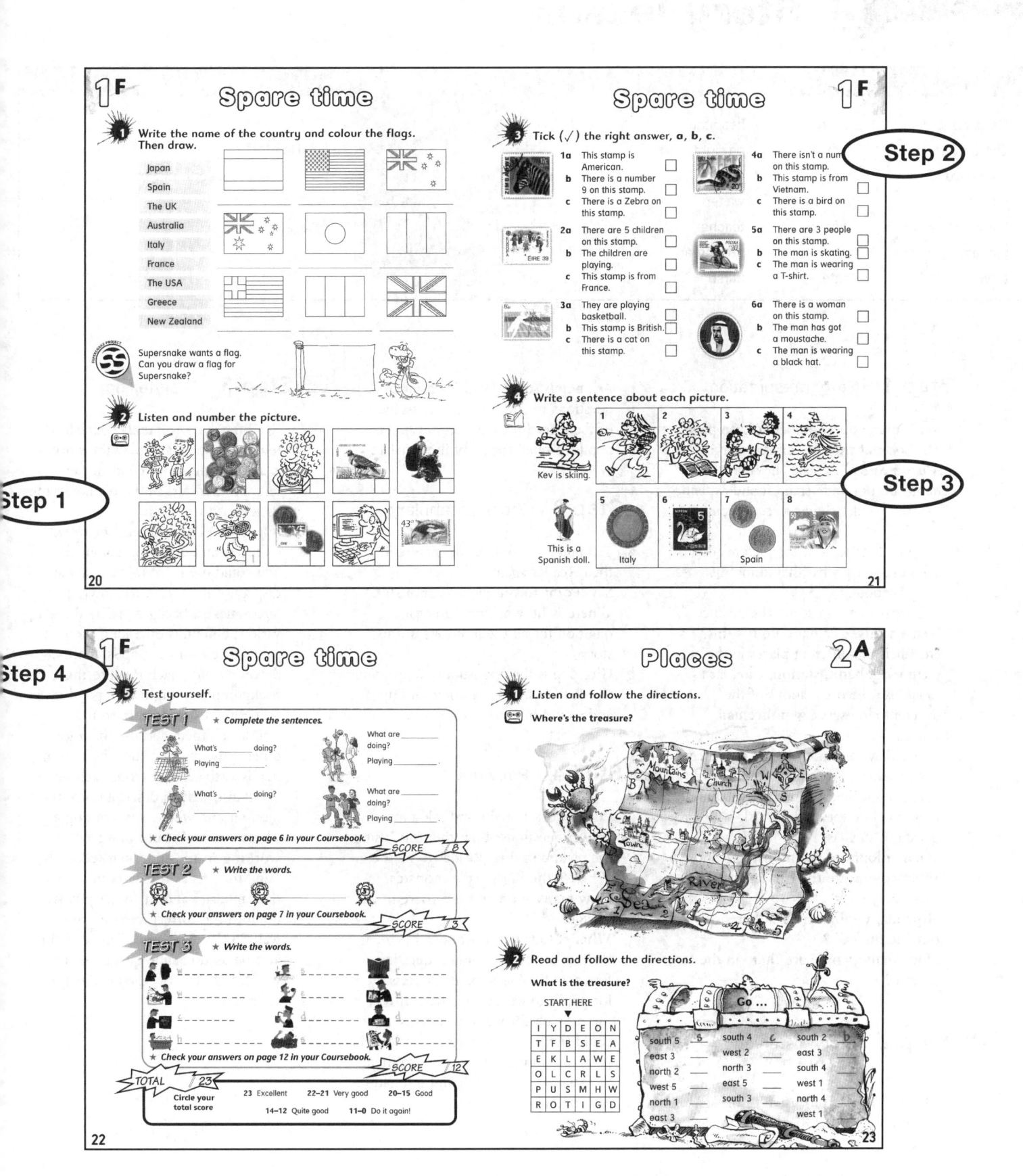

55

2 Story lesson

Main Language Items			Resource File	Materials Needed
Revision: colours	street	hospital		
There is …	school	daylight	25	Reader
There are …	shop	dark	41a	cassette/cassette player
strange	station	waiter	41b	
hairy	cinema	teacher		
places	park	policeman		
town	cafe	nurse		

Step 1 Story presentation

a Say 'Open your Coursebook on page 18. Look at the title of the story: *Monster Street*.' Explain the title if pupils do not understand it and explain that the picture shows a scene from the story.

b Tell pupils to look at the picture and ask in their L1 what they think the story is about.

c Ask what they can see in the picture: 'What's this?', 'What colour's this?', etc. Elicit the different places in the picture e.g. **bank, station, cafe**, etc. Elicit also the occupations of the different monsters e.g. **policeman, nurse**.

d Pupils play a memory game: give them two minutes to remember as much detail about the picture as possible. Tell them to close their books. Ask questions such as:
What colour are the monsters?
What colour are the cars in the picture?
How many monsters are there outside the cafe?
How many people are there in the picture?

Step 2 Story 'listen and read'

a Play the tape. Pupils listen to the story and follow in their Reader at the same time.

b Ask pupils some comprehension questions to check their understanding of the story (in L1 if necessary). Ask pupils to retell the story in their L1.

Step 3 Story vocabulary

a Tell pupils to look at the picture in their Reader again.
Say '**Point to the** *big, blue* **monster. Where is he working?**' Repeat the question for all the monsters in the story.

b Give pupils the opportunity to ask you words they still don't know in English and would like to.

Step 4 Pairwork

Pupils work in pairs and ask and answer questions about the story, using the picture in their Reader to help. e.g.
Where's the big purple monster?
How many monsters are there in the garage?
What colour is the waiter?
Write some of these useful question forms on the blackboard if necessary, for pupils to use as reference. If this is too difficult for weaker students, they could simply read the story out loud in pairs for enjoyment. Encourage them to focus on the rhythm and intonation of the story.

Step 5 Storytelling

Read the story to pupils yourself or rewind the tape and play the story again. Tell pupils to point to the relevant monsters in the picture in their Reader as they listen.

(Optional) Pupils invent their own monsters and draw and colour them. You could use these to make a wall display of the class's very own *Monster Street*: make a background by drawing various buildings on a long piece of paper. Then cut out pupils' monster drawings and attach them to the background. It might be a good idea to use ®Blu-tack to do this, so that you can detach them and use them for other activities, or return them to the pupils at the end of term. Each pupil could also write a description of their monster and where it is working e.g. **There's a small pink monster working in the supermarket.** Each pupil then reads the description of their monster and the other pupils point to the correct monster on the wall display. This wall display could also be used in subsequent lessons in which the story of *Monster Street* is revisited.

Step 1

2 Places

STORY

Monster Street

57

2A Lesson 1

Main Language Items		Resource File	Materials Needed
Which town … ? near mountain		13	cassette/cassette player
Go … north sea		14	
east island			
south river			
west			

Step 1 Presentation

a Ask pupils in their L1 why it is important to be able to read maps and plans. Ask them to list the different instances when this knowledge could be useful, necessary or even crucial.

b Say 'Open your Coursebook on page 20.'

c Play the tape. Pupils listen and read at the same time.

d Then tell pupils to look at the map of Danger Island. Introduce the new vocabulary by asking some questions about the towns on the map:
Is Angerton near the sea?
Which town is near the mountains?
Is Storm Bay in the south of the island?
Which town is near the river?

Step 2 Reading (Task)

a Pupils read the three clues to find out which town Blackbeard's treasure is in.

b Go over the clues with the whole class by asking:
Which towns are near the sea?
Which town is near the mountains?
Which towns are in the north of the island?
Which town is in the south of Danger Island?
Which town is near the river?

c Then pupils read the five clues alongside the treasure map to find the exact location of the treasure.

Step 3 Listening (Task)

Pupils follow the directions around the map on page 23 in the Activity Book to find the location of the treasure.

Tapescript:
Start at the house in the south-east of the map. Go north three squares. // Go west four squares into the mountains. // Now go south one square into the small town by the sea. // Go east three squares // and then north two squares. // Finally go west one square. Where are you?
(Answer: At the church)

Step 4 Pairwork

a All pupils work in pairs, using the map on page 23 of the Activity Book. P1 thinks of a square but does not tell his or her partner. Then, starting at the house in square E5, P1 directs P2 to the mystery square.

b Encourage pupils to use the structure: 'Go north 2 squares.' etc.

c They change roles and repeat the exercise.

Step 5 Puzzle

a Pupils follow the directions around the grid and write down each letter that they land upon to discover the treasure.

b When pupils have finished they can try to make more words for their friends by writing directions from one letter to another.
(**Answers:** sweets, coins, badges)

Step 1

Step 2

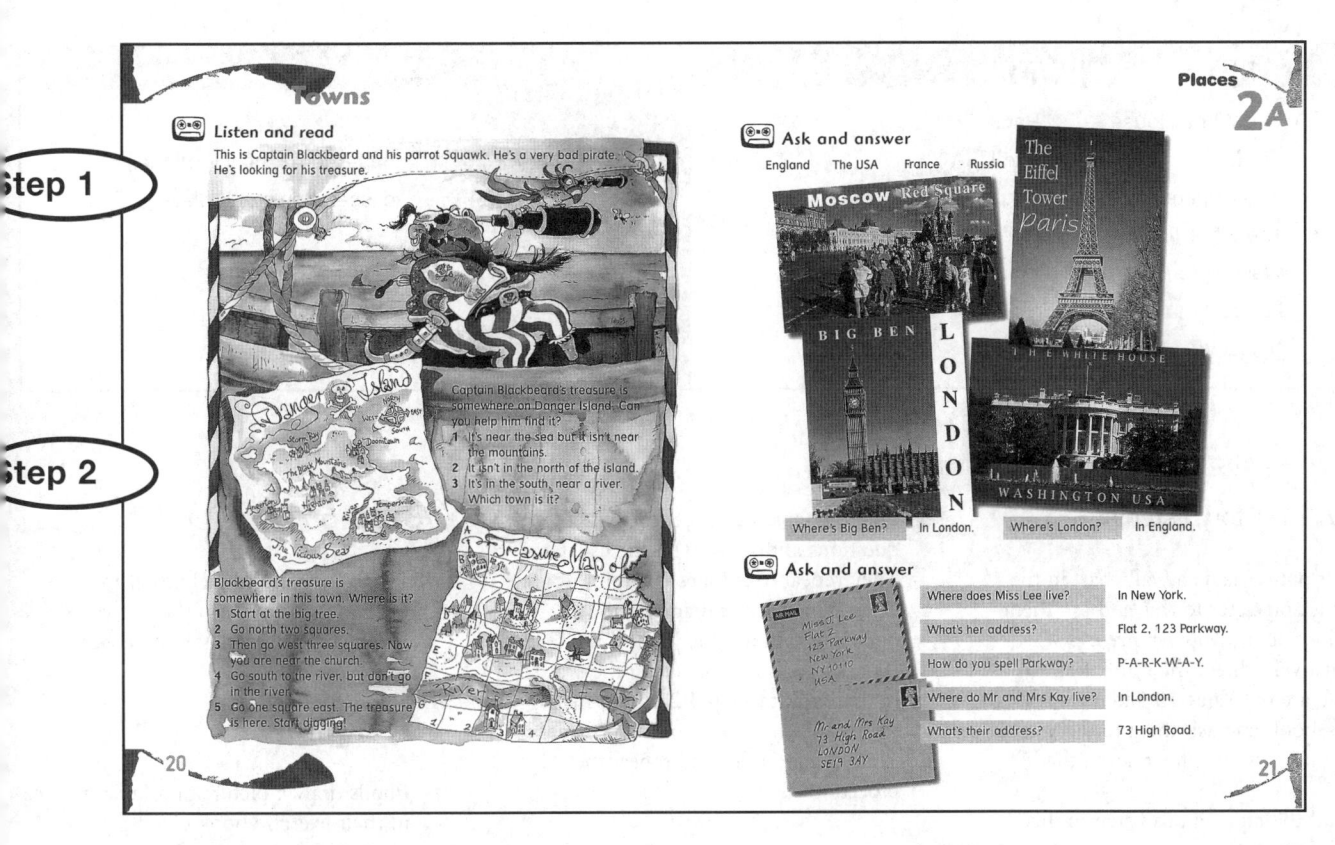

Towns

Listen and read

This is Captain Blackbeard and his parrot Squawk. He's a very bad pirate. He's looking for his treasure.

Captain Blackbeard's treasure is somewhere on Danger Island. Can you help him find it?
1 It's near the sea but it isn't near the mountains.
2 It isn't in the north of the island.
3 It's in the south, near a river. Which town is it?

Blackbeard's treasure is somewhere in this town. Where is it?
1 Start at the big tree.
2 Go north two squares.
3 Then go west three squares. Now you are near the church.
4 Go south to the river, but don't go in the river.
5 Go one square east. The treasure is here. Start digging!

Places 2A

Ask and answer

England   The USA   France   Russia

Moscow — Red Square
The Eiffel Tower — Paris
BIG BEN — LONDON
THE WHITE HOUSE — WASHINGTON USA

Where's Big Ben? — In London.
Where's London? — In England.

Ask and answer

Miss Lee
Flat 2
123 Parkway
New York
NY 10110
USA

Mr and Mrs Kay
73 High Road
LONDON
SE19 3AY

Where does Miss Lee live? — In New York.
What's her address? — Flat 2, 123 Parkway.
How do you spell Parkway? — P-A-R-K-W-A-Y.
Where do Mr and Mrs Kay live? — In London.
What's their address? — 73 High Road.

20 / 21

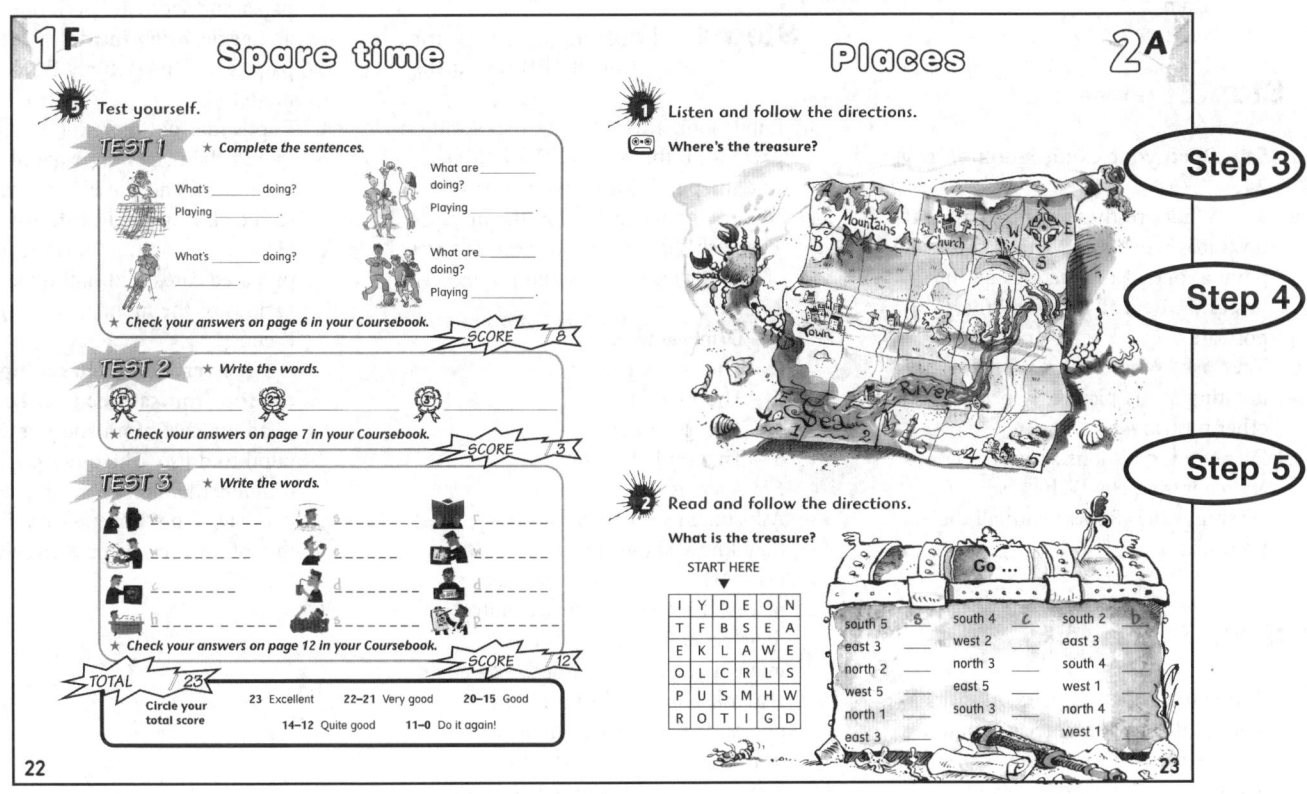

1F Spare time

5 Test yourself.

TEST 1 ★ Complete the sentences.

What's ___ doing?
Playing ___.

What are ___ doing?
Playing ___.

What's ___ doing?
___

What are ___ doing?
Playing ___.

★ Check your answers on page 6 in your Coursebook.

SCORE 8

TEST 2 ★ Write the words.

★ Check your answers on page 7 in your Coursebook.

SCORE 3

TEST 3 ★ Write the words.

★ Check your answers on page 12 in your Coursebook.

SCORE 12

TOTAL 23

Circle your total score:
23 Excellent   22–21 Very good   20–15 Good
14–12 Quite good   11–0 Do it again!

Places 2A

1 Listen and follow the directions.

Where's the treasure?

Step 3

Step 4

Step 5

2 Read and follow the directions.

What is the treasure?

START HERE
▼

I	Y	D	E	O	N
T	F	B	S	E	A
E	K	L	A	W	E
O	L	C	R	L	S
P	U	S	M	H	W
R	O	T	I	G	D

Go ...

south 5 ___ B   south 4 ___ c   south 2 ___ b
east 3 ___   west 2 ___   east 3 ___
north 2 ___   north 3 ___   south 4 ___
west 5 ___   east 5 ___   west 1 ___
north 1 ___   south 3 ___   north 4 ___
east 3 ___   west 1 ___

22 / 23

2A Lesson 2

Main Language Items			Resource File	Materials Needed
Where's … ?	The White House	Paris	7	paper for display (optional)
In …	Big Ben	The USA	8	cassette/cassette player
postcard	Red Square	England	14	
	The Eiffel Tower	Russia	74	
	Washington	France		
	London			
	Moscow			

Step 1 Story listening

a If your pupils made a wall chart in the Story lesson, refer to this and ask them questions about *Monster Street*. Alternatively, direct their attention to the picture on pages 18 and 19 in the Coursebook and ask them to tell you what they can remember about the story.

b Rewind the tape. Pupils listen to the story again.

Step 2 Presentation

a Say '**Open your Coursebook on page 21.**'

b Ask '**What are these?**' and point at the postcards. Then ask '**What's this?**' and point at one of the pictures on the postcards. Repeat with the other postcards.

c Then ask '**Where's the White House?**' pointing at the picture. Repeat with the other postcards.

d Finally ask questions about the cities and countries, e.g. '**Where's Washington?**' Repeat with all the postcards.

Step 3 Pairwork

a Divide the class into pairs. All pairs work at the same time. Say '**Look at the postcards on page 21.**' Cover the questions and answers.

b Play the tape. Pupils repeat the questions and answers in the usual way. They repeat four times changing roles.

c Then pupils ask and answer the questions without the help of the tape. P1 asks the questions using the words in the book to help, P2 answers using only the information on the postcards.

d They change roles and repeat the procedure.

Step 4 Look at the map and number the pictures

Pupils look at the map of the world on page 24 in the Activity Book. Make sure the pupils know the names of the countries labelled 1–6 on the map. Then ask them to number the pictures of famous monuments and places.
Answers:
1 – Disneyland
2 – The Colosseum
3 – The Acropolis
4 – The Pyramids
5 – The Taj Mahal
6 – Ayers Rock
Ask students (in L1 if necessary) what they know about the places on the map. Ask them to list a few more places of interest in their country, in their general area and in their immediate neighbourhood. You could also ask pupils to bring in any postcards they have at home, either from a different country or their own. You could use these to enhance the world map wall display (see **Resource File 7**).

Step 5 Write

Pupils look at the pictures at the bottom of page 24 in the Activity Book and complete the sentences.

Optional

a Pupils draw a picture of a famous place in their exercise book or on a piece of paper and write a description alongside, using the descriptions on page 24 of the Activity Book as a model.

b Pupils find out more information about one of the places on page 24 for homework and present the information to the class in the next lesson.

c Have a competition in class, using pre-prepared cards with information about various of the monuments written on them.
e.g. **It's very tall. It has a big clock at the top. You can see it in London.**
Read out the information or ask a pupil to do so. The other pupils have to guess the monument (Big Ben). If you have more time, ask pupils to write the information cards themselves.

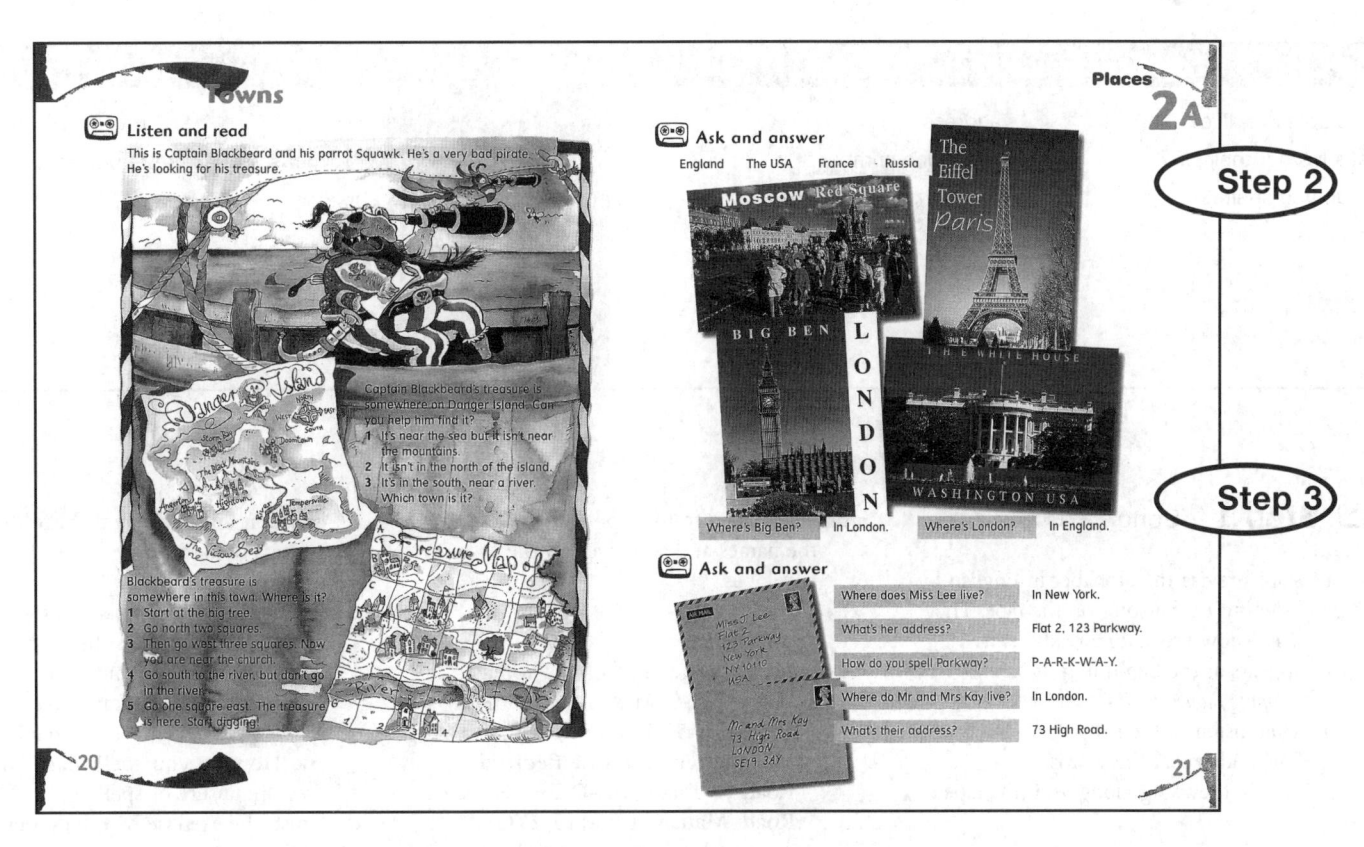

Towns

Listen and read

This is Captain Blackbeard and his parrot Squawk. He's a very bad pirate. He's looking for his treasure.

Captain Blackbeard's treasure is somewhere on Danger Island. Can you help him find it?
1. It's near the sea but it isn't near the mountains.
2. It isn't in the north of the island.
3. It's in the south, near a river.
Which town is it?

Blackbeard's treasure is somewhere in this town. Where is it?
1. Start at the big tree.
2. Go north two squares.
3. Then go west three squares. Now you are near the church.
4. Go south to the river, but don't go in the river.
5. Go one square east. The treasure is here. Start digging!

Places 2A

Ask and answer

England   The USA   France   Russia

Where's Big Ben? — In London.   Where's London? — In England.

Ask and answer

Where does Miss Lee live?	In New York.
What's her address?	Flat 2, 123 Parkway.
How do you spell Parkway?	P-A-R-K-W-A-Y.
Where do Mr and Mrs Kay live?	In London.
What's their address?	73 High Road.

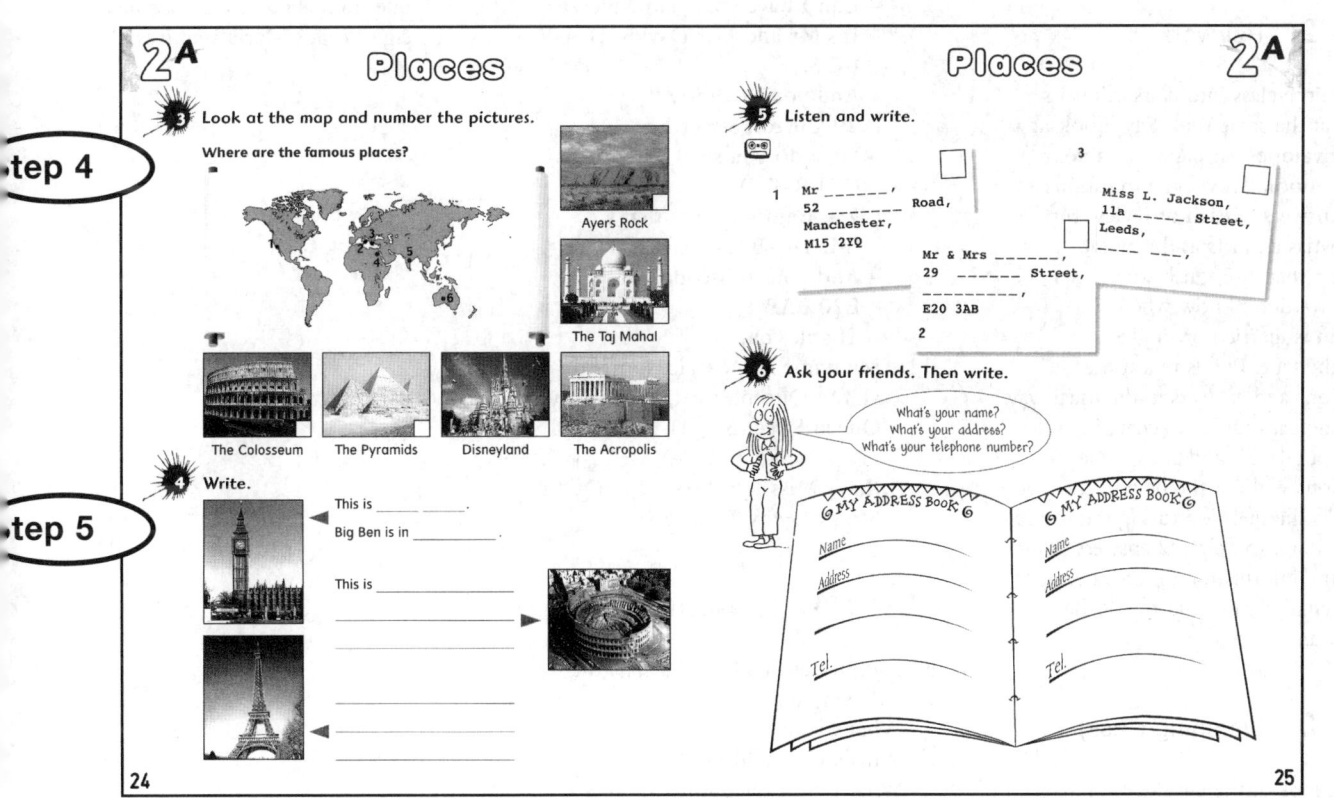

2A Places

3 Look at the map and number the pictures.

Where are the famous places?

Ayers Rock
The Taj Mahal
The Colosseum
The Pyramids
Disneyland
The Acropolis

4 Write.

This is _____.
Big Ben is in _____.

This is _____.
_____

_____
_____

Places 2A

5 Listen and write.

1. Mr _____,
52 _____ Road,
Manchester,
M15 2YQ

2. Mr & Mrs _____,
29 _____ Street,
_____,
E20 3AB

3. Miss L. Jackson,
11a _____ Street,
Leeds,
_____ ___,

6 Ask your friends. Then write.

What's your name?
What's your address?
What's your telephone number?

MY ADDRESS BOOK
Name
Address
Tel.

MY ADDRESS BOOK
Name
Address
Tel.

61

2A Lesson 3

Main Language Items		Resource File	Materials Needed
Where do(es) ... live?	address	38	
What's his/her/their ... ?	telephone number	40	cassette/cassette player
How do you spell ... ?	*Revision: letters of the alphabet*	49b	
Mr	Miss	59	
Mrs	Ms	66	

Step 1 Song

a Pupils revise the alphabet in English by listening to the song on the tape. They may know the song already, as it appears at the beginning of *New Stepping Stones 2*.

b They listen to the song again line by line, and repeat the words.

c Finally they sing along with the tape.

Step 2 Pairwork

a Divide the class into pairs. All pairs work at the same time. Say 'Look at the envelopes on page 21 in your Coursebook. Cover the questions and answers.' Teach or review Mr, Mrs, Miss and Ms at this point. Explain that in English we use Ms when we don't know whether a woman is married or single.

b Play the tape. Pupils repeat the questions and answers in the usual way. They repeat four times changing roles.

c Then pupils ask and answer the questions without the help of the tape. P1 asks the questions using the words in the book to help. P2 answers using only the information on the envelopes.

d They change roles and repeat the procedure.

Step 3 Listening (Task)

a Pupils look at the envelopes on page 25 of the Activity Book.

b They listen to the tape and complete the names and addresses on the envelopes.

Tapescript:

1 My name ... that's Mr Thomas ... that's T-H-O-M-A-S ... and my address is 52 Bedford Road, Manchester ... yes ... Bedford Road ... that's B-E-D-F-O-R-D Road, Manchester M15 2YQ.

2 – Can I have your name please?
– It's Mr and Mrs Davies. D-A-V-I-E-S.
– And your address?
– 29 Curzon Street ...
– How do you spell Curzon? C-U-R-Z-O-N.
– Yes. Edinburgh ... that's E-D-I-N-B-U-R-G-H.
– And your postcode?
– E20 3AB
– Thank you.

3 My name is Miss Jackson and I live at 11a Queen Street, Leeds ... yes, Queen Street is Q-U-E-E-N and my postcode is L-S-2-5-6-X-J ... that's Miss L Jackson, 11a Queen Street, Leeds, LS25 6XJ.

Step 4 Questionnaire

a Ask various pupils in the class the following questions:
What's your name?
What's your address?
What's your telephone number?

b When pupils are familiar with the question forms, direct them to the address book on page 25 of their Activity Book.

c All pupils work simultaneously asking other group members their names, addresses, telephone numbers and writing the information in their Activity Books. Encourage pupils to ask 'How do you spell that?' when they are unsure of spelling.

d Finish the exercise by asking pupils questions about other class members, e.g. 'What's Maria's address?'

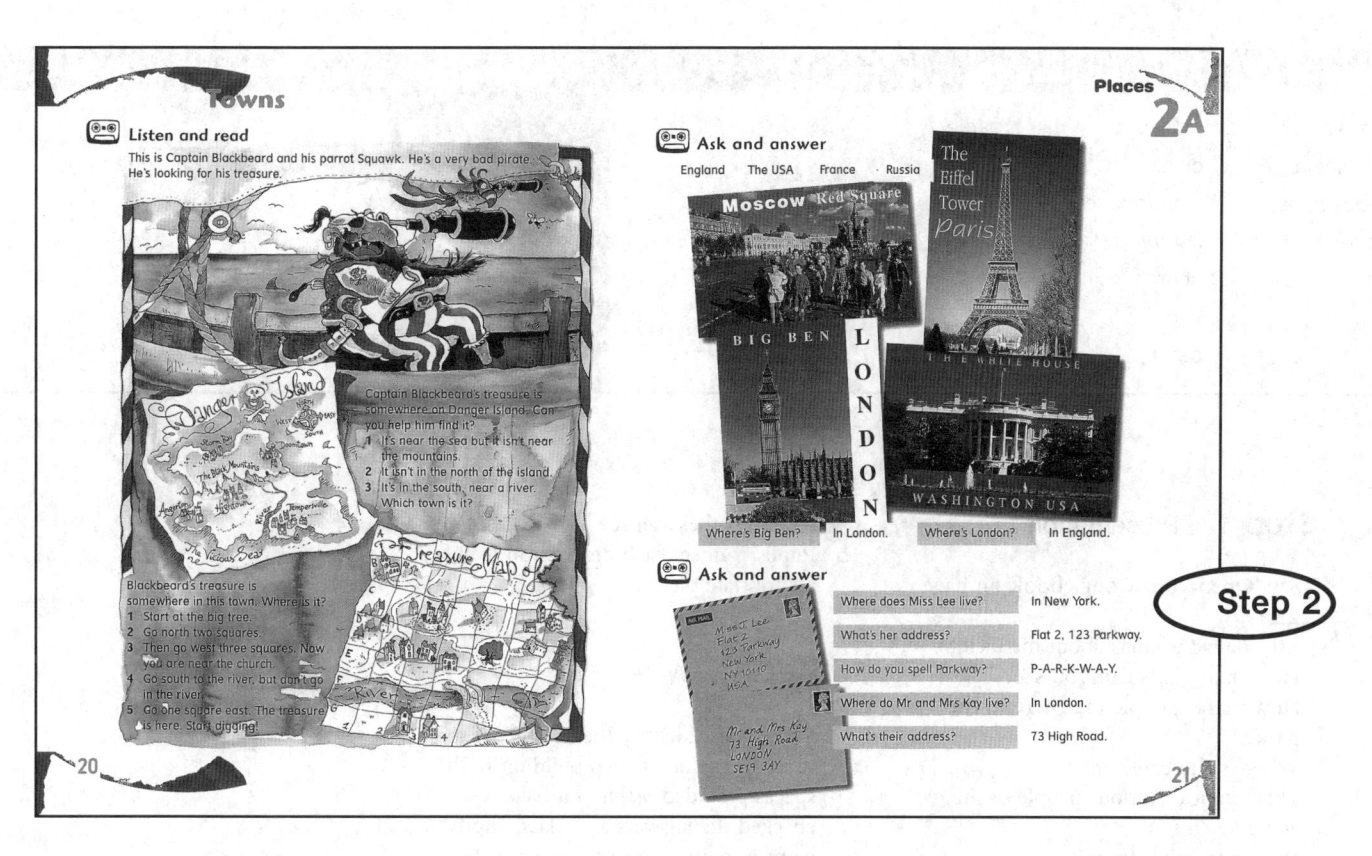

Towns

Listen and read

This is Captain Blackbeard and his parrot Squawk. He's a very bad pirate. He's looking for his treasure.

Captain Blackbeard's treasure is somewhere on Danger Island. Can you help him find it?
1 It's near the sea but it isn't near the mountains.
2 It isn't in the north of the island.
3 It's in the south, near a river.
Which town is it?

Blackbeard's treasure is somewhere in this town. Where's it?
1 Start at the big tree.
2 Go north two squares.
3 Then go west three squares. Now you are near the church.
4 Go south to the river, but don't go in the river.
5 Go one square east. The treasure is here. Start digging!

Places 2A

Ask and answer
England The USA France Russia

Where's Big Ben? In London.   Where's London? In England.

Ask and answer

Where does Miss Lee live? In New York.
What's her address? Flat 2, 123 Parkway.
How do you spell Parkway? P-A-R-K-W-A-Y.
Where do Mr and Mrs Kay live? In London.
What's their address? 73 High Road.

Step 2

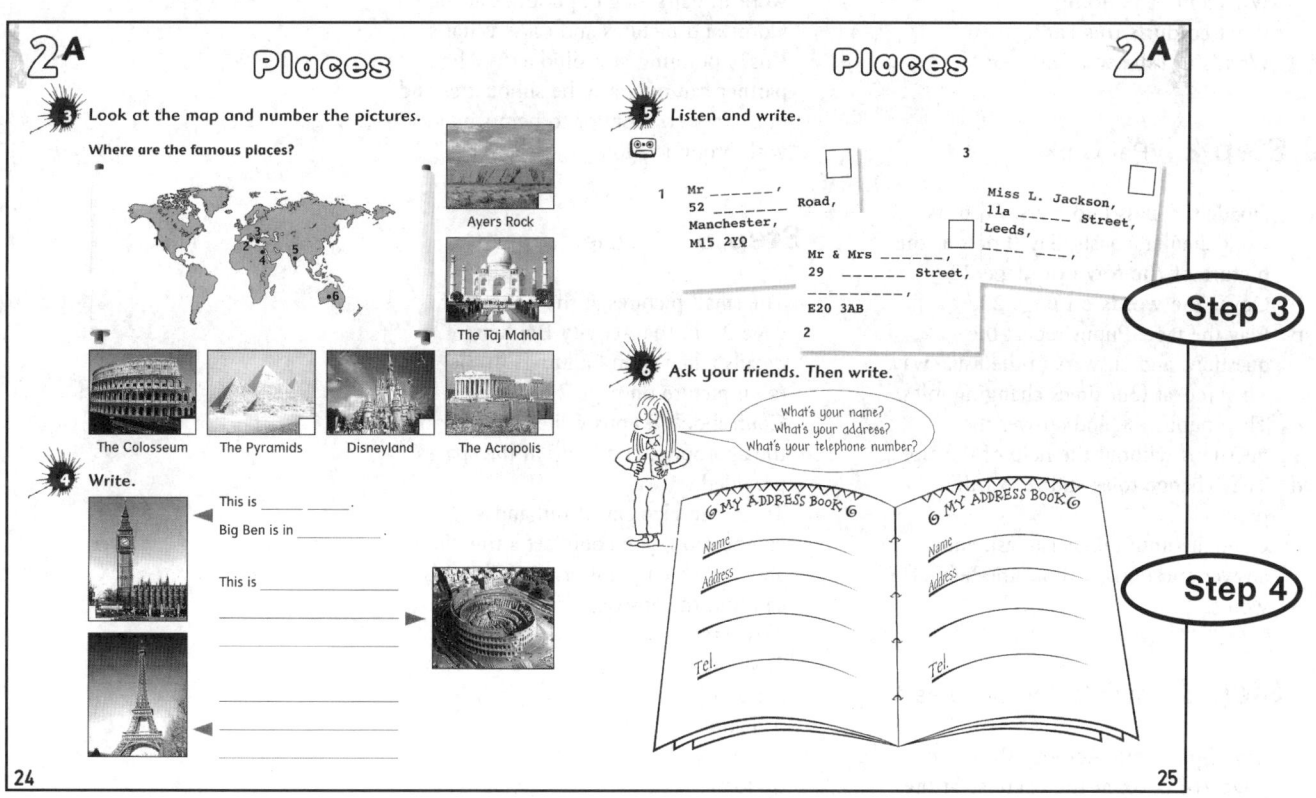

2A Places

3 Look at the map and number the pictures.

Where are the famous places?

Ayers Rock
The Taj Mahal
The Colosseum   The Pyramids   Disneyland   The Acropolis

4 Write.

This is _____ _____.
Big Ben is in _____.

This is _____
_____

Places 2A

5 Listen and write.

1 Mr _____,
   52 _____ Road,
   Manchester,
   M15 2YQ

   Mr & Mrs _____,
   29 _____ Street,
   _____,
   E20 3AB
   2

   3
   Miss L. Jackson,
   11a _____ Street,
   Leeds,
   _____ ___,

Step 3

6 Ask your friends. Then write.

What's your name?
What's your address?
What's your telephone number?

MY ADDRESS BOOK
Name
Address
Tel.

MY ADDRESS BOOK
Name
Address
Tel.

Step 4

63

2B Lesson 1

Main Language Items		Resource File	Materials Needed
Where's ...?	museum park	2	cassette/cassette player
Is ... near ...?	cinema	4	
Prepositions:	supermarket	41	
opposite	library	67	
near	church	74	
by	river		
in	cafe		

Step 1   Presentation

a Say 'Open your Coursebook on page 22.'
b Ask some questions about the picture:
How many cars can you see?
How many people are there in the park?
Where's the cafe? etc.
c Then point to various people or things and ask:
What's he/she doing?
What colour's this car?
What's he/she wearing? etc.

Step 2   Pairwork

a Divide the class into pairs. All pairs work simultaneously. Say 'Look at the **picture of the town on page 22. Cover the words on page 23.**'
b Play the tape. Pupils repeat the questions and answers in the usual way. They repeat four times changing roles.
c Then pupils ask and answer the questions without the help of the tape.
d They change roles and repeat the procedure.
e Continue until pupils can ask and answer questions without the help of words.

Step 3   Words and pictures

a Say 'Open your Activity Book on page 26. Look at the exercise at the top of the page.' Ask pupils what buildings they can see.
b Pupils connect each description to the appropriate picture.

Step 4   Write

Pupils must identify the silhouettes and write the name of each building in the spaces provided. After you have checked the answers as a class, pupils work in pairs; one pupil looks at the words and pictures and asks '**What's this?**', pointing at a silhouette. Their partner can only see the silhouettes and must answer. Monitor to help students with pronunciation.

Step 5   Puzzle

The small pictures at the bottom of page 26 in the Activity Book are details taken from buildings in the town picture on page 22 of the Coursebook. Pupils write the name of the appropriate building in the spaces provided.
To add an element of fun and competition, you could set a time limit and see which pupil or pair of pupils can find the answers first.
Answers:
1 Museum
2 School
3 Station
4 Library
5 Hotel
6 Cinema

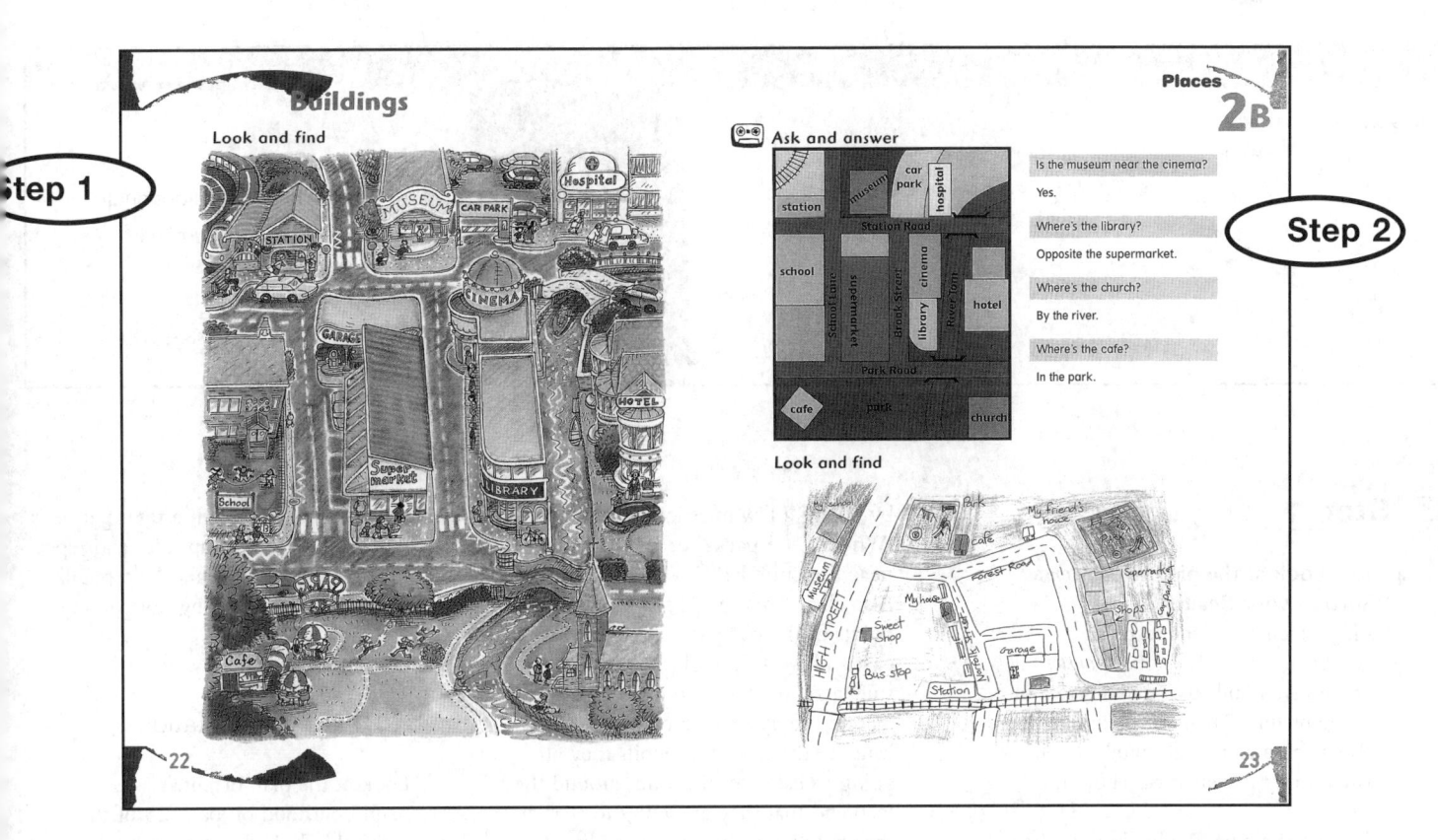

Buildings

Step 1

Look and find

Places 2B

Step 2

Ask and answer

Is the museum near the cinema?
Yes.

Where's the library?
Opposite the supermarket.

Where's the church?
By the river.

Where's the cafe?
In the park.

Look and find

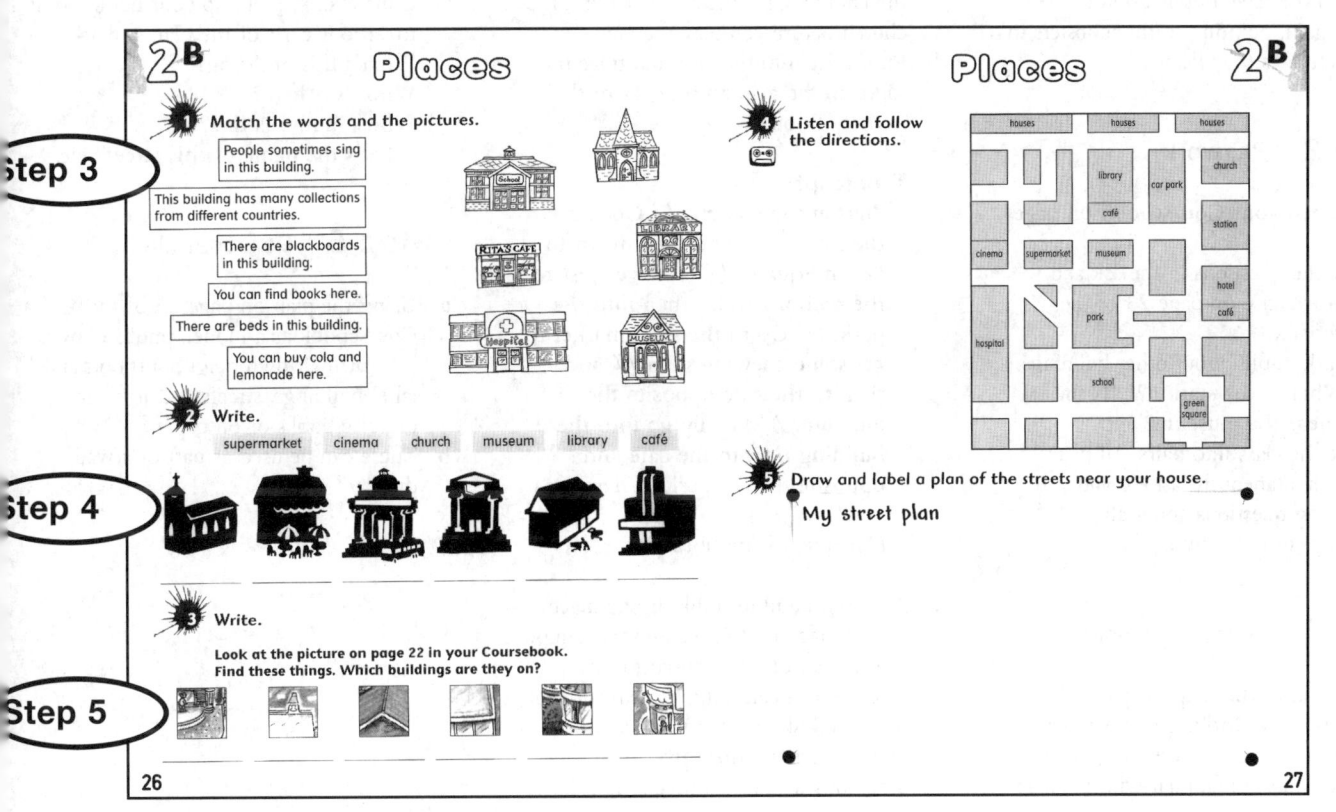

2B Places

Step 3

1 Match the words and the pictures.

- People sometimes sing in this building.
- This building has many collections from different countries.
- There are blackboards in this building.
- You can find books here.
- There are beds in this building.
- You can buy cola and lemonade here.

2 Write.

supermarket   cinema   church   museum   library   café

Step 4

3 Write.

Look at the picture on page 22 in your Coursebook.
Find these things. Which buildings are they on?

Step 5

Places 2B

4 Listen and follow the directions.

5 Draw and label a plan of the streets near your house.

My street plan

26 27

65

2B Lesson 2

Main Language Items		Resource File	Materials Needed
Where's ... ?	plan	1	coloured pencils
	hotel	4a	paper for display (optional)
	hospital	10	cassette/cassette player
	station	14	

Step 1 Story listening

a Say 'Look at the picture of *Monster Street* in your Reader.'
Play a memory game to revise vocabulary from the story *Monster Street*: give pupils two minutes to look at the picture. Then ask them questions about the picture. Ask pupils to tell you what they can remember about the story.

b Rewind the tape. Pupils listen to the story again, pointing to the monsters in the picture as they listen.

Step 2 Pairwork

a Say 'Open your Coursebook on page 22.'
b Revise the questions in the ask and answer exercise on page 23 of the Coursebook.
c Then ask pupils about other buildings, e.g. 'Where's the station?', 'Is the hotel near the museum?' etc.
d Divide the class into pairs. All pairs work simultaneously, asking and answering questions about all the buildings in the picture.

Step 3 Listening (Task)

a Say 'Look at the map on page 27 in your Activity Book.' Ask them what places they can see on the map. Make sure students are familiar with the map by asking a few questions like 'Where's the park?' or 'Is the school near the church?'
Also elicit from the pupils the four points of the compass – **north, south, east** and **west**. It might be useful if students draw these points beside the map to use as a reference while they listen to the tape. Tell pupils they are going to listen to directions around the map and that they are going to start at the church. Give them time to find the church before you play the tape.

b Pupils listen to the tape and trace the route on the map on page 27 of their Activity Book.

Tapescript:
Start at the church. // Go south to the station // and then down to Green Square. // Now go west to the school // and then into the park. // Go to the supermarket to get some chewing gum // and then to the cafe opposite the museum. // Finally go into the building next to the cafe and opposite the car park. Where are you?
(Answer: In the library)

c Ask each pupil to think of one place on the map and to prepare some simple directions from the church to this place. Pupils can write the directions if they need to. Divide the class into pairs. One pupil then gives their directions to their partner, who follows them on the map to find their partner's destination. They swap roles and repeat the activity. Monitor and help pupils when necessary, making note of any common problems.

Step 4 Presentation

Look at the plan of Julie's neighbourhood on page 23 of the Coursebook. Hold up your book, point to various parts of the plan and ask:
What's this building?
Who lives here?
Whose house is this?
What's the name of this street? etc.

Step 5 Personal file

a Using the plan on page 23 of the Coursebook as a model, pupils draw a plan of their own neighbourhood and label buildings, streets, etc. in their exercise books or on paper.
b These can be used as part of a wall display.

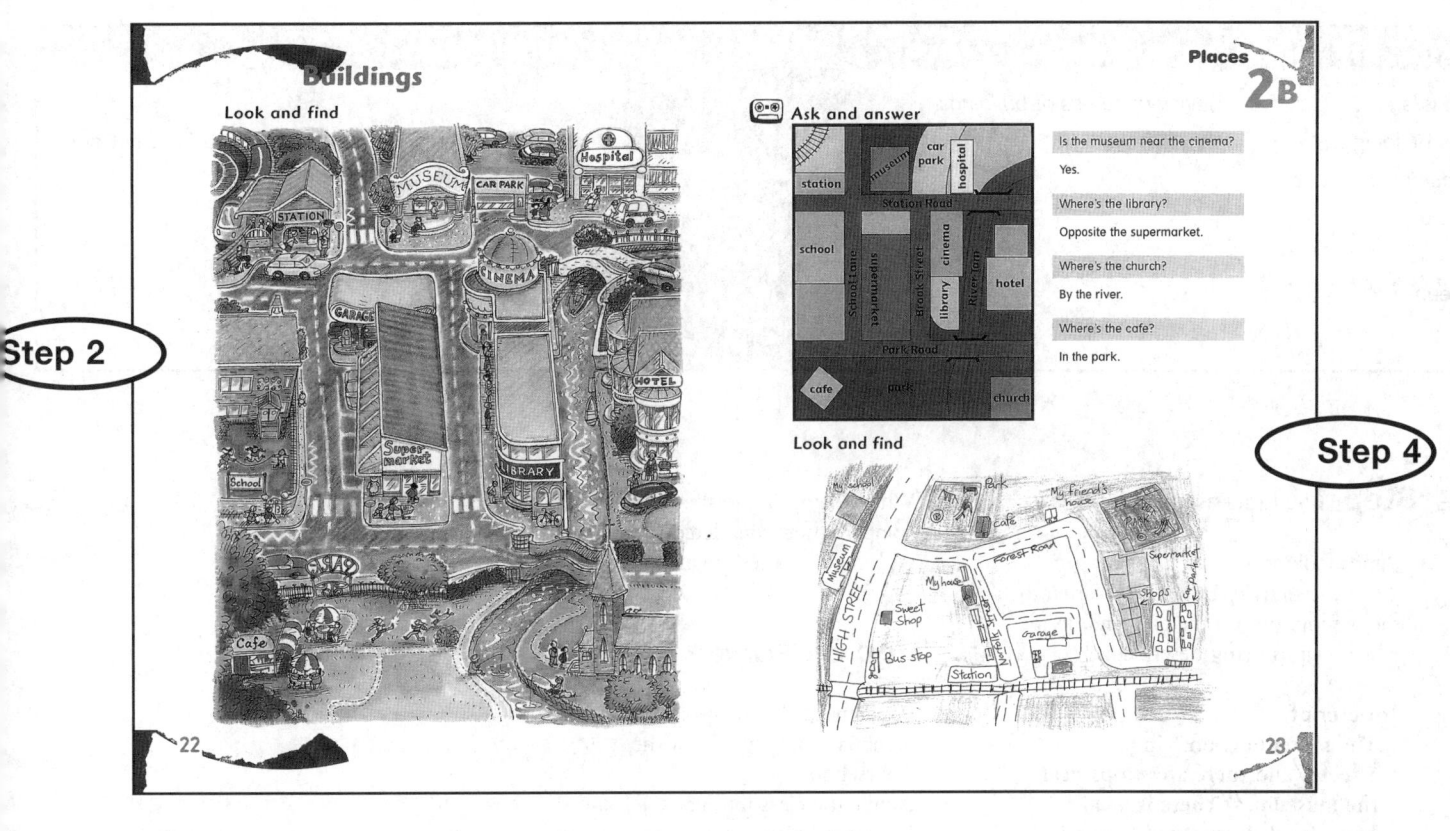

Buildings

Look and find

Places 2B

Ask and answer

Is the museum near the cinema?
Yes.

Where's the library?
Opposite the supermarket.

Where's the church?
By the river.

Where's the cafe?
In the park.

Look and find

Step 2

Step 4

22

23

2B Places

1 Match the words and the pictures.

- People sometimes sing in this building.
- This building has many collections from different countries.
- There are blackboards in this building.
- You can find books here.
- There are beds in this building.
- You can buy cola and lemonade here.

2 Write.

supermarket   cinema   church   museum   library   café

3 Write.

Look at the picture on page 22 in your Coursebook.
Find these things. Which buildings are they on?

Places 2B

4 Listen and follow the directions.

houses | houses | houses
library | car park | church
café | | station
cinema | supermarket | museum | hotel | café
hospital | park
| school
| green square

Step 3

5 Draw and label a plan of the streets near your house.

My street plan

Step 5

26

27

67

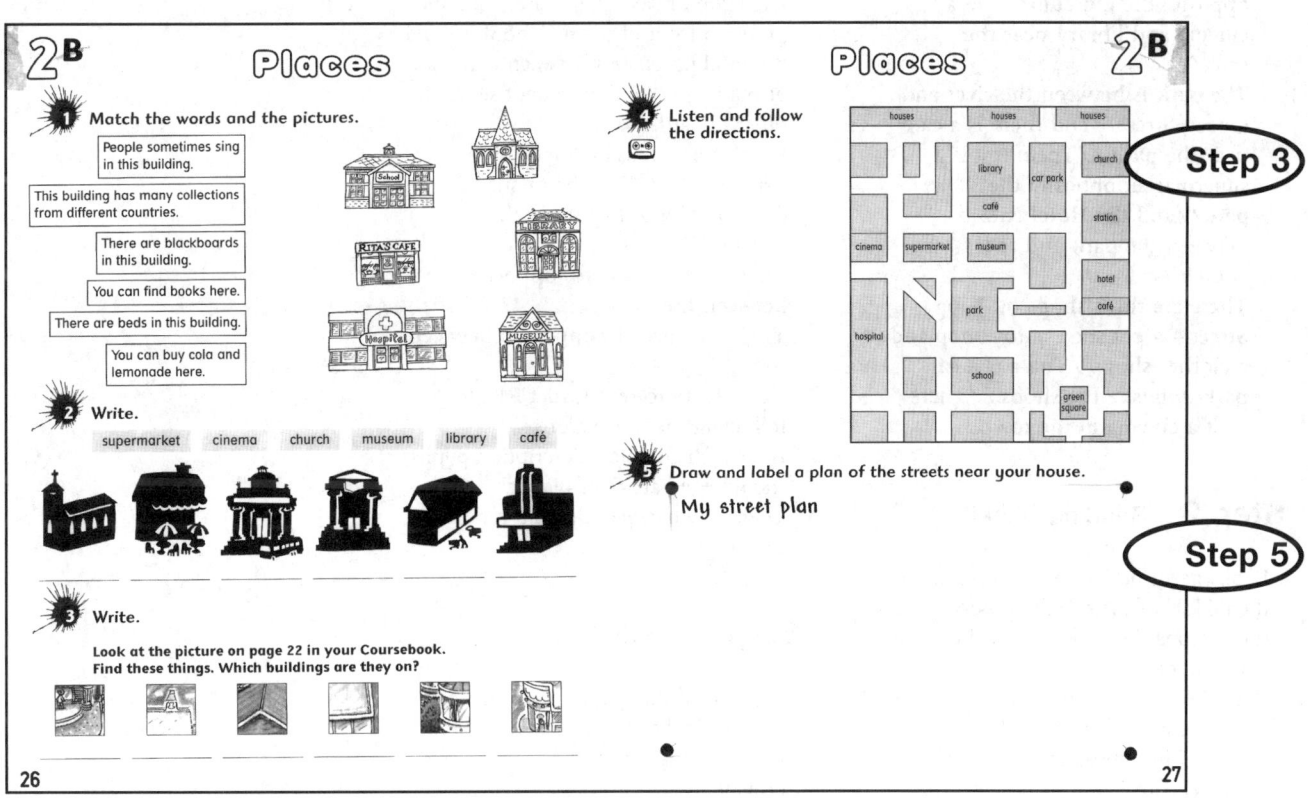

2B Lesson 3

Main Language Items	Resource File	Materials Needed
There is/are … *Revision: names of buildings* Which building …? *Prepositions:* opposite near between	67 77	town pieces (see pull-out section of the Activity Book) cassette/cassette player

Step 1   Listening (Task)

Pupils look at the two maps on page 28 of the Activity Book. They listen to the descriptions on the tape and decide which map is being described.

Tapescript:
1. The museum is on King Street//and there are shops near the museum.//There is a cafe opposite the museum//and a cinema and library near the cafe.//
2. The park is between the river and Queen Street//and there is a cafe near the park.//There is a big supermarket opposite the park//and the Hotel Ritz is between the park and the church.//
3. There are three shops on King Street – a pet shop, a toy shop and a clothes shop.//There is a car park opposite the shops.//There isn't a cinema in the town.

Step 2   Reading (Task)

Pupils need the 25 'town pieces' from the middle of their Activity Books and the baseboard on page 62 of the Coursebook.

a   Pupils read the description on page 28 of the Activity Book and place the pieces in the appropriate location on the baseboard.

b   When they have finished, they should compare their completed town plan with their partner's plans.

Step 3   Pairwork

Pupils need the town pieces and the baseboard on page 62 of the Coursebook.

a   Divide the class into pairs, P1 and P2. Each pupil places their baseboard and pieces in front of them. A book should be stood up on end between each pair of pupils so that they cannot see each other's board.

b   P1 places various buildings on his or her baseboard. Then he or she describes the picture using the structures:
There is a … next to/opposite/between the … .
The … is next to/opposite/between the … .
P2 must try to reconstruct P1's town following the instructions.

c   After each complete description pupils should compare their pictures.

d   Then they change roles and repeat the exercise.

Step 4   Write

Pupils read the questions at the bottom of page 28 of the Activity Book and write the answers in the spaces provided.

2B Places

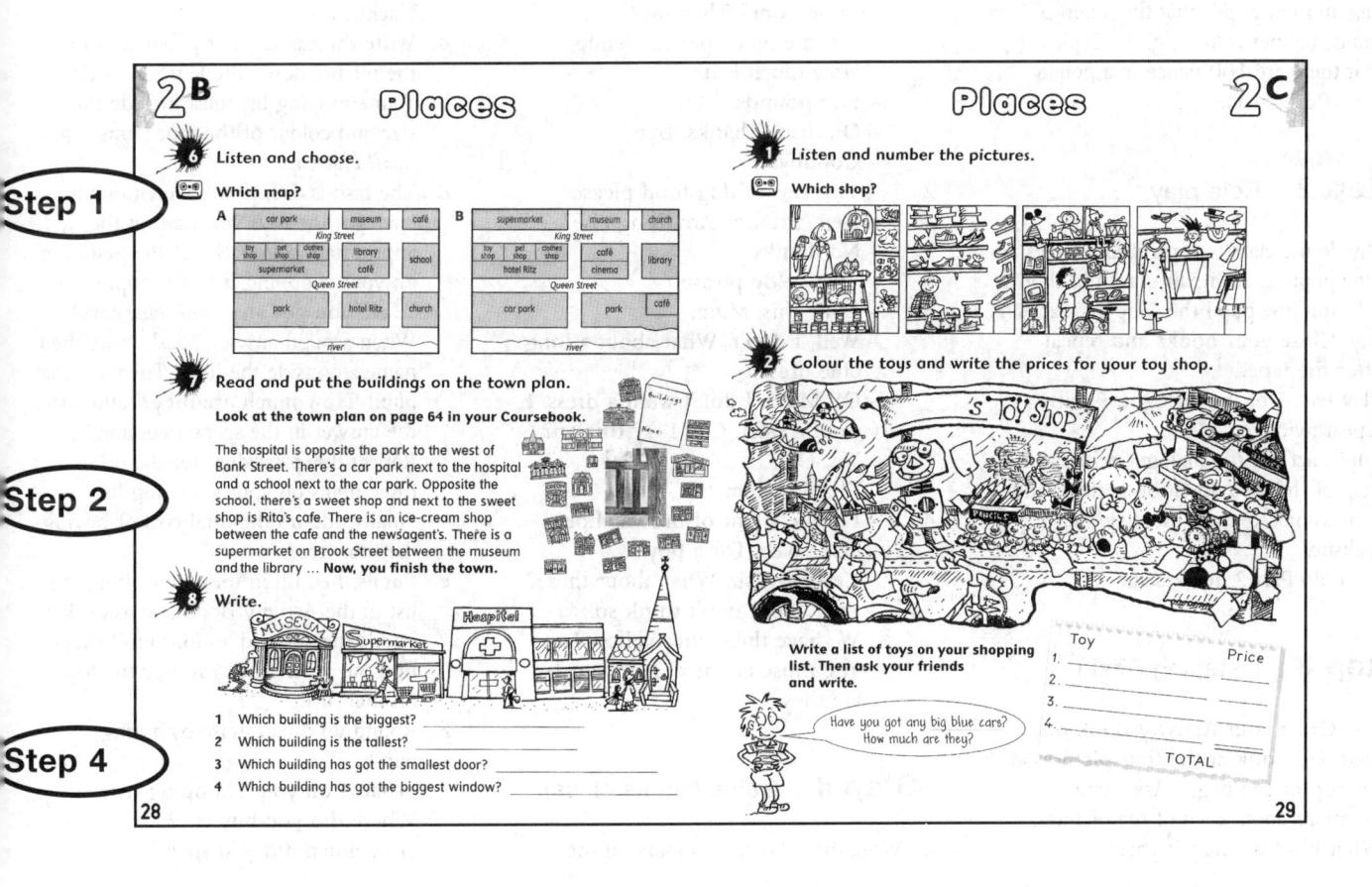

6 Listen and choose.

Which map?

[Map A and Map B showing town layouts with King Street and Queen Street, including car park, museum, café, toy shop, pet shop, clothes shop, library, supermarket, school, park, hotel Ritz, church, cinema, and river]

7 Read and put the buildings on the town plan.

Look at the town plan on page 64 in your Coursebook.

The hospital is opposite the park to the west of Bank Street. There's a car park next to the hospital and a school next to the car park. Opposite the school, there's a sweet shop and next to the sweet shop is Rita's cafe. There is an ice-cream shop between the cafe and the newsagent's. There is a supermarket on Brook Street between the museum and the library ... **Now, you finish the town.**

8 Write.

1 Which building is the biggest? _____
2 Which building is the tallest? _____
3 Which building has got the smallest door? _____
4 Which building has got the biggest window? _____

28

2C Places

1 Listen and number the pictures.

Which shop?

2 Colour the toys and write the prices for your toy shop.

Write a list of toys on your shopping list. Then ask your friends and write.

Have you got any big blue cars? How much are they?

Toy	Price
1.	
2.	
3.	
4.	
TOTAL	

29

2c Lesson 1

Main Language Items			Resource File	Materials Needed
Can I help you?	shop	pound	11	coloured pencils
Have you got ... ?	packet	penny/pence	12	cassette/cassette player
How much ... ?	bag	please	35	
Where can you buy ... ?	bar	thank you	68	
			76b	

Step 1 Presentation

a Say 'Open your Coursebook on page 24. Look at the picture and listen to the tape.' Play the tape.
b Ask some questions about the passage:
   Where is the girl?
   How many people are in the shop?
   What does she buy?
c Explain the meaning of **packet** and **bag** and tell pupils that the letter 'p' stands for **pence** in English. Explain that there are 100 pence in a pound (i.e. 100p = £1).

Step 2 Role play

a Divide the class into pairs. Give roles. One pupil in each pair plays the child's role and one pupil the shop assistant's. Say '**Close your books and repeat after the tape.**'
b Play Part 1 of the dialogue. Pupils repeat twice.
c Pupils act out the dialogue without the help of the tape. Insist on gestures and expressions to make the dialogue realistic.
d Then do Part 2 in the same way.

Step 3 Listening (Task)

a Say '**Open your Activity Book on page 29. Look at the four pictures at the top of the page.**' Ask some questions about each of the pictures: What kind of shop is this? What can you see in the pet shop? etc.
b Then play the tape. Pupils indicate in which shop each conversation is taking place by writing the number of the conversation in the appropriate box.

Tapescript:

1 – Can I see that computer game please?
   – Which one? This one?
   – No, the blue one ... Thanks.
   – How much is it?
   – Five pounds.
   – Oh dear! Thanks. Bye.
   – Goodbye.//
2 – Two tins of dog food please.
   – Here you are. Anything else?
   – No thanks.
   – That's 98p please.//
3 – I like this, Mum.
   – Well, I don't. What about a long blue dress?
   – Oh Mum. I don't want a dress. I want a skirt. Can I try this on?
   – Yes. OK.
   – Thanks Mum.//
4 – I'd like a pair of brown shoes. Size seven. For a boy.
   – Certainly, sir. What about these?
   – Er ... no, I don't think so.
   – We have these with yellow laces.
   – Yes, those are nice. How much are they?

Step 4 Game (whole class)

a Write the following colours on the board: **yellow, green, red, blue, orange, black**. Pupils colour the toys in the picture on page 29 of the Activity Book and write in a price of their choice for each item. They must work individually and not show their partner the prices on their pictures or even the colours, if possible.
b Then copy the shopping list at the bottom of page 29 onto the blackboard.
c Write the names of any four toys from the picture down the left-hand side. Your shopping list must include the size and colour of the four items, e.g. *small blue* car.
d The task is to find out which pupils have got the toys you want in the appropriate colour. Select the first item on your shopping list. Ask pupils '**Have you got any** *small blue* **cars?**' When a pupil answers '**Yes**', write their name alongside the item. Then ask that pupil '**How much are they?**' and write the answer in the second column. Repeat this procedure for the other three items on your shopping list. Finally add up the total cost of buying the four items.
e Pupils then fill in their own shopping list in the Activity Book and ask other pupils the above questions until they find out where they can buy the toys on their list.
f Round up the exercise by asking pupils:
   What is on your shopping list?
   Where did you buy ... ?
   How much did you spend?

70

Shops

Listen and read

Assistant	Good morning. Can I help you?
Child	Have you got any crisps?
Assistant	Yes, how many packets do you want?
Child	Two please.
Assistant	Large or small?
Child	Small please.
Assistant	Anything else?
Child	A bar of chocolate please and a bag of sweets.
Assistant	Here you are.
Child	How much is that?
Assistant	That's 95p please.
Child	Thank you.
Assistant	Thank you very much. Goodbye.

Ask and answer

Where can I buy a newspaper?   At the newsagent's.

a newspaper   bread   a chicken   soap   toothpaste   medicine

Places 2c

Play — The Shopping Game

1. Where can you buy comics?
2. Name three vegetables.
3. One kilo of potatoes is 25p. How much is 3 kilos of potatoes?
4. Name three things you can buy at the newsagent's.
5. Where can you buy soap?
6. Name two shops beginning with the letter 'c'.

1. Where can you buy a rabbit?
2. Name a red fruit.
3. Two kilos of oranges is 86p. How much is one kilo of oranges?
4. Name five things you can buy at the furniture shop.
5. Where can you buy hats?
6. Name two shops beginning with the letter 'b'.

2B Places

6 Listen and choose.

Which map?

A: car park, museum, café / King Street / toy shop, pet shop, clothes shop, library / supermarket, café, school / Queen Street / park, hotel Ritz, church / river

B: supermarket, museum, church / King Street / toy shop, pet shop, clothes shop, café, cinema, library / Queen Street / car park, park, café / river

7 Read and put the buildings on the town plan.

Look at the town plan on page 64 in your Coursebook.

The hospital is opposite the park to the west of Bank Street. There's a car park next to the hospital and a school next to the car park. Opposite the school, there's a sweet shop and next to the sweet shop is Rita's cafe. There is an ice-cream shop between the cafe and the newsagent's. There is a supermarket on Brook Street between the museum and the library ... **Now, you finish the town.**

8 Write.

1. Which building is the biggest? _____
2. Which building is the tallest? _____
3. Which building has got the smallest door? _____
4. Which building has got the biggest window? _____

Places 2c

1 Listen and number the pictures.

Which shop?

2 Colour the toys and write the prices for your toy shop.

Write a list of toys on your shopping list. Then ask your friends and write.

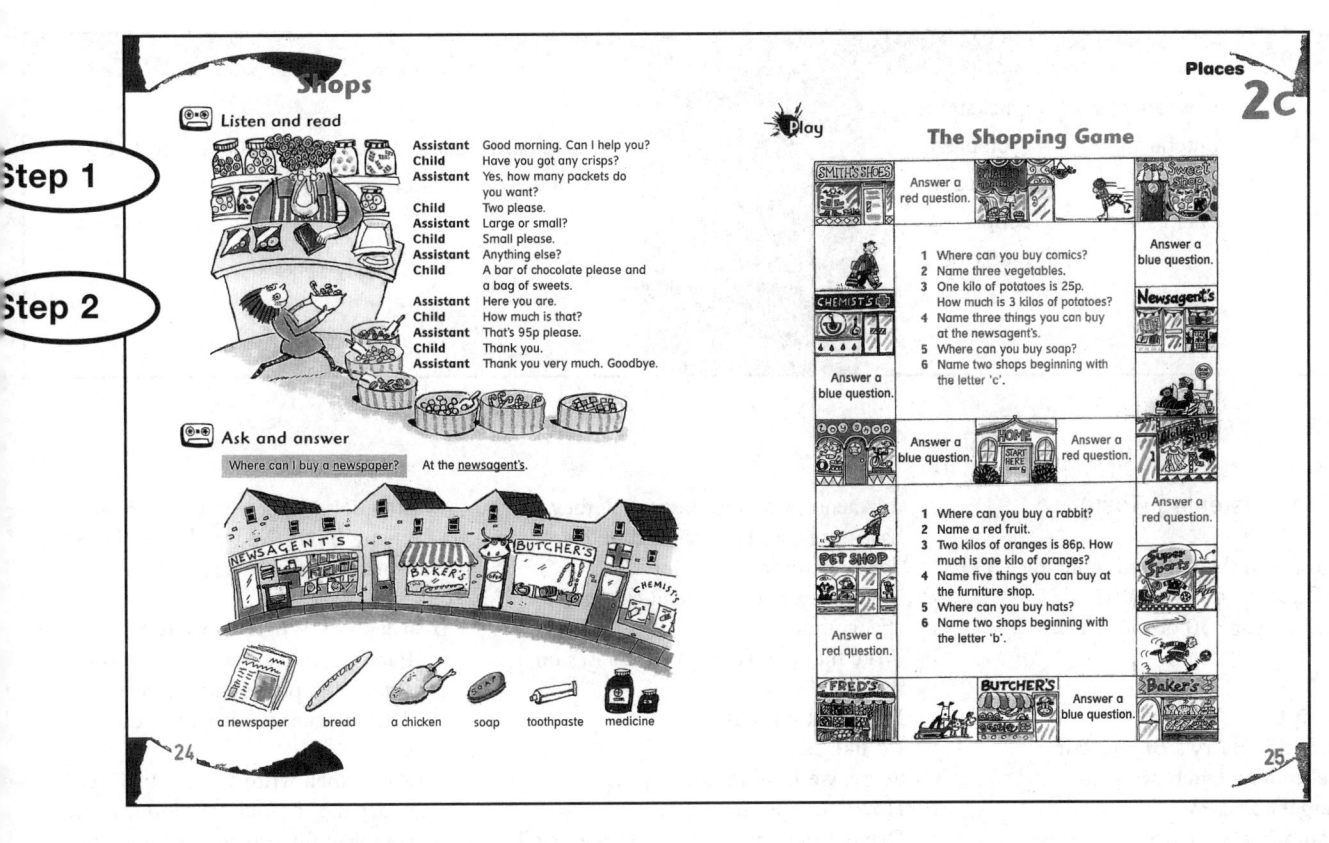

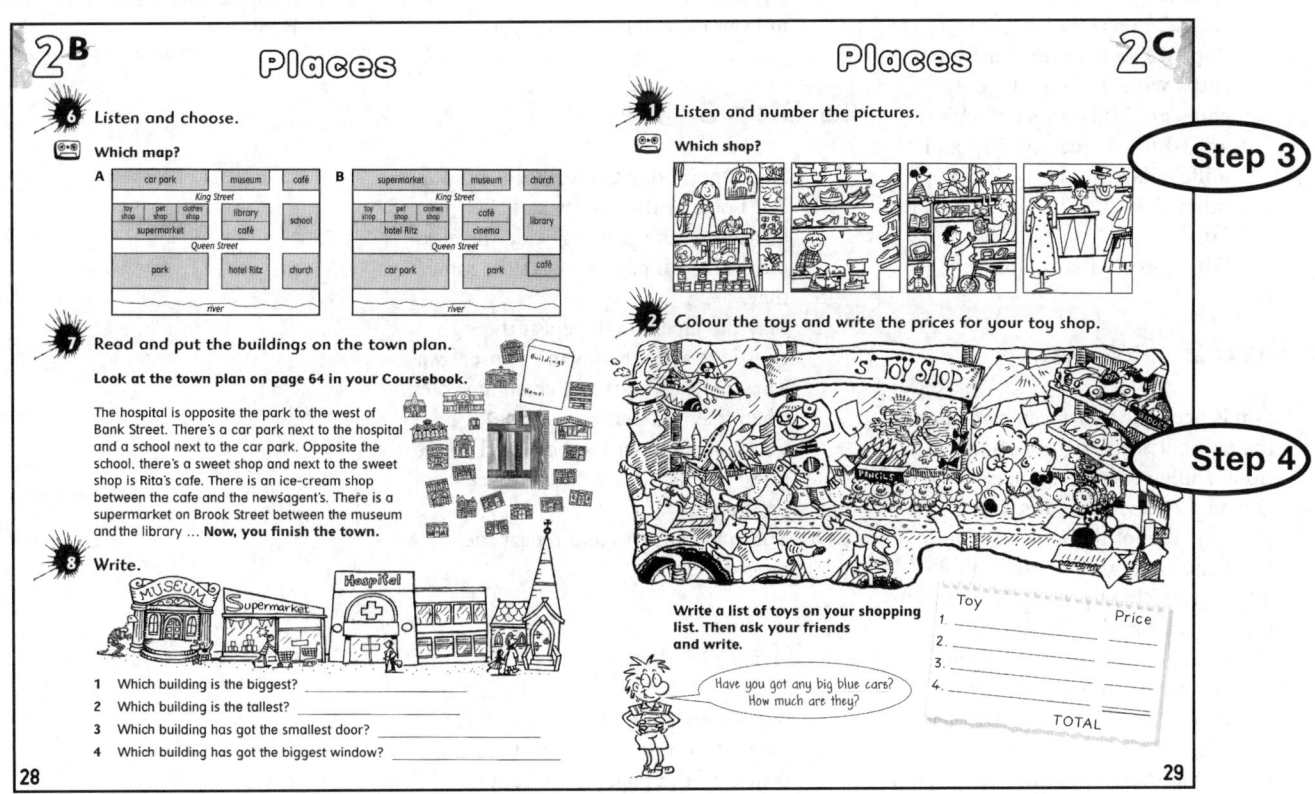

Have you got any big blue cars? How much are they?

Toy	Price
1.	
2.	
3.	
4.	
	TOTAL

2c Lesson 2

Main Language Items			Resource File	Materials Needed
Where can I buy ... ?	newsagent's	chicken	34	menu cards (see pull-out section of the Activity Book)
Have you got ... ?	butcher's	toothpaste	53	cassette/cassette player
I'd like ...	baker's	newspaper	71	
Preposition:	chemist's	soap		
at		medicine		

Step 1 Listening (Task)

Pupils listen to the tape and write the price of each item in the spaces provided on page 30 of the Activity Book.

Tapescript:
— 606785. Harry's Burger Bar.
— Hello, how much are your burgers please?
— Hamburgers are 45p, cheeseburgers and eggburgers are 80p. We've got large and small chips with the burgers. Large chips are 50p and small chips are 30p. Ice-cream is 55p and milkshakes are 35p. All our other drinks, cola, lemonade are 30p.
— Oh ... er ... thank you.

Step 2 Role play

Pupils need the four menu cards from the pull-out section of the Activity Book and an exercise book.

a Divide the class into pairs. One pupil plays the role of the waiter and uses the menu cards as prompts and for information about prices. The other is the customer in the restaurant.
b Before each role play, pupils should decide how much the customer has to spend and they can only order food accordingly.
c Pupils improvise a role play based on the menu cards and the money they have available. The waiter should write down the order each time.
d They select another menu card and change roles.
e Write the following useful phrases on the blackboard:
Have you got any ... ?
I'd like ...
Sorry, we haven't got any ...
How much is/are ... ?
f Demonstrate the activity with one pupil in front of the class before you start.

Step 3 Pairwork

a Say 'Open your Coursebook on page 24. Look at the pictures at the bottom of the page.' Divide the class into pairs. All pairs work at the same time.
b Play the tape. Pupils repeat the questions and answers in the usual way. They repeat four times, changing roles.
c Then they ask and answer the questions without the help of the tape using the pictures in the book as prompts.
d They change roles and repeat the procedure.

Step 4 Write

a Say 'Open your Activity Book on page 30. Look at the words in the centre of the page.' Focus pupils' attention on the vocabulary items by saying 'Find the word *pen*', 'Find the word *cauliflower*.' etc. Repeat with other words.
b Then say 'Where can you buy socks?' Pupils should answer 'At a clothes shop.' Tell pupils they must write 'socks' under the heading 'Clothes shop'.
c Pupils then write all the other items under the appropriate shop name to complete the lists in their Activity Book.

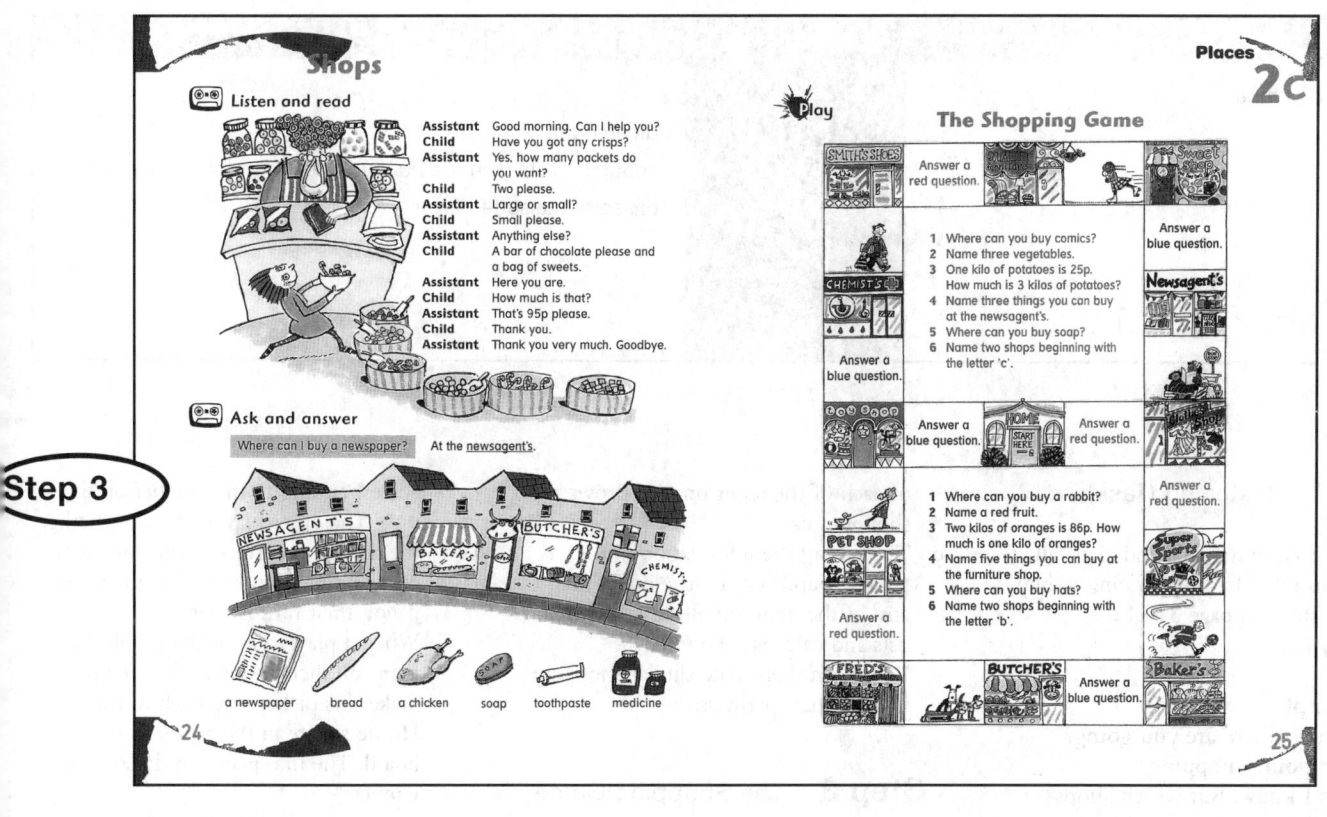

Shops

Listen and read

Assistant	Good morning. Can I help you?
Child	Have you got any crisps?
Assistant	Yes, how many packets do you want?
Child	Two please.
Assistant	Large or small?
Child	Small please.
Assistant	Anything else?
Child	A bar of chocolate please and a bag of sweets.
Assistant	Here you are.
Child	How much is that?
Assistant	That's 95p please.
Child	Thank you.
Assistant	Thank you very much. Goodbye.

Ask and answer

Where can I buy a <u>newspaper</u>? At the <u>newsagent's</u>.

a newspaper   bread   a chicken   soap   toothpaste   medicine

---

Places 2c

Play — The Shopping Game

Answer a red question.

1. Where can you buy comics?
2. Name three vegetables.
3. One kilo of potatoes is 25p. How much is 3 kilos of potatoes?
4. Name three things you can buy at the newsagent's.
5. Where can you buy soap?
6. Name two shops beginning with the letter 'c'.

Answer a blue question.

1. Where can you buy a rabbit?
2. Name a red fruit.
3. Two kilos of oranges is 86p. How much is one kilo of oranges?
4. Name five things you can buy at the furniture shop.
5. Where can you buy hats?
6. Name two shops beginning with the letter 'b'.

Answer a red question.
Answer a blue question.

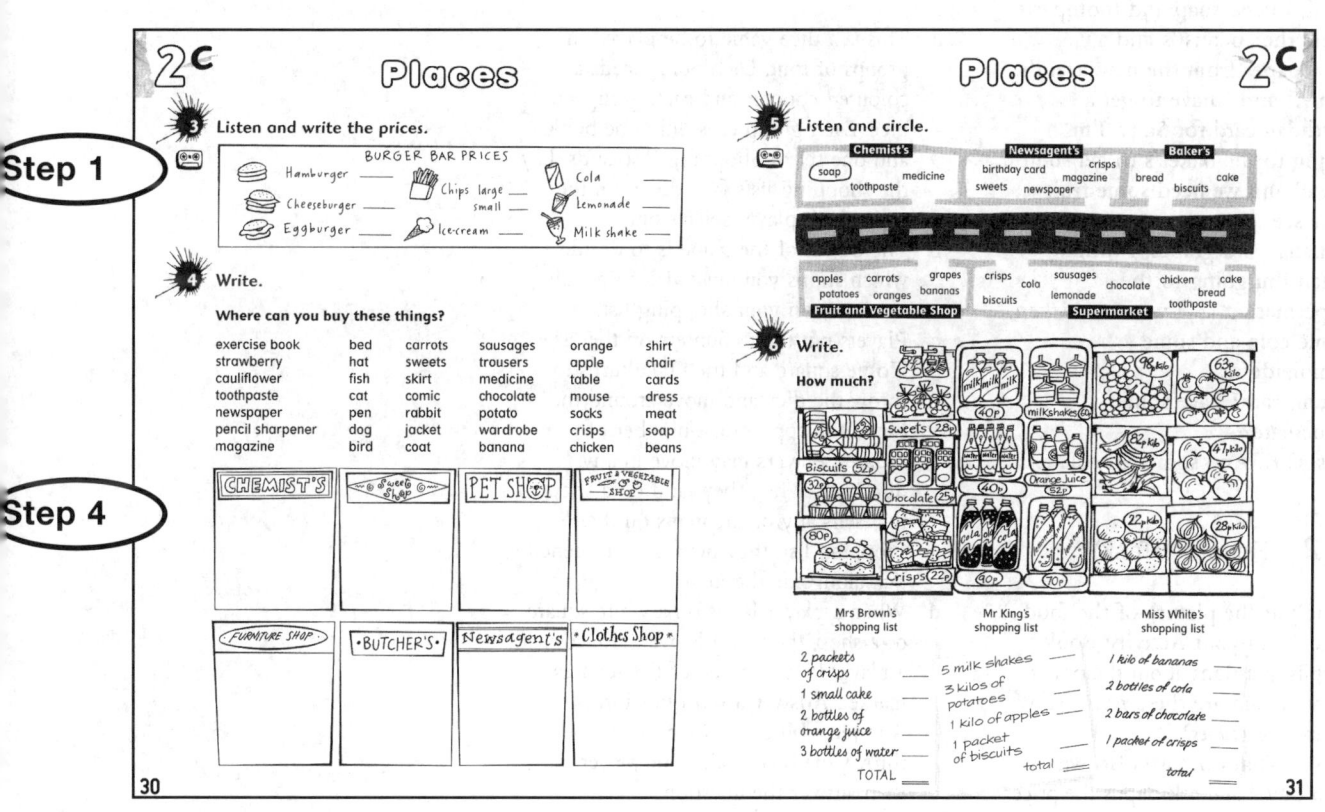

2c Places

3 Listen and write the prices.

BURGER BAR PRICES
- Hamburger ____
- Cheeseburger ____
- Eggburger ____
- Chips large ____ small ____
- Ice-cream ____
- Cola ____
- Lemonade ____
- Milk shake ____

4 Write.

Where can you buy these things?

exercise book	bed	carrots	sausages	orange	shirt
strawberry	hat	sweets	trousers	apple	chair
cauliflower	fish	skirt	medicine	table	cards
toothpaste	cat	comic	chocolate	mouse	dress
newspaper	pen	rabbit	potato	socks	meat
pencil sharpener	dog	jacket	wardrobe	crisps	soap
magazine	bird	coat	banana	chicken	beans

CHEMIST'S   SWEET SHOP   PET SHOP   FRUIT & VEGETABLE SHOP

FURNITURE SHOP   BUTCHER'S   Newsagent's   Clothes Shop

Places 2c

5 Listen and circle.

Chemist's: soap, toothpaste, medicine
Newsagent's: birthday card, magazine, sweets, newspaper, crisps
Baker's: bread, cake, biscuits

Fruit and Vegetable Shop: apples, carrots, grapes, potatoes, oranges, bananas

Supermarket: crisps, cola, biscuits, lemonade, sausages, chocolate, chicken, bread, cake, toothpaste

6 Write. How much?

Mrs Brown's shopping list
- 2 packets of crisps ____
- 1 small cake ____
- 2 bottles of orange juice ____
- 3 bottles of water ____
- TOTAL ____

Mr King's shopping list
- 5 milk shakes ____
- 3 kilos of potatoes ____
- 1 kilo of apples ____
- 1 packet of biscuits ____
- total ____

Miss White's shopping list
- 1 kilo of bananas ____
- 2 bottles of cola ____
- 2 bars of chocolate ____
- 1 packet of crisps ____
- total ____

2c Lesson 3

Main Language Items	ResourceFile	Materials Needed
Revision: food and numbers shopping list	11 12	dice/counters shopping lists (see the pull-out section of the Activity Book) cassette/cassette player

Step 1   Listening (Task)

Pupils listen to the tape and circle all the items that Mrs Kay is going to buy in each shop on page 31 of the Activity Book.

Tapescript:
– Mum, where are you going?
– I'm going shopping.
– Yes I know. But which shops?
– Well, I need soap and toothpaste from the chemist's and a newspaper from the newsagent's. Oh … and I have to get a birthday card for Suzy. I'm going to the baker's to get some bread and we need some fruit … let's see … apples, oranges, bananas and grapes, I think. Then I'm going to the supermarket … I want a chicken, some cola and some lemonade …
– Mum, can I have some chocolate?
– Yes, O.K. And some chocolate.

Step 2   Reading (Task)

a Say 'Look at the picture of the food on page 31 in your Activity Book.' Ask pupils questions about the prices, e.g. 'How much are the *crisps*?' 'How much are the *grapes*?'
b Then ask 'What does Mrs Brown want to buy?' and ask pupils the price of each of the items on Mrs Brown's shopping list.
c Then using the information in the picture, pupils must write down the cost of the items on all three shopping lists and calculate the totals.
d Pupils can then write similar shopping lists for their partners.

Step 3   The Shopping Game

a This is a dice game to be played in groups of four. Each pupil needs a coloured counter and each group a dice. Each group uses only one book and one set of Shopping List cards. Lay the shopping lists face down on the table. Each player selects one.
b The object of the game is to decide which shops you must visit to get all the items on your shopping list.
c Players put their counters on the **Home** square and then take turns to throw the dice and move around the board the appropriate number of squares. Players may move in any direction. When they land on a shop that sells any of the items on their shopping list, they place a small pencil tick alongside the item.
d When a player lands on a white square or a shop, their turn is over. However if a player lands on one of the squares marked **Answer a red question** or **Answer a blue question**, he or she throws the dice again. The player must then answer the question corresponding to the number on the dice. The other players decide whether the answer is correct. If the answer is correct, then the player continues; but if not, their turn is over.
e When a player has ticked off all the items on their shopping list, the player makes his or her way back to the **Home** square in the centre of the board. The first player to do so is the winner.

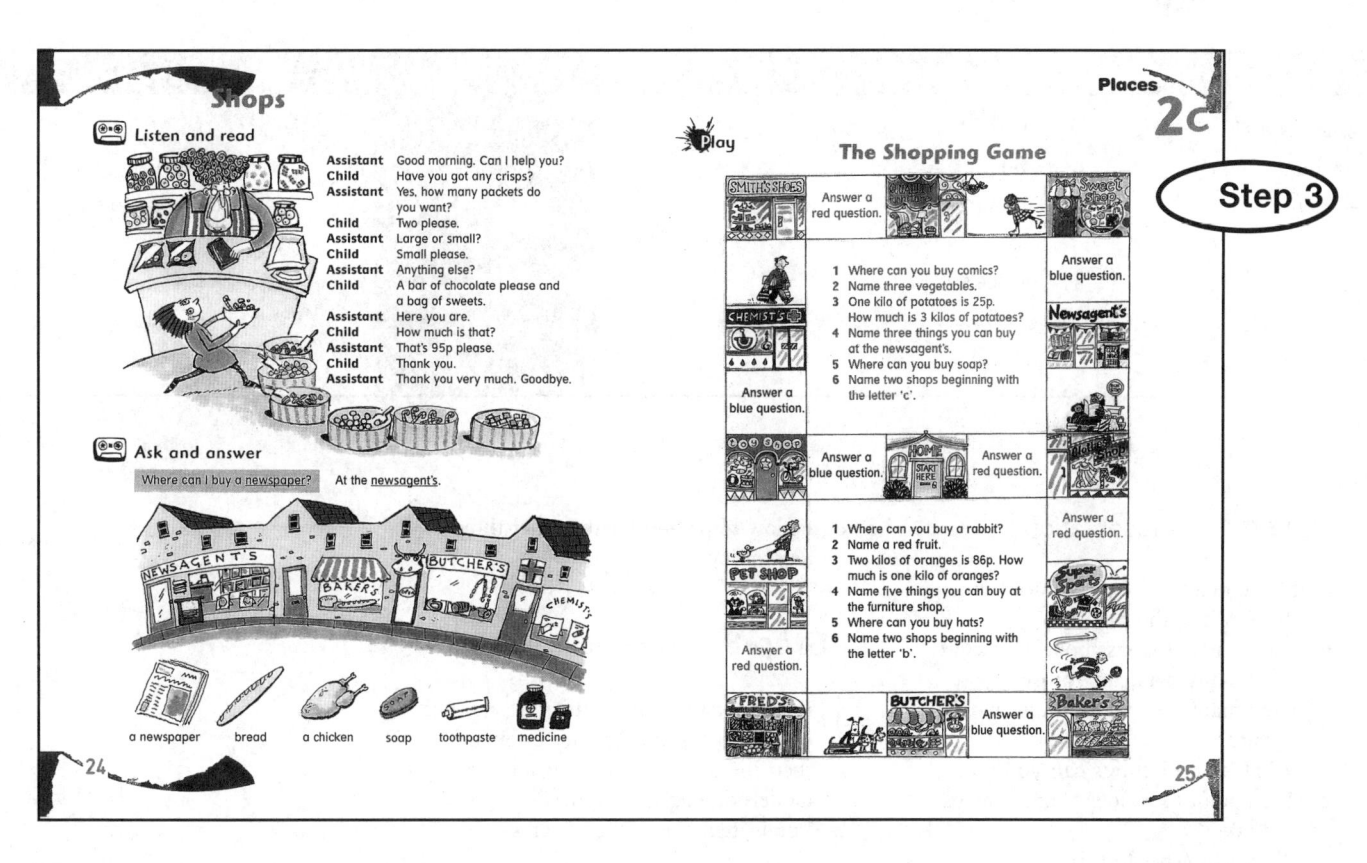

Shops

Listen and read

Assistant	Good morning. Can I help you?
Child	Have you got any crisps?
Assistant	Yes, how many packets do you want?
Child	Two please.
Assistant	Large or small?
Child	Small please.
Assistant	Anything else?
Child	A bar of chocolate please and a bag of sweets.
Assistant	Here you are.
Child	How much is that?
Assistant	That's 95p please.
Child	Thank you.
Assistant	Thank you very much. Goodbye.

Ask and answer

Where can I buy a <u>newspaper</u>? At the <u>newsagent's</u>.

a newspaper   bread   a chicken   soap   toothpaste   medicine

Places 2c

Play — The Shopping Game

1. Where can you buy comics?
2. Name three vegetables.
3. One kilo of potatoes is 25p. How much is 3 kilos of potatoes?
4. Name three things you can buy at the newsagent's.
5. Where can you buy soap?
6. Name two shops beginning with the letter 'c'.

1. Where can you buy a rabbit?
2. Name a red fruit.
3. Two kilos of oranges is 86p. How much is one kilo of oranges?
4. Name five things you can buy at the furniture shop.
5. Where can you buy hats?
6. Name two shops beginning with the letter 'b'.

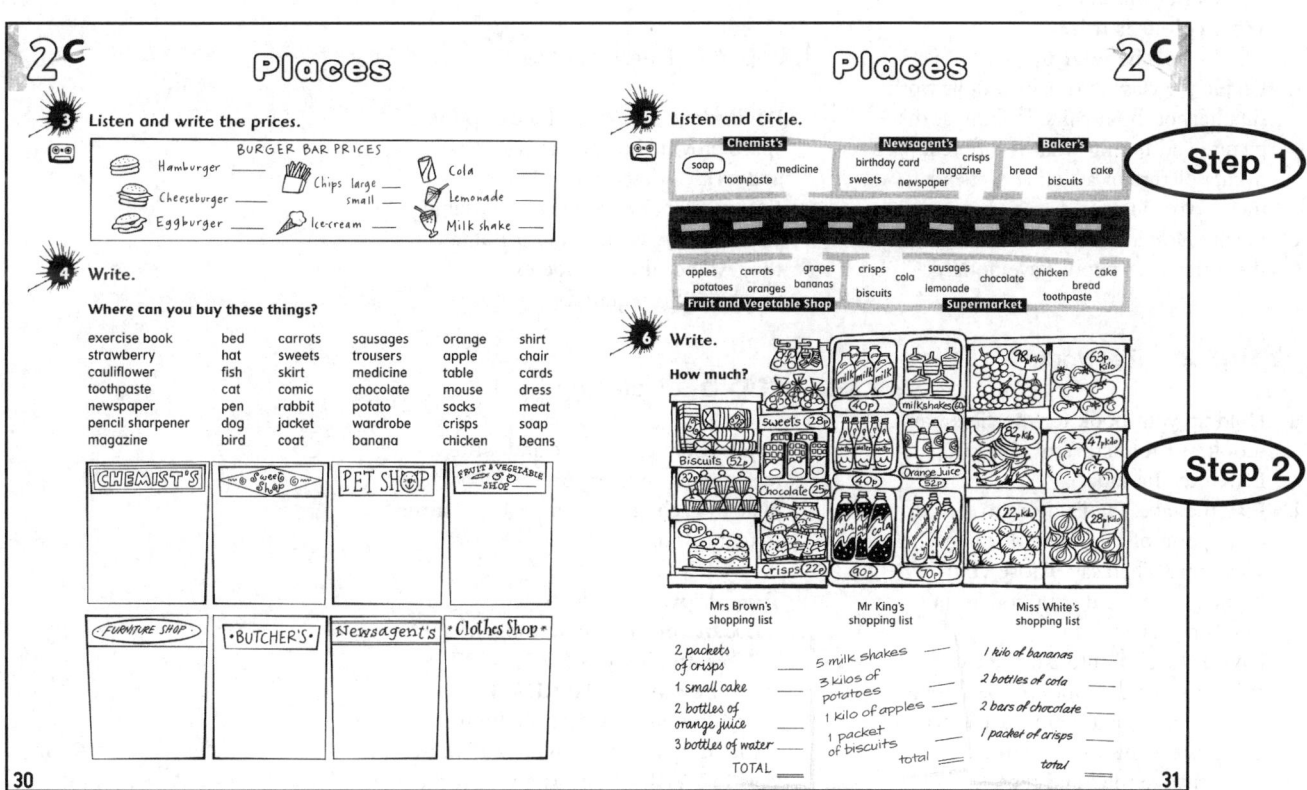

2c Places

3 Listen and write the prices.

BURGER BAR PRICES
- Hamburger ____
- Cheeseburger ____
- Eggburger ____
- Chips large ____ small ____
- Ice-cream ____
- Cola ____
- Lemonade ____
- Milk shake ____

4 Write.

Where can you buy these things?

exercise book	bed	carrots	sausages	orange	shirt
strawberry	hat	sweets	trousers	apple	chair
cauliflower	fish	skirt	medicine	table	cards
toothpaste	cat	comic	chocolate	mouse	dress
newspaper	pen	rabbit	potato	socks	meat
pencil sharpener	dog	jacket	wardrobe	crisps	soap
magazine	bird	coat	banana	chicken	beans

CHEMIST'S   Sweet Shop   PET SHOP   Fruit & Vegetable Shop

FURNITURE SHOP   BUTCHER'S   Newsagent's   Clothes Shop

Places 2c

5 Listen and circle.

Chemist's: soap, toothpaste, medicine, birthday card, crisps
Newsagent's: magazine, sweets, newspaper
Baker's: bread, biscuits, cake

Fruit and Vegetable Shop: apples, carrots, grapes, potatoes, oranges, bananas

Supermarket: crisps, sausages, cola, chicken, cake, biscuits, lemonade, chocolate, bread, toothpaste

6 Write.

How much?

Mrs Brown's shopping list
- 2 packets of crisps ____
- 1 small cake ____
- 2 bottles of orange juice ____
- 3 bottles of water ____
- TOTAL ____

Mr King's shopping list
- 5 milk shakes ____
- 3 kilos of potatoes ____
- 1 kilo of apples ____
- 1 packet of biscuits ____
- total ____

Miss White's shopping list
- 1 kilo of bananas ____
- 2 bottles of cola ____
- 2 bars of chocolate ____
- 1 packet of crisps ____
- total ____

2D Lesson 1

Main Language Items		Resource File	Materials Needed
Comparatives: bigger than faster than	van bus motorbike lorry wheels	41 60	coloured pencils cassette/cassette player

Step 1 Presentation

a Say 'Open your Coursebook on page 26. Look at the picture.'
b Ask some questions about the picture:
How many cars can you see?
How many people are there in the picture?
What kind of shops can you see?
c Then point to various people/things and ask:
What's he/she doing?
What colour is this?
What's he/she wearing? etc.
d Divide the class into pairs. Pupils work simultaneously in pairs, looking at the picture and noting what is different from a picture of a similar scene in their own country.
e Finally have a class discussion about the differences pupils have noticed.

Step 2 Pairwork

a Hold up your book for the class. Say 'Look at the picture of the van. Listen to the tape.'
b Play the tape. Pupils listen to the description of the van and read at the same time. Then say 'Close your books.' Play the description again. Pupils repeat.
c Divide the class into pairs. P1 opens the book. P2 describes the van using only the picture to help. P1 corrects and prompts his or her partner.
d They change roles and repeat.

e Follow steps b–d for the other three descriptions.

Step 3 Write and colour

a Pupils complete the written descriptions on page 32 in the Activity Book and then check their answers against the models on page 26 in the Coursebook.
b Pupils then colour the pictures.

Step 4 Personal file

Pupils draw a picture of a car in the space provided in the Activity Book and write a description alongside. Encourage pupils to draw their family's car, if they have one, and if not, a car they would like. Provide extra vocabulary if required.

Step 5 Listening (Task)

Pupils listen to the tape and write the registration numbers on the number plate of each vehicle on page 33 of the Activity Book.

Tapescript:
– Can you see the numbers?
– Yes, the lorry is N777 WRT.
//The bus is J610 RUA//
and there's a motorbike between the lorry and the bus ...// that's M942 VBI // and the van at the end is P853 GJP.

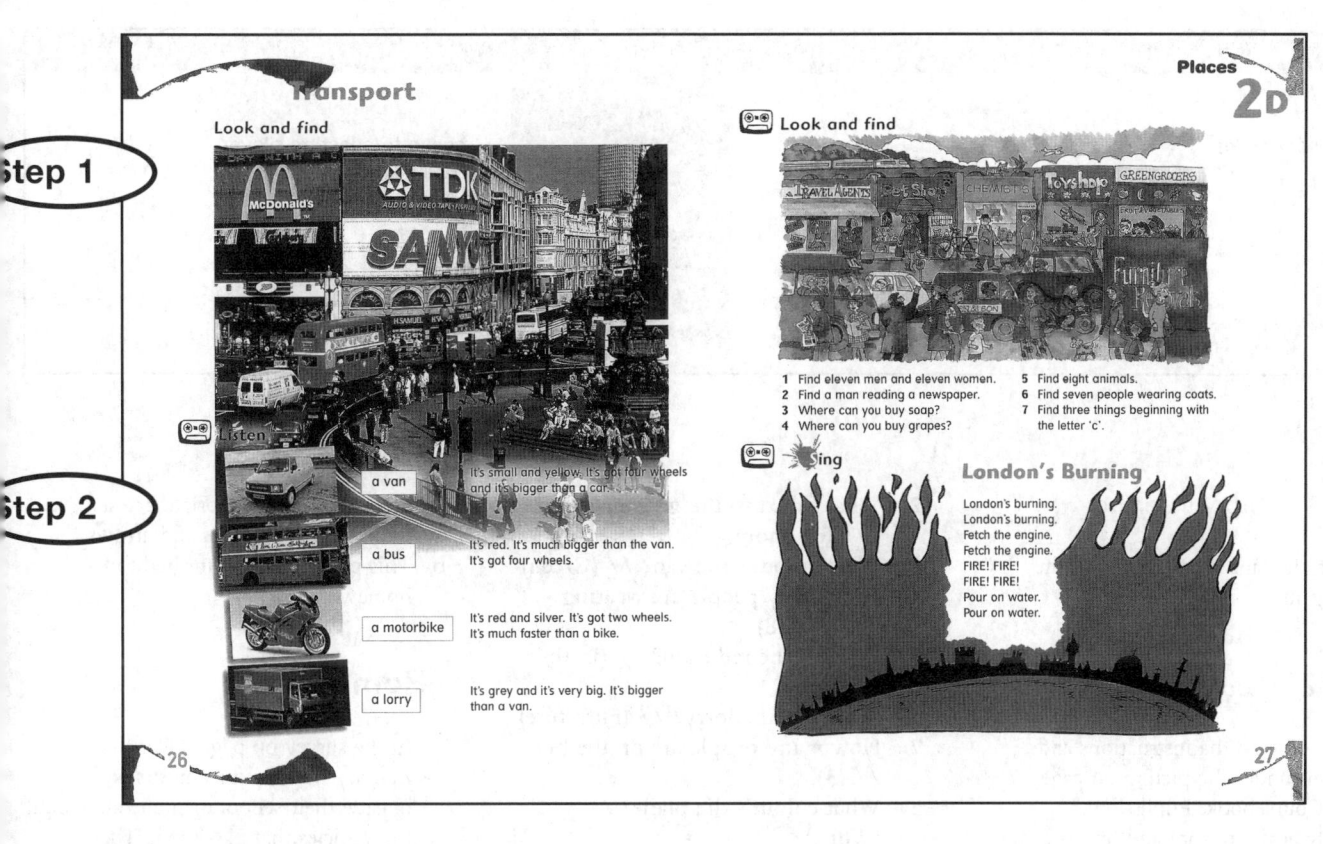

Transport

Look and find

Listen

- a van — It's small and yellow. It's got four wheels and it's bigger than a car.
- a bus — It's red. It's much bigger than the van. It's got four wheels.
- a motorbike — It's red and silver. It's got two wheels. It's much faster than a bike.
- a lorry — It's grey and it's very big. It's bigger than a van.

Places 2D

Look and find

1 Find eleven men and eleven women.
2 Find a man reading a newspaper.
3 Where can you buy soap?
4 Where can you buy grapes?
5 Find eight animals.
6 Find seven people wearing coats.
7 Find three things beginning with the letter 'c'.

Sing — London's Burning

London's burning.
London's burning.
Fetch the engine.
Fetch the engine.
FIRE! FIRE!
FIRE! FIRE!
Pour on water.
Pour on water.

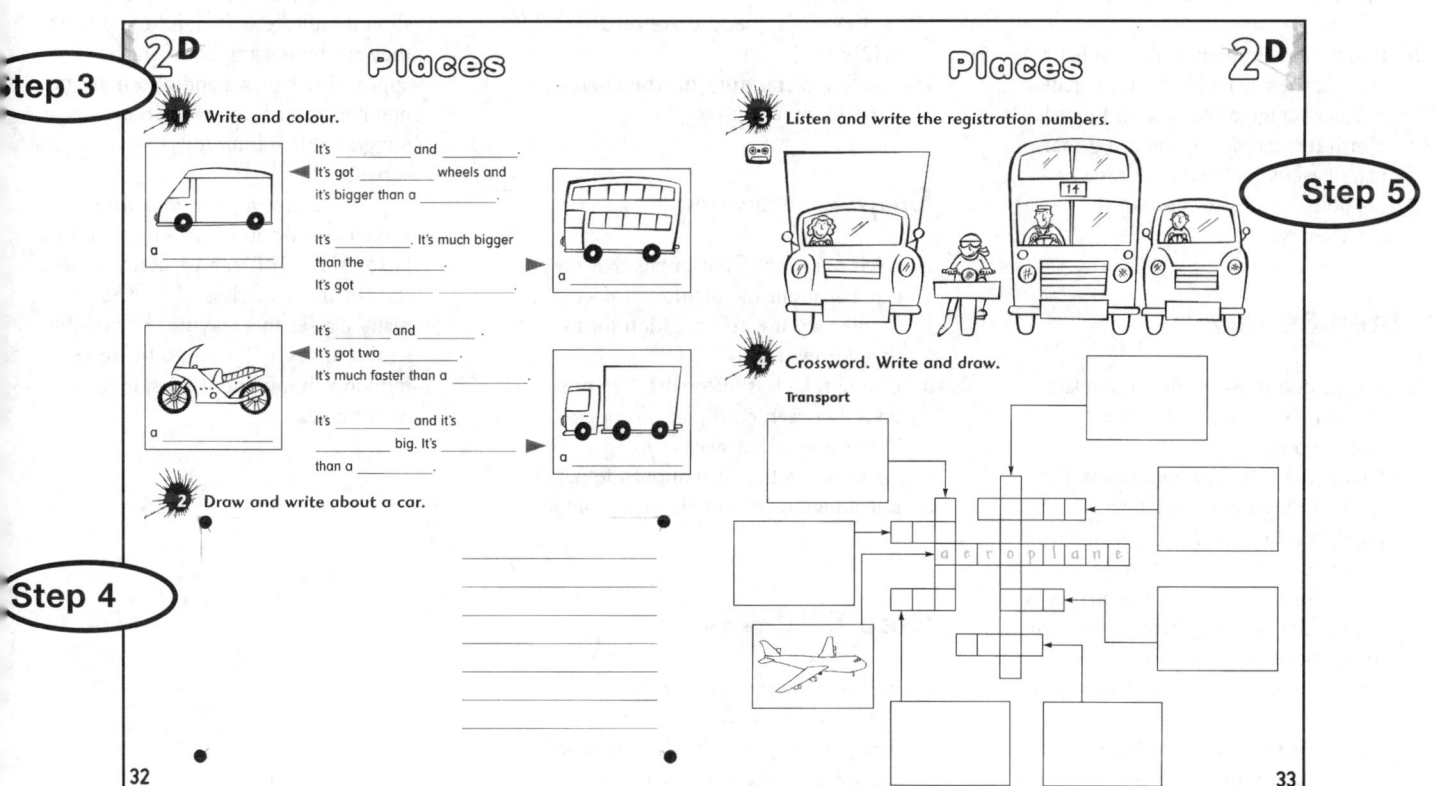

2D Places

1 Write and colour.

It's _____ and _____.
It's got _____ wheels and it's bigger than a _____.
a _____

It's _____. It's much bigger than the _____.
It's got _____.
a _____

It's _____ and _____.
It's got two _____.
It's much faster than a _____.
a _____

It's _____ and it's _____ big. It's _____ than a _____.
a _____

2 Draw and write about a car.

Places 2D

3 Listen and write the registration numbers.

4 Crossword. Write and draw.

Transport

a e r o p l a n e

2D Lesson 2

Main Language Items	Resource File	Materials Needed
Find ... *Revision: names of vehicles*	5 6 41a 41b	cassette/cassette player

Step 1 Story listening

Rewind the tape. Pupils listen to the story again.

Step 2 Look and find

a Direct pupils to the instructions and questions under the picture on page 27 of the Coursebook. Pupils look carefully at the picture and find specific things.
b Pupils work in pairs and complete the tasks in their exercise books. Circulate and encourage discussion in English.
c Finish the activity by checking that pairs have completed each task. Possible answers to question 7 are car, cat, chemist's.

Step 3 Quiz

a All the questions in this quiz relate to the picture on page 27 in the Coursebook.
b Divide the class into two teams. Play the first question on the tape. The first pupil to raise their hand gets a chance to answer, and if correct, wins two points for their team. If the answer is wrong, the opposing team may attempt the question for one point.
c Do all the questions in the same way.

Tapescript (with answers):
1 How many dogs are there? // (2)
2 What's next to the greengrocer's? // (Toy shop)
3 What colour's the van? // (Green)
4 How many people are wearing hats? // (8)
5 Where's the red train? // (In the toy shop)
6 What's in the lorry? // (Furniture)
7 How many people are on the bus? // (3)
8 What colour's the plane? // (White)
9 How many people are reading? // (2)
10 What is standing on the chemist's? // (A cat)

Step 4 Pairwork

a Elicit questions from pupils that they can ask about the picture on page 27. Pupils may use any question forms they know.
b Divide the class into pairs. Use one book between each pair of pupils. Pupils ask and answer as many questions as they can about the picture.
c Encourage them to help and prompt one another.

Step 5 Crossword

a In this crossword puzzle there are no clues, but all the words are means of transport. Pupils write the words in the crossword and draw a picture of each vehicle in the appropriate box as indicated by the lines and arrows.
b This puzzle can be finished for homework.

Homework

In the survey on page 34 of the Activity Book, pupils must stand outside their school or home and count the vehicles that pass them. They should indicate what kind of vehicles they see by putting an 'x' in the appropriate squares and also note the number of men and women drivers. Suggest a time limit for completing the survey.
If possible, it is a good idea to do this survey as a whole-class activity during lesson time. This can be done at the start of the next class. However, for many classes this may not be possible, so the survey will have to be done individually by pupils outside their own homes.

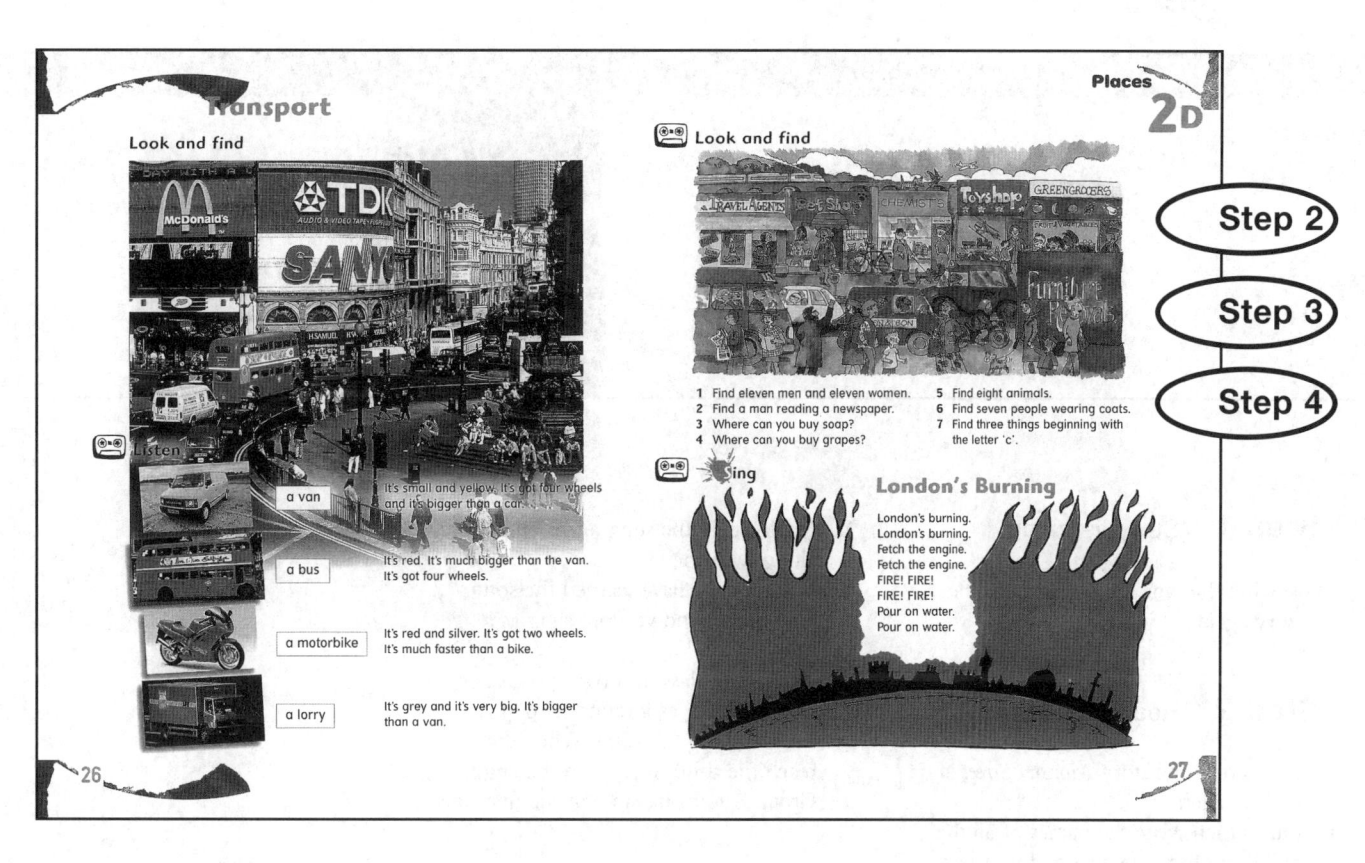

Transport

Look and find

Listen

- a van — It's small and yellow. It's got four wheels and it's bigger than a car.
- a bus — It's red. It's much bigger than the van. It's got four wheels.
- a motorbike — It's red and silver. It's got two wheels. It's much faster than a bike.
- a lorry — It's grey and it's very big. It's bigger than a van.

Places 2D

Look and find

1 Find eleven men and eleven women.
2 Find a man reading a newspaper.
3 Where can you buy soap?
4 Where can you buy grapes?
5 Find eight animals.
6 Find seven people wearing coats.
7 Find three things beginning with the letter 'c'.

Sing — London's Burning

London's burning.
London's burning.
Fetch the engine.
Fetch the engine.
FIRE! FIRE!
FIRE! FIRE!
Pour on water.
Pour on water.

Step 2
Step 3
Step 4

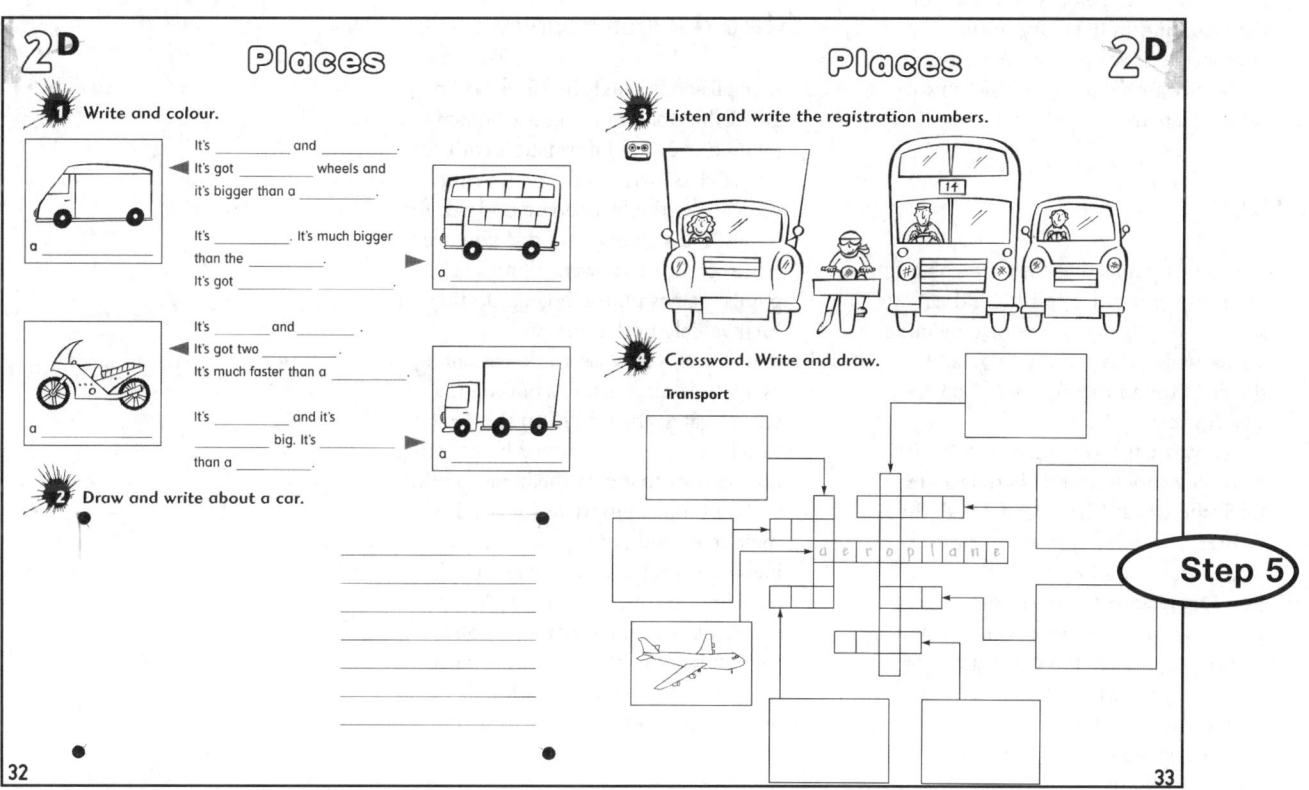

2D Places

1 Write and colour.

It's _____ and _____.
It's got _____ wheels and it's bigger than a _____.

a _____

It's _____. It's much bigger than the _____.
It's got _____.

a _____

It's _____ and _____.
It's got two _____.
It's much faster than a _____.

a _____

It's _____ and it's _____ big. It's _____ than a _____.

a _____

2 Draw and write about a car.

Places 2D

3 Listen and write the registration numbers.

4 Crossword. Write and draw.

Transport

a e r o p l a n e

Step 5

2D Lesson 3

Main Language Items	Resource File	Materials Needed
Story revision burning fetch pour on engine	6 25	Reader cassette/cassette player

Step 1 Story listening

Rewind the tape. Pupils listen to the story again.

Step 2 Read and write

a   Pupils read the story *Monster Street* in their Readers.
b   Pupils then write the names of all the buildings, food, colours and transport they can find in the story in the appropriate space in their Activity Book. Set a time limit to make this more competetive.

Step 3 Song

a   Explain to pupils that they are going to listen to a popular English children's song about the Great Fire of London in 1666, which destroyed a huge area of the city around the Tower of London. The fire started from a baker's oven which was left unattended. Ask pupils who they should call if there is a fire. Elicit the words **'fire engine'** and **'fire fighter'** and ask pupils what the best way to put out a fire is.
b   Say **'Open your Coursebook on page 27. Look at the song at the bottom of the page.'** Play the first version of the song on the tape. Pupils listen and read at the same time.
c   Then listen again line by line and repeat the words.
d   Finally, play the song again. Pupils sing along with the tape.
e   When pupils have learned the song, play the second version, sung as a round.
f   Divide the class into two groups and sing the song as a round. Group A starts singing the song. When they reach the third line, Fetch the engine, Group B joins in, singing the first line.

Step 4 Traffic survey

a   If pupils completed the survey on page 34 of the Activity Book for homework, then go over the information with the whole class. Write the names of the vehicles on the blackboard and ask the pupils **'How many cars did you see?'** etc. Record the answers alongside pupils' names on the board. Do this for each vehicle in the survey.
b   If however, you wish to do the survey as a whole-class activity outside the school gates, then do so in this lesson. Pupils complete the survey by counting the vehicles that pass them and putting an 'x' in the appropriate squares in their chart and noting the number of men and women drivers. Give pupils a time limit of say, 20 minutes. When you're back in the classroom, collate all the results as in step a and see what the most frequent vehicle was. Pupils could make a large wall chart for display.

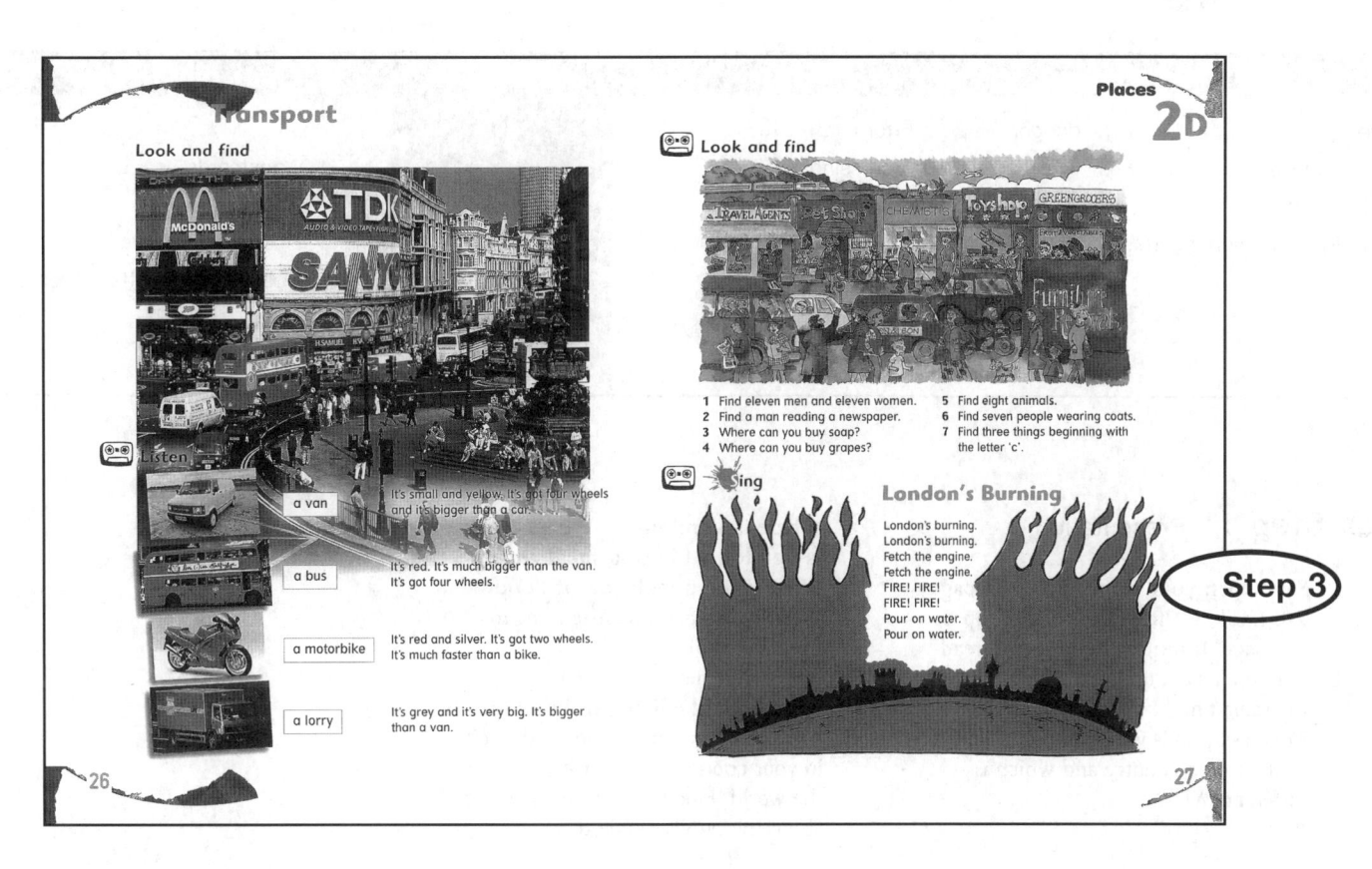

Transport

Look and find

Listen

It's small and yellow. It's got four wheels and it's bigger than a car. — a van

It's red. It's much bigger than the van. It's got four wheels. — a bus

It's red and silver. It's got two wheels. It's much faster than a bike. — a motorbike

It's grey and it's very big. It's bigger than a van. — a lorry

Places 2D

Look and find

1. Find eleven men and eleven women.
2. Find a man reading a newspaper.
3. Where can you buy soap?
4. Where can you buy grapes?
5. Find eight animals.
6. Find seven people wearing coats.
7. Find three things beginning with the letter 'c'.

Sing — London's Burning

London's burning.
London's burning.
Fetch the engine.
Fetch the engine.
FIRE! FIRE!
FIRE! FIRE!
Pour on water.
Pour on water.

Step 3

26   27

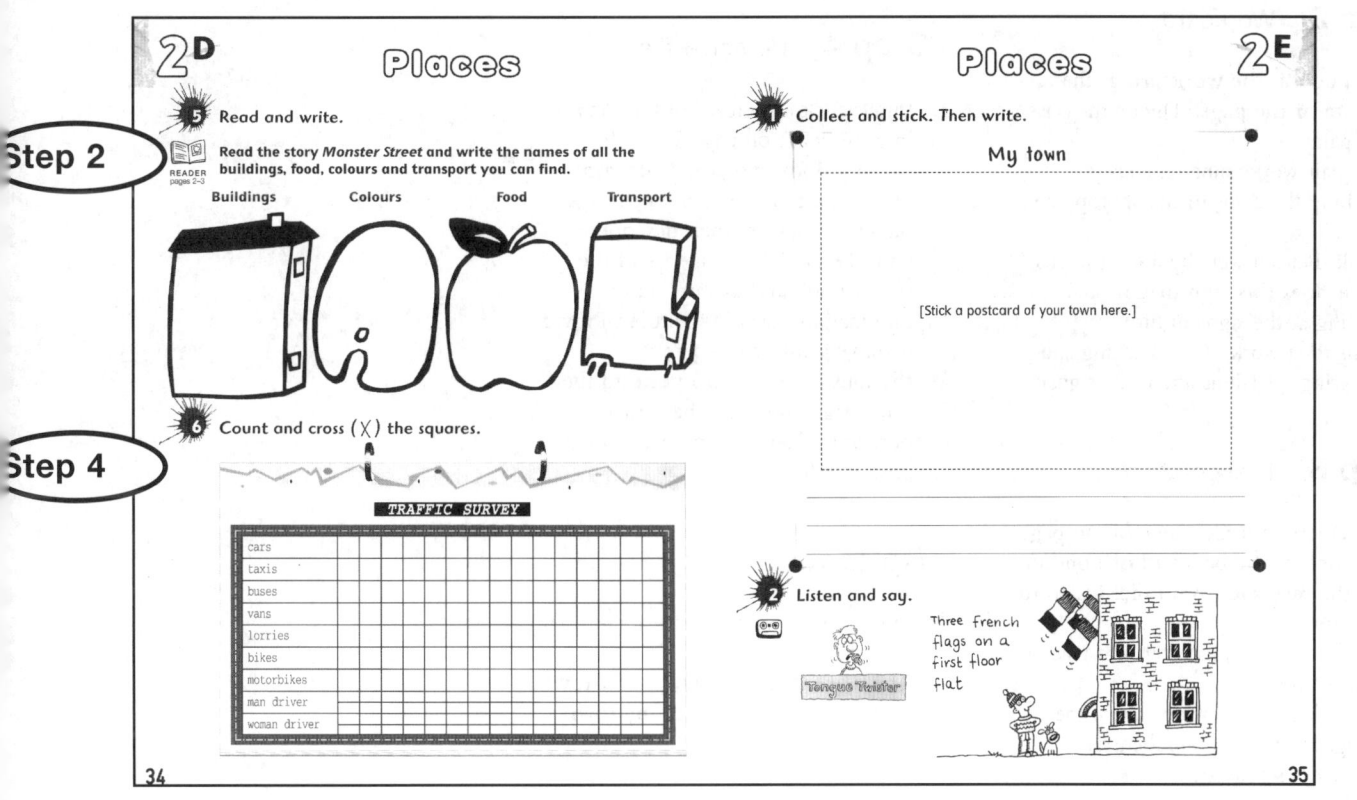

2D Places

Step 2

5 Read and write.

READER pages 2–3

Read the story *Monster Street* and write the names of all the buildings, food, colours and transport you can find.

Buildings   Colours   Food   Transport

Step 4

6 Count and cross (X) the squares.

TRAFFIC SURVEY

| cars |
| taxis |
| buses |
| vans |
| lorries |
| bikes |
| motorbikes |
| man driver |
| woman driver |

Places 2E

1 Collect and stick. Then write.

My town

[Stick a postcard of your town here.]

2 Listen and say.

Tongue Twister

Three french flags on a first floor flat

34   35

81

2E Lesson 1

Main Language Items			Resource File	Materials Needed
drive	danger	turn	8	postcards
right-hand side	wild	crossing	10	glue
left-hand side	roundabout	working	14	coloured pencils
What does this sign mean?	traffic lights	smoking		cassette/cassette player

Step 1 Presentation

a Say 'Open your Coursebook on page 28. Look at the photos at the top of the page, listen to the tape and read.'
b Play the tape. Pupils listen and read at the same time.
c Then ask pupils which photo is similar to their own country and which is different. Why?

Step 2 Workcard

a Say 'Look at the workcard at the bottom of the page.' Divide the class into pairs.
b Each pair works simultaneously, matching the signs to the appropriate words.
c Check their answers by asking pupils 'What does this sign mean?' and pointing at the signs in turn.
d Pupils then work in pairs asking and answering questions about the signs.

Step 3 Presentation

a Say 'Open your Coursebook on page 29. Look at the postcard of London and the message from Julie. Listen to the tape.'
b Play the tape. Pupils listen and read at the same time.
c Then ask some questions about the passage to check comprehension:
Where does Julie live?
Where is London?
Is London a big or a small city?
What is the population of London?
What is the name of the river in London?
Is London near the sea?
Does Julie like living in London?
d Ask similar questions about other cities in your country, or other big cities in the world. Finally, ask some questions about the pupils' home town.

Step 4 Personal file

a Pupils stick a postcard of their town into the space on page 35 of the Activity Book and write a description of the town underneath. Encourage pupils to compare their description with the model on page 29 of the Coursebook and use any other information given in the topic. Provide extra vocabulary if required.
b If pupils do not have a postcard they can design and draw their own postcard. If possible, have a few extra postcards for class use.

Optional

Pupils write five sentences about their town, e.g.
There are three cinemas in my town.
There isn't a museum in my town.

On the Roads

Places 2E

Step 1 — Listen and read
In many countries cars drive on the right-hand side of the road.
In Britain, Malta, Australia and Ireland cars drive on the left-hand side of the road.

Step 2 — WORKCARD
Match the words and the signs.
A Danger – wild animals
B Roundabout
C Traffic lights
D No left turn
E No right turn
F Danger – children crossing
G Danger – men working
H No smoking

Step 3 — Listen and read

Dear Maria,
I live in London. London is a very big city in England. It has a population of about 8 million people. There is a big river in London called the Thames. London is quite near the sea. There are lots of cars and shops in London. I like living in London.
Julie

LONDON

The Stepping Stones Game

The	library	is	opposite		park
	supermarket		near	the	church
	cafe	isn't	next to		cinema
	hotel		in		museum

28
29

2D Places

5 Read and write.
Read the story *Monster Street* and write the names of all the buildings, food, colours and transport you can find.

Buildings Colours Food Transport

6 Count and cross (X) the squares.

TRAFFIC SURVEY

| cars |
| taxis |
| buses |
| vans |
| lorries |
| bikes |
| motorbikes |
| man driver |
| woman driver |

Places 2E

Step 4

1 Collect and stick. Then write.

My town

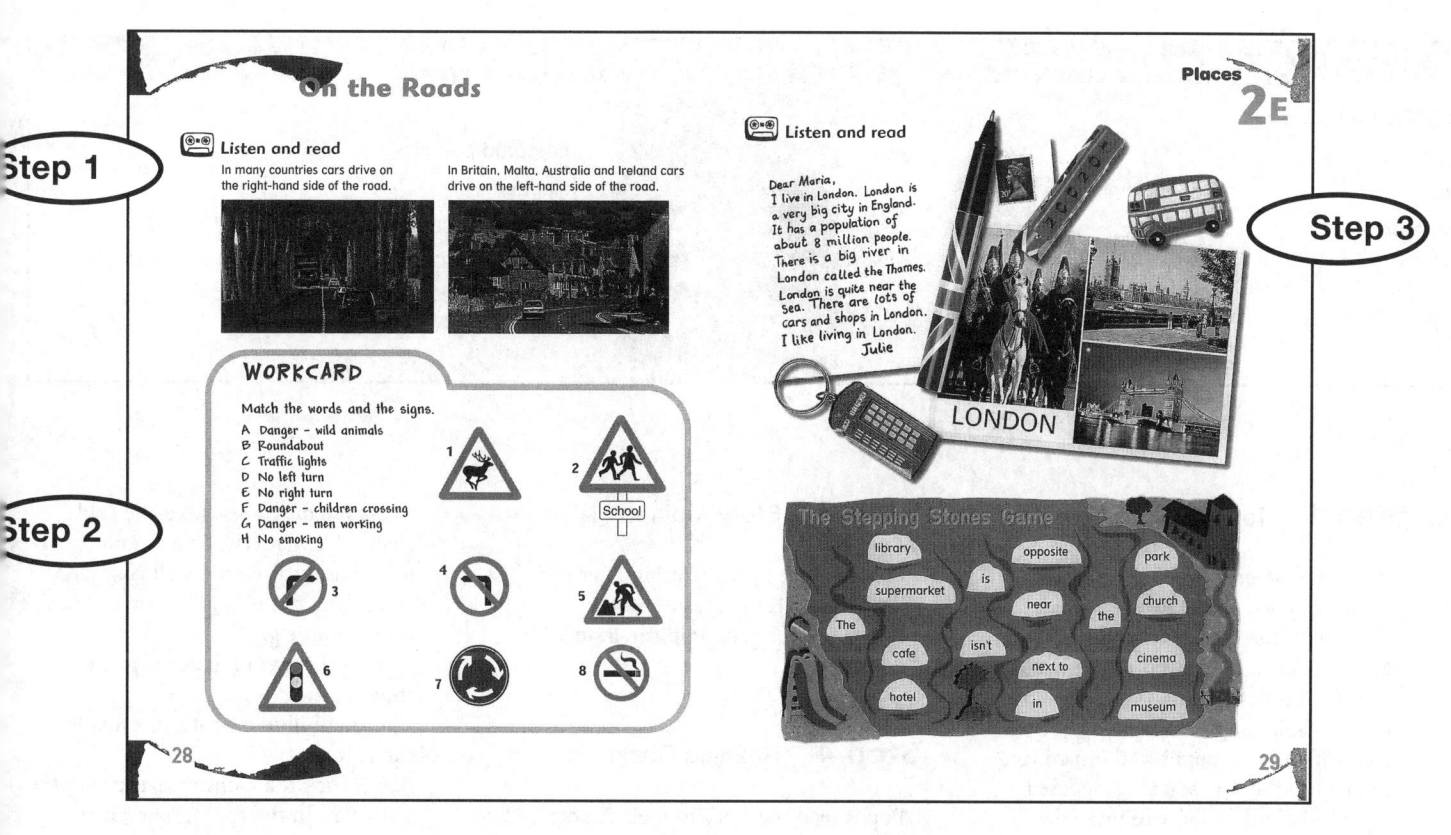

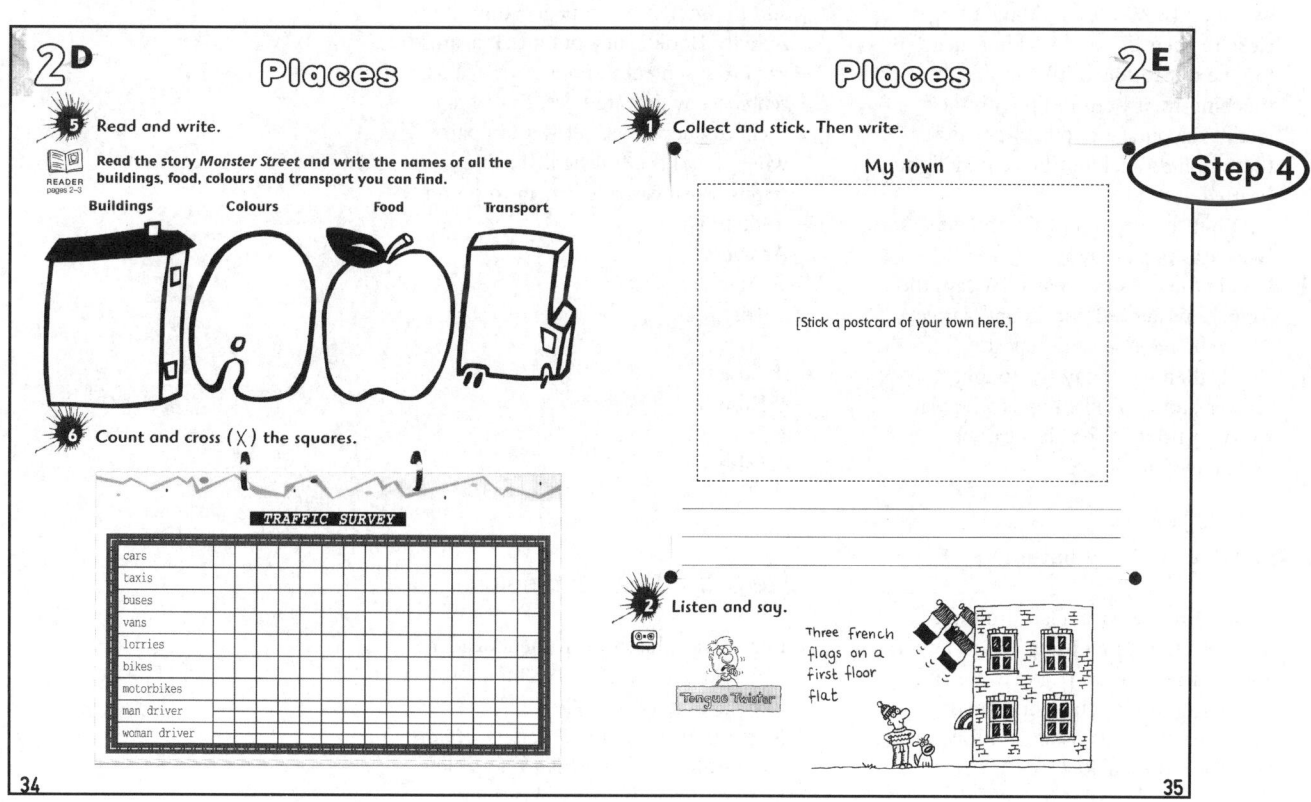

[Stick a postcard of your town here.]

2 Listen and say.

Tongue Twister

Three french flags on a first floor flat

34
35

83

Lesson 2

Main Language Items	Resource File	Materials Needed
Story revision French flag first floor flat	4 25 52	coloured pencils Reader cassette/cassette player

Step 1 Tongue twister

a Play the tape once so pupils can listen to the tongue twister. Play it twice more, with the class repeating.
Note: Focus in on particularly difficult sounds in isolation, and then build up to the whole tongue twister if pupils have difficulty. If pupils find it hard to pronounce the /θ/ sound as opposed to /f/, show them how to make the two sounds: /θ/ (by holding a finger close to their lips and sticking their tongue out to touch it!) and /f/ (by touching their bottom lip with their teeth). Encourage pupils to practise these sounds, making the activity light-hearted and fun.
Beat out the rhythm of the tongue twister as pupils say it.

b Divide the class into pairs. P1 says the tongue twister. P2 checks and corrects. They change roles and repeat.

c Pupils then try to say the tongue twister more quickly. Pupils who want to try in front of the class can be encouraged to do so.

Step 2 Story listening

Quickly revise vocabulary from the story *Monster Street* using the picture in the Coursebook on page 18. Rewind the tape and play the story *Monster Street* again. Pupils listen and follow the story in their Readers.

Step 3 Story 'Join in'

a Play the tape again, pausing after each line for pupils to repeat.
b Play the tape again. Pupils join in with the tape.

Step 4 Reading (Task)

Pupils read the story in their Reader and the sentences on page 36 in their Activity Book. They put a tick against each true sentence and a cross against sentences which are false. Encourage them to check their answers in pairs when they have finished. If some pupils finish early, tell them to go on to Step 5.
Answers:
1 True
2 True
3 True
4 False
5 False
6 True
7 False
8 False

Step 5 Read and colour

Pupils read the story in their Reader and colour the pictures of the monsters in their Activity Book.
(Optional) If you have made a *Monster Street* wall chart, use this to do follow-up work from the story. Ask some true/false questions about the wall chart. Alternatively, detach some of the monsters from the wall chart and hand them out to pupils. Then give instructions e.g.
The big brown monster is in the supermarket.
The small blue monster is outside the cafe.
Pupils stick the monsters back onto the wall chart in the appropriate place.

… Step 1 … Step 2 … Step 3 … Step 4 … Step 5

2 Places

STORY

Monster Street

Places

1 Collect and stick. Then write.

My town

[Stick a postcard of your town here.]

2 Listen and say.

Tongue Twister

Three french flags on a first floor flat

Places

3 Read and tick (✓) or cross (✗).

Read the story *Monster Street*. True (✓) or false (✗)?
READER pages 2-3

1 There is a small pink monster working in the park.
2 The monsters in the garage are big.
3 There are three monsters working in the bank.
4 The nurses are red and blue and brown.
5 The waiter is a small monster.
6 There are two small purple monsters working in the garage.
7 The policeman is a red monster.
8 There are four grey monsters working in the supermarket.

4 Read and colour.

Read the story *Monster Street* and colour the monsters.
READER pages 2-3

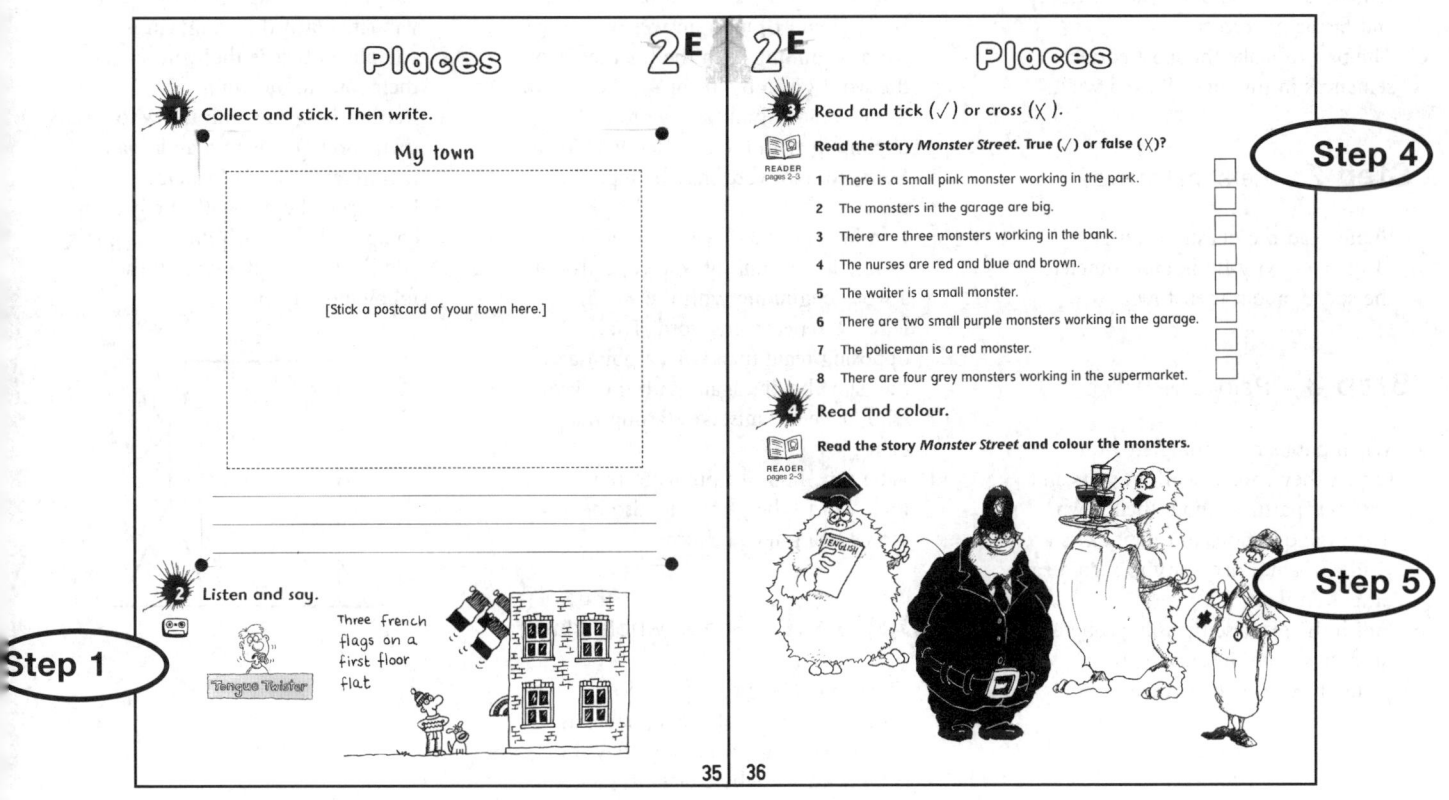

85

2E Lesson 3

Main Language Items			Resource File	Materials Needed
opposite	library	park	10	
near	supermarket	church	14	
next to	cafe	cinema	57	
in	hotel	museum	58	

Step 1 The Stepping Stones Game

a Divide the class into pairs. Pupils write as many sentences as they can in ten minutes from the words in the box. They work from left to right and take one word or pair of words from each column.

b Pupils should refer to the picture on page 22 of their Coursebook. The sentences must be both grammatically and factually correct.

c The pair to make the most correct sentences in the time allowed wins.

Step 2 Personal survey

Pupils read the questions on page 37 of their Activity Book and complete the survey about their town.

Step 3 Pairwork

a When pupils have completed the survey, they should work in pairs and ask their partners about their town, using the questions in the book as a guide. It is not necessary to record each other's answers.

b Finish the exercise by asking pupils questions from the survey about themselves or their partners.

Optional Game (whole class)

a This game is called 'Word Tennis'. Divide the class into two teams. Give each pupil in each team a number. There should be a number one, two, three, etc. in each team. If there are an odd number of pupils in the class, nominate one pupil as scorer.

b The game is a simple vocabulary revision game. P1 in team A begins by calling any English word to P1 in team B. P1 (Team B) must answer with any word beginning with the final letter of the word given by Team A. Then P2 in Team A must think of a word beginning with the final letter of Team B's word. No word may be repeated twice.

c Continue until a player from either team fails to think of a word, calls out a word beginning with the wrong letter or repeats any word. The opposing team then wins a point and the game begins again with the player who made the mistake starting the game.

d Set a time limit for pupils to return their word. The game can also be scored using tennis scores.

Optional Game (whole class)

The game 'Hangman' provides excellent practice of the alphabet as well as revising vocabulary. Play the game with the whole class to establish the rules.

a Think of a word. Represent each letter of your word by a dash on the blackboard, e.g. for the word **lorry** you write _ _ _ _ _.

b Pupils guess letters that might make up the word. Each time a letter is guessed correctly, you write the letter on the appropriate dash. If, however, the guess is incorrect, you add another line to the hangman scoresheet (see below).

c If pupils guess the word before the hangman is complete, they are the winners but if the hangman is completed before the word is guessed, then you are the winner.

d Repeat the game with the whole class, then allow pupils to play in pairs.

Hangman scoring System:
Each game begins with the baseline completed. For each incorrect guess, add lines to the drawing in the following sequence:

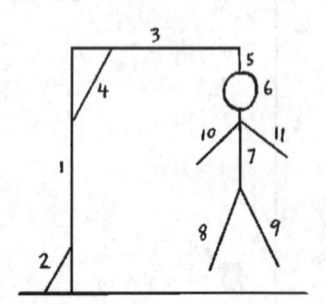

86

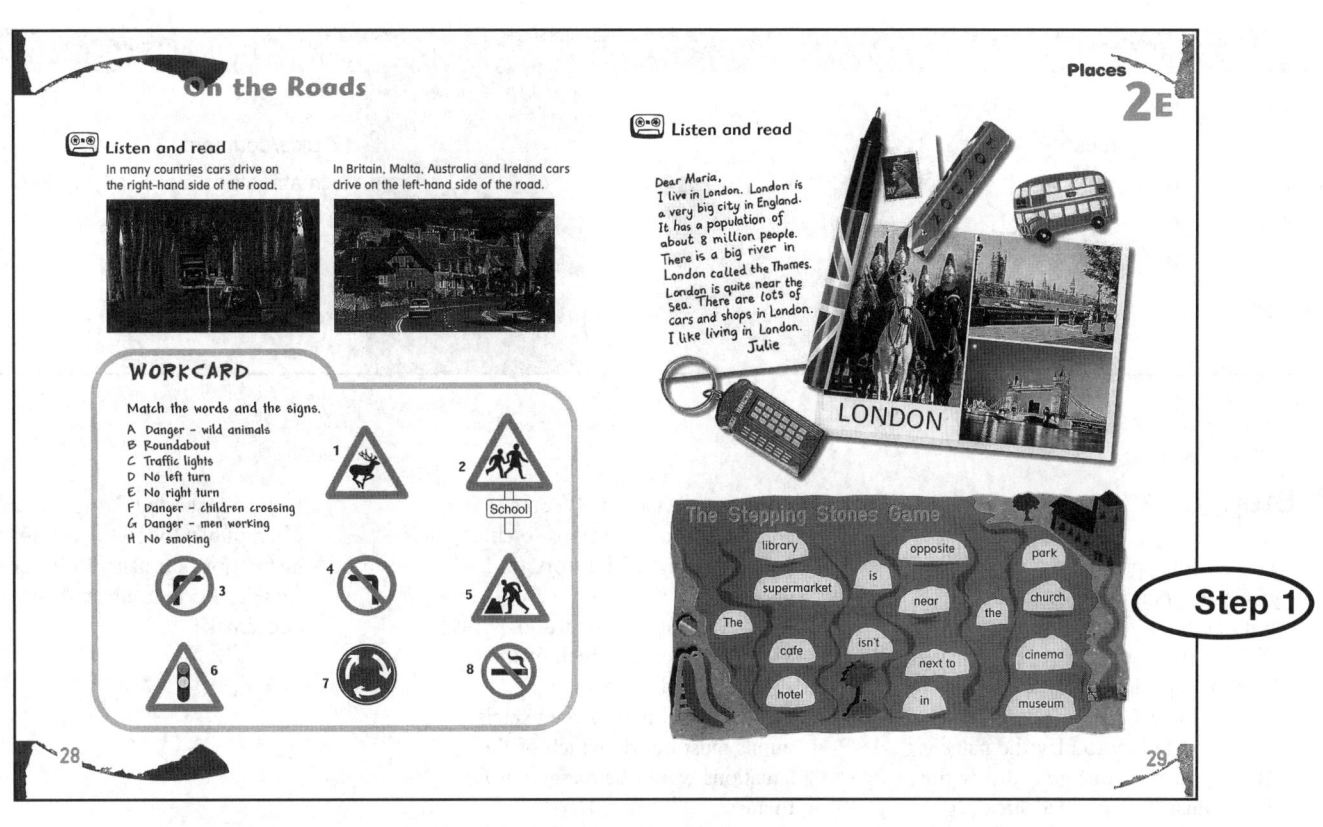

On the Roads

Listen and read

In many countries cars drive on the right-hand side of the road.

In Britain, Malta, Australia and Ireland cars drive on the left-hand side of the road.

WORKCARD

Match the words and the signs.

A Danger – wild animals
B Roundabout
C Traffic lights
D No left turn
E No right turn
F Danger – children crossing
G Danger – men working
H No smoking

Places 2E

Listen and read

Dear Maria,
I live in London. London is a very big city in England. It has a population of about 8 million people. There is a big river in London called the Thames. London is quite near the sea. There are lots of cars and shops in London. I like living in London.
Julie

LONDON

The Stepping Stones Game

library — opposite — park
supermarket — is — near — church
The — the
cafe — isn't — next to — cinema
hotel — in — museum

Step 1

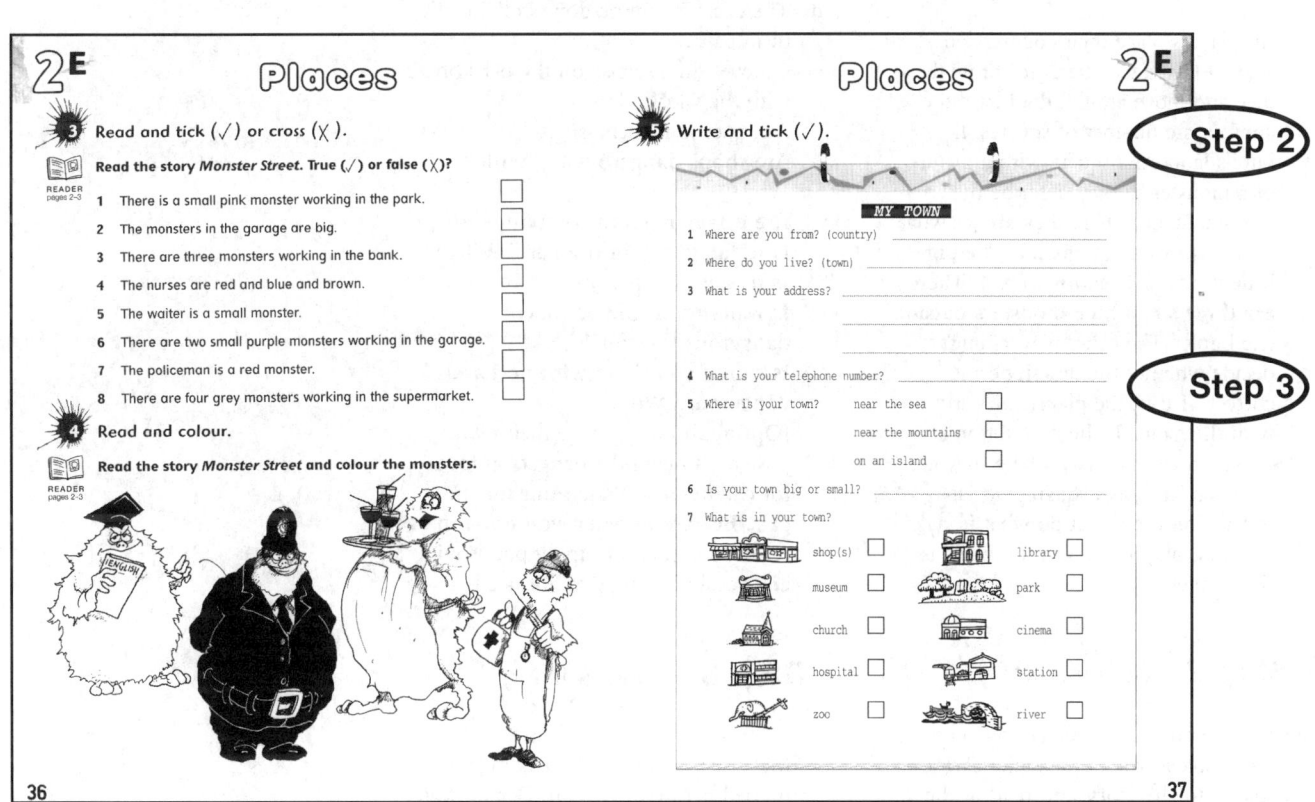

2E Places

3 Read and tick (✓) or cross (✗).

Read the story *Monster Street*. True (✓) or false (✗)?

1 There is a small pink monster working in the park.
2 The monsters in the garage are big.
3 There are three monsters working in the bank.
4 The nurses are red and blue and brown.
5 The waiter is a small monster.
6 There are two small purple monsters working in the garage.
7 The policeman is a red monster.
8 There are four grey monsters working in the supermarket.

4 Read and colour.

Read the story *Monster Street* and colour the monsters.

Places 2E

5 Write and tick (✓).

MY TOWN

1 Where are you from? (country) _____
2 Where do you live? (town) _____
3 What is your address? _____
4 What is your telephone number? _____
5 Where is your town?   near the sea ☐
   near the mountains ☐
   on an island ☐
6 Is your town big or small? _____
7 What is in your town?

shop(s) ☐   library ☐
museum ☐   park ☐
church ☐   cinema ☐
hospital ☐   station ☐
zoo ☐   river ☐

Step 2

Step 3

87

2F Lesson 1

Main Language Items		Resource File	Materials Needed
Story revision	fast		
town	dangerous		dice/counters
be careful	dirty		materials to make a flying Supersnake
watch out	too many		cassette/cassette player
	wrong way		

Step 1 Story game

a This is a dice game to be played in groups of four, using counters, a dice and one book for each group.

b Quickly revise the story *Monster Street*. Play the tape again or ask pupils to tell you the story. Give the pupils some useful vocabulary to play the game e.g. 'It's my turn', 'your go', 'throw the dice', 'miss a turn', 'bad luck', 'go back'.

c All players place their counters on **Start**. Players take turns to throw the dice and move around the board the appropriate number of squares. If pupils land on a square with a picture of a monster/s, they describe the monster/s, i.e. where they are, or what they are doing. e.g. no. 23 **'The big blue monster is eating'**, no. 4 **'There are three small blue monsters outside the bank.'** The other players must decide whether the description is correct. If it is, the player can carry on with the game. If the description is wrong, they must stay where they are. If pupils land on a square with an instruction they must do what it says.

d The first player to reach the finish is the winner.

Step 2 Supersnake

a Say 'Open your Coursebook on page 31. Look at the Supersnake cartoon. Listen to the story and read at the same time.' Ask pupils some comprehension questions to check their understanding of the story (in L1 if necessary).

b Pupils look at the pictures of Willy Worm and decide which of the situations is dangerous.

c In the second part of the exercise, pupils must decide which of the situations would be dangerous for them.

d The exercise can be done individually or in pairs.

e Go over the exercise on the blackboard with the whole class.
Ask questions such as:
Are shops dangerous for Willy? Why?
Are cars dangerous for Willy? Why?
Is it dangerous in the park? Why?
Is reading dangerous?
Is walking on the pavement dangerous for you?
Is riding your bike with no hands dangerous? Why?
(Optional) Pupils make their own posters showing the dangers in town for children e.g. **Watch out for the cars. Be careful when you cross the road.** Monitor and supply pupils with any vocabulary they might need.

Step 3 Make a flying Supersnake

Make sure you have the materials needed before the lesson. Demonstrate how to make the flying Supersnake. Then pupils follow the illustrations and instructions on page 38 in their Activity Book to make their own flying Supersnake.

Step 1

In a Strange, Strange Land
Play
The Monster Street Game

Step 2

Places 2F

SUPERSNAKE

- Hello, Willy. Where are you going? / To town.
- Well, be careful. The cars are very fast.
- The motorbikes are dangerous too.
- And the buses and lorries are very dirty.
- Don't go into the shops. There are too many people.
- Watch out for the dogs and cats.
- There are lots of birds in town, near the museum.
- Be careful in the park.
- Well, have a nice time in town Willy.
- Willy, you're going the wrong way.
- No, I'm not. I'm going home. It's too dangerous in town!

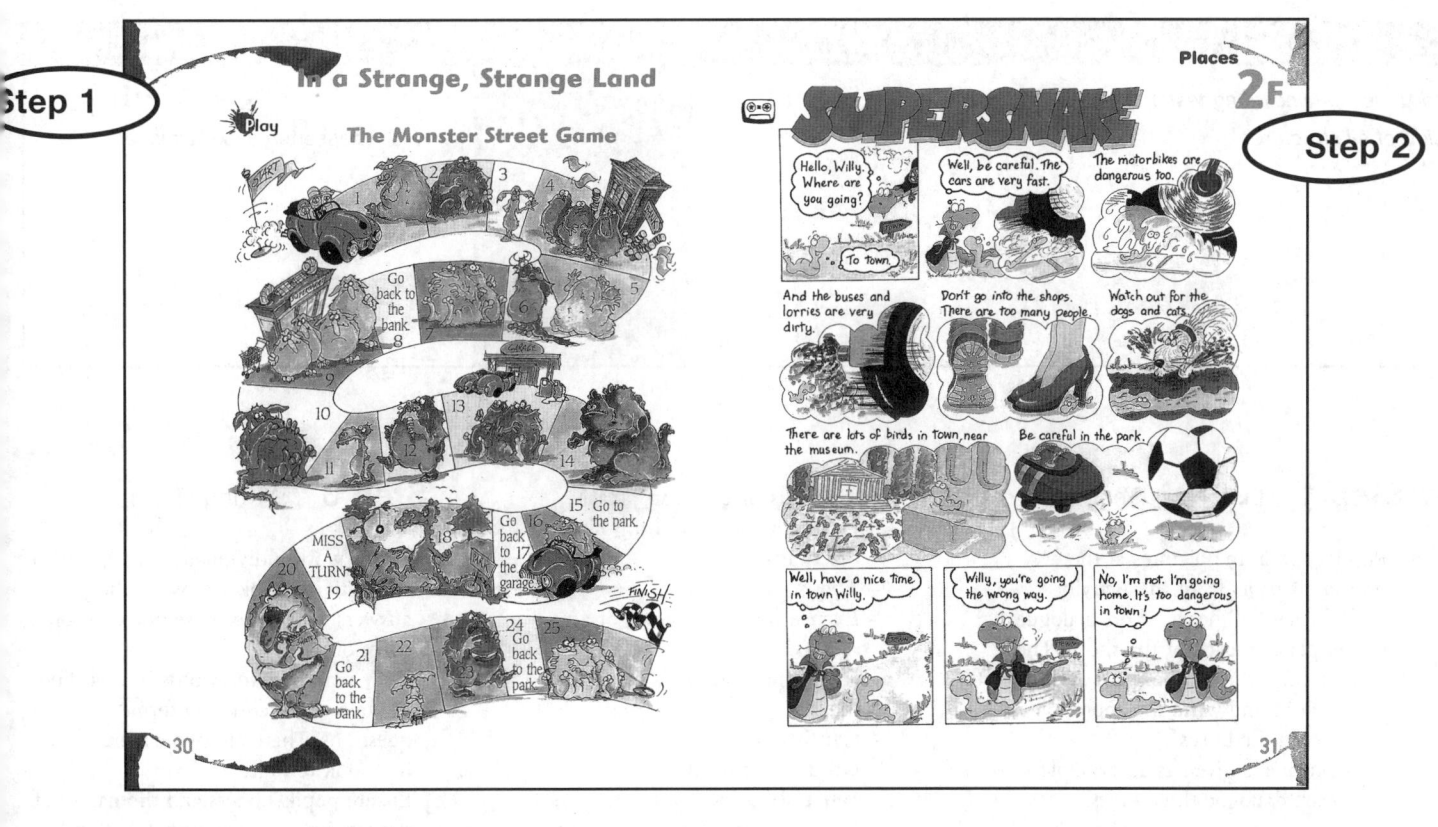

Step 3

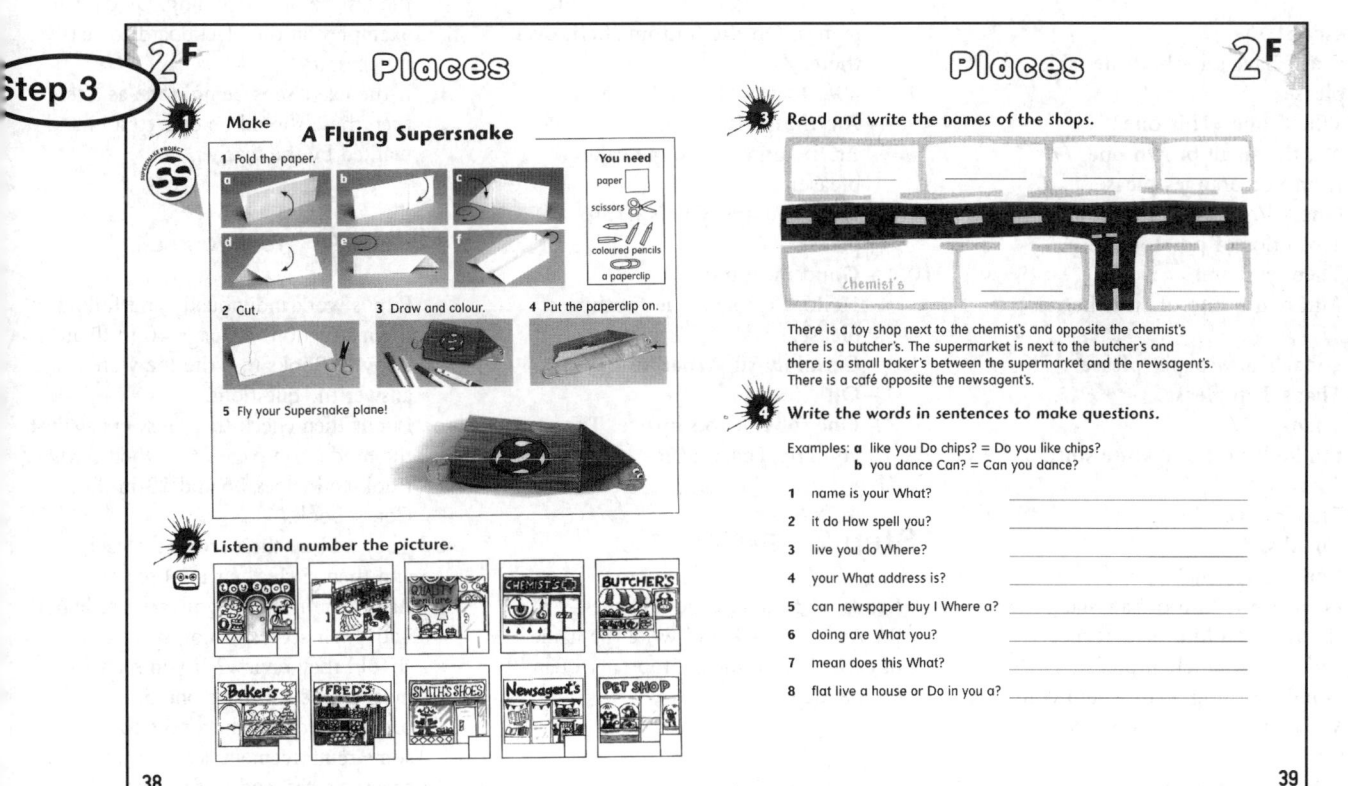

2F Places

1 Make — A Flying Supersnake

1 Fold the paper.
 a   b   c
 d   e   f

You need:
- paper
- scissors
- coloured pencils
- a paperclip

2 Cut.   3 Draw and colour.   4 Put the paperclip on.

5 Fly your Supersnake plane!

2 Listen and number the picture.

(TOY SHOP, CHEMIST'S, BUTCHER'S, Baker's, FRED'S, SMITH'S SHOES, Newsagent's, PET SHOP)

Places 2F

3 Read and write the names of the shops.

chemist's

There is a toy shop next to the chemist's and opposite the chemist's there is a butcher's. The supermarket is next to the butcher's and there is a small baker's between the supermarket and the newsagent's. There is a café opposite the newsagent's.

4 Write the words in sentences to make questions.

Examples: **a** like you Do chips? = Do you like chips?
 b you dance Can? = Can you dance?

1 name is your What? _____
2 it do How spell you? _____
3 live you do Where? _____
4 your What address is? _____
5 can newspaper buy I Where a? _____
6 doing are What you? _____
7 mean does this What? _____
8 flat live a house or Do in you a? _____

89

2F Lesson 2 – Evaluation

Main Language Items	Resource File	Materials Needed
Round-up lesson (including tests) Revision of all structures		cassette/cassette player

Step 1 Listening (Test)

a Pupils look at the pictures at the bottom of page 38 of the Activity Book. They will hear a short dialogue taking place in each of the shops. They must decide which dialogue is taking place where and write the appropriate numbers in the boxes.

b Number one is given as an example. Play each dialogue three times.

Tapescript:

1. – Can I have a look at the table please?
   – Which one? This one?
   – No, the small brown one. //

2. – A kilo of oranges please.
   – One kilo of oranges.
   – Two kilos of potatoes.
   – There you are.
   – And half a kilo of strawberries. //

3. – Today's newspaper please.
   – That's 30p please.
   – Thanks. //

4. – I'm looking for a white shirt. Size 48.
   – They're over there, sir.
   – Thanks. //

5. – Can I help you?
   – I'd like one kilo of sausages, about half a kilo of that meat and a large chicken please.

6. – Good morning. Can I help you?
   – We want a pair of boots. Size six.
   – What colour would you like?
   – Red or green please. //

7. – Two tins of cat food please.
   – Here you are. Anything else?
   – No thanks.
   – That's 92p please. //

8. – Excuse me. Have you got any robots?
   – Only the small grey one over there.
   – Can it talk?
   – No, I don't think so.
   – What about computer games?
   – Yes, we've got lots of computer games. On the bottom shelf, over there. //

9. – Two loaves of bread please.
   – Anything else?
   – Er...a large chocolate cake please.
   – Here you are. That's £1.46 please. //

10. – Good morning.
    – Hello. I'd like some toothpaste please.
    – Certainly sir. What kind?
    – Oh ... any.
    – One tube of toothpaste. There you are. That's 90p.

Step 2 Reading (Test)

Pupils read the passage on page 39 of the Activity Book and write the name of each shop in the appropriate square on the map.

Step 3 Writing (Test)

a Pupils work individually on page 39 of the Activity Book and write the answers in their exercise books or on a sheet of paper.

b They rearrange the words in each line to make eight correctly formed questions. There are two examples in the book to help.

c Ensure pupils understand the nature of the test before beginning. Give further examples on the blackboard to clarify if necessary.

d If the exercise is being done as a test, then these should be collected in and marked by the teacher.

Step 4 Test yourself

a Pupils work individually and follow the instructions on page 40 in their Activity Books to write the words and answer the questions.

b Pupils then check their answers against the models on page 26 of their Activity Book and pages 26 and 23 in the Coursebook.

c They add up their scores for each test and then circle their total score.

d Ask them in their L1 if they are happy with their scores. If not, what areas should they review? If you see that most pupils still have one or several problem areas, make a note to prepare some reinforcement activities for these specific areas, and leaf through the **Resource File** for ideas.

90

2F Places

1 Make — A Flying Supersnake

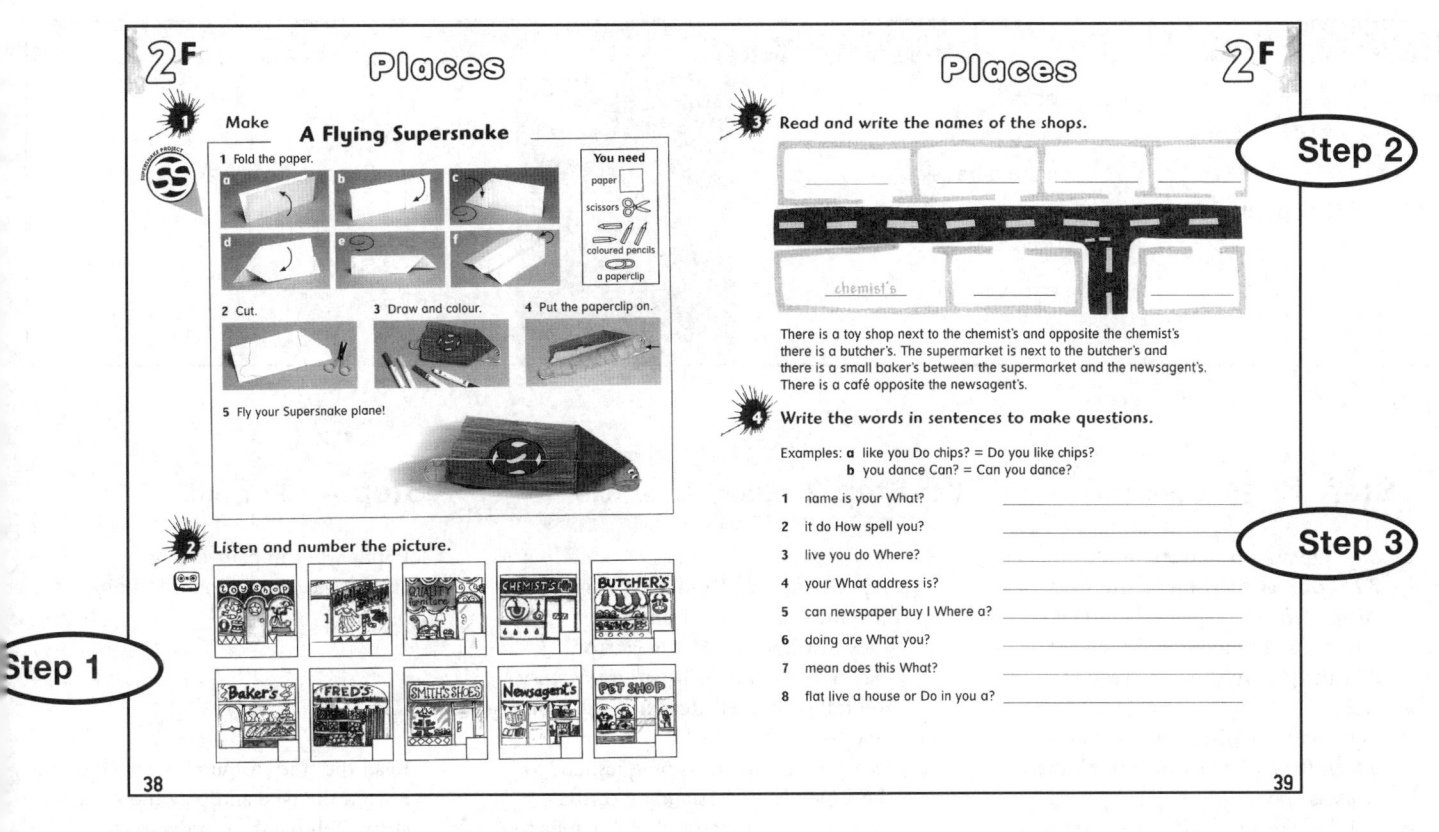

1 Fold the paper.
  a b c
  d e f

You need
- paper
- scissors
- coloured pencils
- a paperclip

2 Cut.
3 Draw and colour.
4 Put the paperclip on.
5 Fly your Supersnake plane!

2 Listen and number the picture.

Step 1

2F Places

3 Read and write the names of the shops.

chemist's

Step 2

There is a toy shop next to the chemist's and opposite the chemist's there is a butcher's. The supermarket is next to the butcher's and there is a small baker's between the supermarket and the newsagent's. There is a café opposite the newsagent's.

4 Write the words in sentences to make questions.

Examples: **a** like you Do chips? = Do you like chips?
          b you dance Can? = Can you dance?

1 name is your What? _____
2 it do How spell you? _____
3 live you do Where? _____
4 your What address is? _____
5 can newspaper buy I Where a? _____
6 doing are What you? _____
7 mean does this What? _____
8 flat live a house or Do in you a? _____

Step 3

2F Places

Step 4

5 Test yourself.

TEST 1 ★ Write the words.
a _____   a _____
a _____   a _____
a _____   a _____

★ Check your answers on page 26 in your Activity Book.   SCORE / 6

TEST 2 ★ Write the words.
a ___   a ___   a ___   a ___

★ Check your answers on page 26 in your Coursebook.   SCORE / 4

TEST 3 ★ Write the answers.

Is the museum near the cinema? _____
Where's the library? _____
Where's the church? _____
Where's the café? _____

★ Check your answers on page 23 in your Coursebook.   SCORE / 10

TOTAL / 20
Circle your total score: 20 Excellent   19–18 Very good   17–15 Good
                        14–12 Quite good   11–0 Do it again!

3A Opposites

1 Write.

What's the opposite of big? Small.

big	small

2 Crossword. Write.

Write the opposite of these words in the crossword.

Across   **Down**
3 small   1 wrong
4 boy   2 last
9 finish   5 hate
10 west   6 brother
11 answer   7 short
13 mother   8 thin
                    12 yes

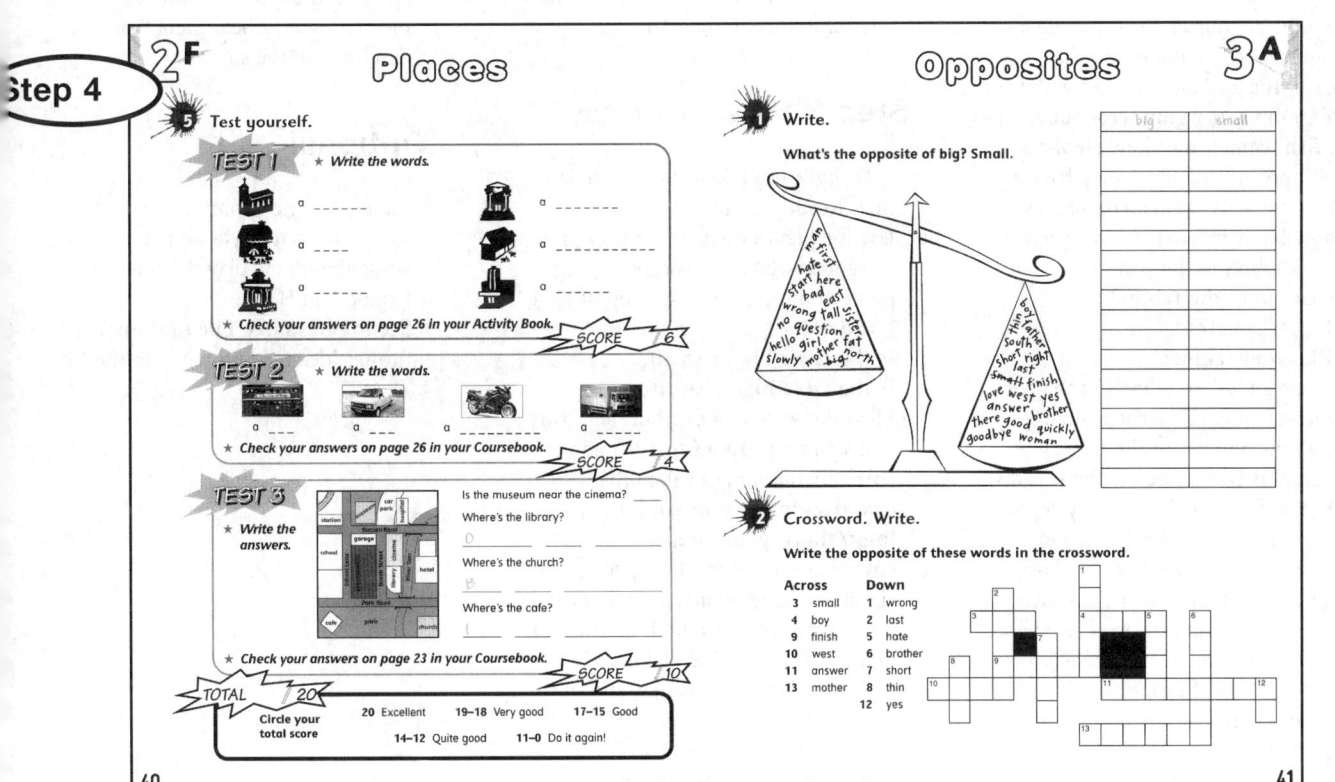

91

3 Story lesson

Main Language Items			Resource File	Materials Needed
mirror	old	opposite	41	Reader
long	enormous	different	55	cassette/cassette player
short	huge	on the other side		
thin	giant	outside		
new	tiny			

Step 1 Story presentation

a Say 'Open your Coursebook on page 32. Look at the title of the story: *The Magic Mirror.*' Explain the title if pupils do not understand it and explain that the picture shows a scene from the story.

b Tell pupils to look at the picture and ask in their L1 what they think the story is about.

c Ask how many pupils have been to a zoo and what animals they saw there. Elicit the names of animals in the picture of the zoo on pages 32 and 33: **giraffe, rabbit, penguin, crocodile, tiger, fish, camel, monkey, elephant, lion, hippo**. Ask pupils if they have a rabbit at home. Ask what colour it is and how big it is. Then ask questions about the rabbit in the picture:
What colour is the rabbit?
Is it big or small?
Is it like your rabbit?
Ask about the other animals in the zoo and elicit from pupils what is strange about all the animals in the zoo e.g.
The camel is blue. The elephants are small. The fish is riding a bicycle.
Pupils work in pairs. Set a time limit and see which pair can find the most strange things in the zoo. Pupils then close their books and try to remember all the strange animals in the zoo.
Tell pupils (in L1 if necessary) that the strange zoo exists on the other side of a magic mirror.

Step 2 Story 'listen and read'

a Say 'Open your Reader on page 4. Listen to the story about a boy who goes through the Magic Mirror.'

b Play the tape. Pupils listen to the story and follow in their Reader at the same time.

c Ask some comprehension questions to check pupils' understanding of the story (in L1 if necessary). Ask pupils to retell the story in their L1.

Step 3 Story vocabulary

a Tell pupils to look at the picture in their Reader again.

b Use the pictures that accompany the story to re-elicit key vocabulary e.g. point to the picture at the top of page 5 and ask:
Is the chair big or small?
Is the table big or small?
Elicit the words '**enormous**' and '**tiny**'. Ask similar questions to elicit and check the meaning of the other adjectives in the story: **old/new, long/short, giant, huge**.

c Give pupils the opportunity to ask you about any other words they don't understand, but set a limit on the number of words. The aim of this lesson is for pupils to enjoy the story so don't focus in too much detail on vocabulary that isn't essential to understanding the gist of the story.

Step 4 Pairwork

Pupils work in pairs and ask and answer questions about the story pictures.

Step 5 Storytelling

Read the story to pupils yourself or rewind the tape and play the story again. Tell pupils to point at the pictures as they hear them being described in the story.

Optional

Pupils get into groups and read the story. One pupil will be the narrator, while the others play the roles of Arnold and Bob.
See the **Resource File** (55) for a further idea for following up the story.

3 Opposites

STORY

The Magic Mirror

Step 1

3A Lesson 1

Main Language Items		Resource File	Materials Needed
Revision: opposites and classroom language		4	cassette/cassette player
When teacher says … laugh	cry	15	
I say … hello	goodbye	54	
stupid	clever		
always	never		
opposite			

Step 1   Presentation

a Pupils listen to the poem on page 34 of the Coursebook twice through without stopping. Coursebooks must be closed.

b Ask some questions to check comprehension, e.g.
What does the boy say when the teacher says 'Hello'?
What does the boy say when the teacher says 'You're stupid'?
What does the boy do when the teacher says 'Stand'?

Step 2   Poem

a Listen to the poem again. Pupils should repeat each line.

b Pupils act out the poem as a class, with the teacher giving instructions.

c Pupils act out the poem in pairs, taking turns in the role of the teacher.

d (Optional) Ask pupils to think of another sentence for the poem. Write suggestions on the blackboard. Pupils can replace 'teacher' with each other's names, e.g. 'When *Carlos* says "Run", I always walk', 'When *Maria* says "Quiet", I always talk.' Make as many verses as possible. All the verses can be collected and displayed as a class poem on the wall.

Step 3   Action game

a Bring four pupils and four chairs to the front of the class. Revise the instructions for the Action game introduced in previous levels of the course.

b Explain that in this game the pupils must do the opposite of what they are told. For example, if you say '**Stand up**' then they should sit; if you say '**Sit down**' then they should stand. Practise a few times.

c Play the game with the whole class. Possible instructions are: '**Stand up**', '**Sit down**', '**Look up/down**', '**Turn to the north/south/east/west**', '**Pick up/put down your pen/book**', '**Open/close your bag/book**', etc.

Step 4   Write

a Say '**Open your Activity Book on page 41.**' The task is to find opposite words on each side of the scales. Do a few examples orally with the class.

b Round up by asking the class their answers: '**What's the opposite of bad?**' etc. Pupils then complete the list in their Activity Book.

Step 5   Crossword

a Pupils complete the crossword on page 41 of the Activity Book.

b (Optional) Divide the class into pairs and tell them to look at the crossword. P1 asks the Across clues, e.g. '**What's the opposite of "small"?**', and P2 asks the Down clues, e.g. '**What's the opposite of "wrong"?**' Both pupils write down each answer in the crossword.

Step 1

Step 2

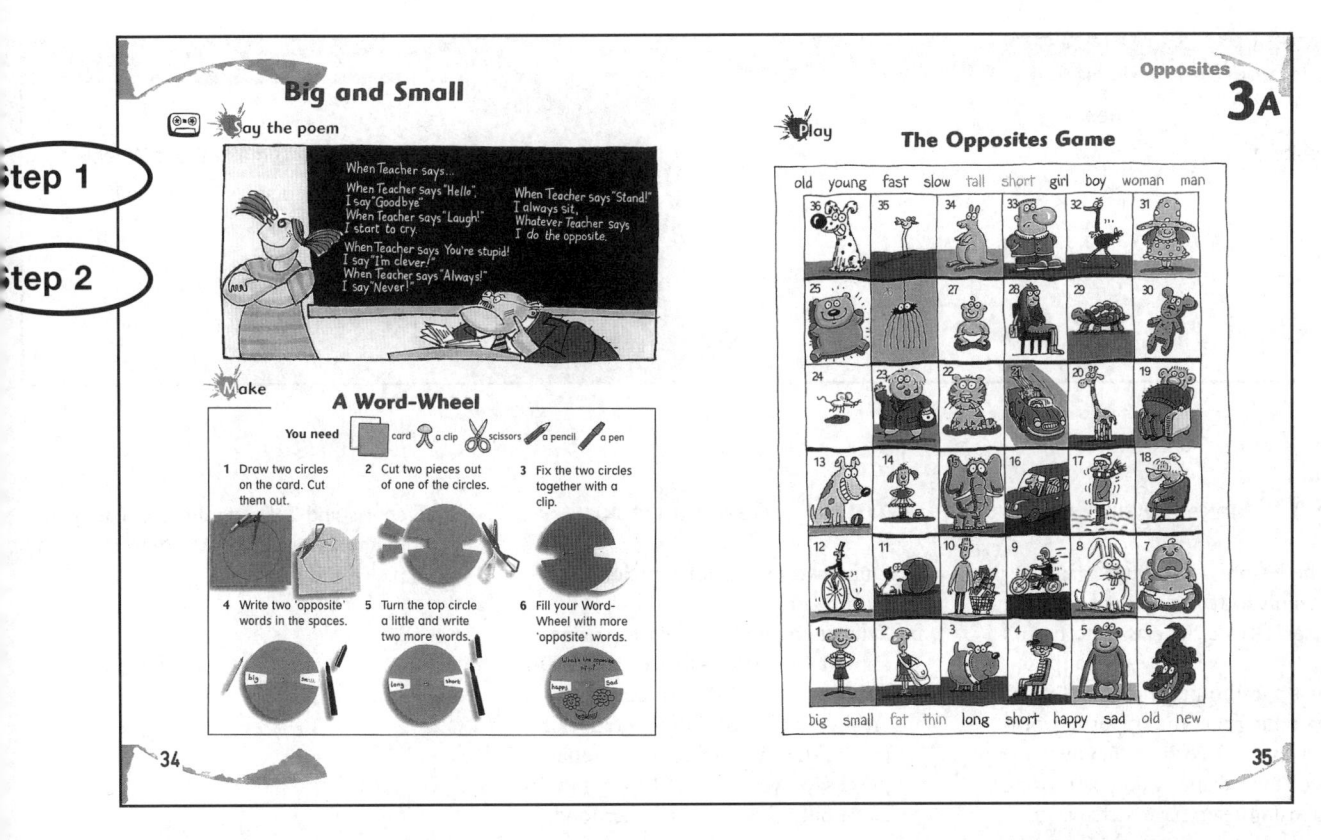

Big and Small

Say the poem

When Teacher says...
When Teacher says "Hello",
I say "Goodbye".
When Teacher says "Laugh!"
I start to cry.
When Teacher says "You're stupid!"
I say "I'm clever!"
When Teacher says "Always!"
I say "Never!"

When Teacher says "Stand!"
I always sit,
Whatever Teacher says
I do the opposite.

Make — A Word-Wheel

You need: card, a clip, scissors, a pencil, a pen

1. Draw two circles on the card. Cut them out.
2. Cut two pieces out of one of the circles.
3. Fix the two circles together with a clip.
4. Write two 'opposite' words in the spaces.
5. Turn the top circle a little and write two more words.
6. Fill your Word-Wheel with more 'opposite' words.

Play — The Opposites Game

Opposites 3A

old young fast slow tall short girl boy woman man

big small fat thin long short happy sad old new

34 / 35

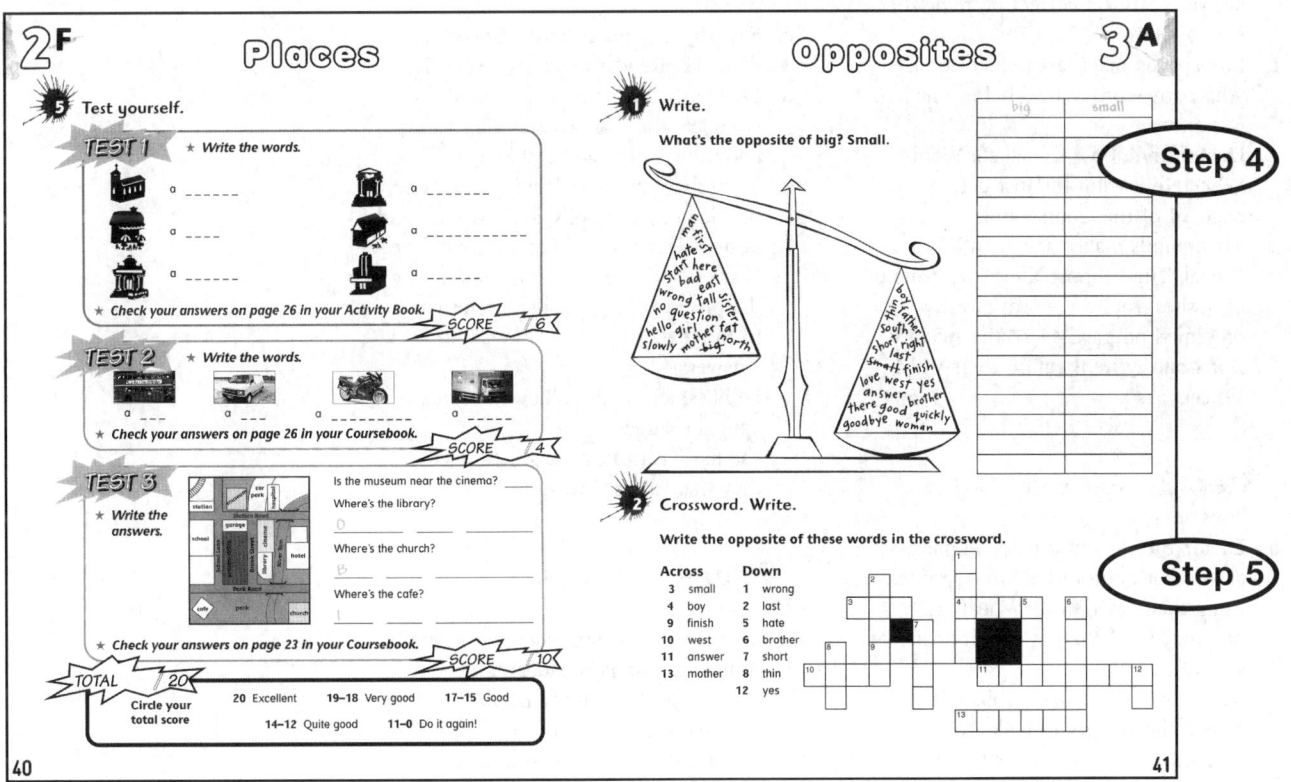

2F Places

5 Test yourself.

TEST 1 ★ Write the words.
a _ _ _ _ _ _ _ _
a _ _ _ _
a _ _ _ _ _ _ _
a _ _ _ _ _ _ _ _ _ _
a _ _ _ _ _ _ _ _ _
a _ _ _ _ _ _ _ _ _

★ Check your answers on page 26 in your Activity Book.
SCORE / 6

TEST 2 ★ Write the words.
a _ _ _   a _ _   a _ _ _ _ _ _ _ _   a _ _ _

★ Check your answers on page 26 in your Coursebook.
SCORE / 4

TEST 3 ★ Write the answers.

Is the museum near the cinema? ___
Where's the library?
D
Where's the church?
B
Where's the cafe?

★ Check your answers on page 23 in your Coursebook.
SCORE / 10

TOTAL / 20

Circle your total score:
20 Excellent 19–18 Very good 17–15 Good
14–12 Quite good 11–0 Do it again!

Opposites 3A

1 Write.

What's the opposite of big? Small.

(balance scale with words: man, first, hate, start here, bad, wrong, east, no question, tall, hello, girl, sister, slowly, mother, fat, big, north / boy, father, this, south, right, short, last, small, finish, love, west, yes, answer, there, good, brother, goodbye, quickly, woman)

big	small

Step 4

2 Crossword. Write.

Write the opposite of these words in the crossword.

Across
3 small
4 boy
9 finish
10 west
11 answer
13 mother

Down
1 wrong
2 last
5 hate
6 brother
7 short
8 thin
12 yes

Step 5

40 / 41

3A Lesson 2

Main Language Items	Resource File	Materials Needed
Revision: food wheel What's the opposite of … ? I/you/we like …	19 44 54	materials to make Word-Wheels paper for display (optional)

Step 1   Make a Word-Wheel

a Start the lesson with a quick game of word-tennis to revise pairs of opposites. Divide the class into two teams. Say an adjective e.g. **'happy'**. The first pupil to put their hand up can answer, telling you the opposite word **(sad)**. If they are correct, they win a point for their team. If they are wrong, the opposing team have a chance to answer. Insist on correct pronunciation for the point.

b Prepare the materials needed to make your own Word-Wheel before the lesson.

c Demonstrate how to make a Word-Wheel, following the instructions on page 34 of the Coursebook.

d Then pupils make their own Word-Wheel. They choose their own pairs of opposites from the words already presented on page 41 of the Activity Book and write them on their Word-Wheel.

Step 2   Pairwork

a Divide the class into pairs. Pupils ask each other questions about opposites, using their own Word-Wheels as prompts, e.g. **'What is the opposite of short?'**

b (Optional) More able pupils can extend the activity to make full sentences. P1 says **'I've got a big bike.'** P2 replies **'No you've got a small bike.'** etc.

Step 3   Reading (Task)

a Draw two interlocking circles on the blackboard.

b Select two pupils. Write their names above each circle. Ask each pupil **'Do you like chips?'** If both pupils say **'Yes'**, write **'chips'** in the interlocking part of the two circles. If only one pupil says **'yes'**, write **'chips'** in their circle only. Repeat with other food items.

c Say **'Open your Activity Book on page 42. Read the passage silently.'**

d Divide the class into pairs. Pupils complete the diagram showing Kong's and Tong's likes and dislikes.

e Then draw two interlocking circles on the board. Ask pupils about Kong's and Tong's likes and dislikes and write the answers into the circles. If there is any disagreement, get pupils to refer back to the text.

Answers:
he likes: ice-cream, cake, chocolate, apples, oranges
she likes: carrots, potatoes, beans
they like: cheese, biscuits

Step 4   Pairwork

Divide the class into pairs. Each pupil completes the likes and dislikes diagram in the Activity Book by asking their partner **'Do you like …?'** Questions need not be restricted to food. Pupils can ask about games, sports and TV programmes. The final diagrams can be copied onto coloured paper and displayed.

Big and Small

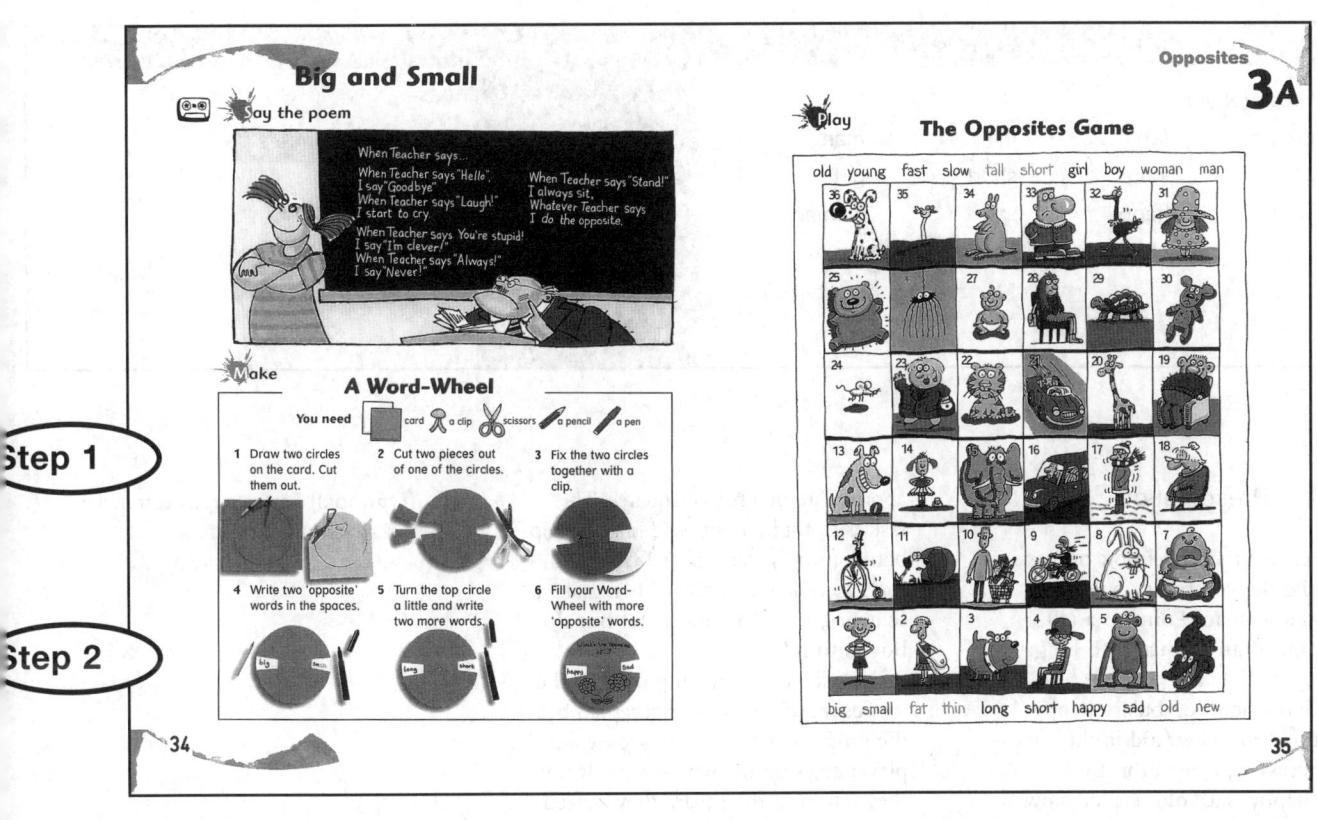

Opposites 3A

Say the poem

When Teacher says...
When Teacher says "Hello",
I say "Goodbye".
When Teacher says "Laugh!"
I start to cry.
When Teacher says "You're stupid!"
I say "I'm clever!"
When Teacher says "Always!"
I say "Never!"

When Teacher says "Stand!"
I always sit.
Whatever Teacher says
I do the opposite.

Make — A Word-Wheel

You need: card, a clip, scissors, a pencil, a pen

1 Draw two circles on the card. Cut them out.
2 Cut two pieces out of one of the circles.
3 Fix the two circles together with a clip.
4 Write two 'opposite' words in the spaces.
5 Turn the top circle a little and write two more words.
6 Fill your Word-Wheel with more 'opposite' words.

Play — The Opposites Game

old young fast slow tall short girl boy woman man

big small fat thin long short happy sad old new

34

35

3A Opposites

3 Read and write.

Kong Mouse is a fat, greedy mouse. He's always eating. He loves cheese and biscuits. He also likes ice-cream, cake, chocolate, apples and oranges. The only things Kong doesn't like are vegetables. His sister, Tong, is just the opposite. She eats very little. She never eats fruit, cake, chocolate or ice-cream, but she does like cheese and biscuits. She also likes carrots, potatoes and beans.

he likes / they like / she likes

4 Ask your friend. Then write.

Do you like ...?

I like / we like / _____ likes

Opposites 3A

5 Ask and answer. Then write.

Find someone who is tall. _____
Find someone who is short. _____
Find someone who has got long hair. _____
Find someone who has got short hair. _____
Find someone who can swim. _____
Find someone who can't swim. _____
Find someone who likes ice-cream. _____
Find someone who doesn't like ice-cream. _____

6 Write.

1 CHOCOLATE
2 _____

1 _____
2 _____

1 _____
2 _____

7 Write. Then draw.

Take the third letter in _____
The second letter in _____
The second letter in _____
The fourth letter in _____
The last letter in _____
The sixth letter in _____
And the first letter in _____
What have you got?

Draw your answer here.

42

43

97

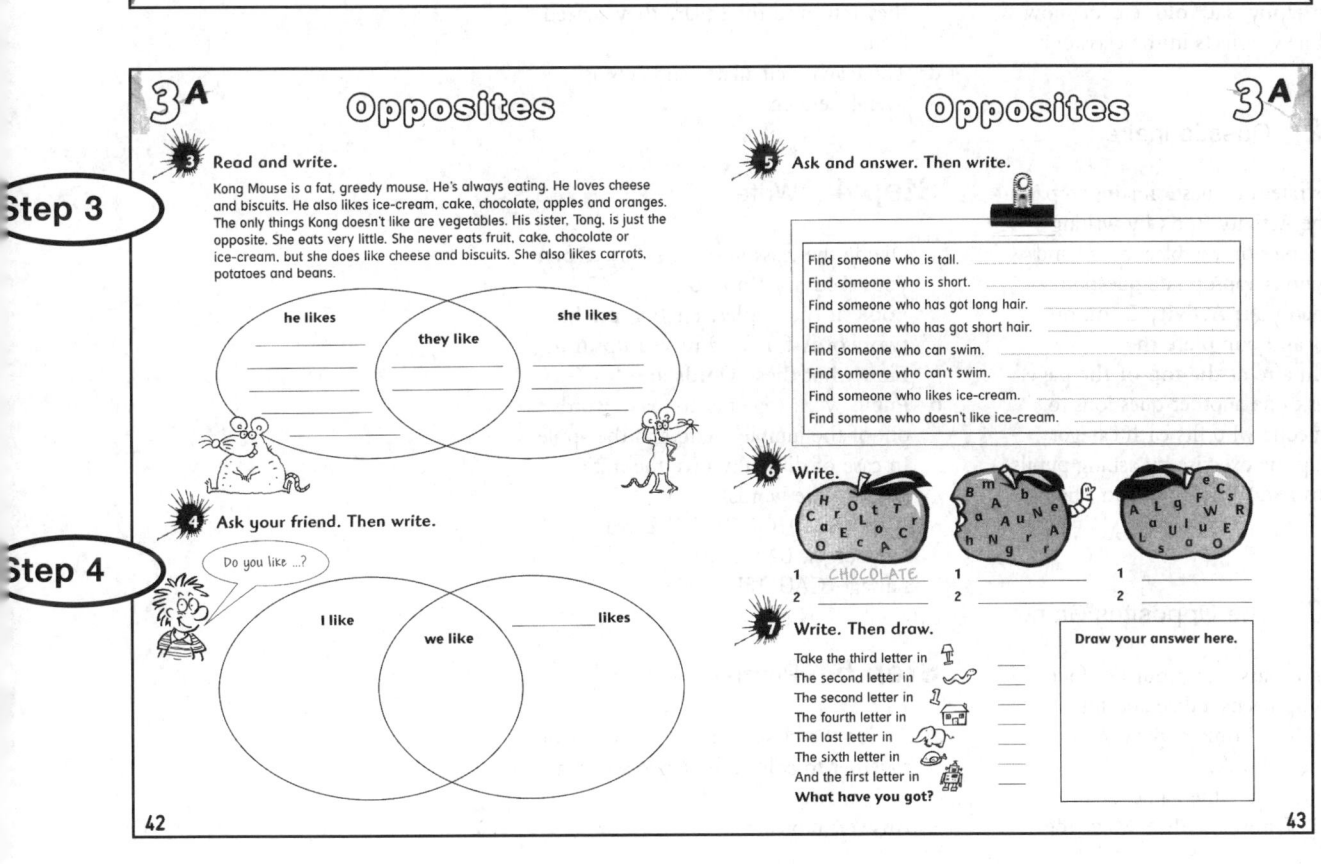

3A Lesson 3

Main Language Items				Resource File	Materials Needed
Revision: physical descriptions				15	dice/counters
Find someone who ...	fat	thin	man	44	
He/she is ...	long	short	girl	53	
Can you ... ?	happy	sad	woman		
Do you like ... ?	old	new	boy		
Point to ...					
He/she's got ...					

Step 1 Presentation

a Say 'Open your Coursebook on page 35.' Revise the vocabulary by saying 'Point to a woman. Point to a tall man. Point to an animal with long legs.' etc.

b Introduce the new vocabulary **happy/sad, young/old, new/old** in the same way. If necessary, extend this by miming **happy, sad, old**, etc. or show old and new objects in the classroom.

Step 2 Questionnaire

a Demonstrate the questionnaire on page 43 of the Activity Book by writing two examples on the blackboard and asking pupils appropriate questions.

b Say 'Open your Activity Book on page 43 and complete the questionnaire at the top of the page.' Pupils ask one another questions to find someone who fits each category.

c Round up the exercise by asking pupils questions like '**Who's got long hair?**' etc.

Step 3 The Opposites Game

a Divide the class into groups of four. Each group needs a dice and four counters. Say '**Look at page 35 in your Coursebook.**'

b First demonstrate the game. Start at Square 1. Throw the dice. Move the appropriate number of squares. The task is to find an opposite relationship between the square started from and the square landed on and then make a sentence, e.g. '**The dog is fat but the boy is thin.**'

c Pupils play the game in groups. If the 'opposite' relationship is accepted by the other members of the group, the player stays on the new square. If not, they return to the square they started from.

d The teacher circulates and acts as overall referee.

Step 4 Write

a Divide the class into pairs. Say '**Open your Activity Book on page 43. Look at the apples. Each apple has two words for food mixed up in it. Find what these words are.**'

b Pupils work together to make words out of the jumbled letters in the apples. In case of difficulty give the initial letter of the words.
Answers: CHOCOLATE, carrot; hamburger, BANANA; sausage, CAULIFLOWER

Step 5 Puzzle

a Divide the class into pairs. Pupils work together to solve the puzzle and draw their answer.
Answer: monster

b (**Optional**) Faster pupils can make puzzles for their friends.

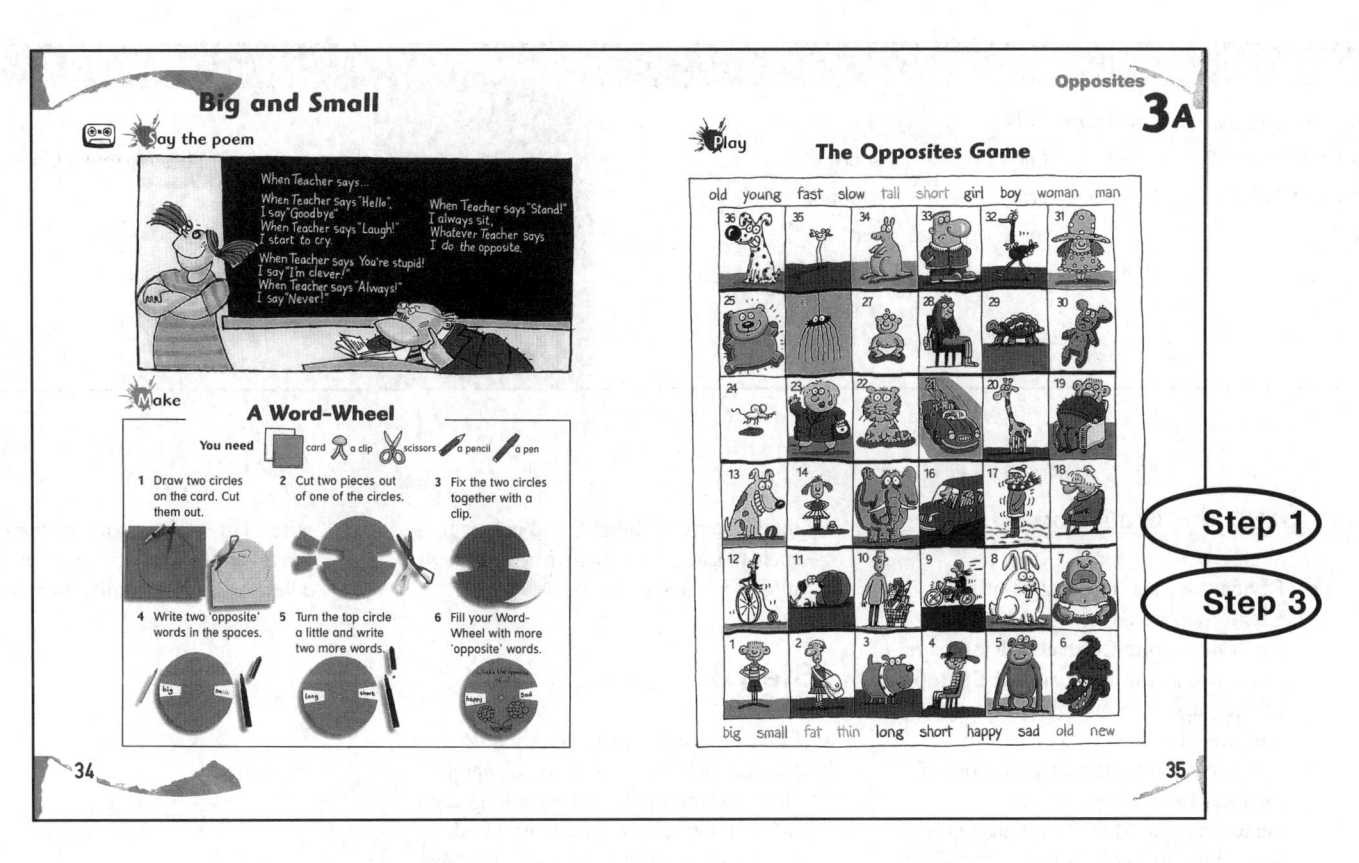

Big and Small

Say the poem

When Teacher says...
When Teacher says "Hello",
I say "Goodbye".
When Teacher says "Laugh!"
I start to cry.
When Teacher says "You're stupid!"
I say "I'm clever!"
When Teacher says "Always!"
I say "Never!"
When Teacher says "Stand!"
I always sit,
Whatever Teacher says
I do the opposite.

Make — A Word-Wheel

You need: card, a clip, scissors, a pencil, a pen

1 Draw two circles on the card. Cut them out.
2 Cut two pieces out of one of the circles.
3 Fix the two circles together with a clip.
4 Write two 'opposite' words in the spaces.
5 Turn the top circle a little and write two more words.
6 Fill your Word-Wheel with more 'opposite' words.

Opposites — 3A

Play — The Opposites Game

old young fast slow tall short girl boy woman man

big small fat thin long short happy sad old new

Step 1
Step 3

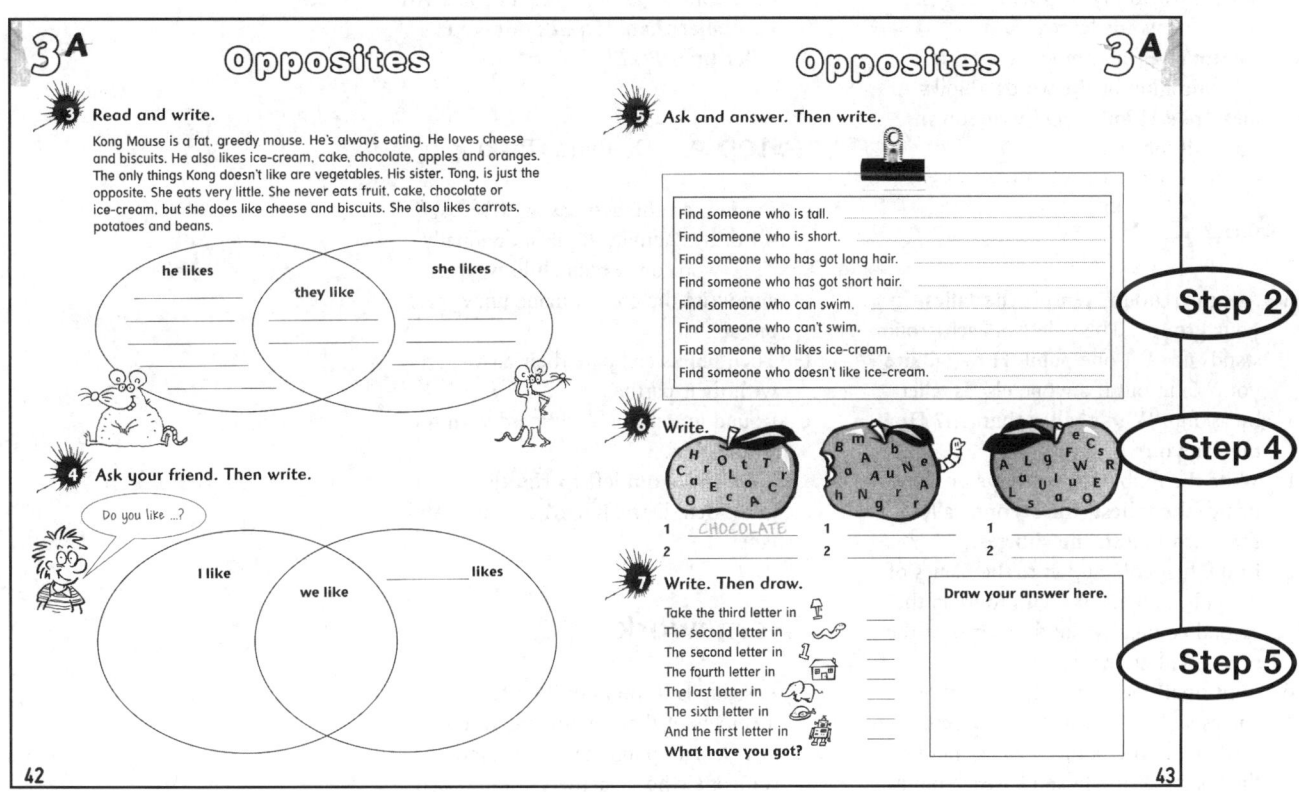

3A Opposites

3 Read and write.

Kong Mouse is a fat, greedy mouse. He's always eating. He loves cheese and biscuits. He also likes ice-cream, cake, chocolate, apples and oranges. The only things Kong doesn't like are vegetables. His sister, Tong, is just the opposite. She eats very little. She never eats fruit, cake, chocolate or ice-cream, but she does like cheese and biscuits. She also likes carrots, potatoes and beans.

he likes / they like / she likes

4 Ask your friend. Then write.

Do you like ...?

I like / we like / _____ likes

Opposites 3A

5 Ask and answer. Then write.

Find someone who is tall. _____
Find someone who is short. _____
Find someone who has got long hair. _____
Find someone who has got short hair. _____
Find someone who can swim. _____
Find someone who can't swim. _____
Find someone who likes ice-cream. _____
Find someone who doesn't like ice-cream. _____

Step 2

6 Write.

1 CHOCOLATE
2 _____

1 _____
2 _____

1 _____
2 _____

Step 4

7 Write. Then draw.

Take the third letter in 🪔
The second letter in 🪱
The second letter in 🏠
The fourth letter in 🏠
The last letter in 🐕
The sixth letter in
And the first letter in 🤖
What have you got?

Draw your answer here.

Step 5

3B Lesson 1

Main Language Items		Resource File	Materials Needed
Revision: comparatives and superlatives		5	string/rulers for measuring
Who's the tallest?	tall short	44	
Are you taller than … ?	first second	54	
	third last		

Step 1 Groupwork

a Divide the class into groups of four. Each group needs string and a ruler. Say '**Open your Coursebook on page 36. Look at the workcard at the top of the page.**' Go over the instructions with the class.

b Ask one pupil to come to the front of the class to be measured as a demonstration. Make sure that pupils know how to say heights in English: revise the words '**metre**' and '**centimetres**' and model the correct pronunciation of the words. Pupils measure each other and write down how tall they are.

Step 2 Survey

a Ask each group '**Who is the tallest in your group?**' The tallest in each group stands up. Ask one pupil '**How tall are you?**' Find out if anyone else is taller by asking '**Who's taller than …? How tall are you?**'

b Write the following headings on the board: **the tallest, the second tallest, the third tallest, the shortest.**

c In the first column, write the names of the tallest pupils in each group; in the second column, write the names of the second tallest and so on.

d (**Optional**) Prepare a block graph with names and heights as the two axes. Write in all the pupils' names, and in the course of the lesson let each pupil mark their own height, and colour in their block. Pupils then copy the graph into their exercise books.

Step 3 Speaking activity

a Erase the list from the blackboard.

b Pupils must line up in order of height, checking their positions by asking each other '**How tall are you?**' etc. Guide the pupils by asking questions like '**Are you taller than** *Maria*?', '**Are you taller than** *Paul*?'

Step 4 Reading (Task)

a Pupils read the two passages on page 44 of the Activity Book individually. They work out which child is which and write the correct name under each picture.

b Then pupils compare their answers with their partner.

c Round up on the blackboard with the whole class.
Solution (from left to right):
John, Ben, Dave, Jim, Mary, Tina, Ann, Jane

Homework

Ask pupils to find out how tall members of their family are. In the next lesson, pupils can do a 'Find someone who …' activity, asking each other '**How tall is your** *brother/sister*?' etc. to find out who has the tallest or shortest family members.

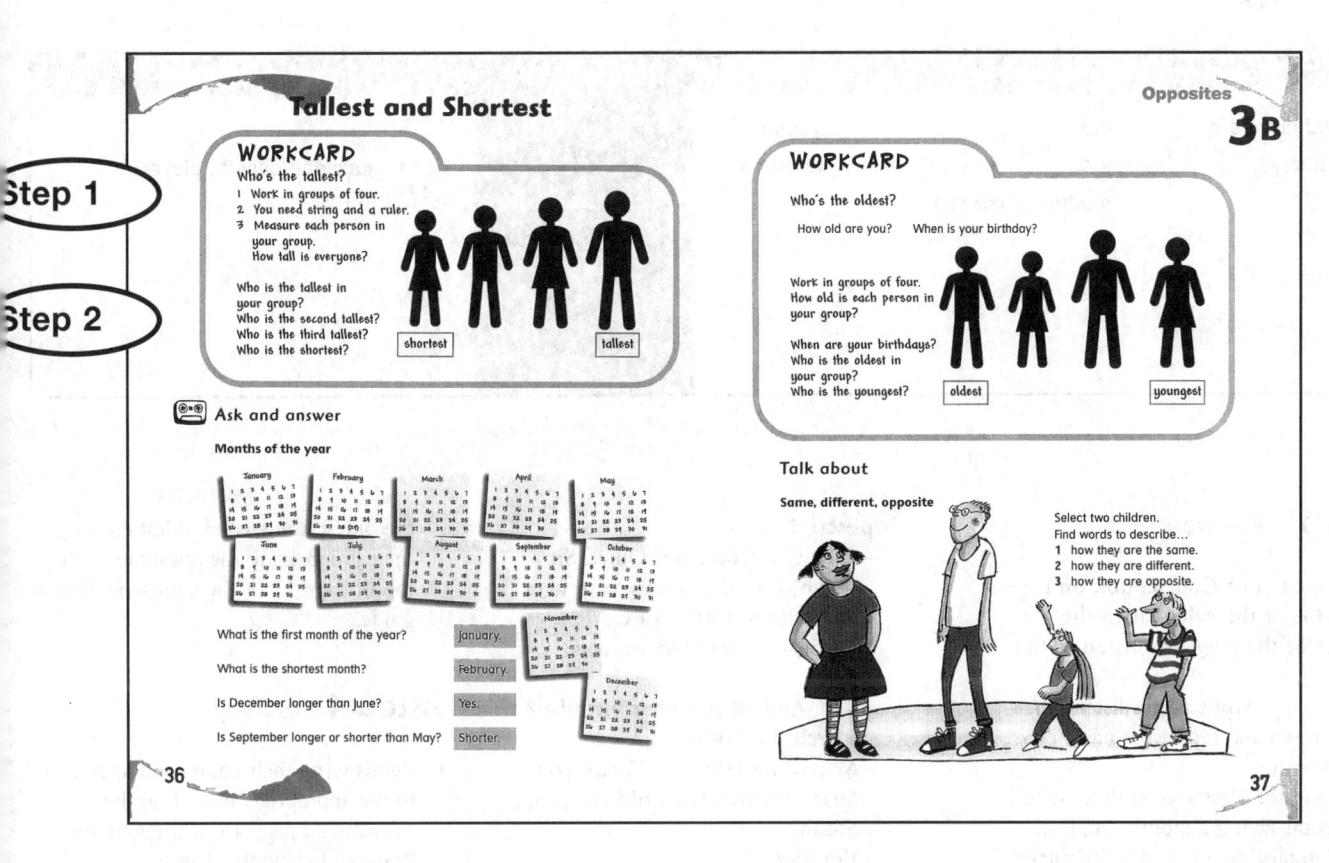

Tallest and Shortest

WORKCARD

Who's the tallest?
1. Work in groups of four.
2. You need string and a ruler.
3. Measure each person in your group.
   How tall is everyone?

Who is the tallest in your group?
Who is the second tallest?
Who is the third tallest?
Who is the shortest?

shortest — tallest

Ask and answer

Months of the year

What is the first month of the year?	January.
What is the shortest month?	February.
Is December longer than June?	Yes.
Is September longer or shorter than May?	Shorter.

Opposites 3B

WORKCARD

Who's the oldest?

How old are you? When is your birthday?

Work in groups of four.
How old is each person in your group?

When are your birthdays?
Who is the oldest in your group?
Who is the youngest?

oldest — youngest

Talk about

Same, different, opposite

Select two children.
Find words to describe…
1. how they are the same.
2. how they are different.
3. how they are opposite.

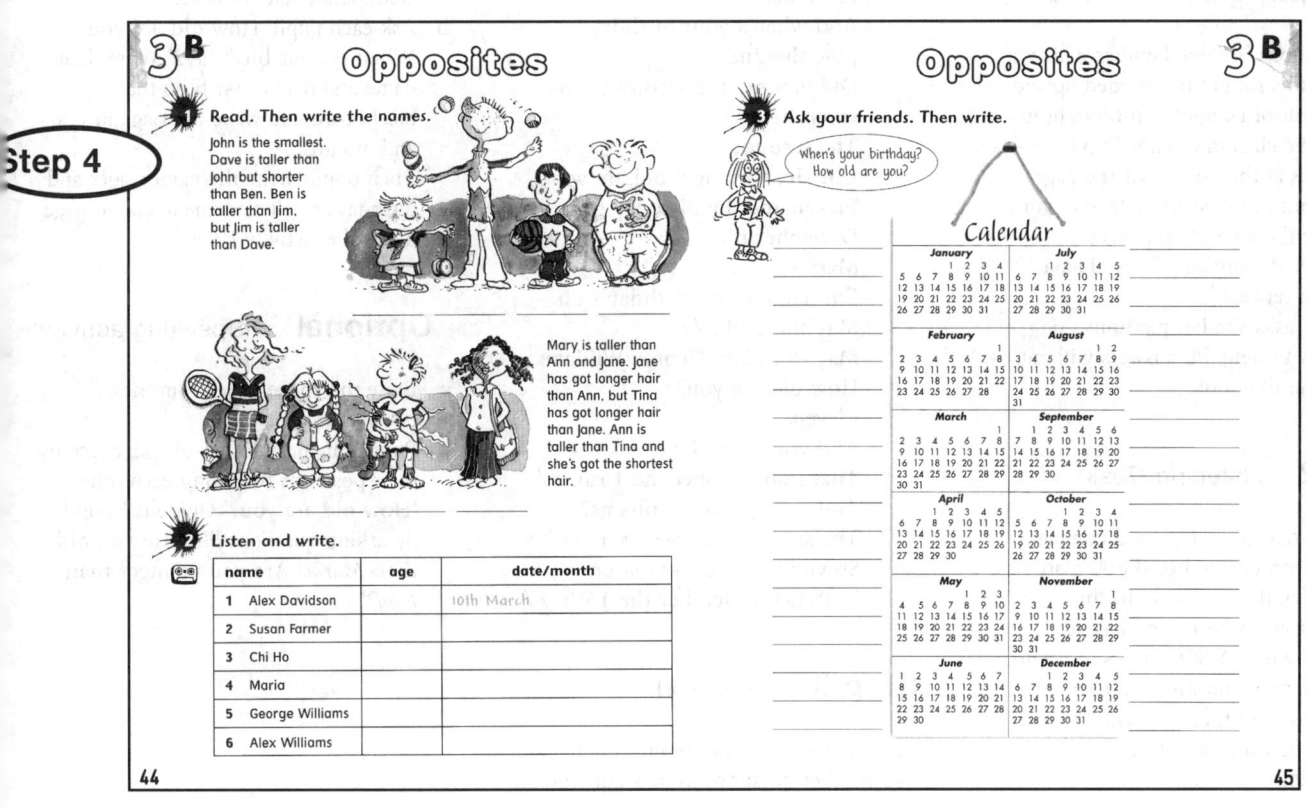

3B Opposites

1 Read. Then write the names.

John is the smallest. Dave is taller than John but shorter than Ben. Ben is taller than Jim, but Jim is taller than Dave.

Mary is taller than Ann and Jane. Jane has got longer hair than Ann, but Tina has got longer hair than Jane. Ann is taller than Tina and she's got the shortest hair.

2 Listen and write.

name	age	date/month
1 Alex Davidson		10th March
2 Susan Farmer		
3 Chi Ho		
4 Maria		
5 George Williams		
6 Alex Williams		

Opposites 3B

3 Ask your friends. Then write.

When's your birthday?
How old are you?

Calendar

3B Lesson 2

Main Language Items		Resource File	Materials Needed
Revision: age and numbers	old	young	
When's your birthday?	long	short	21
How old are you?	months of the year		22	cassette/casette player
Who's the oldest?			38a	
Are you older than … ?			75	

Step 1   Pairwork

a   Say 'Open your Coursebook on page 36. Look at the calendar in the middle of the page and listen to the tape.'
Play the tape while pupils listen. Then pupils listen and repeat the name of each month.

b   Go round the class several times with each pupil saying a month. Pupil A says '**January**', pupil B says '**February**', etc.
As the pupils become familiar with the months this should be speeded up and an element of competition brought in.

c   Divide the class into pairs. Pupils cover the words at the bottom of the page. Tell them to look at the calendar while you play the tape. P1 repeats the questions. P2 answers. They change roles and repeat.

d   Then P1 asks similar questions using the book to help. P2 answers without looking at the book.

Step 2   Listening (Task)

Pupils listen to the tape and complete the chart on page 44 of the Activity Book. Play the tape straight through twice pausing where necessary for pupils to write. Advise pupils to listen for one kind of information each time it is played and fill in the chart with ages the first time and birthdays the second time.

Tapescript:
– All right. Come on. Quiet. Sit down. I need to know your ages and date of birth. Alex. Alex Davidson. How old are you?
– Ten.
– Ten. And when's your birthday?
– March the 10th.
– March the 10th. // Thank you. Susan Farmer. How old are you, Susan?
– I'm nine. //
– And when's your birthday?
– June the 2nd.
– Did you say the second or the seventh?
– The second.
– Chi Ho. Chi, how old are you?
– Eleven and my birthday's on December the 21st. //
– Maria?
– I'm ten and my birthday's on May the 12th. //
– May the 12th. George Williams. How old are you?
– Eleven.
– And your birthday?
– That's on October the 15th. //
– And finally. Alex Williams?
– The same as George, we're twins.
– So you're eleven and your birthday is October the 15th. //

Step 3   Groupwork

Divide the class into groups. Pupils ask each other questions to find out who is the oldest, the second oldest etc. in their group using the questions at the top of page 37 of the Coursebook as a guide.

Step 4   Survey

a   Pupils write their names and ages next to the appropriate month on the calendar on page 45 of the Activity Book and circle the date.

b   Ask each pupil '**How old are you? When is your birthday?**' Write their name and date of birth on the blackboard and write their age in years and months.
Then pupils write the names, ages and birthdays of all class members on page 45 of the Activity Book.

Optional   (Speaking activity)

a   Erase the above dates from the blackboard.

b   Pupils line up in order of age, checking their positions by asking each other '**How old are you?**' Guide the pupils by asking questions like '**Are you older than** *Maria*? **Are you younger than** *Paul*?'

102

Tallest and Shortest

WORKCARD

Who's the tallest?
1. Work in groups of four.
2. You need string and a ruler.
3. Measure each person in your group.
   How tall is everyone?

Who is the tallest in your group?
Who is the second tallest?
Who is the third tallest?
Who is the shortest?

shortest   tallest

Step 1

🎧 Ask and answer

Months of the year

January, February, March, April, May, June, July, August, September, October, November, December

What is the first month of the year? — January.
What is the shortest month? — February.
Is December longer than June? — Yes.
Is September longer or shorter than May? — Shorter.

36

Opposites **3B**

WORKCARD

Who's the oldest?

How old are you? When is your birthday?

Work in groups of four.
How old is each person in your group?

When are your birthdays?
Who is the oldest in your group?
Who is the youngest?

oldest   youngest

Step 3

Talk about

Same, different, opposite

Select two children.
Find words to describe...
1. how they are the same.
2. how they are different.
3. how they are opposite.

37

3B Opposites

1 Read. Then write the names.

John is the smallest.
Dave is taller than
John but shorter
than Ben. Ben is
taller than Jim,
but Jim is taller
than Dave.

Mary is taller than
Ann and Jane. Jane
has got longer hair
than Ann, but Tina
has got longer hair
than Jane. Ann is
taller than Tina and
she's got the shortest
hair.

2 Listen and write.

name	age	date/month
1 Alex Davidson		10th March
2 Susan Farmer		
3 Chi Ho		
4 Maria		
5 George Williams		
6 Alex Williams		

Step 2

44

Opposites **3B**

3 Ask your friends. Then write.

When's your birthday?
How old are you?

Calendar

January, February, March, April, May, June, July, August, September, October, November, December

Step 4

45

103

3B Lesson 3

Main Language Items		Resource File	Materials Needed
Revision: physical description and clothes		4	
I am older than …	same	53	cassette/cassette player
I've got longer hair than …	different		
We/they are wearing …	opposite		
	matches		

Step 1   Quiz

Ask pupils questions about the class using the information gathered in this unit. Pupils can refer to their Activity Book.
Ask questions like:
Who's the oldest/tallest/youngest in the class?
Is *Paul* older or younger than *Maria*?
Who is the *second oldest* in the class?

Step 2   Personal survey

a Pupils individually complete the sentences on page 46 of the Activity Book.

b (Optional) In pairs or groups pupils write a series of sentences describing someone in the class. The other members of the class then guess who is referred to e.g. 'He is taller than *Maria* but shorter than *Paul*,' 'He is older than *John* but younger than *Maria*,' 'His birthday is in *January*' etc. The riddles can be displayed and a competition held to see who can guess the greatest number correctly.

Step 3   Presentation

a Say 'Open your Coursebook on page 37. Look at the four children at the bottom of the page.' Ask questions about any two of these children. 'How are they the same?', 'How are they different?', 'How are they opposite?'

b Repeat with other pairs (of the four children) until all combinations have been covered.
Note: There may be some confusion about which are 'opposite' and which are 'different'. Example: 'Red and blue are different, but black and white are opposite.' This should provoke discussion in the class. Encourage pupils to come up with more pairs of 'different' and 'opposite'.

Step 4   Pairwork

a Divide the class into pairs. Pupils must find three ways that they are the same as, different from and opposite to each other.

b Round up with the whole class. Note common areas of sameness and difference on the blackboard, for example, ages, heights, sexes, birthdays, clothes, likes and dislikes.

Step 5   Workcard

Pupils do the workcard on page 46 of the Activity Book either individually or in pairs.

Homework

Ask pupils to find magazine pictures of their favourite actors, actresses, musicians, sportsmen, etc. In the next lesson, pupils compare their pictures, saying how they are the same, opposite or different. Pupils work in pairs or groups to make a poster, writing sentences comparing their pictures.

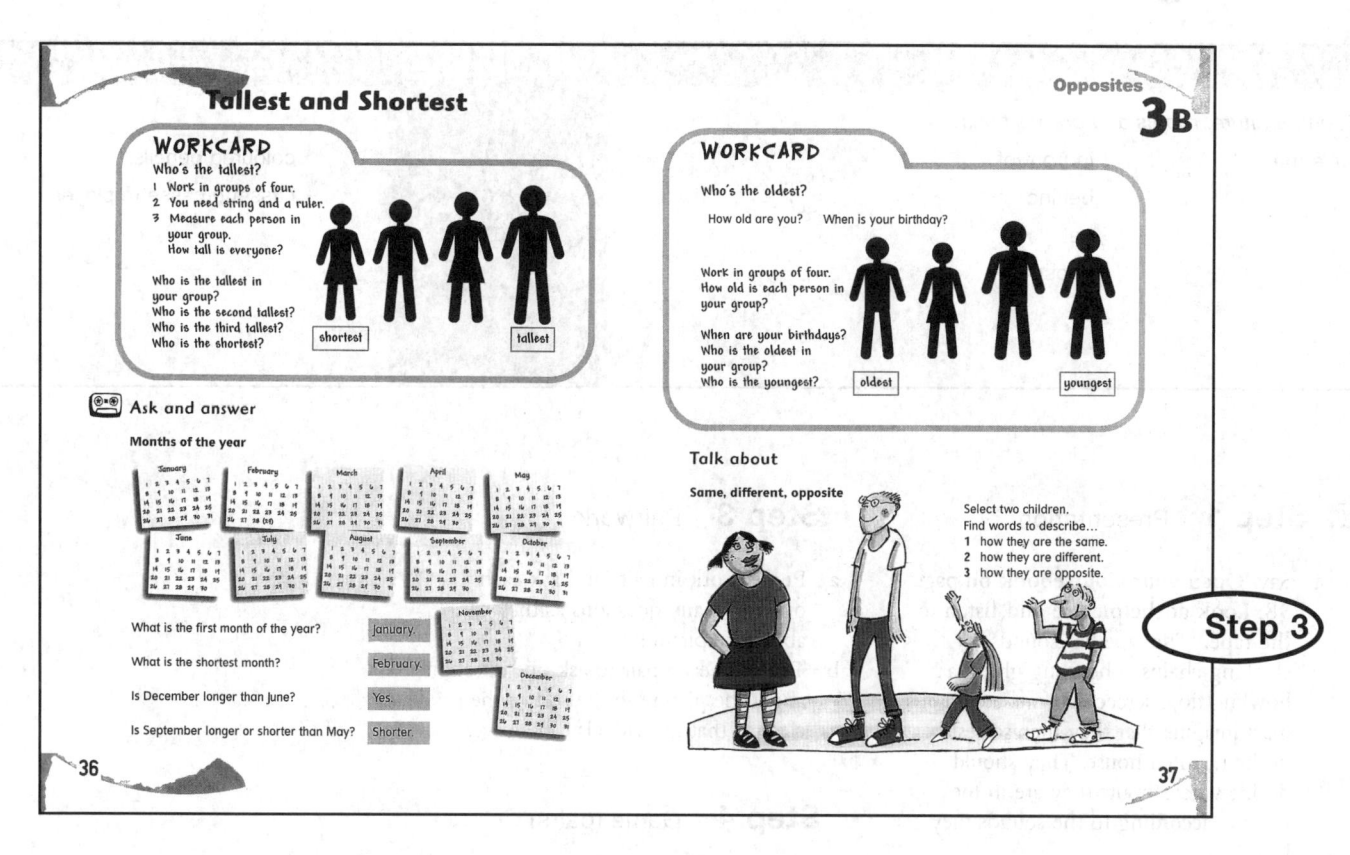

Tallest and Shortest

3B Opposites

WORKCARD
Who's the tallest?
1. Work in groups of four.
2. You need string and a ruler.
3. Measure each person in your group.
   How tall is everyone?

Who is the tallest in your group?
Who is the second tallest?
Who is the third tallest?
Who is the shortest?

shortest   tallest

WORKCARD
Who's the oldest?
How old are you?   When is your birthday?

Work in groups of four.
How old is each person in your group?

When are your birthdays?
Who is the oldest in your group?
Who is the youngest?

oldest   youngest

Ask and answer

Months of the year

What is the first month of the year? — January.
What is the shortest month? — February.
Is December longer than June? — Yes.
Is September longer or shorter than May? — Shorter.

Talk about

Same, different, opposite

Select two children.
Find words to describe…
1. how they are the same.
2. how they are different.
3. how they are opposite.

Step 3

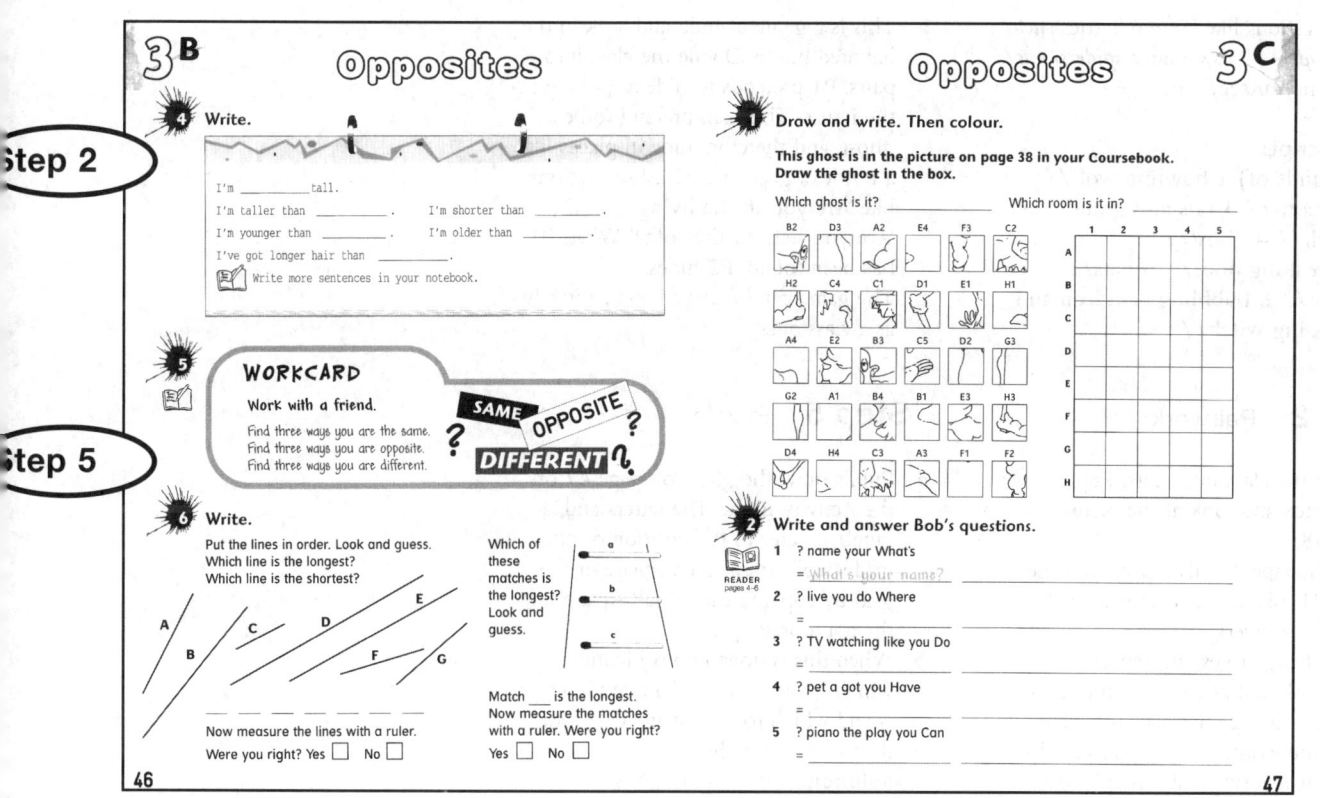

3B Opposites

4 Write.

I'm _____ tall.
I'm taller than _____ .   I'm shorter than _____ .
I'm younger than _____ .   I'm older than _____ .
I've got longer hair than _____ .
Write more sentences in your notebook.

Step 2

5 **WORKCARD**
Work with a friend.
Find three ways you are the same.
Find three ways you are opposite.
Find three ways you are different.

SAME OPPOSITE DIFFERENT

Step 5

6 Write.
Put the lines in order. Look and guess.
Which line is the longest?
Which line is the shortest?

A B C D E F G

Now measure the lines with a ruler.
Were you right? Yes ☐ No ☐

Which of these matches is the longest?
Look and guess.

a b c

Match ___ is the longest.
Now measure the matches with a ruler. Were you right?
Yes ☐ No ☐

Opposites 3C

1 Draw and write. Then colour.

This ghost is in the picture on page 38 in your Coursebook.
Draw the ghost in the box.

Which ghost is it? _____   Which room is it in? _____

	B2	D3	A2	E4	F3	C2
H2	C4	C1	D1	E1	H1
A4	E2	B3	C5	D2	G3
G2	A1	B4	B1	E3	H3
D4	H4	C3	A3	F1	F2

	1	2	3	4	5
A					
B					
C					
D					
E					
F					
G					
H					

2 Write and answer Bob's questions.

1 ? name your What's
  = What's your name? _____
2 ? live you do Where
  = _____
3 ? TV watching like you Do
  = _____
4 ? pet a got you Have
  = _____
5 ? piano the play you Can
  = _____

46   47

105

3c Lesson 1

Main Language Items	Resource File	Materials Needed
Revision: furniture, rooms and prepositions Where's the … ? in front of behind bat ghost	24 27 41	coloured pencils cassette/cassette player

Step 1 Presentation

a Say 'Open your Coursebook on page 38. Look at the picture and listen to the tape.' The tape has sounds of clanking chains, a howling ghost, a howling dog, screeching rats etc. Pupils must imagine that they themselves are in the haunted house. They should decide whereabouts they are in the picture, according to the sounds they hear.

b Ask questions like 'Where's the *witch/bed/spider?*', 'How many *spiders/rats/bats* can you see?' etc.

Tapescript:
(Sounds of) 1 howling wolf//
2 chains// 3 rats and grandfather clock// 4 ghost//
5 creaking door// 6 bats//
7 cat// 8 bubbling cauldron and cackling witch//

Step 2 Pairwork

a Divide the class into pairs. Pupils cover the words and look at the picture on page 38.
b Play the tape. Pupils repeat after the tape. P1 asks the questions after the tape. P2 answers.
c They change roles and repeat.
d Pupils ask and answer the questions without the tape. P1 asks the questions using the words in the book to help. P2 answers using only the pictures.

Step 3 Pairwork

a Pupils work in pairs and ask each other as many questions as they can about the picture.
b Then ask each pair to ask one question about the picture to the rest of the class so that individuals can answer.

Step 4 Game (pairs)

a This is a game of hide-and-seek in the haunted house. Divide the class into pairs. P1 pretends to hide anywhere in the house. They can pretend to be a ghost, and therefore hide in places like a bottle, a glass etc. P2 asks questions like 'Are you in the living room?', 'Are you behind the sofa?' When P1 has been found, P2 hides.
b The game can be played competitively as a class quiz.

Step 5 Puzzle

a Pupils draw the ghost on page 47 of the Activity Book. The letters and numbers refer to the position on the grid. Pupils fill in each square of the grid by copying each small square into the appropriate place.
b When this is done pupils identify which ghost from the haunted house it is and which room it is in. They can then colour the ghost.
Solution: It is the pink ghost in the kitchen.

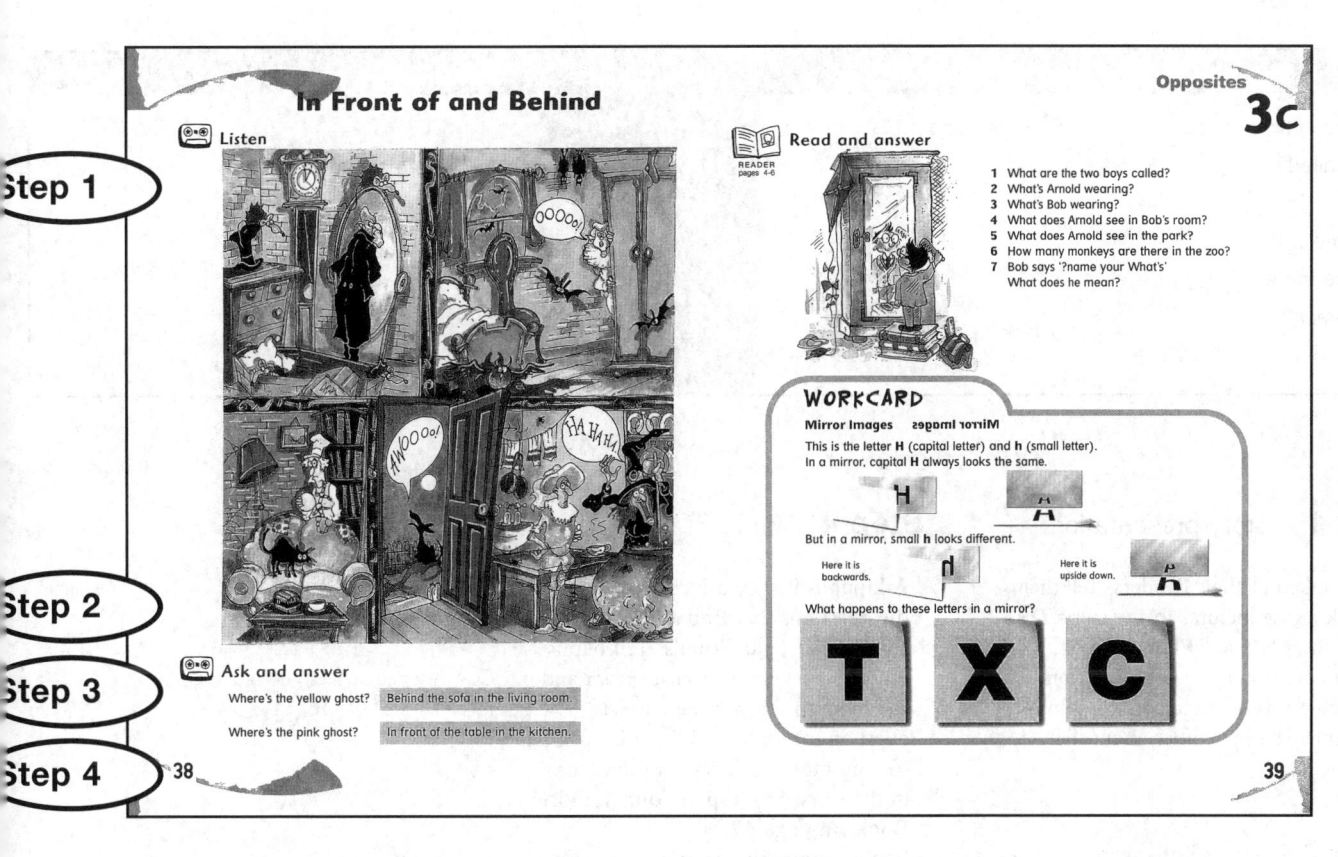

In Front of and Behind

Step 1

Listen

Ask and answer

Where's the yellow ghost? — Behind the sofa in the living room.

Where's the pink ghost? — In front of the table in the kitchen.

Step 2
Step 3
Step 4

38

Opposites 3c

Read and answer

READER pages 4-6

1 What are the two boys called?
2 What's Arnold wearing?
3 What's Bob wearing?
4 What does Arnold see in Bob's room?
5 What does Arnold see in the park?
6 How many monkeys are there in the zoo?
7 Bob says '?name your What's'
   What does he mean?

WORKCARD

Mirror Images   Mirror Images

This is the letter **H** (capital letter) and **h** (small letter).
In a mirror, capital **H** always looks the same.

But in a mirror, small **h** looks different.

Here it is backwards.   Here it is upside down.

What happens to these letters in a mirror?

T   X   C

39

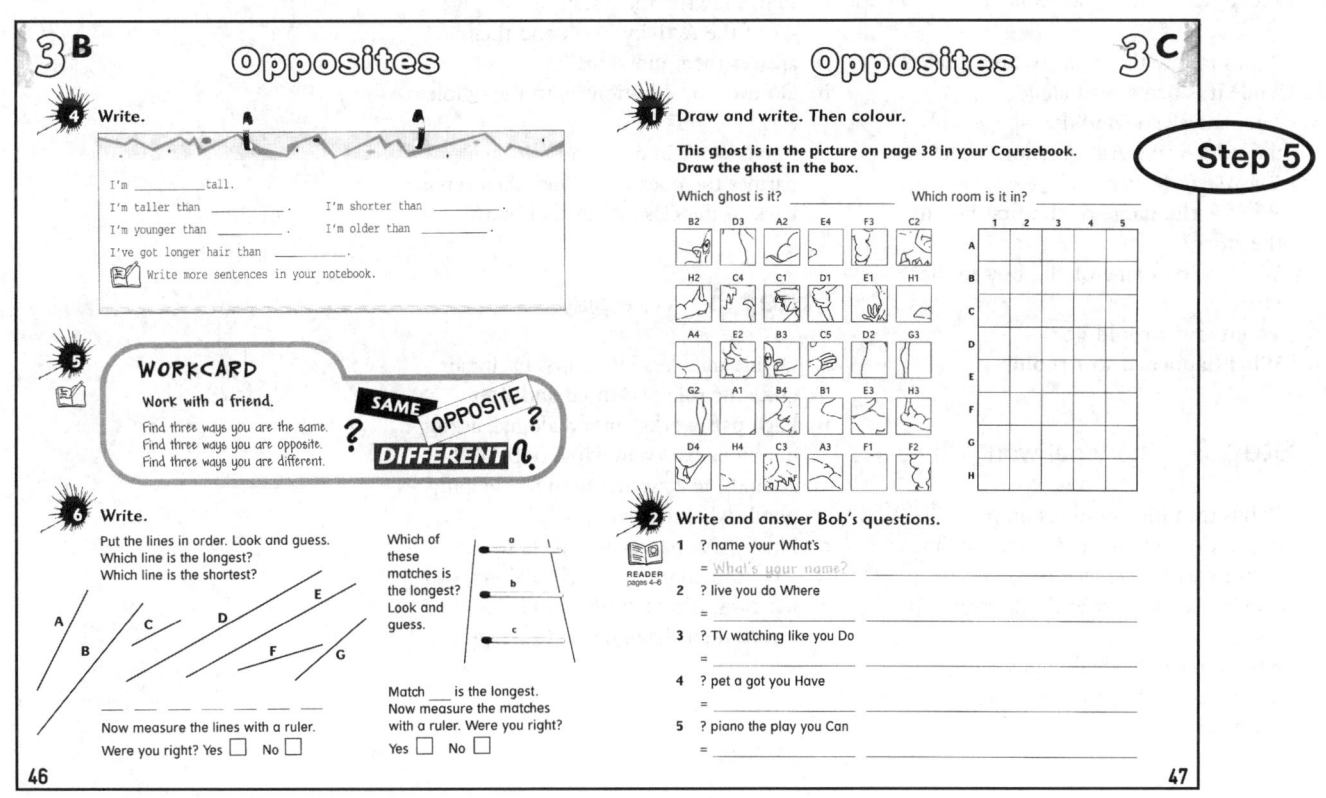

3B Opposites

4 Write.

I'm _____ tall.
I'm taller than _____.   I'm shorter than _____.
I'm younger than _____.   I'm older than _____.
I've got longer hair than _____.
Write more sentences in your notebook.

5 WORKCARD

Work with a friend.
Find three ways you are the same.
Find three ways you are opposite.
Find three ways you are different.

SAME OPPOSITE DIFFERENT

6 Write.

Put the lines in order. Look and guess.
Which line is the longest?
Which line is the shortest?

A B C D E F G

Now measure the lines with a ruler.
Were you right? Yes ☐ No ☐

Which of these matches is the longest? Look and guess.

a b c

Match ___ is the longest.
Now measure the matches with a ruler. Were you right?
Yes ☐ No ☐

46

Opposites 3c

1 Draw and write. Then colour.

This ghost is in the picture on page 38 in your Coursebook.
Draw the ghost in the box.

Which ghost is it? _____   Which room is it in? _____

B2 D3 A2 E4 F3 C2
H2 C4 C1 D1 E1 H1
A4 E2 B3 C5 D2 G3
G2 A1 B4 B1 E3 H3
D4 H4 C3 A3 F1 F2

	1	2	3	4	5
A					
B					
C					
D					
E					
F					
G					
H					

Step 5

2 Write and answer Bob's questions.

READER pages 4-6

1 ? name your What's
   = What's your name? _____
2 ? live you do Where
   = _____
3 ? TV watching like you Do
   = _____
4 ? pet a got you Have
   = _____
5 ? piano the play you Can
   = _____

47

3c Lesson 2

Main Language Items	Resource File	Materials Needed
Revision: question forms *Story revision* What are they called? What's he wearing? What does he see ... ? How many ... are there? What does he mean?	41 52	cassette/cassette player Reader

Step 1   Story presentation

Pupils take out their Readers. Tell them to look at the pictures in the story *The Magic Mirror*. Ask '**What can you see?**' Elicit as much vocabulary from the pictures as possible and ask pupils what they can remember about the story.

Step 2   Story listening

Pupils follow the story in their Reader while it is being read aloud. Alternatively, rewind the tape and play the story again. Ask questions about *The Magic Mirror* e.g.
What is the name of the first boy in the story?
What is the name of the boy in the mirror?
Where did Arnold go?
What happened to Arnold?

Step 3   Story pairwork

a   Pupils read the questions on page 39 of the Coursebook and work out the answers with reference to the Reader.
b   Pupils ask and answer the questions in pairs.
c   Finally ask individual pupils the questions. Discuss the answers if necessary.

Step 4   Write

Ask pupils if they can remember any of the questions that Bob asked Arnold. e.g. '?name your What's' Tell pupils that the question is back-to-front and ask them to tell you the correct question in English. Tell pupils to look for any other back-to-front questions in the story. Say '**Open your Activity Book on page 47.**'

a   Pupils rewrite the questions on page 47 of the Activity Book and then answer them individually.
b   Go over the questions with the whole class.
c   Pupils work in pairs and ask their partner the questions. They then report back to the class about their partner.

Step 5   Role play

a   Divide the class into pairs. Each pair takes the role of Arnold and Bob.
b   Each pair works out a dialogue, asking questions backwards like Bob. Walk around the class and monitor, helping pupils when necessary.
c   Finally, ask one or two pairs to volunteer to present their dialogues to the class. Alternatively, pupils can record their dialogues onto a tape.

In Front of and Behind

Listen

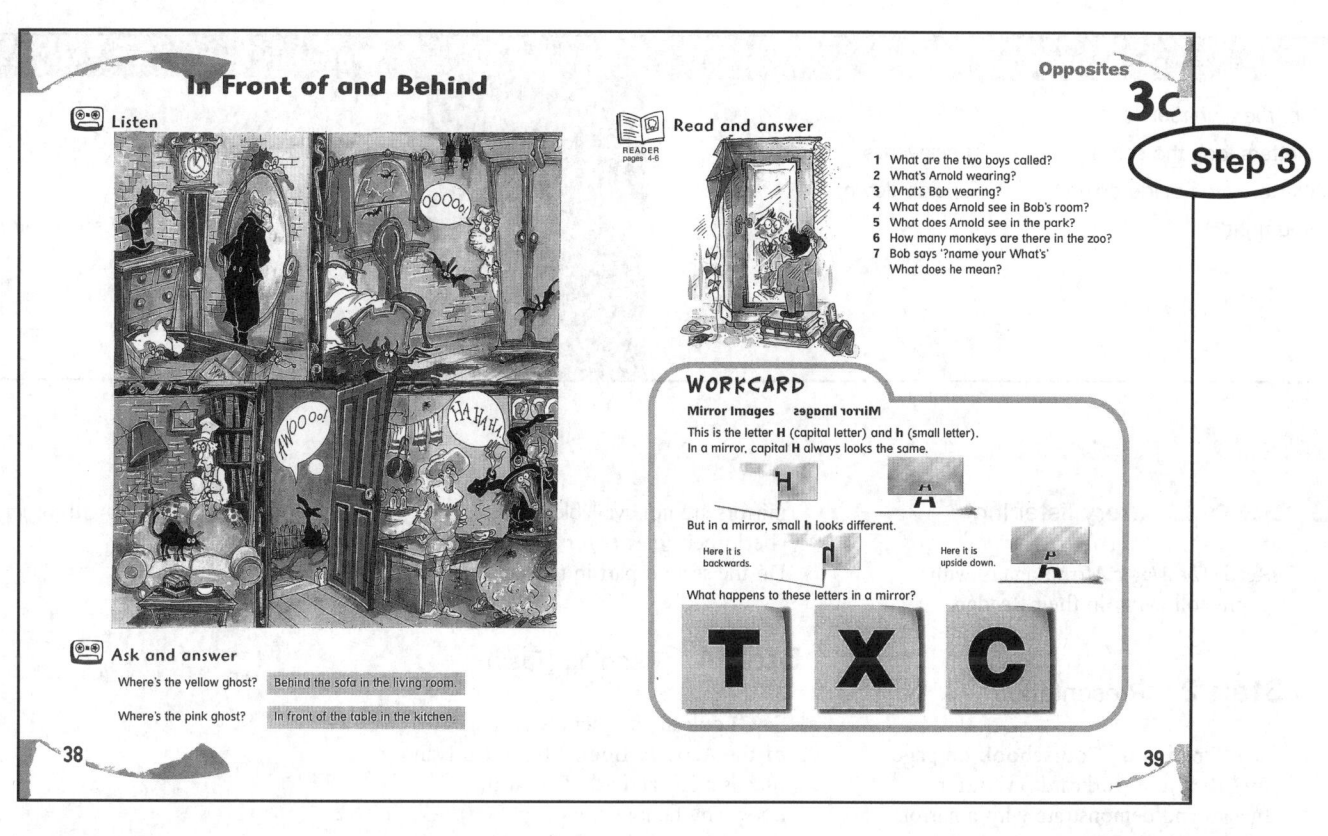

Ask and answer
- Where's the yellow ghost? — Behind the sofa in the living room.
- Where's the pink ghost? — In front of the table in the kitchen.

38

3c Opposites

Read and answer
READER pages 4-6

1. What are the two boys called?
2. What's Arnold wearing?
3. What's Bob wearing?
4. What does Arnold see in Bob's room?
5. What does Arnold see in the park?
6. How many monkeys are there in the zoo?
7. Bob says '?name your What's' What does he mean?

Step 3

WORKCARD

Mirror Images   *Mirror Images*

This is the letter **H** (capital letter) and **h** (small letter).
In a mirror, capital **H** always looks the same.

But in a mirror, small **h** looks different.
Here it is backwards.   Here it is upside down.

What happens to these letters in a mirror?

T   X   C

39

3B Opposites

4 Write.

I'm _____ tall.
I'm taller than _____ .   I'm shorter than _____ .
I'm younger than _____ . I'm older than _____ .
I've got longer hair than _____ .
Write more sentences in your notebook.

5 WORKCARD

Work with a friend.
Find three ways you are the same.
Find three ways you are opposite.
Find three ways you are different.

SAME   OPPOSITE   DIFFERENT

6 Write.

Put the lines in order. Look and guess.
Which line is the longest?
Which line is the shortest?

A B C D E F G

_____
Now measure the lines with a ruler.
Were you right? Yes ☐ No ☐

Which of these matches is the longest? Look and guess.

a b c

Match ___ is the longest.
Now measure the matches with a ruler. Were you right?
Yes ☐ No ☐

46

3C Opposites

1 Draw and write. Then colour.

This ghost is in the picture on page 38 in your Coursebook.
Draw the ghost in the box.

Which ghost is it? _____   Which room is it in? _____

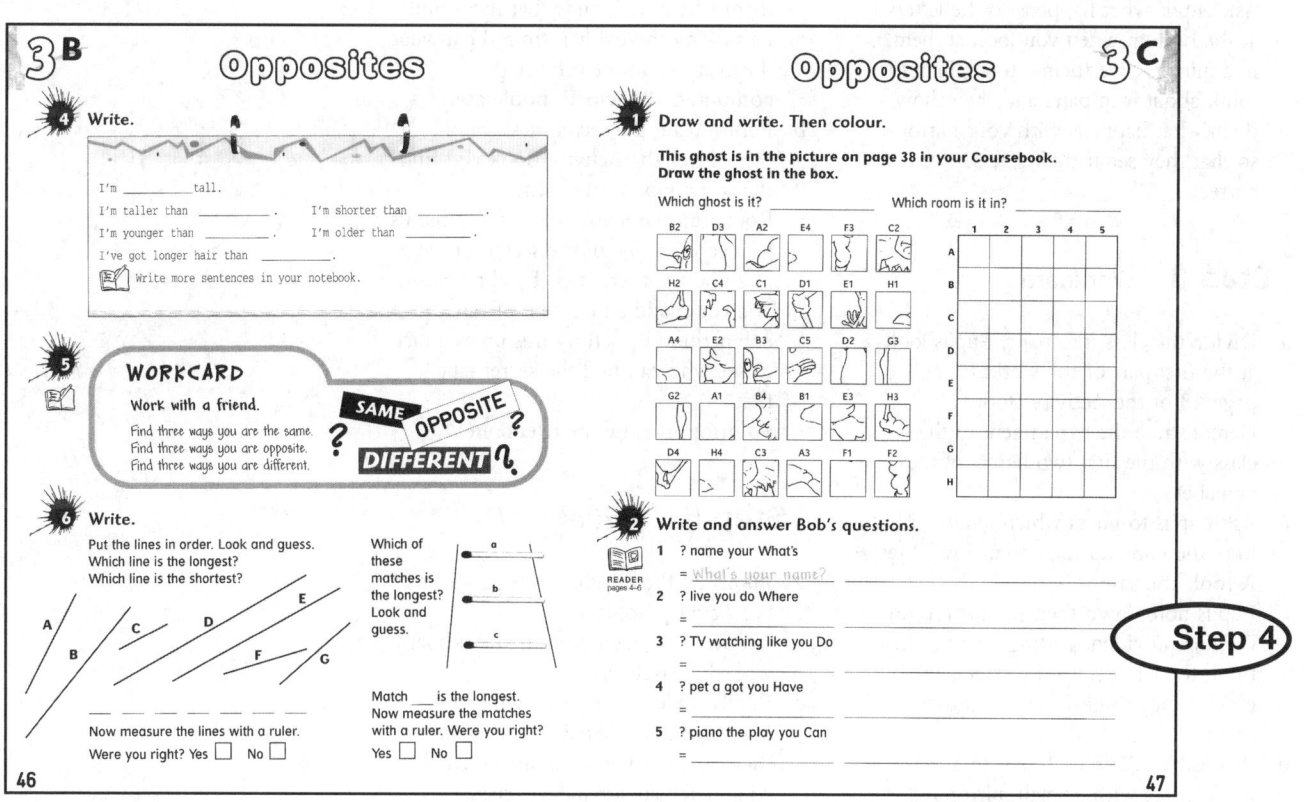

B2 D3 A2 E4 F3 C2
H2 C4 C1 D1 E1 H1
A4 E2 B3 C5 D2 G3
G2 A1 B4 B1 E3 H3
D4 H4 C3 A3 F1 F2

	1	2	3	4	5
A					
B					
C					
D					
E					
F					
G					
H					

2 Write and answer Bob's questions.
READER pages 4-6

1 ? name your What's
   = What's your name? _____
2 ? live you do Where
   = _____
3 ? TV watching like you Do
   = _____
4 ? pet a got you Have
   = _____
5 ? piano the play you Can
   = _____

Step 4

47

3c Lesson 3

Main Language Items		Resource File	Materials Needed
Revision: the alphabet		18	cassette/cassette player
Which letters look the same?	backwards	43	Reader
Which letters are upside down?	upside down	48	large mirror or a number of small mirrors
Were you right?		51	

Step 1 Story listening

Read *The Magic Mirror* again, with pupils following in their Readers.

Step 2 Presentation

Say 'Open your Coursebook on page 39.' Read the workcard on Mirror Images and demonstrate with a mirror. Ask pupils what happens to the letters at the bottom when you look at them in a mirror. Give them a few minutes to think about it in pairs and then show them what happens with your mirror so that they see if their guesses were correct.

Step 3 Workcard

a Divide the class into pairs. Pupils look at the first part of the workcard on page 48 of the Activity Book. Demonstrate the experiment to the class with the first two letters of the alphabet.
b Ask pupils to guess which letters still look the same upside down. Say '**Does A look the same?**' etc.
c Pupils note down their predictions on the line provided, putting a tick if they think the letter stays the same and a cross if they think it will be upside down.
d If possible, allow each pair to check the answers with a small mirror. If mirrors are not available, pupils can check their guesses for homework.
e Do the second part in the same way.

Step 4 Reading (Task)

a Say 'Look at the picture on page 49 of the Activity Book.' Tell them Ivan Idea is a spy and ask them if they know any famous spies (e.g. 007). Ask them where he is and what they think he's doing there. Elicit from them what they can see in the office e.g. **computer, rug, clock, bookcase.**
b Pupils 'read' the secret message on page 49 of the Activity Book and find the secret tape for Ivan Idea.
c Round up the mystery by asking pupils to read each line of the secret message and find the secret tape by elimination. You could add an element of fun and competition by setting this up as a race to see who can find the secret tape first.
Solution: It is by the telephone.

Step 5 Puzzles

a Pupils do the puzzles on page 49 of the Activity Book.
b Go over the puzzles on the blackboard with the whole class.
c Pupils could make their own puzzles like the one in exercise 5 and give them to a partner to complete. Or they could circulate around the class, exchanging puzzles with other class members.

In Front of and Behind

Listen

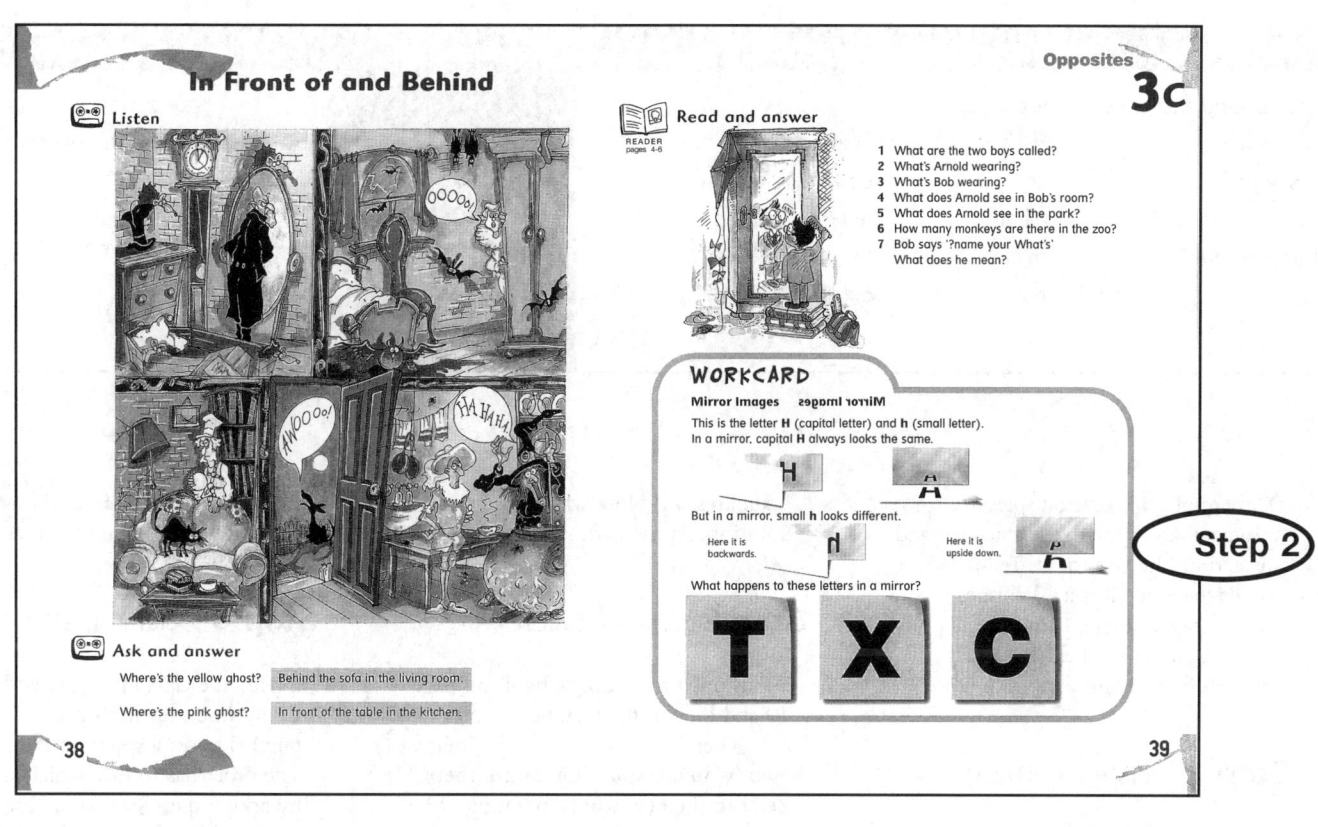

Ask and answer

Where's the yellow ghost? — Behind the sofa in the living room.

Where's the pink ghost? — In front of the table in the kitchen.

Opposites 3c

Read and answer

READER pages 4-6

1. What are the two boys called?
2. What's Arnold wearing?
3. What's Bob wearing?
4. What does Arnold see in Bob's room?
5. What does Arnold see in the park?
6. How many monkeys are there in the zoo?
7. Bob says '?name your What's' What does he mean?

WORKCARD

Mirror Images

This is the letter **H** (capital letter) and **h** (small letter).
In a mirror, capital **H** always looks the same.

But in a mirror, small **h** looks different.

Here it is backwards.   Here it is upside down.

What happens to these letters in a mirror?

T   X   C

Step 2

Opposites 3c

WORKCARD

ABCDEFGHIJKLMN
OPQRSTUVWXYZ

A Look at these letters in the mirror.

A|A
A B

The letter **A** is upside down.
The letter **B** is the same.

What happens to the other letters of the alphabet?

1. GUESS – Which letters do you **think** look the same?
2. CHECK – Now look in a mirror. Were you right?

	A	B	C	D	E	F	G	H	I	J	K	L	M	N	O	P	Q	R	S	T	U	V	W	X	Y	Z
GUESS																										
CHECK																										

B Look at these letters in the mirror.

AB

The letter **A** looks the same.
The letter **B** is backwards.

What happens to the other letters of the alphabet?

1. GUESS – Which letters do you **think** look the same?
2. CHECK – Now look in a mirror. Were you right?

	A	B	C	D	E	F	G	H	I	J	K	L	M	N	O	P	Q	R	S	T	U	V	W	X	Y	Z
GUESS																										
CHECK																										

C What happens to small letters and numbers in a mirror?

Step 3

Opposites 3c

Read and find. Then write.

Ivan Idea is a spy. Help him find the secret tape. It's _____

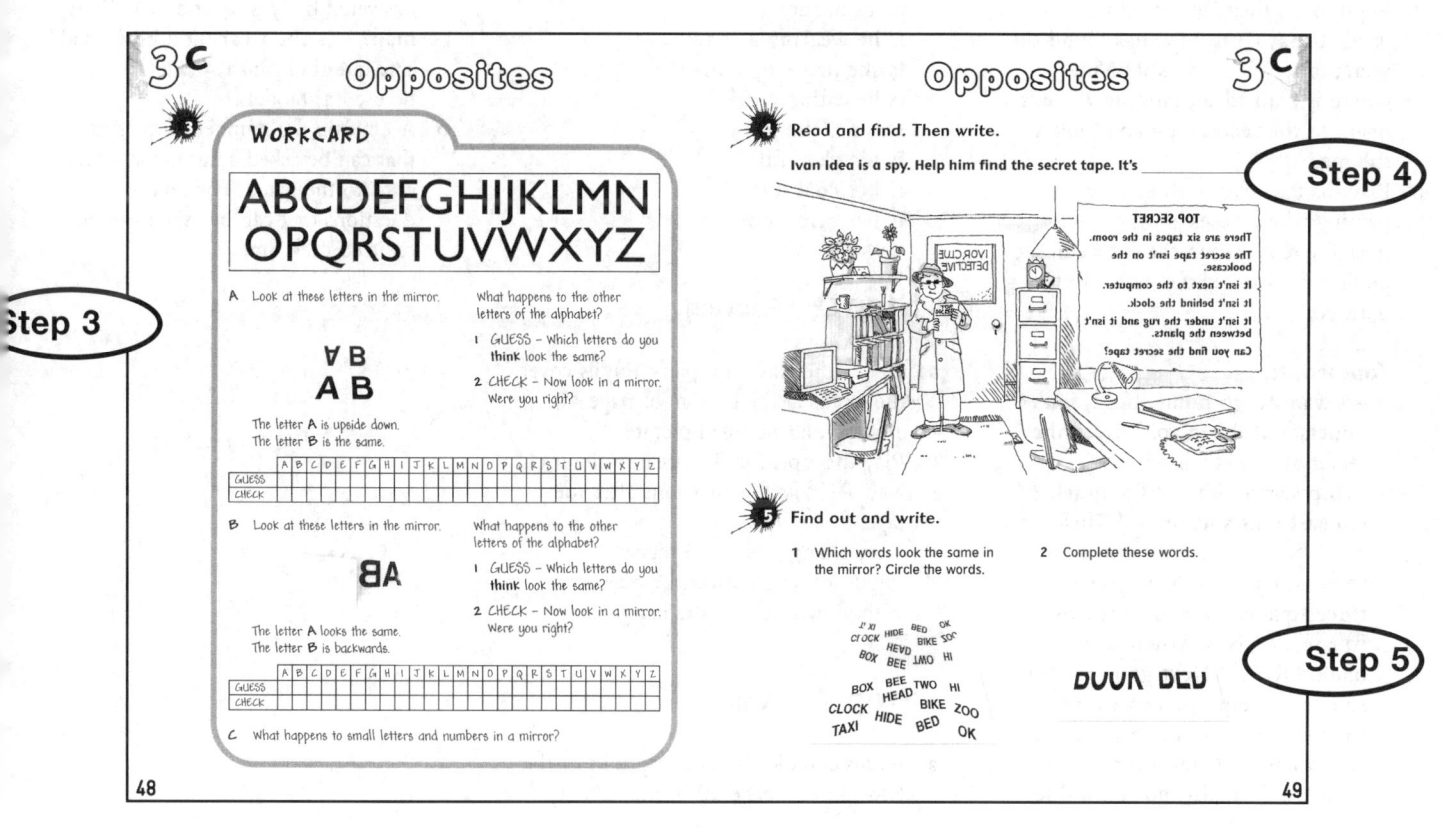

TOP SECRET
There are six tapes in the room.
The secret tape isn't on the bookcase.
It isn't next to the computer.
It isn't behind the clock.
It isn't under the rug and it isn't between the plants.
Can you find the secret tape?

Step 4

Find out and write.

1. Which words look the same in the mirror? Circle the words.

   BOX BEE TWO HI
   CLOCK HEAD BIKE ZOO
   TAXI HIDE BED OK

2. Complete these words.

   DOOR BED

Step 5

3D Lesson 1

Main Language Items			Resource File	Materials Needed
Revision: building and physical descriptions			18	cassette/cassette player
Is he/she wearing … ?	full	empty	27	
Has he/she got … ?	light	dark	41	
Is he/she drinking … ?	clean	dirty	51	
Is his/her glass *full*?	thick	thin		
	hot	cold		

Throughout this unit on spies, try to create an atmosphere of excitement and mystery in the classroom. Tell the pupils they are all spies. Whisper instructions to them. Bring instructions out of secret envelopes. (Even disguise yourself by wearing dark glasses!)

Step 1   Listening (Task)

a   Pupils open their Activity Books on page 50. Say 'Ivan Idea has found the secret tape. Where was it? Now where is Ivan Idea going next? Let's listen to the secret tape and look at the map.'

b   Play the tape two or three times, pausing where necessary for pupils to trace the route. Then check that all the pupils have worked out where Ivan must go.

Tapescript:
   – I want to go home, but I don't understand this map. Ah yes, the secret tape. Let's listen …
   – Top secret. Start at the hotel. // Go east four squares. // Then go north four squares // and west three squares. // Now go south three squares // and west two squares. // Now you're at the bank. OK? // Next go north two squares // and then east three squares. // From there go north two squares // and then east one square. // Finally, go south three squares. // Now where are you?
Solution: At the cafe.

Step 2   Presentation

Pupils open their Coursebook on page 40 and look at the pictures of spies. Ask general questions e.g. 'How many men/women/spies/tables are there?' Refer to the new words, pointing at particular spies:
Is he wearing a coat?
Is she drinking coffee?
Is he eating a cake?
Has he/she got …?
Is his glass full?
Is her coat dirty?
Is her drink hot? etc.

Step 3   Pairwork

a   Divide the class into pairs. Pupils cover the words at the bottom of page 40 and look at the small picture.
b   Play the tape. Pupils repeat in the usual way: P1 asks the questions after the tape. P2 answers.
c   They change roles and repeat.
d   Pupils ask and answer the questions without the help of the tape.

Step 4   Write

a   Pupils complete the descriptions of the two spies on page 50 of the Activity Book, using words from the box.
b   Go over the exercise with the class.

Step 5   Game (pairs)

a   Divide the class into pairs with the Coursebook open on page 40. One pupil chooses a spy from the picture. The other has to find which spy it is by asking questions which can only be answered by 'yes' or 'no', e.g. 'Is it a man?', 'Is she wearing a blue coat?' The questions in the Coursebook can be used as models.
b   A limit on the number of questions that can be asked adds a competitive edge to the game. The number of questions that can be asked can be reduced each time.

Inside and Outside

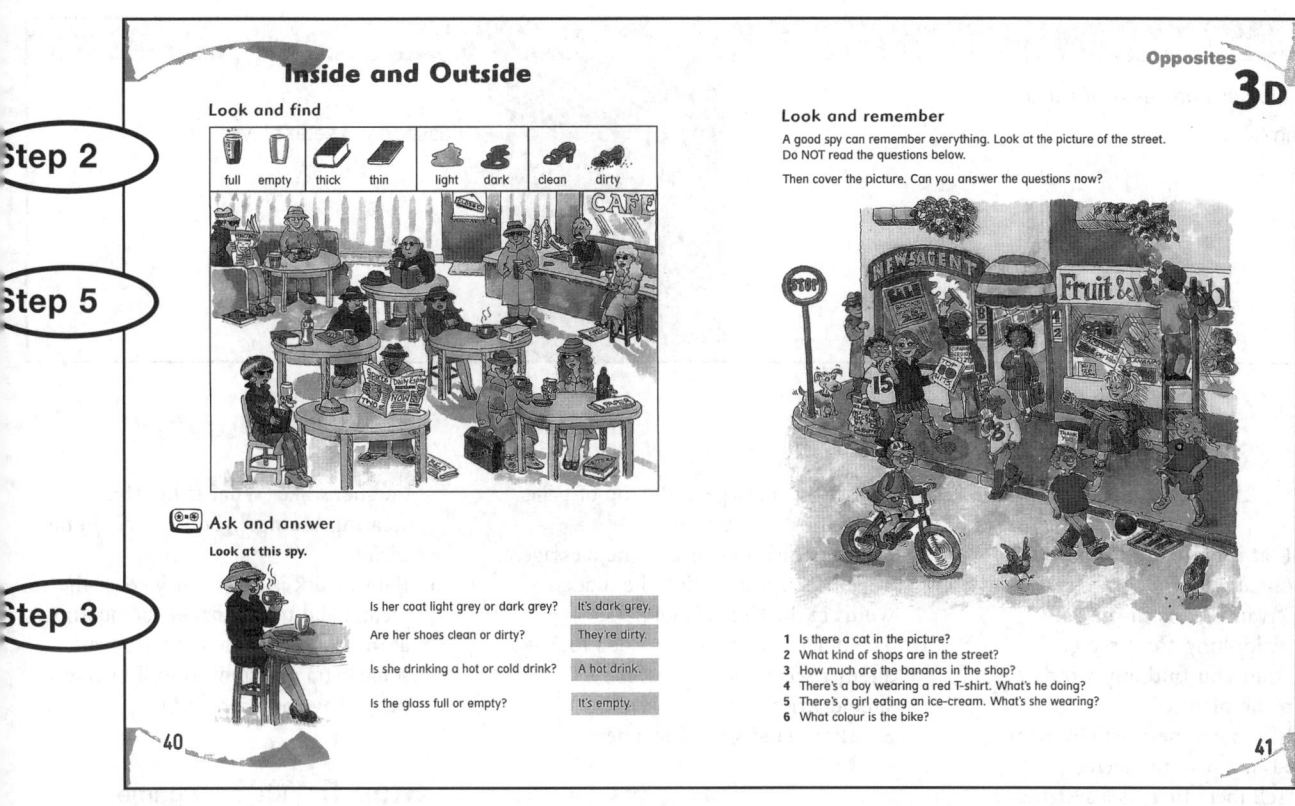

Look and find

full | empty | thick | thin | light | dark | clean | dirty

Ask and answer

Look at this spy.

Is her coat light grey or dark grey?	It's dark grey.
Are her shoes clean or dirty?	They're dirty.
Is she drinking a hot or cold drink?	A hot drink.
Is the glass full or empty?	It's empty.

40

Opposites 3D

Look and remember

A good spy can remember everything. Look at the picture of the street. Do NOT read the questions below.

Then cover the picture. Can you answer the questions now?

1. Is there a cat in the picture?
2. What kind of shops are in the street?
3. How much are the bananas in the shop?
4. There's a boy wearing a red T-shirt. What's he doing?
5. There's a girl eating an ice-cream. What's she wearing?
6. What colour is the bike?

41

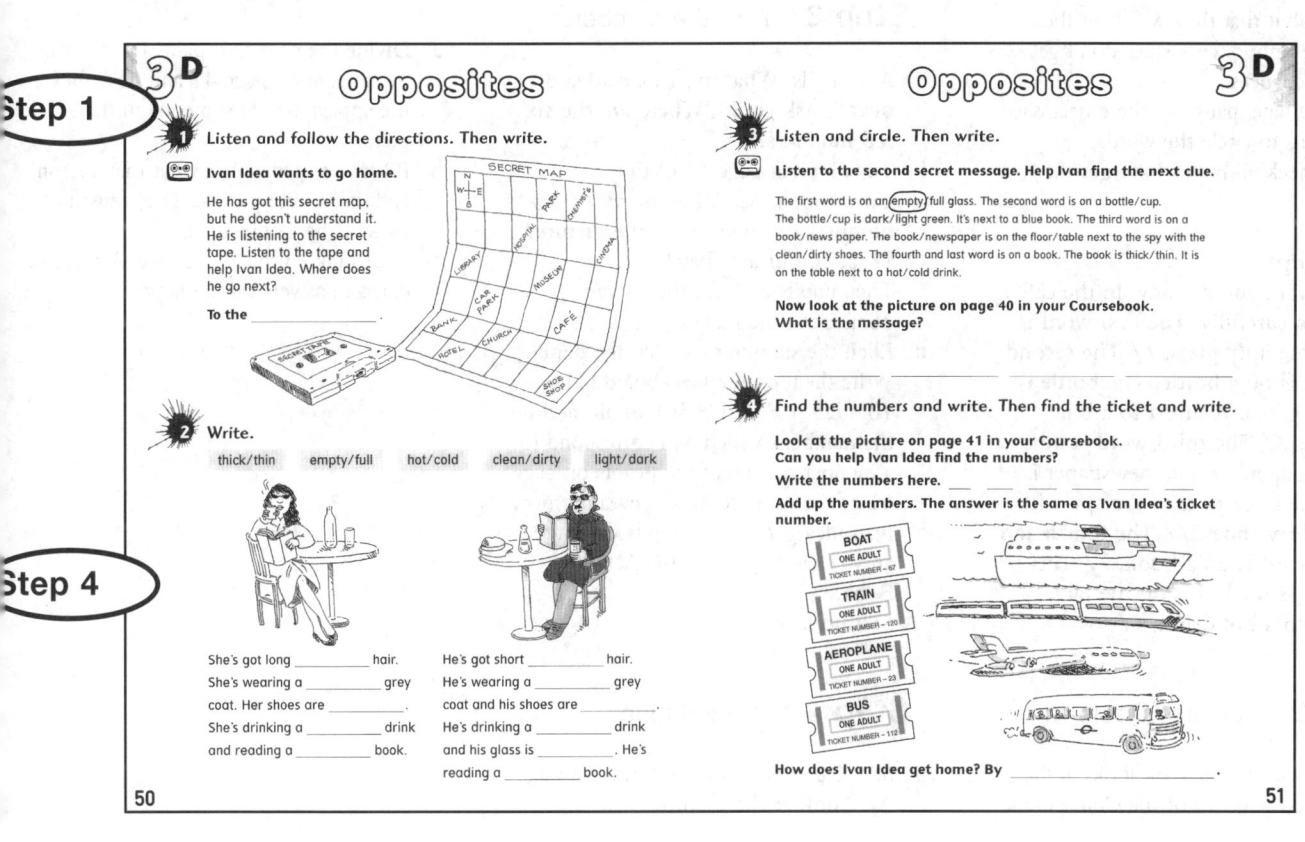

3D Opposites

1 Listen and follow the directions. Then write.

Ivan Idea wants to go home.

He has got this secret map, but he doesn't understand it. He is listening to the secret tape. Listen to the tape and help Ivan Idea. Where does he go next?

To the _____

2 Write.

thick/thin   empty/full   hot/cold   clean/dirty   light/dark

She's got long _____ hair.
She's wearing a _____ grey coat. Her shoes are _____.
She's drinking a _____ drink and reading a _____ book.

He's got short _____ hair.
He's wearing a _____ grey coat and his shoes are _____.
He's drinking a _____ drink and his glass is _____. He's reading a _____ book.

50

Opposites 3D

3 Listen and circle. Then write.

Listen to the second secret message. Help Ivan find the next clue.

The first word is on an (empty)/full glass. The second word is on a bottle/cup. The bottle/cup is dark/light green. It's next to a blue book. The third word is on a book/news paper. The book/newspaper is on the floor/table next to the spy with the clean/dirty shoes. The fourth and last word is on a book. The book is thick/thin. It is on the table next to a hot/cold drink.

Now look at the picture on page 40 in your Coursebook.
What is the message?

_____

4 Find the numbers and write. Then find the ticket and write.

Look at the picture on page 41 in your Coursebook.
Can you help Ivan Idea find the numbers?
Write the numbers here. ____ ____ ____ ____
Add up the numbers. The answer is the same as Ivan Idea's ticket number.

BOAT ONE ADULT TICKET NUMBER – 67
TRAIN ONE ADULT TICKET NUMBER – 120
AEROPLANE ONE ADULT TICKET NUMBER – 23
BUS ONE ADULT TICKET NUMBER – 112

How does Ivan Idea get home? By _____.

51

3D Lesson 2

Main Language Items	Resource File	Materials Needed
Revision: vehicles, clothes and verbs of action What's he/she doing? What's he/she wearing?	18 27 41a 41b	cassette/cassette player

Step 1   Listening (Task)

a   Say '**Look at the picture on page 40 of the Coursebook.**'
b   Then say '**Ivan Idea is in the cafe now. He is looking for a secret message. Can you find any words hidden in the picture?**'
c   Tell pupils to open their Activity Book on page 51 and read the secret message. Tell them there is a secret tape to help, but that they will hear the message only once – spies don't get second chances.
d   Play the tape, pausing where necessary for pupils to circle the words.
e   Then check all pupils have got the message.

Tapescript:
Yes Ivan, you are now in the cafe. Listen carefully. The first word is on an empty glass. // The second word is on a bottle. The bottle is light green. It's next to a blue book. // The third word is on a newspaper. // The newspaper is on the floor next to the spy with the dirty shoes. // The fourth and last word is on a book. // The book is thick. It's on the table next to a hot drink. //

Step 2   Reading (Task)

a   Pupils work in pairs. P1 looks at the picture on page 40 of the Coursebook. P2 has the message at the top of page 51 of the Activity Book.
b   P2 reads each sentence of the message. Together they must find the hidden words in the Coursebook.
c   The hidden words are revealed to make another secret message, which P1 should write out.
Solution: Find six red numbers.

Step 3   Find the numbers

a   Ask pupils '**What must Ivan Idea do next?**' Ask pupils '**Where are the six red numbers?**'
b   Then look at page 41 of the Coursebook. Ask '**How many numbers can you see in the picture? What colour are they?**'
c   Then pupils look for the six red numbers in the picture.
d   Elicit the six numbers from the pupils. Write them on the blackboard (41 + 10 + 25 + 8 + 6 + 30). Pupils add up the numbers, which will correspond to a number on one of the tickets on page 51 of the Activity Book, revealing how Ivan Idea gets home. Pupils write the answer on page 51 of the Activity Book.
Solution: By train

Step 4   Presentation

a   Say '**Open your Coursebook on page 41. Look at the picture.**' Ask questions like '**What is he/she wearing/doing?**' about people in the picture.
b   Pupils work in pairs. They cover the picture and try to answer the questions at the bottom of the page. (Prepare some extra questions as well in case pupils have been practising!)

Step 5   Memory game

a   Divide the class into pairs. P1 looks at the picture on page 41 and describes the appearance of someone in the picture.
b   P2 tries to remember what that person is doing in the picture. They must not look at the Coursebook.
c   Pupils take turns to describe. A score of correct answers can be kept.

Inside and Outside

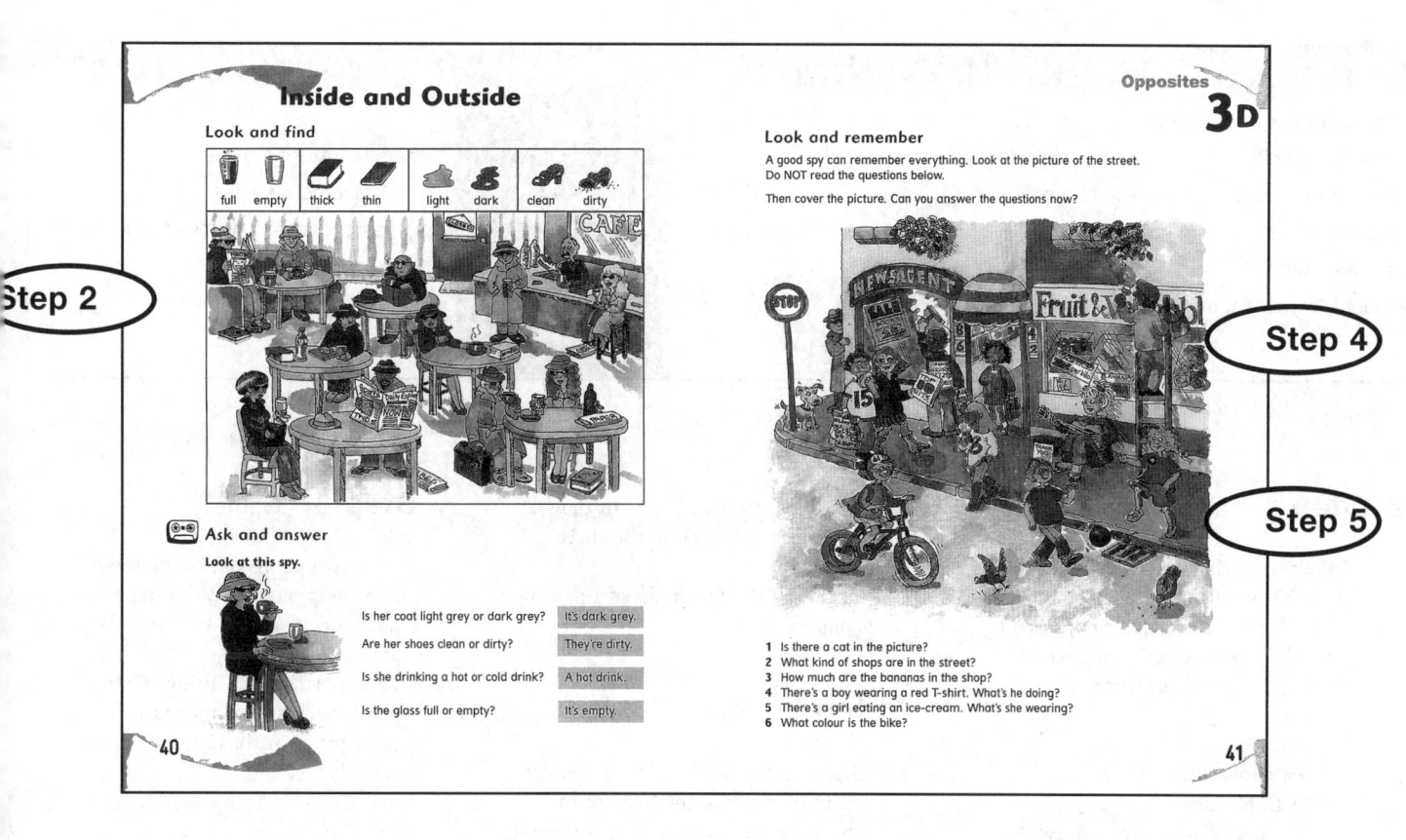

Look and find

full empty thick thin light dark clean dirty

Ask and answer

Look at this spy.

Is her coat light grey or dark grey?	It's dark grey.
Are her shoes clean or dirty?	They're dirty.
Is she drinking a hot or cold drink?	A hot drink.
Is the glass full or empty?	It's empty.

40

Opposites 3D

Look and remember

A good spy can remember everything. Look at the picture of the street. Do NOT read the questions below.

Then cover the picture. Can you answer the questions now?

1. Is there a cat in the picture?
2. What kind of shops are in the street?
3. How much are the bananas in the shop?
4. There's a boy wearing a red T-shirt. What's he doing?
5. There's a girl eating an ice-cream. What's she wearing?
6. What colour is the bike?

41

3D Opposites

1 Listen and follow the directions. Then write.

Ivan Idea wants to go home.

He has got this secret map, but he doesn't understand it. He is listening to the secret tape. Listen to the tape and help Ivan Idea. Where does he go next?

To the _____

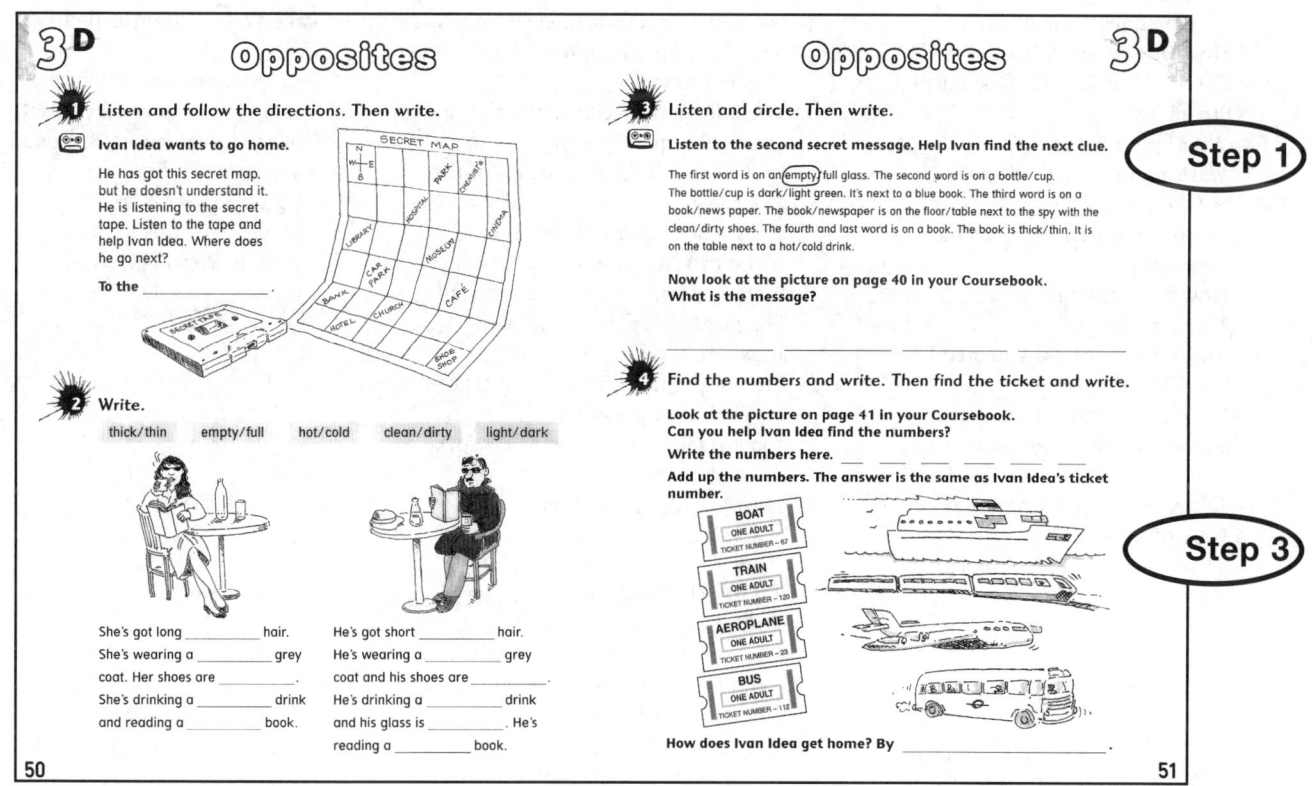

2 Write.

thick/thin   empty/full   hot/cold   clean/dirty   light/dark

She's got long _____ hair.
She's wearing a _____ grey coat. Her shoes are _____.
She's drinking a _____ drink and reading a _____ book.

He's got short _____ hair.
He's wearing a _____ grey coat and his shoes are _____.
He's drinking a _____ drink and his glass is _____. He's reading a _____ book.

50

Opposites 3D

3 Listen and circle. Then write.

Listen to the second secret message. Help Ivan find the next clue.

The first word is on an (empty)/full glass. The second word is on a bottle/cup. The bottle/cup is dark/light green. It's next to a blue book. The third word is on a book/news paper. The book/newspaper is on the floor/table next to the spy with the clean/dirty shoes. The fourth and last word is on a book. The book is thick/thin. It is on the table next to a hot/cold drink.

Now look at the picture on page 40 in your Coursebook.
What is the message?

_____ _____ _____ _____

4 Find the numbers and write. Then find the ticket and write.

Look at the picture on page 41 in your Coursebook.
Can you help Ivan Idea find the numbers?
Write the numbers here. ___ ___ ___ ___

Add up the numbers. The answer is the same as Ivan Idea's ticket number.

BOAT ONE ADULT TICKET NUMBER – 67
TRAIN ONE ADULT TICKET NUMBER – 120
AEROPLANE ONE ADULT TICKET NUMBER – 23
BUS ONE ADULT TICKET NUMBER – 112

How does Ivan Idea get home? By _____.

51

115

3D Lesson 3

Main Language Items		Resource File	Materials Needed
Revision: personal information		18	cassette/cassette player
What's your name?	passport	43a	glue/coloured pencils
What's your address?	nationality	64	pupils need small photos of themselves
Where are you from?			
How tall are you?			
How much do you weigh?			

Step 1 Listening (Task)

Pupils open their Activity Books on page 52. Pupils must listen to the tape and fill in the details on the passport. Play the tape as often as necessary, pausing for pupils to write.

Tapescript:
- Passport. Name?
- Ivan O. Idea
- What's your home address?
- 61 Document Street.
- How do you spell 'Document'?
- D-O-C-U-M-E-N-T. Document Street. //
- What town is that in?
- Washington. That's W-A-S-H-I-N-G-T-O-N.
- So you're American, are you?
- That's right. //
- How tall are you?
- 1 metre 86.
- And how much do you weigh?
- 76 Kilos. //
- Let me see. Hair, dark brown and what colour are your eyes?
- Grey. //
- And your passport number?
- IMA 6549302 SPY
- Thank you Mr Idea. You can go. Have a nice day. //

Step 2 Write

a Pupils complete the passport on page 52 of the Activity Book with their own details.

b They should stick a photo or draw a picture of themselves in the space provided.

c **(Optional)** Pupils can make a passport if time permits.

Step 3 Game

a Choose a group of four to six pupils and bring them to the front of the class. Give them a cassette. Let them go out of the class for a moment so that one of the group can hide the cassette on their person.

b When the group returns, the class asks questions requiring a 'yes' or 'no' answer to individual members of the group, e.g.
   Does a boy have the cassette?
   Is the cassette in someone's pocket?
   Is the person with the cassette tall?
   The members of the group must answer truthfully.

c After a specified number of questions, the class must guess who the spy is. You can take a class vote or ask for a show of hands.

d Then play the game in groups of four or six. Each group can take turns playing against another group.

e **(Optional)** The game can be played with one person as 'detective' and the whole class as 'spies'. The detective leaves the room and one pupil takes the tape. Find out who is the best detective – who can find the tape by asking the fewest questions.

Step 4 Game

Send two pupils out of the room. The remaining pupils have to describe, in as much detail as possible, what the two are wearing. Write up the descriptions on the blackboard. Bring the two pupils back and compare the descriptions with what the pupils are actually wearing.

Step 5 Game (I-spy)

In groups of four, pupils play **I-spy**, using the pictures on pages 40 and 41 of the Coursebook. One pupil says '**I spy with my little eye, something beginning with "b".**' The rest of the group take turns to guess what the pupil is referring to. The pupil who guesses correctly 'spies' next.

Inside and Outside

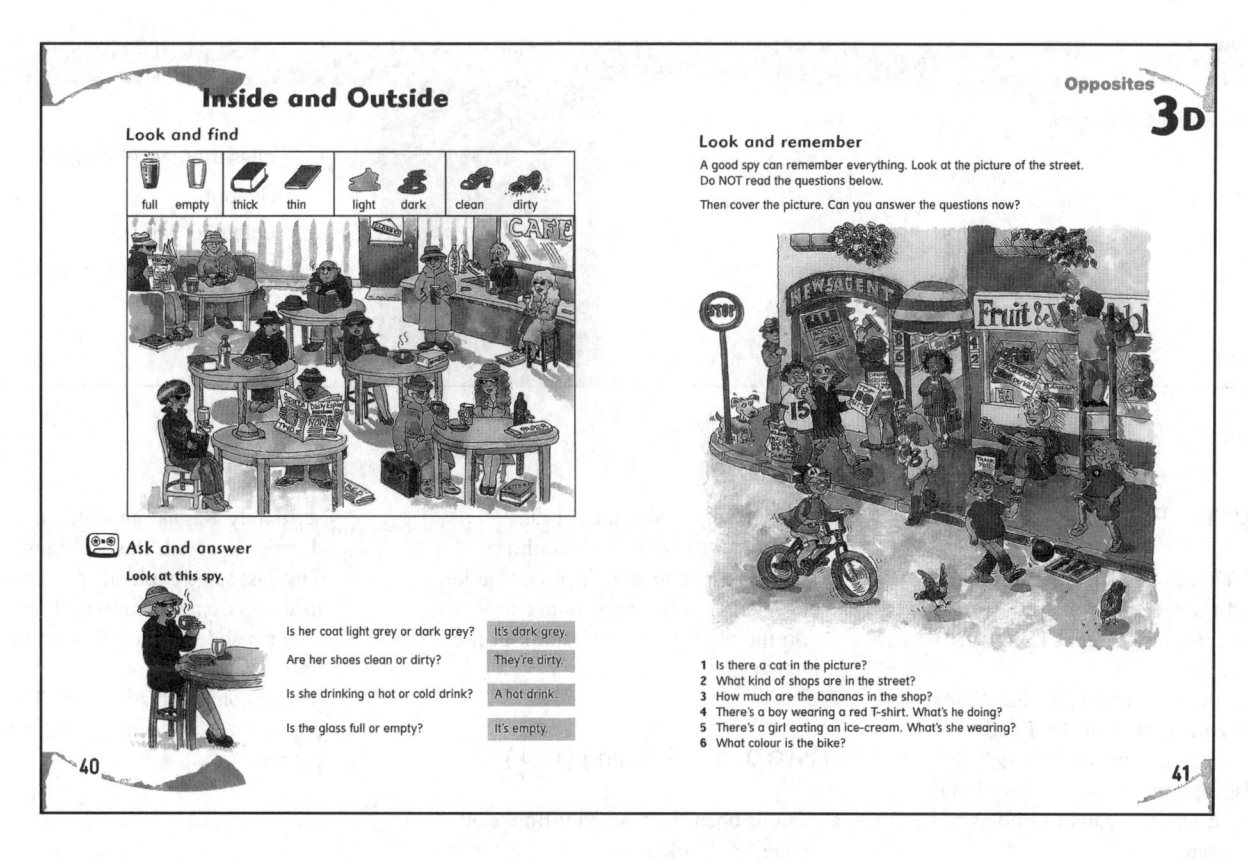

Opposites 3D

Look and find

full · empty · thick · thin · light · dark · clean · dirty

Ask and answer

Look at this spy.

Is her coat light grey or dark grey?	It's dark grey.
Are her shoes clean or dirty?	They're dirty.
Is she drinking a hot or cold drink?	A hot drink.
Is the glass full or empty?	It's empty.

Look and remember

A good spy can remember everything. Look at the picture of the street. Do NOT read the questions below.

Then cover the picture. Can you answer the questions now?

1. Is there a cat in the picture?
2. What kind of shops are in the street?
3. How much are the bananas in the shop?
4. There's a boy wearing a red T-shirt. What's he doing?
5. There's a girl eating an ice-cream. What's she wearing?
6. What colour is the bike?

3D Opposites

Step 1

5 Listen and write.

Now that Ivan Idea knows how to get home he needs a passport.

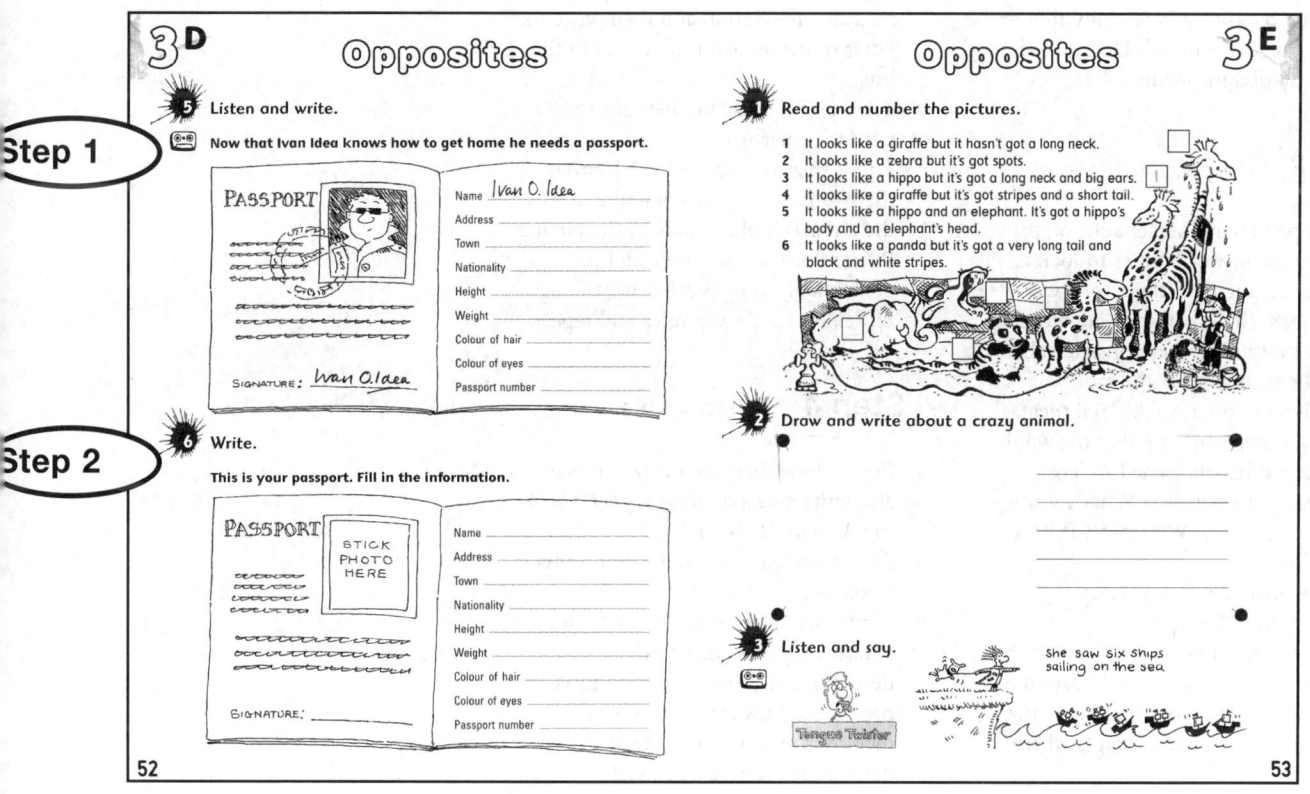

PASSPORT
Name: Ivan O. Idea
Address:
Town:
Nationality:
Height:
Weight:
Colour of hair:
Colour of eyes:
SIGNATURE: Ivan O. Idea
Passport number:

Step 2

6 Write.

This is your passport. Fill in the information.

PASSPORT — STICK PHOTO HERE
Name:
Address:
Town:
Nationality:
Height:
Weight:
Colour of hair:
Colour of eyes:
SIGNATURE:
Passport number:

Opposites 3E

1 Read and number the pictures.

1. It looks like a giraffe but it hasn't got a long neck.
2. It looks like a zebra but it's got spots.
3. It looks like a hippo but it's got a long neck and big ears.
4. It looks like a giraffe but it's got stripes and a short tail.
5. It looks like a hippo and an elephant. It's got a hippo's body and an elephant's head.
6. It looks like a panda but it's got a very long tail and black and white stripes.

2 Draw and write about a crazy animal.

3 Listen and say.

Tongue Twister

She saw six ships sailing on the sea

3E Lesson 1

Main Language Items	Resource File	Materials Needed
Revision: animals and descriptions It looks like … It's got/hasn't got … because ('cos)	4 10 41 52	cassette/cassette player Reader coloured pencils paper for display (optional)

Step 1 Pairwork

a Read *The Magic Mirror* again or rewind the tape and listen to the story without stopping. Pupils follow in their Readers.
b Divide the class into pairs. Say '**Look at the zoo picture in the Reader. How many things are wrong?**' Get pupils to point out one or two things, and then work in pairs to find as many as they can.
c Round up by asking how many things various pairs have found. Discuss and clarify any disagreements.

Step 2 Poem

a Pupils open their Coursebooks on page 42. Give them two minutes to look at the pictures, then ask them to close their books. Give them one minute to tell you everything they can remember about the picture. Play the tape while they follow in their books. Tell them before you play the tape that the word **because** is often shortened to **'cos**.
b Then ask questions like '**What's wrong with the camel?**', '**Why can't it be a rabbit?**' etc.
c Play the poem again, with pupils repeating after the tape.
d Divide the class into pairs. P1 reads the first line of each verse and P2 says the other two lines without looking at the book. P1 corrects and prompts where necessary.
e They change roles and repeat.
f Go round the class and monitor, helping the pupils with pronunciation as required. Encourage pupils to focus on the rhythm and intonation of the poem.

Step 3 Reading (Task)

a Pupils open their Activity Books on page 53. Working individually, they read the description and then write the letter of the animal it describes in the box.
b Then pupils compare their answers with their partner.
c Pupils then work in pairs. P1 covers the words and tries to describe one of the animals looking only at the picture. P2 can look at the words and the picture and prompts P1 if he/she has difficulty. They swap roles and repeat.

Step 4 Personal file

a Pupils draw their own crazy animal and write a description on page 53 of the Activity Book, using the descriptions in the Reader and Activity Book as prompts.
b (**Optional**) Then they can draw the animal on paper with a brief description of it on a separate piece of paper. The finished crazy animals pictures can form a wall display. The descriptions can be displayed separately. Pupils can match the descriptions with the drawings. This last stage could also be done as a listening exercise: collect all the pupils' pictures and pin them around the wall. Each pupil keeps their written description and reads it out. The other pupils listen and point to the correct picture.

Can and Can't

Say the poem

It Looks Like a Camel

It looks like a camel
But it can't be a camel
Because it's blue!

It looks like a hippo
But it can't be a hippo
Because it jumps like a kangaroo!

It looks like a penguin
But it can't be a penguin
Because it's climbing up a tree!

It looks like a rabbit
But it can't be a rabbit
Because it's bigger than you and me!

Opposites 3E

Read and answer

READER pages 4-6

1. How many pens were there in Bob's room?
2. What were the boys in the park doing?
3. Was the girl riding a bike?
4. What colour were the cats?
5. What colour was the rabbit?
6. Which animals were climbing trees?
7. What does 'huge' mean?
8. What does 'tiny' mean?

The Stepping Stones Game

Crocodiles / Elephants / Giraffes / Tigers **are** bigger / smaller / faster / taller / longer **than** snakes / penguins / rabbits / hippos

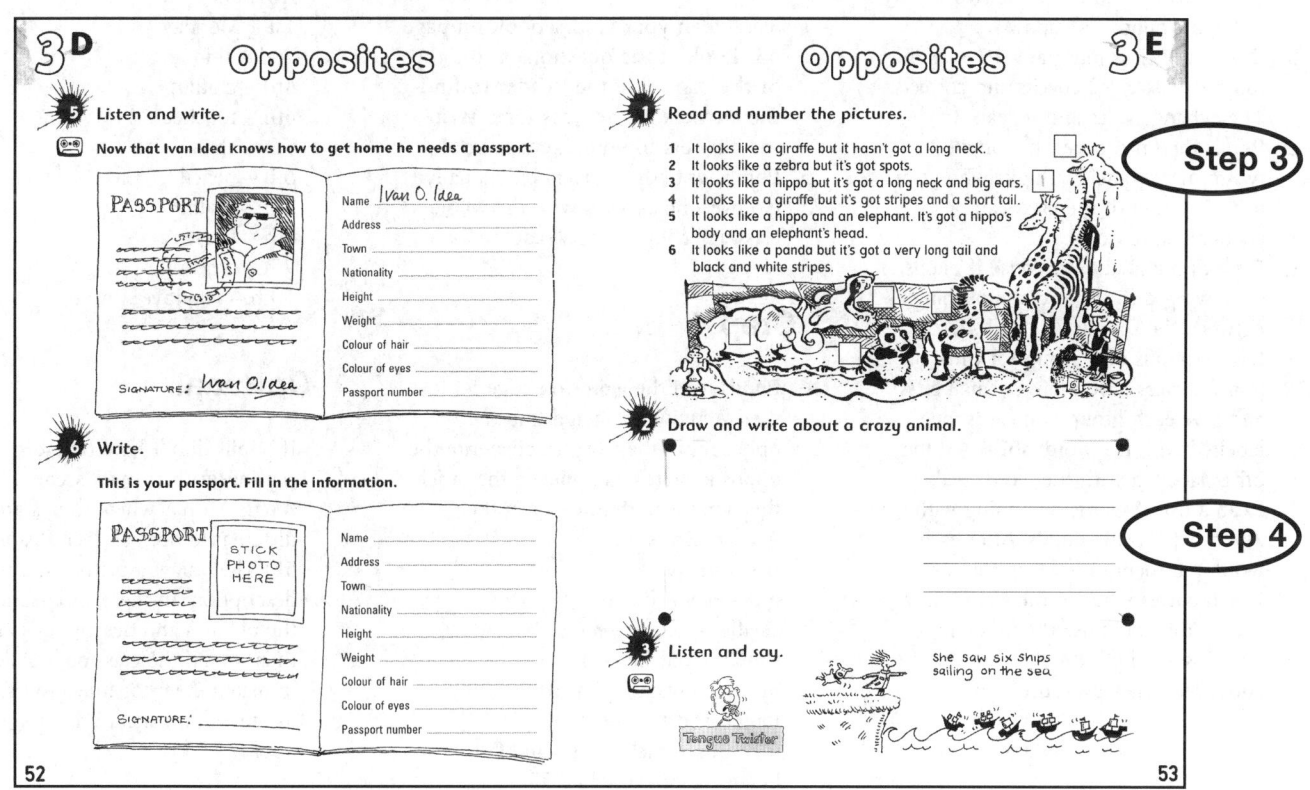

3D Opposites

5 Listen and write.

Now that Ivan Idea knows how to get home he needs a passport.

PASSPORT
Name: Ivan O. Idea
Address:
Town:
Nationality:
Height:
Weight:
Colour of hair:
Colour of eyes:
Passport number:
SIGNATURE: Ivan O. Idea

6 Write.

This is your passport. Fill in the information.

PASSPORT — STICK PHOTO HERE
Name:
Address:
Town:
Nationality:
Height:
Weight:
Colour of hair:
Colour of eyes:
SIGNATURE:
Passport number:

Opposites 3E

1 Read and number the pictures.

1. It looks like a giraffe but it hasn't got a long neck.
2. It looks like a zebra but it's got spots.
3. It looks like a hippo but it's got a long neck and big ears.
4. It looks like a giraffe but it's got stripes and a short tail.
5. It looks like a hippo and an elephant. It's got a hippo's body and an elephant's head.
6. It looks like a panda but it's got a very long tail and black and white stripes.

2 Draw and write about a crazy animal.

3 Listen and say.

Tongue Twister

She saw six ships sailing on the sea

3E Lesson 2

Main Language Items	Resource File	Materials Needed
Revision: comparatives and question forms was were	52 55	cassette/cassette player Reader

Step 1 Tongue twister

a Play the tape once so pupils can listen to the tongue twister. Play it twice more, with the class repeating. Follow the same procedure as for the other tongue twisters if pupils have difficulty with pronunciation. Focus particularly on **'six ships'** and make pupils aware that the 'x' is reduced to a /k/ when the words are said very quickly. Show the pupils how to make the two different sounds /s/ and /ʃ/.

b Divide the class into pairs. P1 says the tongue twister. P2 checks and corrects. They change roles and repeat.

c Pupils then try to say the tongue twister more quickly. Pupils who want to try in front of the class can be encouraged to do so.

d Do a discrimination exercise if pupils are having difficulties distinguishing between the sounds /s/ and /ʃ/. Divide pupils into groups of three or four (or pairs if you have a small class) and give each group two cards, one labelled with the word **'ship'** and the other labelled with the word **'sea'**. Read a list of words beginning with /s/ or /ʃ/ to the pupils. After each word, tell them to hold up the card which corresponds to the sound they heard. You could use the following words: **sell/shell, Sue/shoe, see/she, saw/sure**.

Step 2 Story 'Join In'

Read *The Magic Mirror* again or rewind the tape and play the story without stopping. Pupils follow in their Readers. If they are familiar enough with the story, volunteers can play the roles of the characters.

Step 3 Read and answer

a Say 'Open your Coursebook on page 43. Look at the questions at the top of the page. Use the Reader to find the answers to the questions. Write the answers in your exercise book.'

b Pupils write the answers individually.

c Go over the answers with the whole class, referring to the Reader.

Step 4 Write

Pupils read the words on page 54 in their Activity Book and find the opposites in the story. Pupils write the opposite words and lines in the order they appear in the Reader in their Activity Book.
Answers:
girl – boy – line 6
smaller – bigger – line 21
slowly – quickly – line 53
inside – outside – line 36
long – short – line 41
forwards – backwards – line 53
hello – goodbye – line 55

Step 5 Write

Pupils complete the sentences in their Activity Book and then check their answers in the Reader.

Step 6 Write

Pupils write the words in the order they appear in the Reader (1st to 10th).
Answers:
1st – Monday
2nd – thin
3rd – clothes
4th – touched
5th – chair
6th – pencil
7th – mother
8th – horse
9th – crocodiles
10th – goodbye

Optional

If pupils didn't have time before, they can invent their own 'scene' from the *Magic Mirror*, where things are different to normal. (See **Resource File 55**) They draw a picture and write a description. In the next lesson, separate the pictures and descriptions and pin them round the classroom. Ask pupils to match them together. You can then use these to make a class *Magic Mirror* book.

Can and Can't

Say the poem

It Looks Like a Camel

It looks like a camel
But it can't be a camel
Because it's blue!

It looks like a hippo
But it can't be a hippo
Because it jumps like a kangaroo!

It looks like a penguin
But it can't be a penguin
Because it's climbing up a tree!

It looks like a rabbit
But it can't be a rabbit
Because it's bigger than you and me!

Opposites 3E

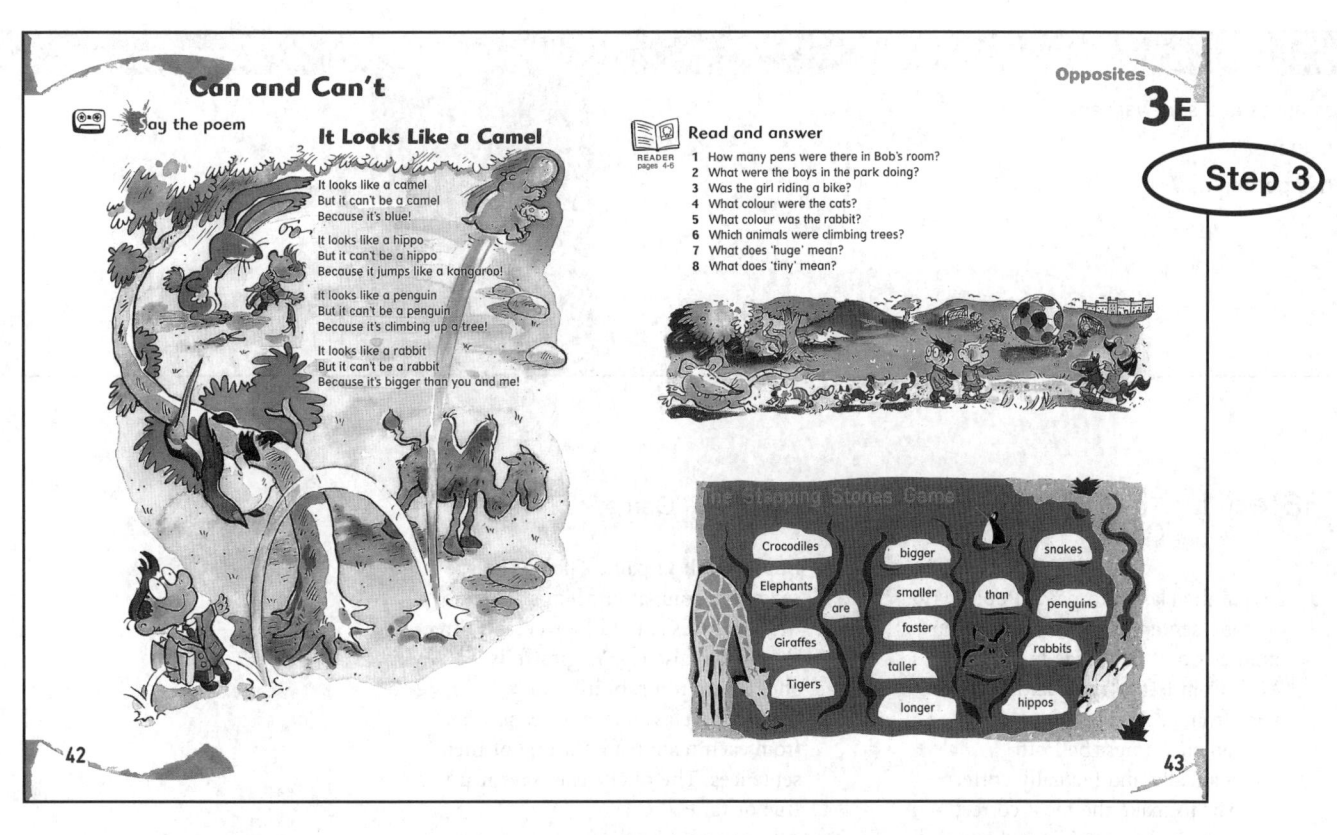

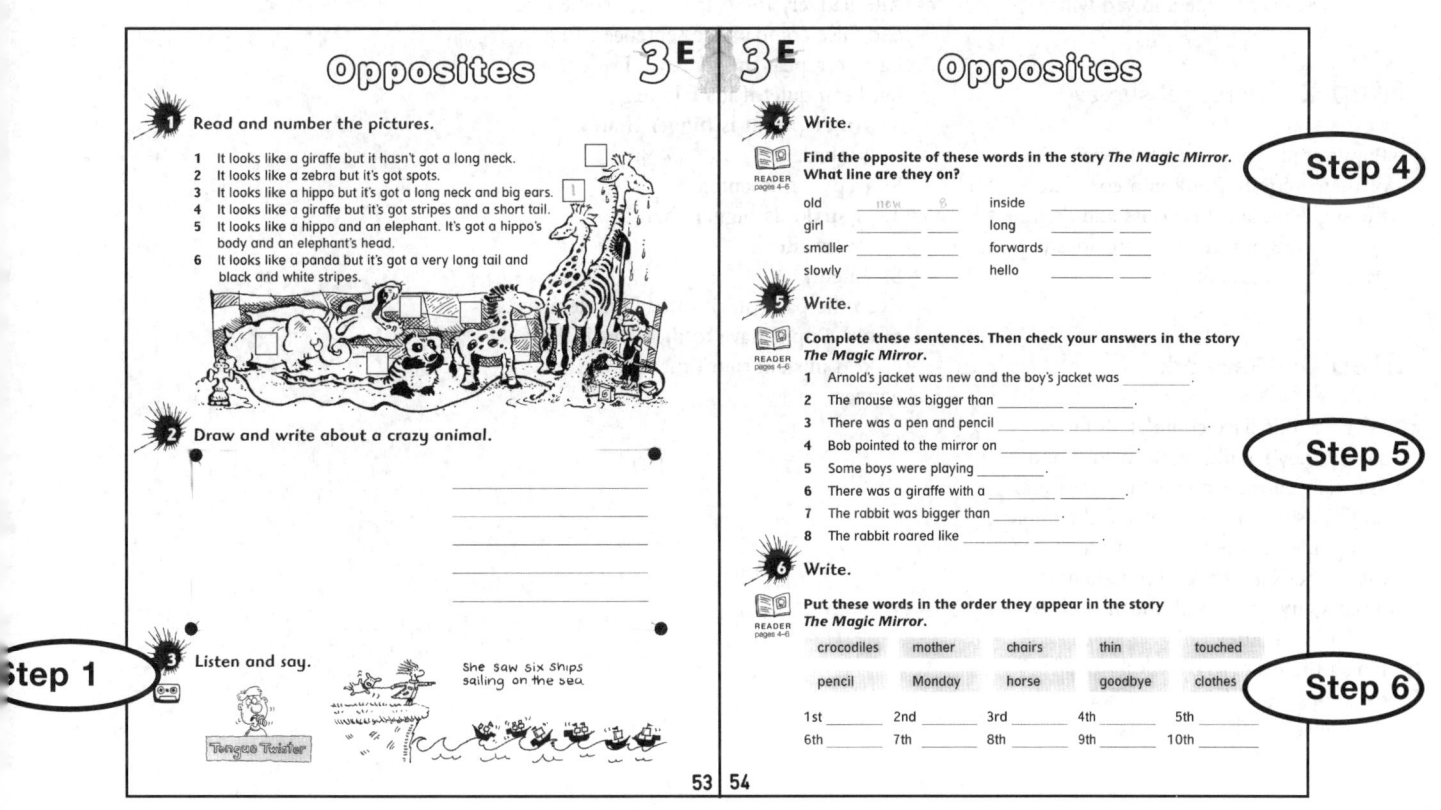

Read and answer
(READER pages 4–6)

1. How many pens were there in Bob's room?
2. What were the boys in the park doing?
3. Was the girl riding a bike?
4. What colour were the cats?
5. What colour was the rabbit?
6. Which animals were climbing trees?
7. What does 'huge' mean?
8. What does 'tiny' mean?

The Stepping Stones Game

Crocodiles / Elephants / Giraffes / Tigers — are — bigger / smaller / faster / taller / longer — than — snakes / penguins / rabbits / hippos

42 / 43

Opposites 3E

1 Read and number the pictures.

1. It looks like a giraffe but it hasn't got a long neck.
2. It looks like a zebra but it's got spots.
3. It looks like a hippo but it's got a long neck and big ears.
4. It looks like a giraffe but it's got stripes and a short tail.
5. It looks like a hippo and an elephant. It's got a hippo's body and an elephant's head.
6. It looks like a panda but it's got a very long tail and black and white stripes.

2 Draw and write about a crazy animal.

3 Listen and say.

Tongue Twister: She saw six ships sailing on the sea.

Opposites 3E

4 Write.

Find the opposite of these words in the story *The Magic Mirror*. What line are they on?
(READER pages 4–6)

old	new	8	inside	___	___
girl	___	___	long	___	___
smaller	___	___	forwards	___	___
slowly	___	___	hello	___	___

5 Write.

Complete these sentences. Then check your answers in the story *The Magic Mirror*.
(READER pages 4–6)

1. Arnold's jacket was new and the boy's jacket was _____.
2. The mouse was bigger than _____ _____.
3. There was a pen and pencil _____ _____ _____.
4. Bob pointed to the mirror on _____ _____.
5. Some boys were playing _____.
6. There was a giraffe with a _____ _____.
7. The rabbit was bigger than _____.
8. The rabbit roared like _____ _____.

6 Write.

Put these words in the order they appear in the story *The Magic Mirror*.
(READER pages 4–6)

| crocodiles | mother | chairs | thin | touched |
| pencil | Monday | horse | goodbye | clothes |

1st ___ 2nd ___ 3rd ___ 4th ___ 5th ___
6th ___ 7th ___ 8th ___ 9th ___ 10th ___

53 / 54

121

3E Lesson 3

Main Language Items	Resource File	Materials Needed
Comparatives and superlatives Who is the ... ? Who has got the ... ?	10	

Step 1 The Stepping Stones Game

a Divide the class into pairs. Pupils write as many sentences as they can in ten minutes from the words in the box. Work from left to right and take one word from each column.
b The sentences must be both grammatically and factually correct.
c The pair to make the most correct sentences in the time allowed wins.

Step 2 Personal survey

Pupils read the questions on page 55 of their Activity Book and complete the survey about their class and their family, using information previously gathered in the unit.

Step 3 Pairwork

a When pupils have completed the survey they should work in pairs and ask their partners about their class and family, using the questions in the book as a guide. It is not necessary to record each other's answers. Pupils should discuss any answers about their class that they disagree on!
b Finish the exercise by asking pupils questions from the survey about themselves or their partners.

Step 4 Game

a Pupils work in pairs. They write six sentences comparing things. Three of the sentences should be true and three should be false e.g. **'A giraffe is shorter than a rabbit!'**.
b Divide the class into two teams. Pairs from each team read out one of their sentences. The other team says if it is true or false.
c Alternatively the teacher says some true and false comparative sentences. Pupils have to repeat the sentence if it's true, but keep quiet if it's false e.g.
  T: **An elephant is bigger than a mouse.**
  S: (repeat the sentence)
  T: **A snake is bigger than a crocodile.**
  S: (silent)
Keep the pace quick to add an element of fun. Pupils have to drop out if they make a mistake, until there is just one winner.

Can and Can't

🔊 Say the poem

It Looks Like a Camel

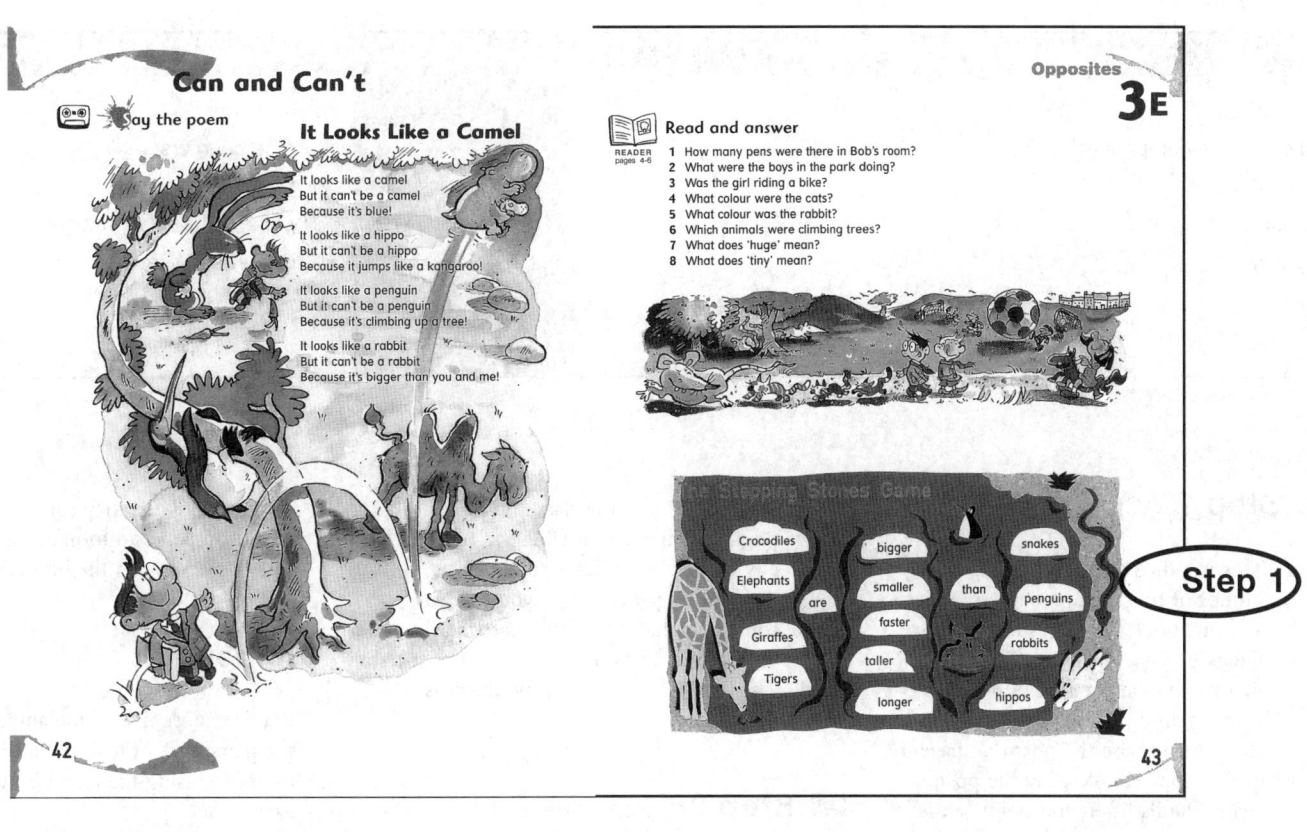

It looks like a camel
But it can't be a camel
Because it's blue!

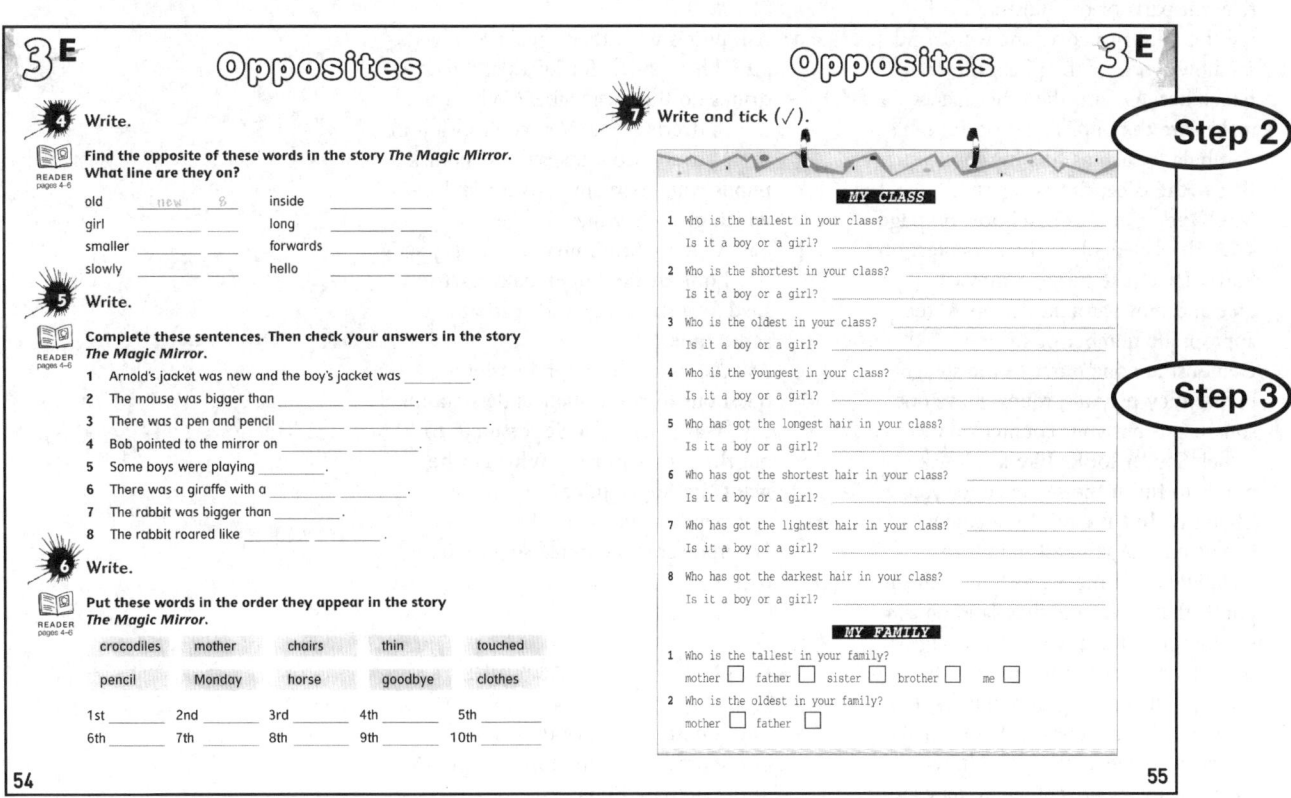

It looks like a hippo
But it can't be a hippo
Because it jumps like a kangaroo!

It looks like a penguin
But it can't be a penguin
Because it's climbing up a tree!

It looks like a rabbit
But it can't be a rabbit
Because it's bigger than you and me!

Opposites 3E

Read and answer (READER pages 4–6)

1. How many pens were there in Bob's room?
2. What were the boys in the park doing?
3. Was the girl riding a bike?
4. What colour were the cats?
5. What colour was the rabbit?
6. Which animals were climbing trees?
7. What does 'huge' mean?
8. What does 'tiny' mean?

The Stepping Stones Game

Crocodiles / Elephants / Giraffes / Tigers — are — bigger / smaller / faster / taller / longer — than — snakes / penguins / rabbits / hippos

Step 1

3E Opposites

4 Write.

Find the opposite of these words in the story *The Magic Mirror*. What line are they on? (READER pages 4–6)

old	new 8	inside	____ ____
girl	____ ____	long	____ ____
smaller	____ ____	forwards	____ ____
slowly	____ ____	hello	____ ____

5 Write.

Complete these sentences. Then check your answers in the story *The Magic Mirror*. (READER pages 4–6)

1. Arnold's jacket was new and the boy's jacket was _____.
2. The mouse was bigger than _____ _____.
3. There was a pen and pencil _____ _____.
4. Bob pointed to the mirror on _____ _____.
5. Some boys were playing _____.
6. There was a giraffe with a _____ _____.
7. The rabbit was bigger than _____.
8. The rabbit roared like _____ _____.

6 Write.

Put these words in the order they appear in the story *The Magic Mirror*. (READER pages 4–6)

crocodiles / mother / chairs / thin / touched
pencil / Monday / horse / goodbye / clothes

1st _____ 2nd _____ 3rd _____ 4th _____ 5th _____
6th _____ 7th _____ 8th _____ 9th _____ 10th _____

Opposites 3E

7 Write and tick (✓).

MY CLASS

1. Who is the tallest in your class? _____
   Is it a boy or a girl? _____
2. Who is the shortest in your class? _____
   Is it a boy or a girl? _____
3. Who is the oldest in your class? _____
   Is it a boy or a girl? _____
4. Who is the youngest in your class? _____
   Is it a boy or a girl? _____
5. Who has got the longest hair in your class? _____
   Is it a boy or a girl? _____
6. Who has got the shortest hair in your class? _____
   Is it a boy or a girl? _____
7. Who has got the lightest hair in your class? _____
   Is it a boy or a girl? _____
8. Who has got the darkest hair in your class? _____
   Is it a boy or a girl? _____

MY FAMILY

1. Who is the tallest in your family?
   mother ☐ father ☐ sister ☐ brother ☐ me ☐
2. Who is the oldest in your family?
   mother ☐ father ☐

Step 2

Step 3

3F Lesson 1

Main Language Items	Resource File	Materials Needed
Story revision Why did … swim/jump/climb … ? the longest … the tallest … the highest …	4	dice/counters coloured pencils paper for display (optional) cassette/cassette player

Step 1 Story game

a This is a dice game to be played in groups of four, using counters, a dice and one book for each group.

b Quickly revise the story *The Magic Mirror*; rewind the tape and play the story again or ask pupils to tell you the story. Also revise the poem on page 42 of the Coursebook. Play the poem again. Pupils listen and point to the relevant parts of the illustration. Then tell the pupils to cover the words and see how much of the poem they can remember. As with the other games, make sure the pupils have useful vocabulary, such as 'it's my/your turn, throw the dice, throw again…'.

c Say 'Open your Coursebook on page 44.' All players place their counters on Start. They take turns to throw the dice and move around the board the appropriate number of squares. Demonstrate one move to the students before they play in groups: move one square and put your counter on the camel. Say 'It looks like a …'. Ask pupils to finish the sentence for you. Then say 'but it can't be a camel because …'. Again, ask pupils to complete the sentence for you. Tell the pupils that each time they land on a square they must say what's wrong with the animal in the picture. The other pupils in the group must decide whether they are correct. If they make a correct sentence, they can throw again. If not, they stay where they are.

Monitor around the class and help pupils when necessary. Make a note of any common problems pupils have during the game, so that you can do some remedial work later, particularly with pronunciation.

d The first player to reach the finish is the winner.

Step 2 Supersnake

a Ask pupils what their favourite adverts are. What adverts for juices and fizzy drinks do they remember? What do these adverts stress? You could bring in some adverts from magazines and ask pupils what each advert is for and which ones they like/dislike.

b Say 'Open your Coursebook on page 45. Look at the Supersnake cartoon. Listen to the story and read at the same time.'

c Ask pupils some comprehension questions to check their understanding, e.g. 'Was it easy for Supersnake to get the Super Juice?' 'Why did he want the Super Juice?' Ask pupils to imagine what Superpowers they think Super Juice has.

Step 3 Draw and write

a Pupils design an advertisement for one of the products at the top of page 56 in the Activity Book.

b (Optional) Then they can draw the advert on paper to form a wall display. Pupils can vote on the best advert.

Homework

Pupils choose five of the animals from the game and write a sentence about each one, using the poem on page 42 as a model.

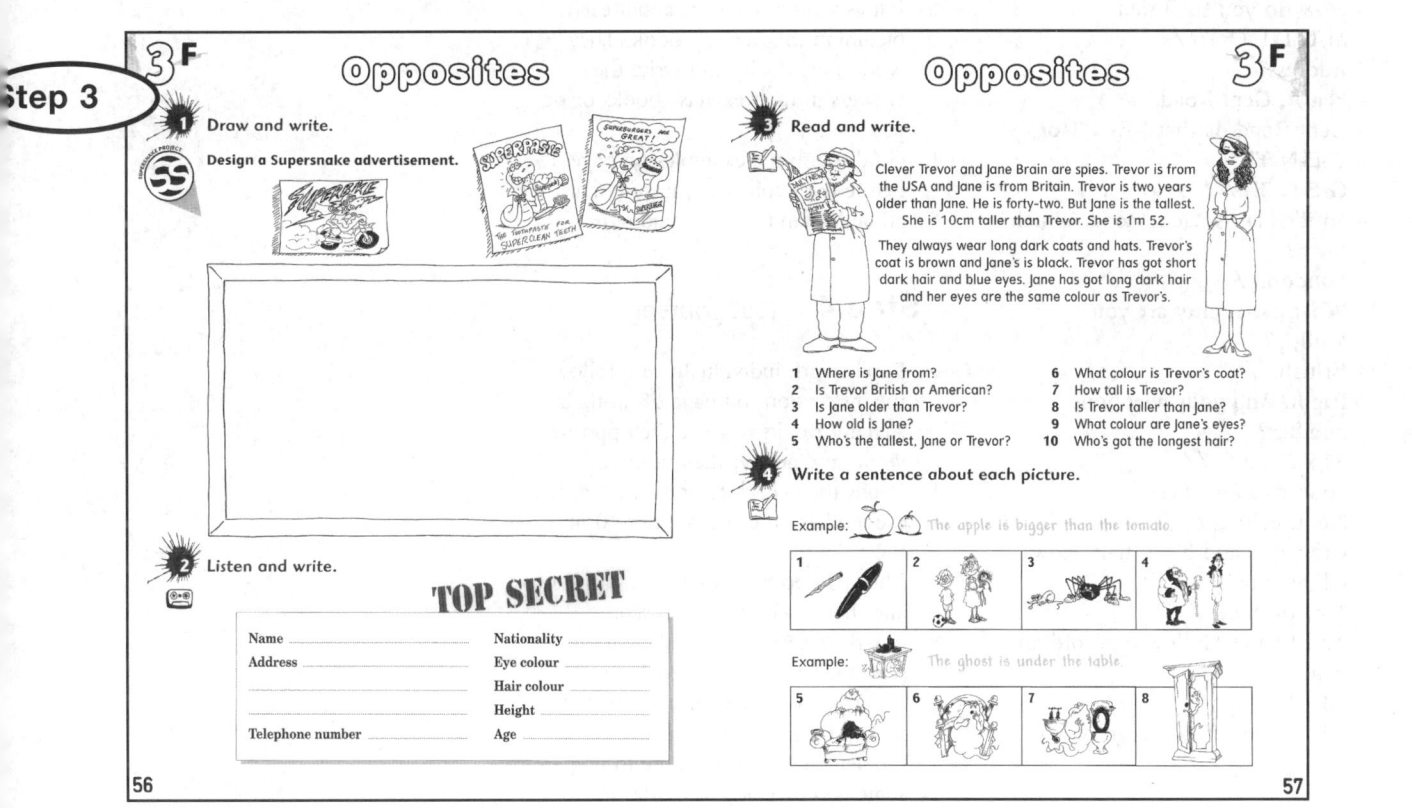

Step 1

Everything is Different
The Magic Mirror Game

page 44

Step 2

Supersnake — Opposites 3F

Last week Supersnake went to Viper TV studios to make an advertisement.

Supersnake was advertising a new drink called 'Super Juice'.

WHY DID SUPERSNAKE SWIM THE LONGEST RIVER...

...JUMP THE TALLEST BUILDING...

...AND CLIMB THE HIGHEST MOUNTAIN?

FOR SUPER JUICE, THE SUPER NEW ORANGE DRINK!

This is the poster.

NEW! SUPER JUICE The drink for Superheroes!

My hero!

page 45

Step 3

Opposites 3F

1 Draw and write.

Design a Supersnake advertisement.

2 Listen and write.

TOP SECRET

Name _____ Nationality _____
Address _____ Eye colour _____
_____ Hair colour _____
_____ Height _____
Telephone number _____ Age _____

Opposites 3F

3 Read and write.

Clever Trevor and Jane Brain are spies. Trevor is from the USA and Jane is from Britain. Trevor is two years older than Jane. He is forty-two. But Jane is the tallest. She is 10cm taller than Trevor. She is 1m 52.

They always wear long dark coats and hats. Trevor's coat is brown and Jane's is black. Trevor has got short dark hair and blue eyes. Jane has got long dark hair and her eyes are the same colour as Trevor's.

1 Where is Jane from?
2 Is Trevor British or American?
3 Is Jane older than Trevor?
4 How old is Jane?
5 Who's the tallest, Jane or Trevor?
6 What colour is Trevor's coat?
7 How tall is Trevor?
8 Is Trevor taller than Jane?
9 What colour are Jane's eyes?
10 Who's got the longest hair?

4 Write a sentence about each picture.

Example: The apple is bigger than the tomato

Example: The ghost is under the table.

pages 56, 57

125

3F Lesson 2 - Evaluation

Main Language Items	Resource File	Materials Needed
Round-up lesson (including tests) Revision of all vocabulary and structures		cassette/cassette player

Step 1 Listening (Test)

Say 'Open your Activity Book on page 56. Listen to the tape and fill in the information on the form.' Play the tape three times pausing where necessary for pupils to write.

Tapescript:
- Right. Name?
- Mulloy.
- How do you spell that?
- M-U-L-L-O-Y.//
- Address?
- Flat A, Gent Road.
- Gent Road. Is that J-E-N-T or G-E-N-T?
- G-E-N-T.//
- So it's Flat A, Gent Road. Which town?
- London.//
- What nationality are you, Mulloy?
- British.//
- Right. And your telephone number?
- 315 269007.//
- Your eyes are blue?
- No, they're grey.//
- Grey eyes and black hair. How tall are you?
- 1 metre 89.//
- And finally Mulloy. How old are you?
- 34.//
- OK Mulloy. You can go now.//

Step 2 Reading (Test)

Pupils read the text on page 57 of the Activity Book and answer the questions. The work should be done individually and the answers written into exercise books or on paper.

Step 3 Writing (Test)

a Pupils write a sentence about each picture in the Activity Book. They work individually and write the answers in their exercise books or on paper.
b Go through the examples on page 57 before the pupils start. Ensure that they all understand what is required.

Step 4 Test yourself

a Pupils work individually and follow the instructions on page 58 in their Activity Books to write the opposite words and answer the questions.
b Pupils then check their answers against the models on pages 35 and 40 in their Coursebook.
c They add up their scores for each test and then circle their total score.
d Ask them in their L1 if they are happy with their scores. If not, what areas should they review? If you see that most pupils still have one or several problem areas, make a note to prepare some reinforcement activities for these specific areas, and leaf through the **Resource File** for ideas.

3F Opposites

1 Draw and write.

Design a Supersnake advertisement.

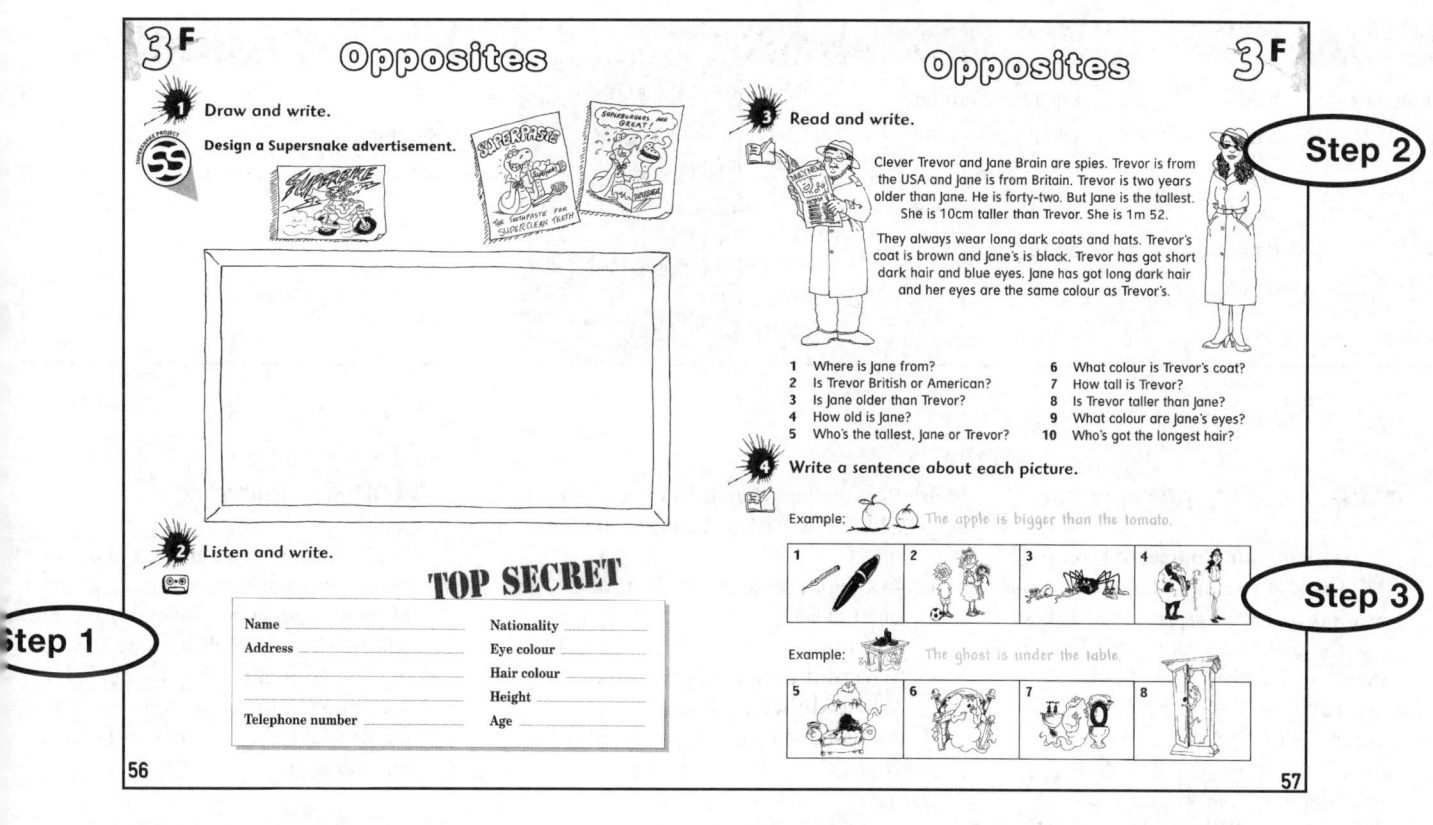

2 Listen and write.

TOP SECRET

Name	Nationality
Address	Eye colour
	Hair colour
	Height
Telephone number	Age

Step 1

56

3F Opposites

3 Read and write.

Clever Trevor and Jane Brain are spies. Trevor is from the USA and Jane is from Britain. Trevor is two years older than Jane. He is forty-two. But Jane is the tallest. She is 10cm taller than Trevor. She is 1m 52.

They always wear long dark coats and hats. Trevor's coat is brown and Jane's is black. Trevor has got short dark hair and blue eyes. Jane has got long dark hair and her eyes are the same colour as Trevor's.

1 Where is Jane from?
2 Is Trevor British or American?
3 Is Jane older than Trevor?
4 How old is Jane?
5 Who's the tallest, Jane or Trevor?
6 What colour is Trevor's coat?
7 How tall is Trevor?
8 Is Trevor taller than Jane?
9 What colour are Jane's eyes?
10 Who's got the longest hair?

Step 2

4 Write a sentence about each picture.

Example: The apple is bigger than the tomato.

1	2	3	4

Example: The ghost is under the table.

5	6	7	8

Step 3

57

3F Opposites

5 Test yourself.

TEST 1 ★ Write the opposites of these words.

big	_____	young	_____
fat	_____	fast	_____
new	_____	tall	_____
happy	_____	boy	_____
long	_____	man	_____

★ Check your answers on page 35 in your Coursebook.
SCORE /10

TEST 2 ★ Look at the spy. Write the answers.

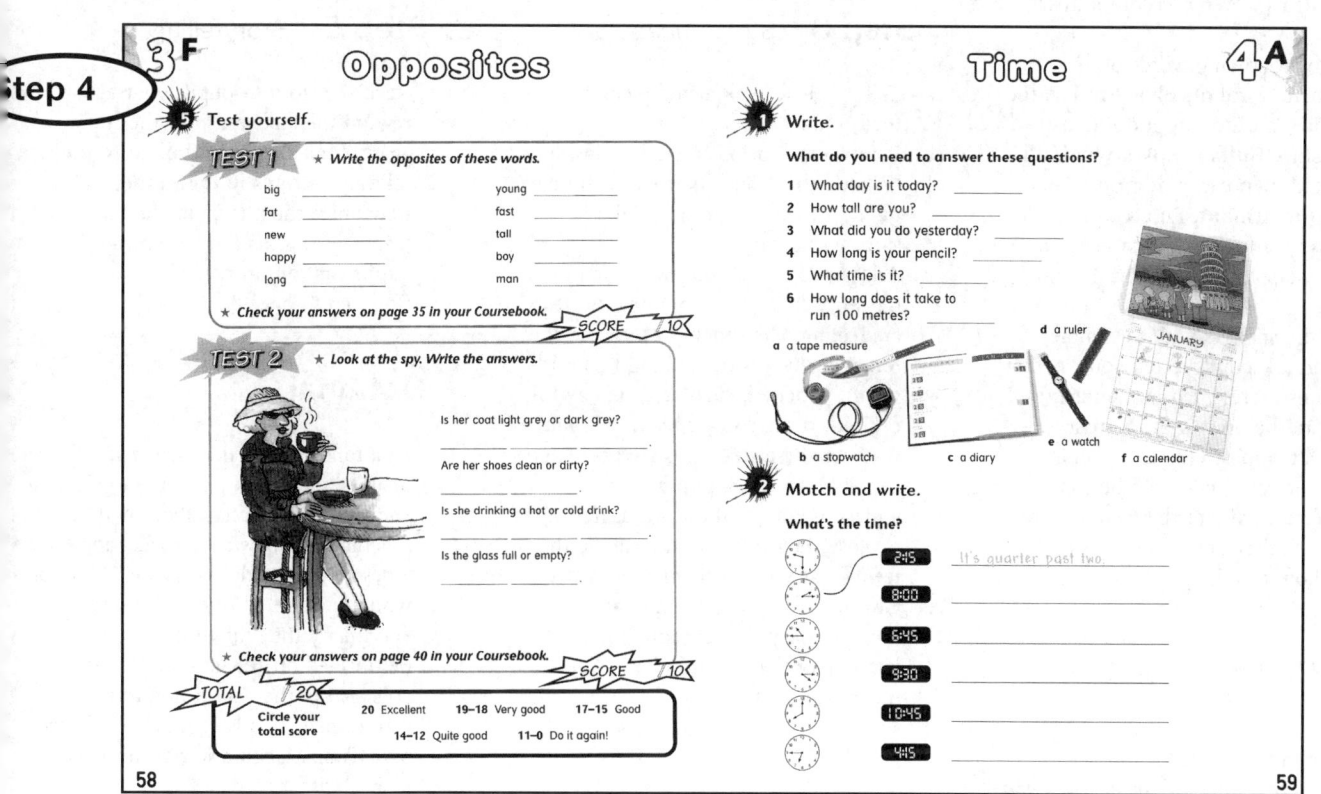

Is her coat light grey or dark grey?
_____
Are her shoes clean or dirty?
_____
Is she drinking a hot or cold drink?
_____
Is the glass full or empty?
_____

★ Check your answers on page 40 in your Coursebook.
SCORE /10

TOTAL /20
Circle your total score
20 Excellent 19–18 Very good 17–15 Good
14–12 Quite good 11–0 Do it again!

Step 4

58

4A Time

1 Write.

What do you need to answer these questions?

1 What day is it today? _____
2 How tall are you? _____
3 What did you do yesterday? _____
4 How long is your pencil? _____
5 What time is it? _____
6 How long does it take to run 100 metres? _____

a a tape measure
b a stopwatch
c a diary
d a ruler
e a watch
f a calendar

2 Match and write.

What's the time?

2:45 — It's quarter past two.
8:00 _____
6:45 _____
9:30 _____
10:45 _____
4:45 _____

59

127

4 Story lesson

Main Language Items			Resource File	Materials Needed
Time machine	field	knights in armour	31	Reader
future	plant	windmill	41	cassette/cassette player
switch	dry	pirate ships		
earth	dead	horse-drawn car		
sky	dinosaur	dodo		
river	dangerous			

Step 1 Story presentation

a Say 'Open your Coursebook on page 46. Look at the title of the story: *Jim and Jean and the Time Machine*.' Explain that the picture shows a scene from the story.
b Tell pupils to look at the picture and ask in their L1 what they think the story is all about.
c Ask what they can see in the picture, 'What's this?' 'What colour's this?', etc.
d Write the following words on the blackboard: **a robot, Elvis Presley, the Pyramids, a dinosaur, a dodo, a pirate ship, Buffalo Bill, a windmill, a horse-drawn car, a dog on wheels, knights in armour**. Pupils work in pairs and try to match each word to one of the pictures on pages 46 and 47.
e Check the answers with the whole class and ask pupils to tell you whether the things represented in the pictures belong to the present or the past. Draw pupils' attention to Jim and Jean in their Time Machine in the bottom right-hand corner of the picture. Tell pupils that they are going to listen to a story about travelling in time.

Step 2 Story 'listen and read'

a Say 'Open your Reader on page 7. Listen to the story of *Jim and Jean and the Time Machine*.'
b Play the tape. Pupils listen to the story and follow in their Reader at the same time.
c Ask pupils some comprehension questions e.g.
Did Jim and Jean like the future?
What did they see in the past?
Why did they go home?
d Ask pupils to retell the story in their L1.

Step 3 Story vocabulary

a Tell pupils to look at the picture in their Reader again.
b Point to the various pictures and ask 'What's this?' and 'Is it from the past or the future?' to recap on the key story vocabulary.
c Ask pupils to pick out the words from the story that show how Jim and Jean are feeling. Help them to pick out the following words by miming them: **it's great!, shocked, surprised, it's awful, excited, tired**. Ask pupils to tell you whether these adjectives are positive or negative. To check pupils' understanding of these words, tell them to close their books and to mime the feelings as you say them.
d Give pupils the opportunity at this stage to ask you about any other vocabulary they would like to know the meaning of.

Step 4 Pairwork

Pupils work in pairs and ask and answer questions about the story. More able pupils may like to try to re-tell the story in English, using the pictures as prompts. Pupils could also read through the story in groups, with pupils taking the roles of the narrator, Jim and Jean.

Step 5 Storytelling

Read the story to pupils yourself or rewind the tape and play the story again. Pupils listen and point to the relevant pictures in the Reader. Encourage them to mime Jim and Jean's feelings as they listen too. All pupils can join in with the countdown from ten to one.

Optional

As a follow-up to the story, pupils imagine their own journey into the past and future and design their own Time Machine. Pupils work in pairs and write a description of their drawing. Monitor while they are writing and provide any vocabulary they might need. This can be finished off for homework and collected in the next lesson to make a wall display. Pupils could also 'tell' their own Time Machine stories to the class if they wish.

4 Time

STORY

Jim and Jean and the Time Machine

Step 1

4A Lesson 1

Main Language Items		Resource File	Materials Needed
What's the time?	day	clock(s)	
o'clock	week	watch(es)	20	calendar
quarter (past/to)	month	diary/diaries	36	cassette/cassette player
half (past)	year		37	
second	measure		45	
minute	calendar(s)			
hour	opposite			

Step 1 Presentation

a Ask various pupils 'How old are you?' Write the answers on the blackboard. Then ask the pupils what the numbers mean. If a pupil answers 'I'm ten', ask 'Ten what?' and write on the blackboard ' ... is ten years old.' Direct pupils to the words on page 48 of the Coursebook.

b Ask 'What is a year?' and then 'How many months are there in a year?' and then 'How many weeks in a year?', 'How many days in a week?' etc.

c Then ask pupils 'How old are you in months?', 'How old are you in weeks?', 'How old are you in days?' etc. Give them a few minutes to calculate their answers on paper.

d Ask pupils 'How many days in a year?' If they answer 365 ask 'Are there 365 days in every year?' Then explain that there are 366 days in a leap year, and that a leap year occurs every four years. If the last two digits of a year are divisible by four, then that is a leap year. Write some years on the blackboard. Say 'Is this a leap year?'

e Point to various objects in the photo on page 48 and ask 'What's this?' Then ask, 'Which of these is used to measure seconds?', 'Which of these is used to measure hours?' etc.

Step 2 Reading (Task)

a Individually, pupils complete the exercise on page 59 of the Activity Book by writing the appropriate letter next to each question. Check the answers in pairs.

b Round up the exercise by asking 'How do we measure seconds?', 'What do we use to measure hours?' etc.

Step 3 Pairwork

a Ask pupils what other instruments can be used to measure time. What did the ancient Greeks and Romans measure time with? How can you tell the time when you haven't got a watch?

b Divide the class into pairs. Say 'Open your Coursebook on page 48. Look at the clocks at the bottom of the page. Cover the words.'

c Pupils repeat after the tape. One pupil repeats the questions, pointing at the appropriate clock, the other answers. They repeat four times changing roles.

d Then pupils ask and answer the questions without the help of the tape.

e They change roles and repeat the procedure.

Step 4 Action game

a Use your arms to represent the hands of a clock. Tell pupils that in this exercise the right hand will always be the hour hand. Put one hand straight up and one hand straight down. Ask pupils 'What's the time?'

b Repeat with your arms in different positions.

c Then tell individual pupils to 'Stand up. Put your arms at quarter past nine.' Repeat with other pupils and change the times in the instructions. Practise briefly with the whole class.

d Divide the class into two teams. The first player from each team stands up. Say a time. The first player to put their arms into the appropriate position to indicate the time wins a point for their team. Repeat until all pupils have had at least one go.

Step 5 Write

On page 59 of the Activity Book pupils connect the clock faces to the corresponding digital time and then write out the time in full.

Step 1

Measuring Time

Look and find

seconds
minutes
hours
days
weeks
months
years

Ask and answer

What's the time?

Ten past six.
Twenty to five.

Time 4A

Ask and answer

What's the time?

o'clock
five · five
ten · ten
quarter · quarter
to · past
twenty · twenty
twenty-five · twenty-five
half

Make — A Calendar

You need: card, a ruler, scissors, tape, a pen

1 Draw three lines on the card.
2 Fold the card along each line.
3 Tape the edges at the front.
4 Cut out ten pieces of card 6 cm by 3.5 cm. Write the days and months.
5 Cut out sixteen pieces of card 3 cm by 3.5 cm. Write the dates.
6 What's the date today? Put the cards in your calendar.

Step 3

Ask and answer

What's the time?

Four o'clock.   Quarter past ten.   Half past one.   Quarter to six.

48

49

3F Opposites

5 Test yourself.

TEST 1 ★ Write the opposites of these words.

big _____   young _____
fat _____   fast _____
new _____   tall _____
happy _____   boy _____
long _____   man _____

★ Check your answers on page 35 in your Coursebook.   SCORE /10

TEST 2 ★ Look at the spy. Write the answers.

Is her coat light grey or dark grey? _____
Are her shoes clean or dirty? _____
Is she drinking a hot or cold drink? _____
Is the glass full or empty? _____

★ Check your answers on page 40 in your Coursebook.   SCORE /10

TOTAL /20
Circle your total score
20 Excellent   19–18 Very good   17–15 Good
14–12 Quite good   11–0 Do it again!

Time 4A

1 Write.

What do you need to answer these questions?

1 What day is it today? _____
2 How tall are you? _____
3 What did you do yesterday? _____
4 How long is your pencil? _____
5 What time is it? _____
6 How long does it take to run 100 metres? _____

a a tape measure   d a ruler
b a stopwatch   c a diary   e a watch   f a calendar

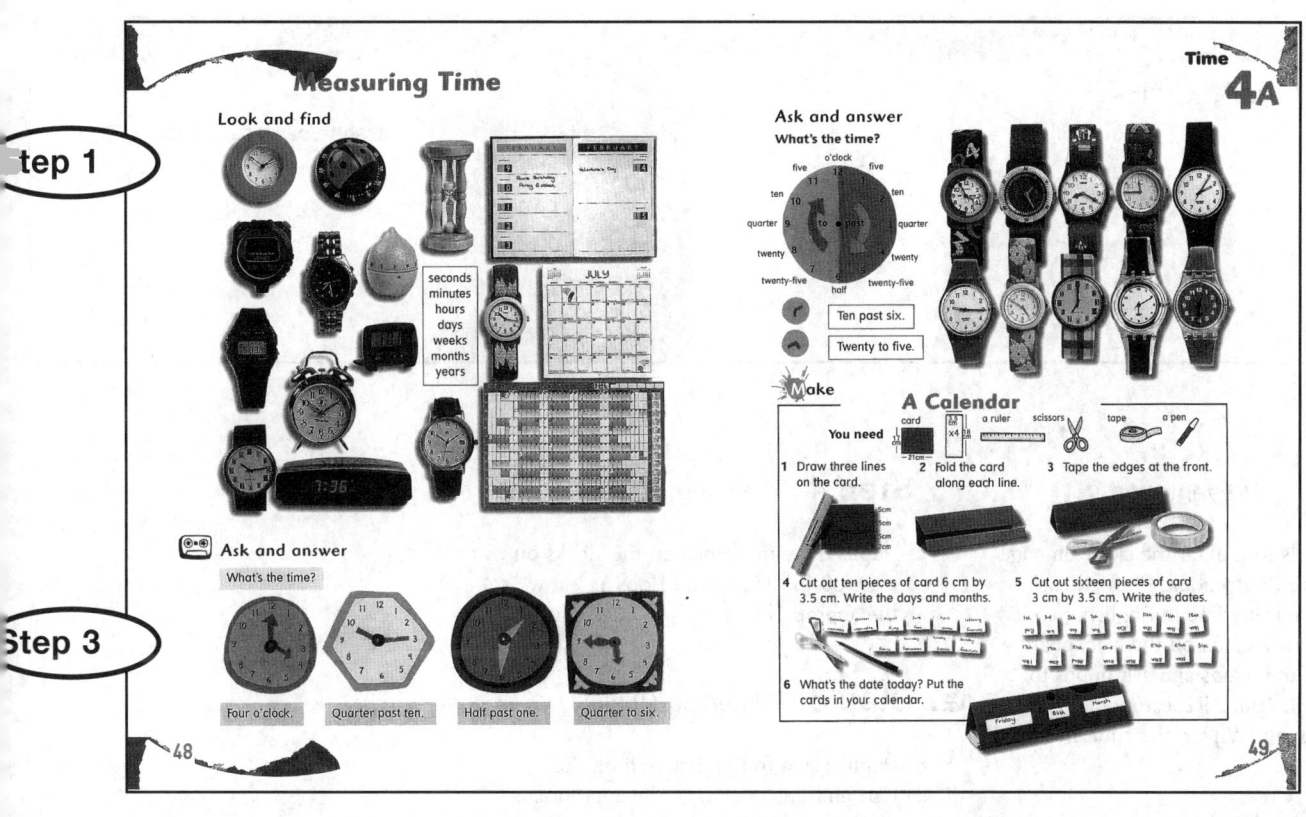

Step 2

Step 5

2 Match and write.

What's the time?

2:45 — It's quarter past two.
8:00 _____
6:45 _____
9:30 _____
10:45 _____
4:45 _____

58

59

131

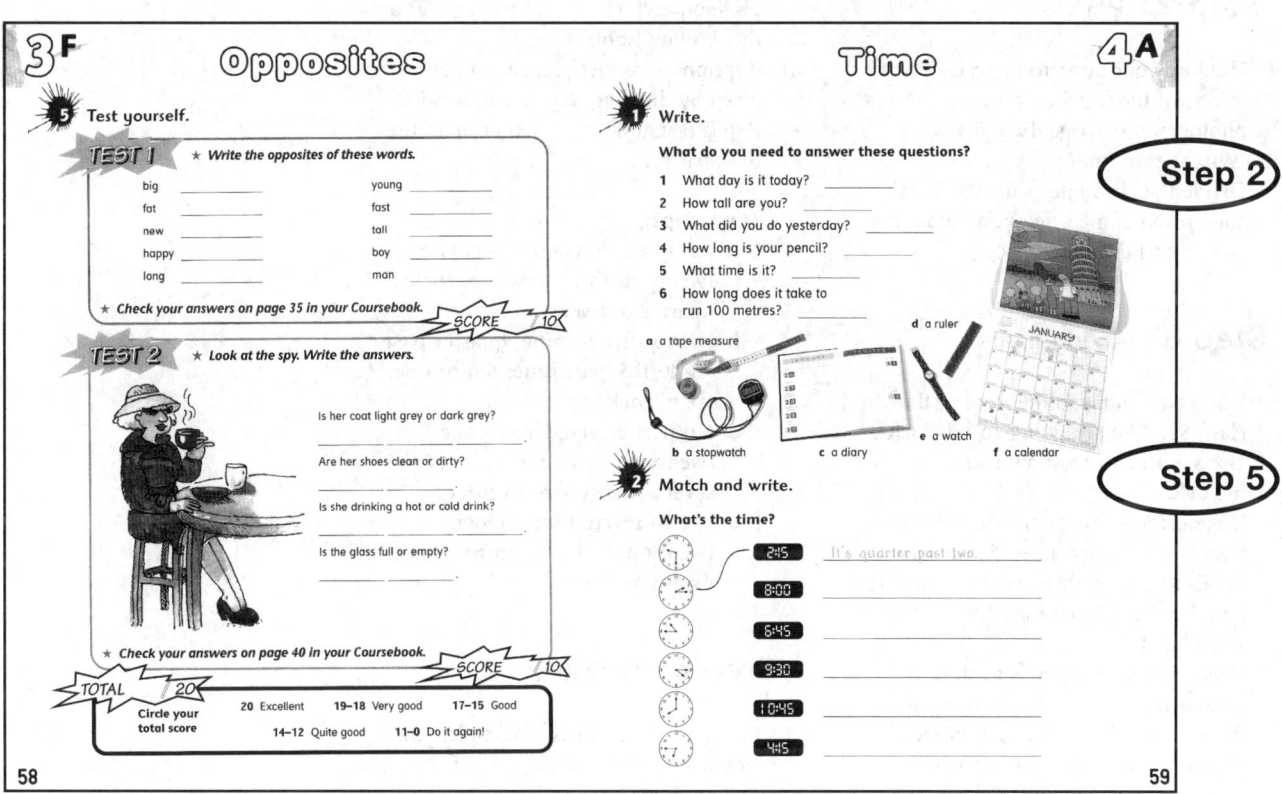

4A Lesson 2

Main Language Items		Resource File	Materials Needed
Telling the time	to	36	cassette/cassette player
What's the time?	past	37	
Is that correct?	nearly	45	
		46	

Step 1 Presentation

a Tell pupils to look at the clock on page 49 of the Coursebook. Show them how to tell the time in English.

b Then draw a clock on the blackboard. Draw in the hands and ask pupils to tell you the time. Repeat around the clock asking 'What's the time now?'

Step 2 Pairwork

a Hold up your book to the class. Point to one of the watches in the photograph on page 49 and ask 'What's the time?'

b Divide the class into pairs. Pupils ask and answer similar questions about the other watches in the photograph.

Step 3 Action game

a Bring two pupils to the front of the class. Say 'We are going to be clocks. Use your arms to show three o'clock.'

b Demonstrate. The pupils should copy. Repeat with other times. (Note: tell pupils to extend their hand for 'the big hand' and to clench their fist for 'the small hand'.)

c Then ask the two pupils to show various times without your help. Ask the rest of the class 'Is that correct?' Repeat the exercise with the whole class. Encourage pupils to check each other's responses.

Step 4 Reading (Task)

Pupils draw the hands on the clocks on page 60 in the Activity Book to show the appropriate time.

Step 5 Listening (Task)

a Pupils listen to the dictation on the tape and draw hands in the appropriate place on each clock face on page 60 of the Activity Book.

b (**Optional**) Further practice can be given by dividing the class into pairs. Pupils take turns in dictating times to their partners.

Tapescript:

a ten to eight; twenty past two; twenty to three; seven o'clock; quarter to twelve.

b twenty-five to nine; quarter past eight; five past nine; ten to one; six o'clock.

c ten past eleven; five to one; twenty-five past ten; quarter to seven; twenty-five to three.

d five to seven; four o'clock; twenty past three; ten to seven; twenty to nine.

Step 6 Crossword

Pupils write the times to complete the crossword puzzle on page 61 of the Activity Book.

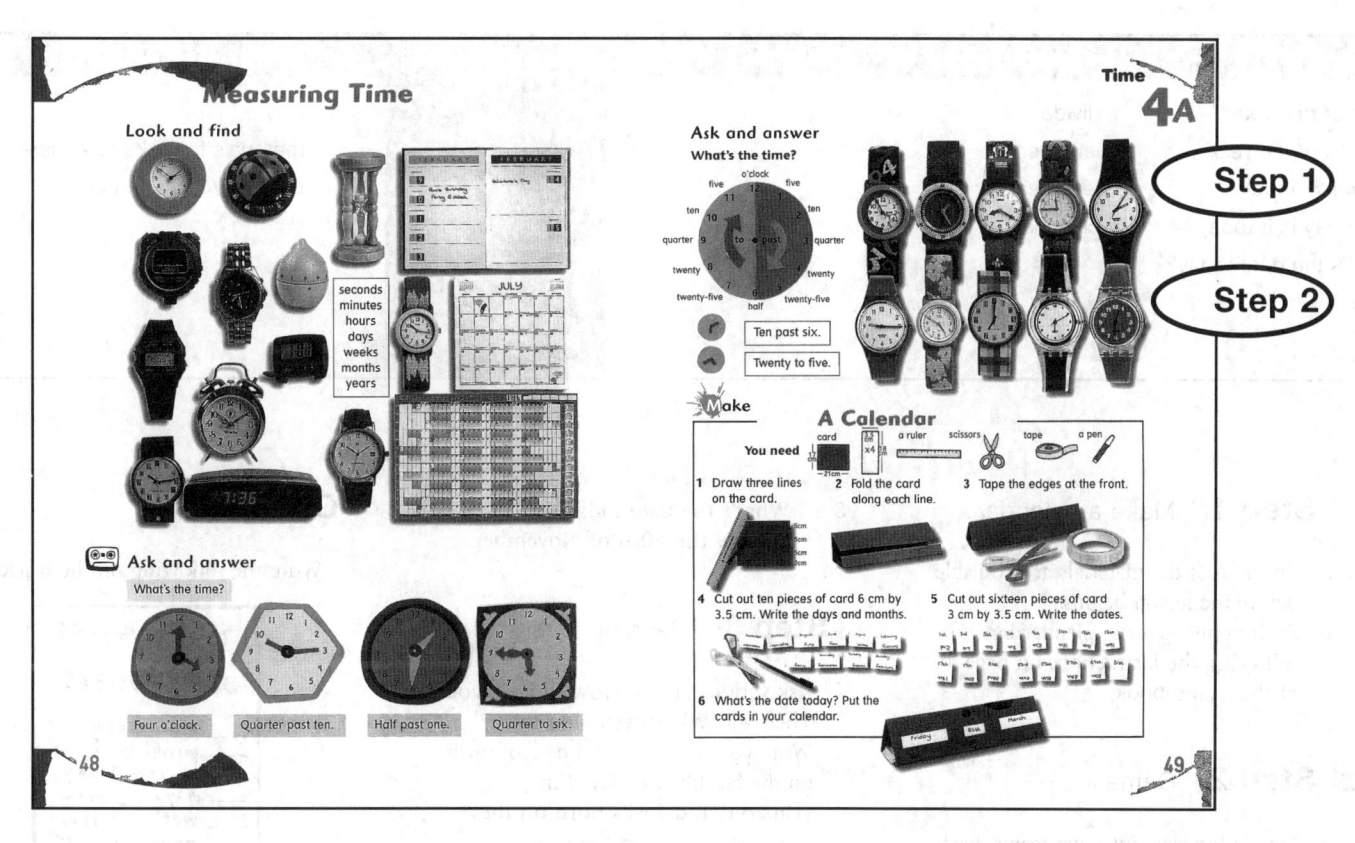

Measuring Time

Look and find

seconds
minutes
hours
days
weeks
months
years

Ask and answer

What's the time?

Four o'clock. Quarter past ten. Half past one. Quarter to six.

Ask and answer

What's the time?

five o'clock five
ten ten
quarter to past quarter
twenty twenty
twenty-five half twenty-five

Ten past six.
Twenty to five.

Make — A Calendar

You need: card x4 (21cm), a ruler, scissors, tape, a pen

1 Draw three lines on the card.
2 Fold the card along each line.
3 Tape the edges at the front.
4 Cut out ten pieces of card 6 cm by 3.5 cm. Write the days and months.
5 Cut out sixteen pieces of card 3 cm by 3.5 cm. Write the dates.
6 What's the date today? Put the cards in your calendar.

48 / 49

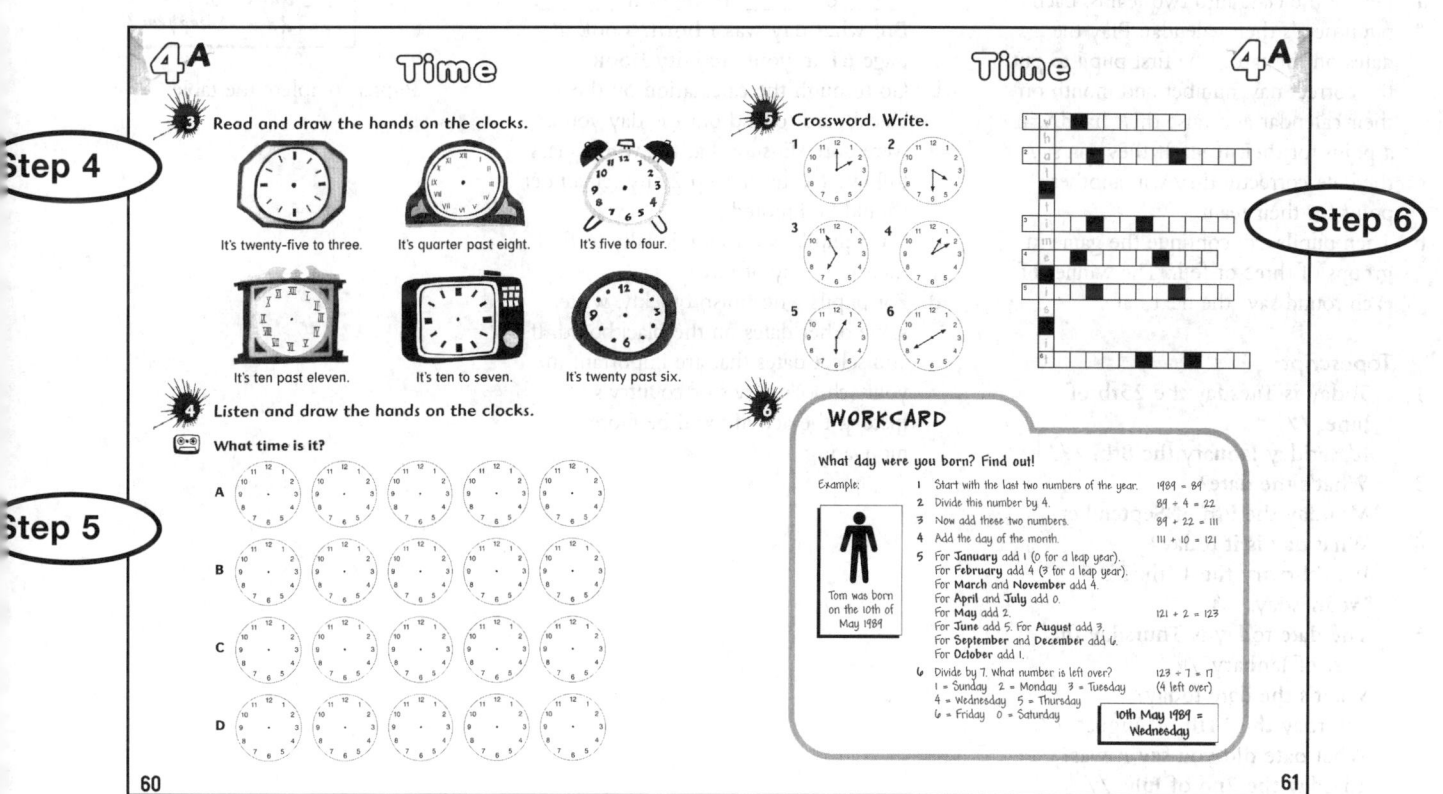

4A Time

3 Read and draw the hands on the clocks.

It's twenty-five to three. It's quarter past eight. It's five to four.
It's ten past eleven. It's ten to seven. It's twenty past six.

4 Listen and draw the hands on the clocks.

What time is it?

A B C D

5 Crossword. Write.

1 2 3 4 5 6

6 WORKCARD

What day were you born? Find out!

Example:
Tom was born on the 10th of May 1984

1 Start with the last two numbers of the year. 1984 = 84
2 Divide this number by 4. 84 ÷ 4 = 22
3 Now add these two numbers. 84 + 22 = 111
4 Add the day of the month. 111 + 10 = 121
5 For **January** add 1 (0 for a leap year).
   For **February** add 4 (3 for a leap year).
   For **March** and **November** add 4.
   For **April** and **July** add 0.
   For **May** add 2. 121 + 2 = 123
   For **June** add 5. For **August** add 3.
   For **September** and **December** add 6.
   For **October** add 1.
6 Divide by 7. What number is left over? 123 ÷ 7 = 17
   1 = Sunday 2 = Monday 3 = Tuesday (4 left over)
   4 = Wednesday 5 = Thursday
   6 = Friday 0 = Saturday

10th May 1984 = Wednesday

60 / 61

133

4A Lesson 3

Main Language Items		Resource File	Materials Needed
Days of the week	divide	21	materials to make calendars
Months of the year	left over	22	cassette/cassette player
Ordinal numbers	leap year	75	
What day is it today?	calendar		
What's the date today?			
born			
add			

Step 1   Make a calendar

a Ensure that the materials are available before the lesson begins.
b Each pupil makes a calendar by following the instructions on page 49 of the Coursebook.

Step 2   Game

a Divide the class into two teams. Each pupil needs their calendar. Play the dates on the tape. The first pupil to put the correct day, number and month on their calendar and raise their hand wins a point for their team. If they can say the date correctly they win another point for their team.
b Then pupils can continue the game in groups of three or four. The winner of each round says the next date.

Tapescript:
1 Today is Tuesday the 25th of June. //
2 It's Friday January the 8th. //
3 What's the date?
   Monday the 9th of September. //
4 What day is it today?
   It's February the 12th. It's a Wednesday. //
5 The date today is Thursday the 21st of January. //
6 What's the date today?
   Saturday the 11th of August. //
7 What date did you say it was?
   Tuesday the 2nd of July. //
8 What's the date today?
   Sunday the 20th of November.

Step 3   Reading (Task)

a Ask various pupils 'How old are you?' Then ask 'When were you born?' Write your own age and date of birth on the blackboard. Say 'I'm ____ years old and I was born on the ____ of ____ in the year ____. But what day was I born? Look at page 61 in your Activity Book.'
b Go through the calculation on the blackboard to find out the day you were born. Ensure that the whole class follows. (Note: at Step 2 any remainder should be ignored.)
c Then pupils work individually to find their own day of birth.
d For pupils who finish quickly, write some other dates on the blackboard. If you select dates that are important in your school's, city's or country's history, the activity will be more motivating.

Optional

Write the following on the blackboard:

```
7  24  60  52
366  60  365

____ seconds = 1 minute
____ minutes = 1 hour
____ hours = 1 day
____ days = 1 week
____ weeks = 1 year
____ days = 1 year
____ days = 1 leap year
```

Pupils complete the table.

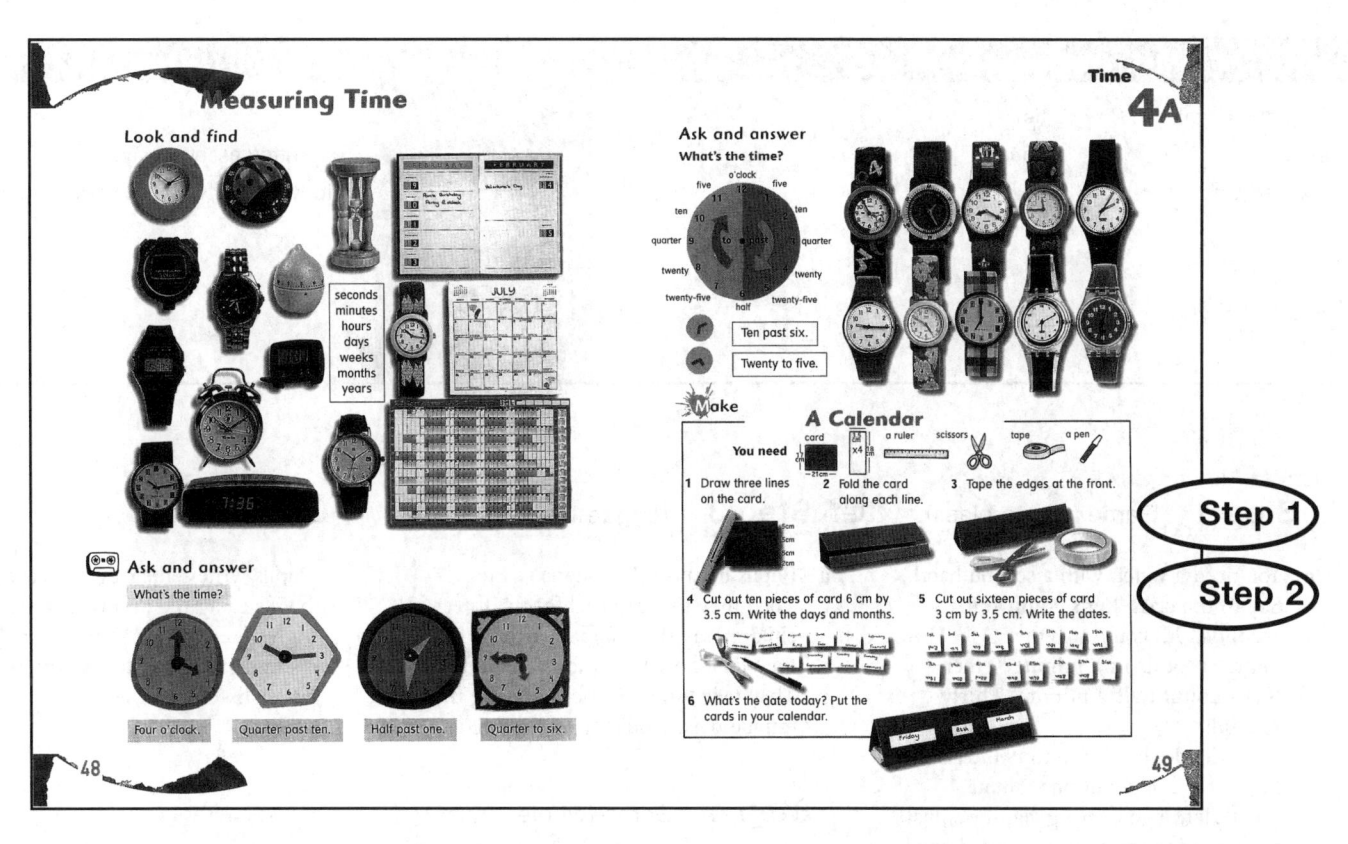

Measuring Time

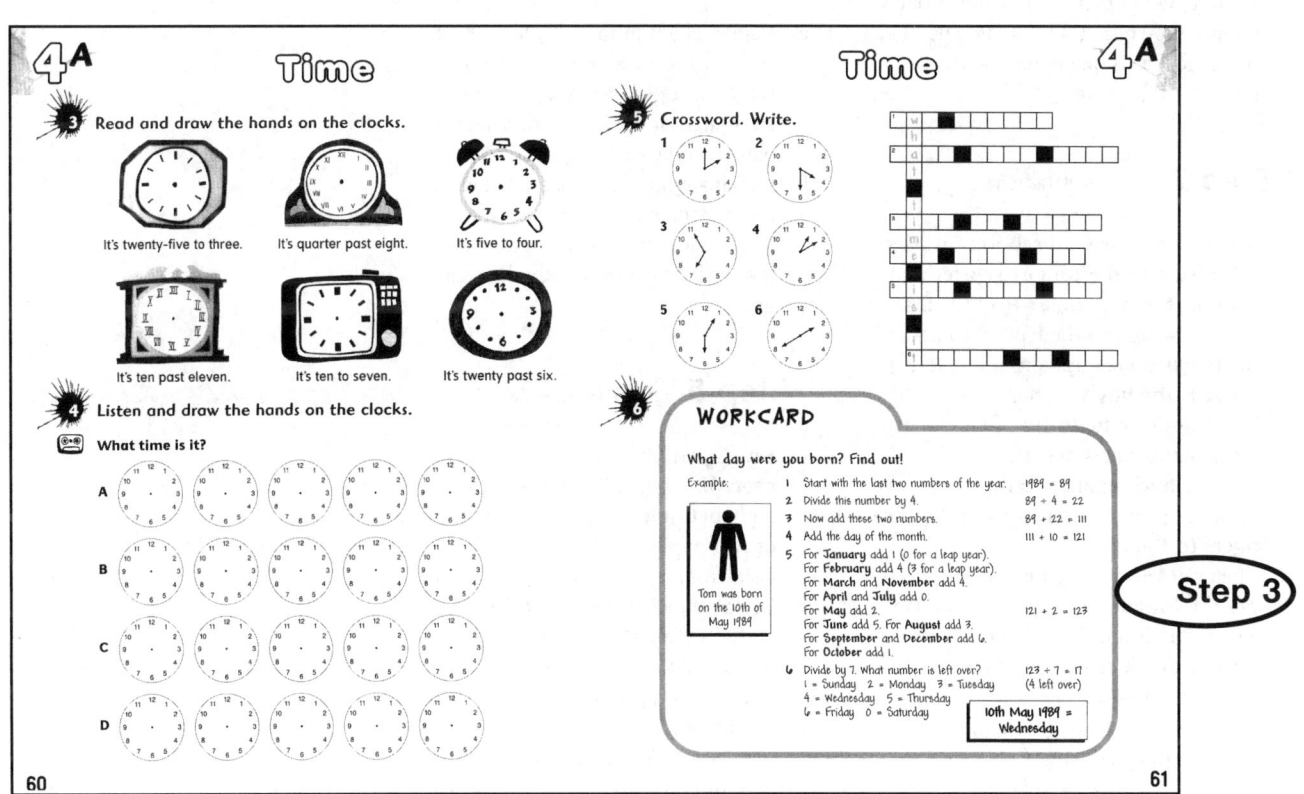

Look and find

seconds
minutes
hours
days
weeks
months
years

Ask and answer

What's the time?

Four o'clock. Quarter past ten. Half past one. Quarter to six.

Ask and answer

What's the time?

Ten past six.
Twenty to five.

Make — A Calendar

You need: card, a ruler, scissors, tape, a pen

1 Draw three lines on the card.
2 Fold the card along each line.
3 Tape the edges at the front.
4 Cut out ten pieces of card 6 cm by 3.5 cm. Write the days and months.
5 Cut out sixteen pieces of card 3 cm by 3.5 cm. Write the dates.
6 What's the date today? Put the cards in your calendar.

Time — 4A

3 Read and draw the hands on the clocks.

It's twenty-five to three.
It's quarter past eight.
It's five to four.
It's ten past eleven.
It's ten to seven.
It's twenty past six.

4 Listen and draw the hands on the clocks.

What time is it?

A B C D

5 Crossword. Write.

1 2 3 4 5 6

6 WORKCARD

What day were you born? Find out!

Example: Tom was born on the 10th of May 1984.

1 Start with the last two numbers of the year. 1984 = 84
2 Divide this number by 4. 84 ÷ 4 = 22
3 Now add these two numbers. 84 + 22 = 111
4 Add the day of the month. 111 + 10 = 121
5 For **January** add 1 (0 for a leap year).
For **February** add 4 (3 for a leap year).
For **March** and **November** add 4.
For **April** and **July** add 0.
For **May** add 2. 121 + 2 = 123
For **June** add 5. For **August** add 3.
For **September** and **December** add 6.
For **October** add 1.
6 Divide by 7. What number is left over? 123 ÷ 7 = 17 (4 left over)
1 = Sunday 2 = Monday 3 = Tuesday
4 = Wednesday 5 = Thursday
6 = Friday 0 = Saturday

10th May 1984 = Wednesday

4B Lesson 1

Main Language Items		Resource File	Materials Needed
How long does it take … ?	tie	45	cassette/cassette player
It takes …	count	61	stopwatch or watch with second hand
Ready, steady, go!	spell		

Step 1 Game (whole class)

a You need a watch with a second hand. Say to the class 'Let's count ten seconds.' All count together. Ask 'How many seconds in a minute?', then say 'Let's count half a minute. Thirty seconds.'

b Then divide the class into two teams. Pupils have to count one minute silently once you have given the signal to start. When they have counted one minute they raise their hands. The pupil closest to one minute wins a point for their team.

Step 2 Presentation

a Say 'Open your Coursebook on page 50. Listen to the tongue twister and read at the same time.' Play the first tongue twister on the tape, then ask the pupils some questions about it, e.g.
What is the boy's name?
What does he tie to the tree?
How many tigers are there?
Are the trees small or tall?
How long does it take him to tie the tigers to the trees?

b Then say 'How long does it take to say the tongue twister?' Play the tape again. Pupils must decide how long each of the three children take and who is the fastest.

c Then say the tongue twister yourself. Pupils count how long it takes.

Step 3 Tongue twister

a Pupils listen to the tongue twister.
b Then they listen to each of the three children say the tongue twister. In pairs they time how long the children take.
c They take turns to practise saying the tongue twister quickly and correctly.

Step 4 Game (whole class)

a Pupils take it in turns to come to the front of the class and say the tongue twister as quickly as they can. Use a stopwatch or a watch with a second hand to time each pupil.

b Nominate one pupil as a timekeeper, one as scorer to note times on the blackboard, and one as starter. Teach the starter the phrase 'Ready, steady, go!'

Step 5 Game (pairs)

a Say 'Open your Activity Book on page 62.' Ask 'Who can say the alphabet quickly in English?' Let one or two pupils try. Time them. Try other tasks from the grid with other pupils.

b Divide the class into pairs. Pupils perform the tasks in pairs. Their partners time them, either with a watch or by counting, and record the answers.

c Go over the exercise with the whole class. Say '*Alex*, how long did you take to count to twenty in English?' etc.

Optional

Pupils write sentences in their exercise books using the information from the above exercise, e.g. **It takes me […] seconds to count to twenty in English.**

How Long Does It Take?

Time 4B

Say the tongue twister

Tiny Trevor takes twenty-two and two-thirds of a second
to tie two tired tigers to two tall trees.
How long does it take Tiny Trevor
to tie two tired tigers to two tall trees?

How long does it take you to say the tongue twister?

Listen

Maureen's Morning

6 asleep | 7 got up / got washed / cleaned teeth / got dressed | 8 had breakfast | 9 watched TV | walked to school | at school | 10 | 11 | 12 had lunch

Ask and answer

What time did Maureen get up?	At five to seven.
What time did she have breakfast?	At ten to eight.
What time did she go school?	At quarter to nine.
What time did she get to school?	At ten past nine.

Sing

I Jump out of Bed in the Morning

I jump out of bed in the morning
I jump out of bed in the morning
I jump out of bed in the morning
I hope it's a very nice day!

I jump out of bed
and stretch myself in the morning
(3 times)

I jump out of bed
and stretch myself
and step in the bath ... in the morning
(3 times)

... and wash myself
... and dress myself
... and brush my teeth
... and comb my hair
... and eat my toast
... and wave goodbye
... and walk to school ... in the morning

I hope it's a very nice day!

What did you do this morning? Sing the song again.

4B Time

1 WORKCARD

How long does it take you to ...

	minutes	seconds
1 Count. ... count to twenty in English?		
... say the alphabet in English?		
... say the months in English?		
... say the days in English?		
... spell your name backwards in English?		
... write your name?		
... write the English alphabet?		

2 Write. It takes me _____ seconds to count to twenty in English.

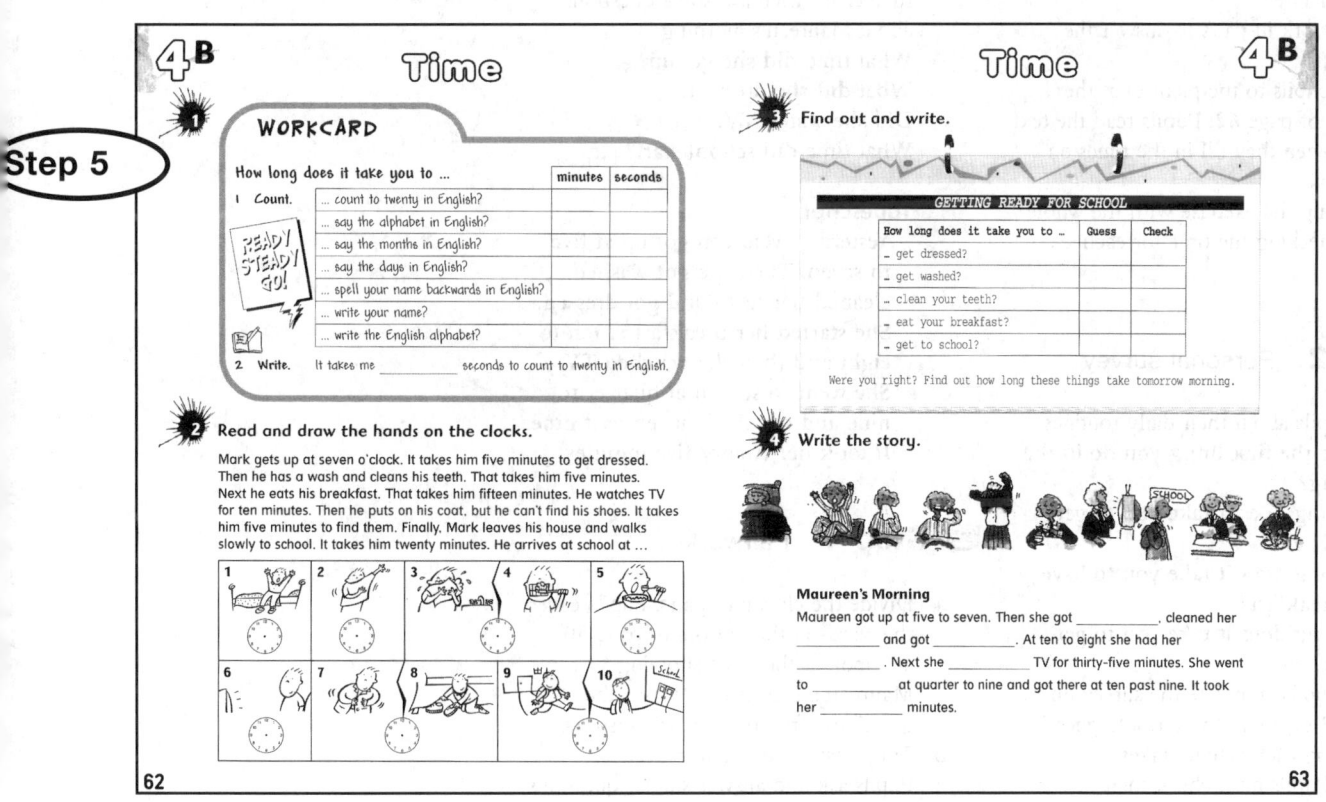

2 Read and draw the hands on the clocks.

Mark gets up at seven o'clock. It takes him five minutes to get dressed. Then he has a wash and cleans his teeth. That takes him five minutes. Next he eats his breakfast. That takes him fifteen minutes. He watches TV for ten minutes. Then he puts on his coat, but he can't find his shoes. It takes him five minutes to find them. Finally, Mark leaves his house and walks slowly to school. It takes him twenty minutes. He arrives at school at ...

3 Find out and write.

GETTING READY FOR SCHOOL

How long does it take you to ...	Guess	Check
get dressed?		
get washed?		
clean your teeth?		
eat your breakfast?		
get to school?		

Were you right? Find out how long these things take tomorrow morning.

4 Write the story.

Maureen's Morning

Maureen got up at five to seven. Then she got _____, cleaned her _____ and got _____. At ten to eight she had her _____. Next she _____ TV for thirty-five minutes. She went to _____ at quarter to nine and got there at ten past nine. It took her _____ minutes.

4B Lesson 2

Main Language Items			Resource File	Materials Needed
Simple past tense	got	started	16	cassette/cassette player
What time did ... ?	watched	went	17	
			26	
			39	

Step 1 Reading (Task)

a Say 'Open your Activity Book on page 62.' Read the text to the class. Then ask:
What does Mark do first?
What time does he get up?
Then what does he do?
Write the following on the blackboard:
What time does he get to school?
School starts at five to nine. Is he early or late?
Pupils work in pairs to answer the questions.

b Direct pupils to the pictures at the bottom of page 62. Pupils read the text again. Then they fill in the times on the clocks.

c Round up the exercise with the whole class, checking the time for each picture.

Step 2 Personal survey

a Ask pupils about their daily routines.
What is the first thing you do in the morning?
How long does it take you to get washed?
How long does it take you to have your breakfast?
How long does it take you to get dressed? etc.

b Then pupils complete the survey on page 63 of the Activity Book, guessing how long each activity takes.
(Note: Pupils must check their answers the next morning to complete the grid.)

Step 3 Presentation

a Say 'Open your Coursebook on page 50. Look at the pictures in the middle of the page and listen to the tape.'

b Make sure that pupils understand the time chart, then ask some questions about Maureen's morning.
What time did she get up?
What did she do next?
Did she watch TV?
What time did school start? etc.

Tapescript:
Yesterday Maureen got up at five to seven. Then she got washed, cleaned her teeth and got dressed. She started her breakfast at ten to eight and then she watched TV. She went to school at quarter to nine and got there at ten past nine. It took her twenty-five minutes.

Step 4 Pairwork

a Divide the class into pairs. Pupils cover the words at the bottom of page 50 and look at the chart showing **Maureen's Morning**. P1 asks the questions after the tape. P2 answers.

b They change roles and repeat.

c Pupils ask and answer similar questions about **Maureen's Morning**.

Step 5 Write

Using the information given in the Coursebook, pupils complete the description of **Maureen's Morning** on page 63 of the Activity Book.

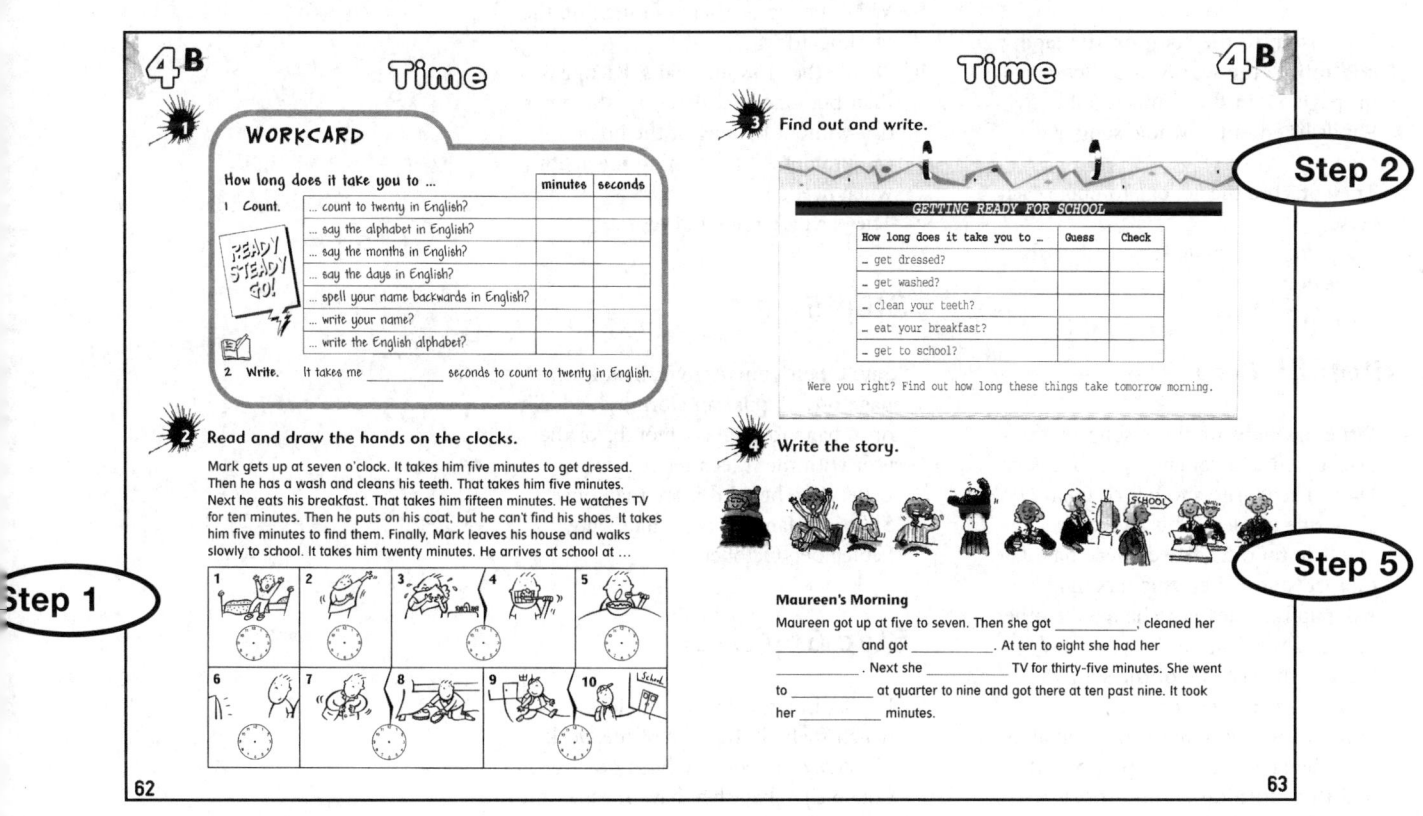

How Long Does It Take?

Say the tongue twister

Tiny Trevor takes twenty-two and two-thirds of a second
to tie two tired tigers to two tall trees.
How long does it take Tiny Trevor
to tie two tired tigers to two tall trees?

How long does it take you to say the tongue twister?

Listen

Maureen's Morning

6 — asleep
7 — got up / got washed / cleaned teeth / got dressed
8 — had breakfast / watched TV
9 — walked to school / at school
12 — had lunch

Ask and answer

What time did Maureen get up?	At five to seven.
What time did she have breakfast?	At ten to eight.
What time did she go school?	At quarter to nine.
What time did she get to school?	At ten past nine.

Time 4B

Sing — I Jump out of Bed in the Morning

I jump out of bed in the morning
I jump out of bed in the morning
I jump out of bed in the morning
I hope it's a very nice day!

I jump out of bed
and stretch myself in the morning
(3 times)

I jump out of bed
and stretch myself
and step in the bath ... in the morning
(3 times)

... and wash myself
... and dress myself
... and brush my teeth
... and comb my hair
... and eat my toast
... and wave goodbye
... and walk to school ... in the morning

I hope it's a very nice day!

What did you do this morning? Sing the song again.

4B Time

1. WORKCARD

How long does it take you to ...	minutes	seconds
1 Count. ... count to twenty in English?		
... say the alphabet in English?		
... say the months in English?		
... say the days in English?		
... spell your name backwards in English?		
... write your name?		
... write the English alphabet?		

READY STEADY GO!

2 Write. It takes me _____ seconds to count to twenty in English.

2 Read and draw the hands on the clocks.

Mark gets up at seven o'clock. It takes him five minutes to get dressed. Then he has a wash and cleans his teeth. That takes him five minutes. Next he eats his breakfast. That takes him fifteen minutes. He watches TV for ten minutes. Then he puts on his coat, but he can't find his shoes. It takes him five minutes to find them. Finally, Mark leaves his house and walks slowly to school. It takes him twenty minutes. He arrives at school at ...

Time 4B

3 Find out and write.

| GETTING READY FOR SCHOOL |
How long does it take you to ...	Guess	Check
_ get dressed?		
_ get washed?		
_ clean your teeth?		
_ eat your breakfast?		
_ get to school?		

Were you right? Find out how long these things take tomorrow morning.

4 Write the story.

Maureen's Morning

Maureen got up at five to seven. Then she got _____, cleaned her _____ and got _____. At ten to eight she had her _____. Next she _____ TV for thirty-five minutes. She went to _____ at quarter to nine and got there at ten past nine. It took her _____ minutes.

4B Lesson 3

Main Language Items	Resource File	Materials Needed
Simple present and simple past	16	
jump(ed) dress(ed) wave(d)	39	cassette/cassette player
stretch(ed) brush(ed) walk(ed)	49	
step(ped) comb(ed) hope(d)	53	
wash(ed) eat/ate is/was		

Step 1   Personal file

Pupils draw a time line of their own morning on page 64 of the Activity Book, using the example in the Coursebook to help. Tell them to think about the questions next to the chart in the Activity Book as they do this.

Step 2   Song

a   Say 'Listen to the song on the tape and follow the words and pictures on page 51 in the Coursebook.' Pupils listen to the whole song and then to each verse.

b   They practise the actions to mime each verse.

c   They sing the whole song and perform the actions.

Step 3   Song

a   Write the verbs from the song on the blackboard in a column headed '**Every Day**'. Then write another column alongside headed '**This Morning**'.

b   Say '**I jump out of bed every day. I jumped out of bed this morning.**' Ask pupils if they can change the other verses of the song in the same way. Change the last line of the song to '**And it was a very nice day.**'

c   Sing the new version of the song along with the tape. (i.e. '**I jumped out of bed this morning ... and it was a very nice day.**')

Step 4   Pairwork

a   Say 'Close your books. What did the boy in the song do? First he ... ?' Mime the actions to prompt the pupils if they are having difficulty remembering. Continue with the other verses of the song prompting pupils with the following questions: '**What did he do next? Then what did he do?**' Write the words **then** and **next** on the blackboard.

b   Divide the class into pairs. P1 opens their book and P2 describes the boy's day without looking at the book. P1 can prompt P2 by miming the actions when needed.

c   They change roles and repeat.

Step 5   Puzzle

Say '**Open your Activity Book on page 64.**' Pupils can work individually or in pairs to spell six months of the year with the fifteen letters given. Letters can be used more than once.
Solution: January, May, June, July, September, October.

Step 6   Puzzle

Pupils should colour in the letters which spell all the days of the week. ('Monday' has already been done as an example.) When they have finished the shaded squares should spell out a word.
Solution: Friday

140

How Long Does It Take?

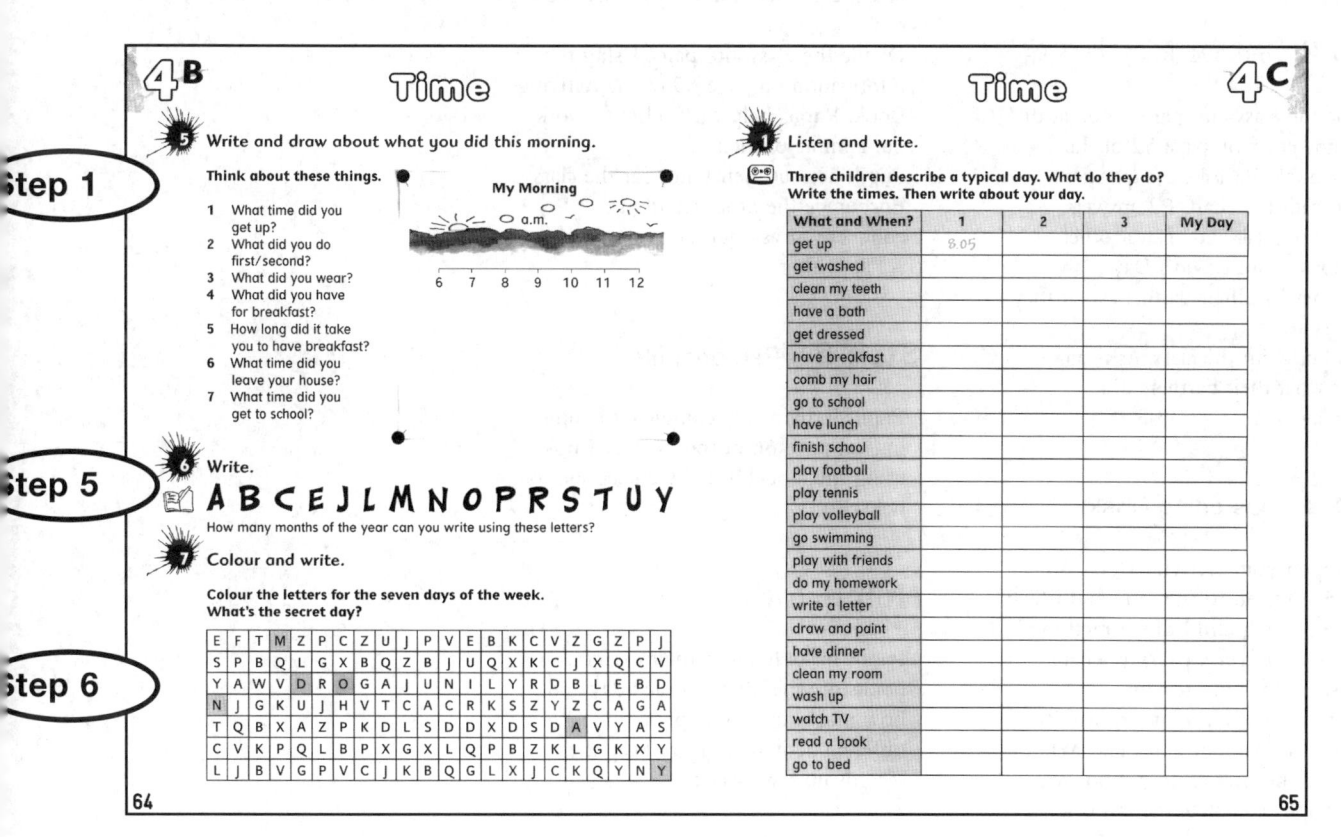

Say the tongue twister

Tiny Trevor takes twenty-two and two-thirds of a second to tie two tired tigers to two tall trees.
How long does it take Tiny Trevor to tie two tired tigers to two tall trees?

How long does it take you to say the tongue twister?

Listen

Maureen's Morning

6 7 8 9 10 11 12

asleep | got up | got washed / cleaned teeth / got dressed | had breakfast | watched TV | walked to school | at school | had lunch

Ask and answer

What time did Maureen get up?	At five to seven.
What time did she have breakfast?	At ten to eight.
What time did she go school?	At quarter to nine.
What time did she get to school?	At ten past nine.

Time 4B

Sing

I Jump out of Bed in the Morning

I jump out of bed in the morning
I jump out of bed in the morning
I jump out of bed in the morning
I hope it's a very nice day!

I jump out of bed
and stretch myself in the morning
(3 times)

I jump out of bed
and stretch myself
and step in the bath ... in the morning
(3 times)

... and wash myself
... and dress myself
... and brush my teeth
... and comb my hair
... and eat my toast
... and wave goodbye
... and walk to school ... in the morning

I hope it's a very nice day!

What did you do this morning? Sing the song again.

4B Time

5 Write and draw about what you did this morning.

Think about these things.

1 What time did you get up?
2 What did you do first/second?
3 What did you wear?
4 What did you have for breakfast?
5 How long did it take you to have breakfast?
6 What time did you leave your house?
7 What time did you get to school?

My Morning
a.m.
6 7 8 9 10 11 12

6 Write.

A B C E J L M N O P R S T U Y

How many months of the year can you write using these letters?

7 Colour and write.

Colour the letters for the seven days of the week.
What's the secret day?

E	F	T	M	Z	P	C	Z	U	J	P	V	E	B	K	C	V	Z	G	Z	P	J
S	P	B	Q	L	G	X	B	Q	Z	B	J	U	Q	X	K	C	J	X	Q	C	V
Y	A	W	V	D	R	O	G	A	J	U	N	I	L	Y	R	D	B	L	E	B	D
N	J	G	K	U	J	H	V	T	C	A	C	R	K	S	Z	Y	Z	C	A	G	A
T	Q	B	X	A	Z	P	K	D	L	S	D	D	X	D	S	D	A	V	Y	A	S
C	V	K	P	Q	L	B	P	X	G	X	L	Q	P	B	Z	K	L	G	K	X	Y
L	J	B	V	G	P	V	C	J	K	B	Q	G	L	X	J	C	K	Q	Y	N	Y

Time 4C

1 Listen and write.

Three children describe a typical day. What do they do?
Write the times. Then write about your day.

What and When?	1	2	3	My Day
get up	8.05			
get washed				
clean my teeth				
have a bath				
get dressed				
have breakfast				
comb my hair				
go to school				
have lunch				
finish school				
play football				
play tennis				
play volleyball				
go swimming				
play with friends				
do my homework				
write a letter				
draw and paint				
have dinner				
clean my room				
wash up				
watch TV				
read a book				
go to bed				

4c Lesson 1

Main Language Items		Resource File	Materials Needed
Simple past tense What did ... do ... ?	morning afternoon evening	10 16 26 39	cassette/cassette player

Step 1 Presentation

a Ask pupils questions about what they did earlier today and yesterday, e.g. **'What time did you get to school this morning?'**

b Then say **'Open your Coursebook on page 52.'** Ask questions about what David did, e.g. **'What time did he get up?'**, **'Did he watch TV?'** etc.

Step 2 Pairwork

a Divide the class into pairs. Look at the time-line chart on page 52 of the Coursebook. P1 asks the questions underneath the chart. P2 answers.

b Then pupils ask and answer other questions about David's Day.

c Then they ask their partners what they did yesterday.

d Round up with the class. Ask some pupils what their partners did yesterday.

Step 3 Listening (Task)

a Say **'Open your Activity Book on page 65. Listen to the tape and fill in the times each child did something.'** Play the tape twice, pausing where necessary for pupils to write.

b Check in pairs and round up with the whole class. Ask questions like **'What time did the first child get up?'** etc.

c Then pupils complete the last column on the page with the times of the things they did yesterday. (See tapescript on page 178.)

Step 4 Action game

a Mime a series of actions showing the things you did yesterday, e.g. wake up, get washed, get dressed, go to school, teach, eat lunch. Pupils say what you did.

b Divide the class into pairs. Using the information on page 65 of the Activity Book. Pupils help each other to work out a mime of their day.

c Pupils act out their mime for the class. Encourage the other children to comment or ask questions about what is happening.

Step 5 Personal file

Pupils individually complete the time line on page 66 of the Activity Book using the model in the Coursebook to help.

Homework

Pupils make notes in their exercise books of what they do each day and how much time they spend on different activities. Try to keep these records up for a week.

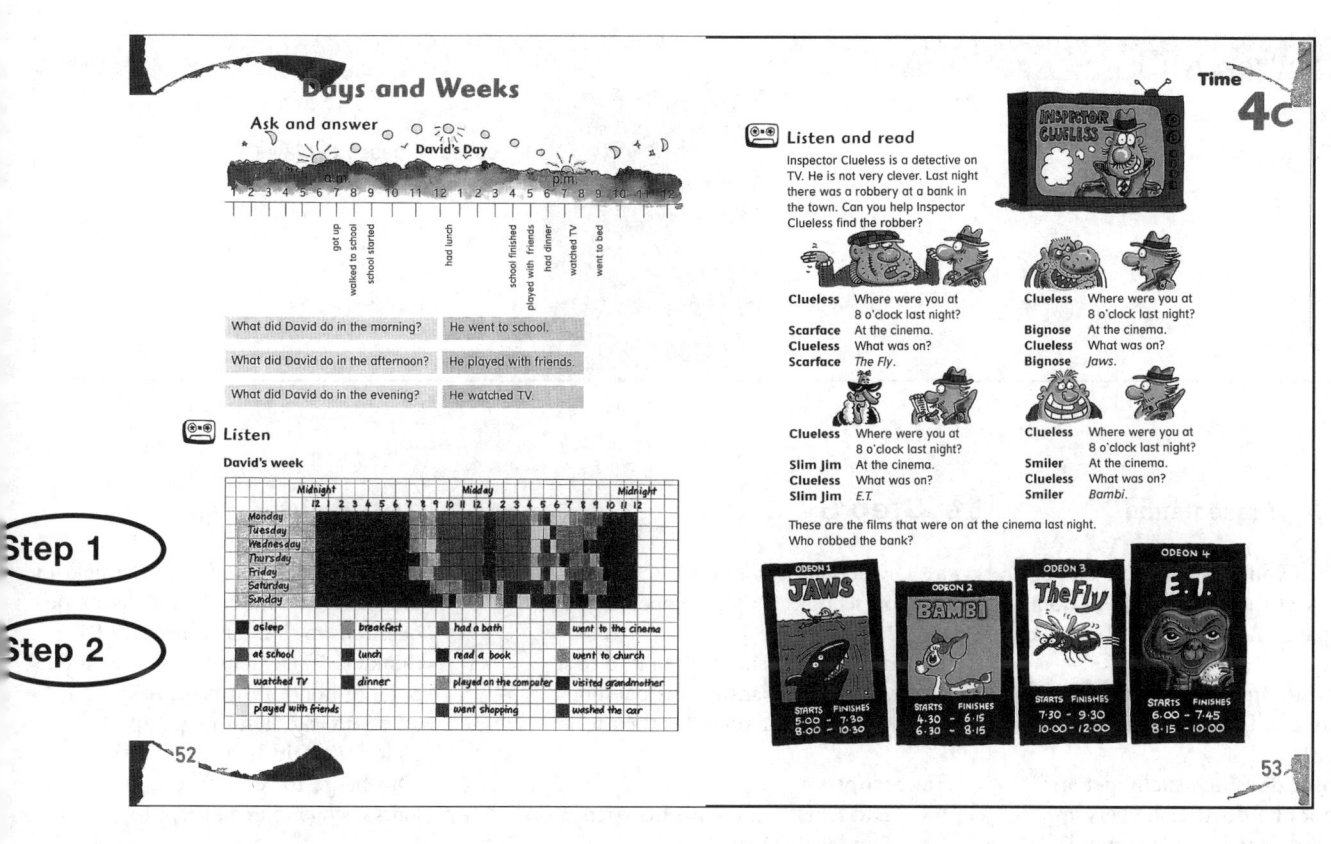

Days and Weeks

Ask and answer

David's Day

a.m. 1 2 3 4 5 6 7 8 9 10 11 12 p.m. 1 2 3 4 5 6 7 8 9 10 11 12

got up / walked to school / school started / had lunch / school finished / played with friends / had dinner / watched TV / went to bed

What did David do in the morning?	He went to school.
What did David do in the afternoon?	He played with friends.
What did David do in the evening?	He watched TV.

Listen

David's week

Midnight 12 1 2 3 4 5 6 7 8 9 10 11 Midday 12 1 2 3 4 5 6 7 8 9 10 11 Midnight 12

Monday / Tuesday / Wednesday / Thursday / Friday / Saturday / Sunday

- asleep
- breakfast
- had a bath
- went to the cinema
- at school
- lunch
- read a book
- went to church
- watched TV
- dinner
- played on the computer
- visited grandmother
- played with friends
- went shopping
- washed the car

52

Time 4c

Listen and read

Inspector Clueless is a detective on TV. He is not very clever. Last night there was a robbery at a bank in the town. Can you help Inspector Clueless find the robber?

Clueless Where were you at 8 o'clock last night?
Scarface At the cinema.
Clueless What was on?
Scarface *The Fly.*

Clueless Where were you at 8 o'clock last night?
Bignose At the cinema.
Clueless What was on?
Bignose *Jaws.*

Clueless Where were you at 8 o'clock last night?
Slim Jim At the cinema.
Clueless What was on?
Slim Jim *E.T.*

Clueless Where were you at 8 o'clock last night?
Smiler At the cinema.
Clueless What was on?
Smiler *Bambi.*

These are the films that were on at the cinema last night. Who robbed the bank?

ODEON 1 — JAWS — STARTS FINISHES 5·00 – 7·30 8·00 – 10·30
ODEON 2 — BAMBI — STARTS FINISHES 4·30 – 6·15 6·30 – 8·15
ODEON 3 — The Fly — STARTS FINISHES 7·30 – 9·30 10·00 – 12·00
ODEON 4 — E.T. — STARTS FINISHES 6·00 – 7·45 8·15 – 10·00

53

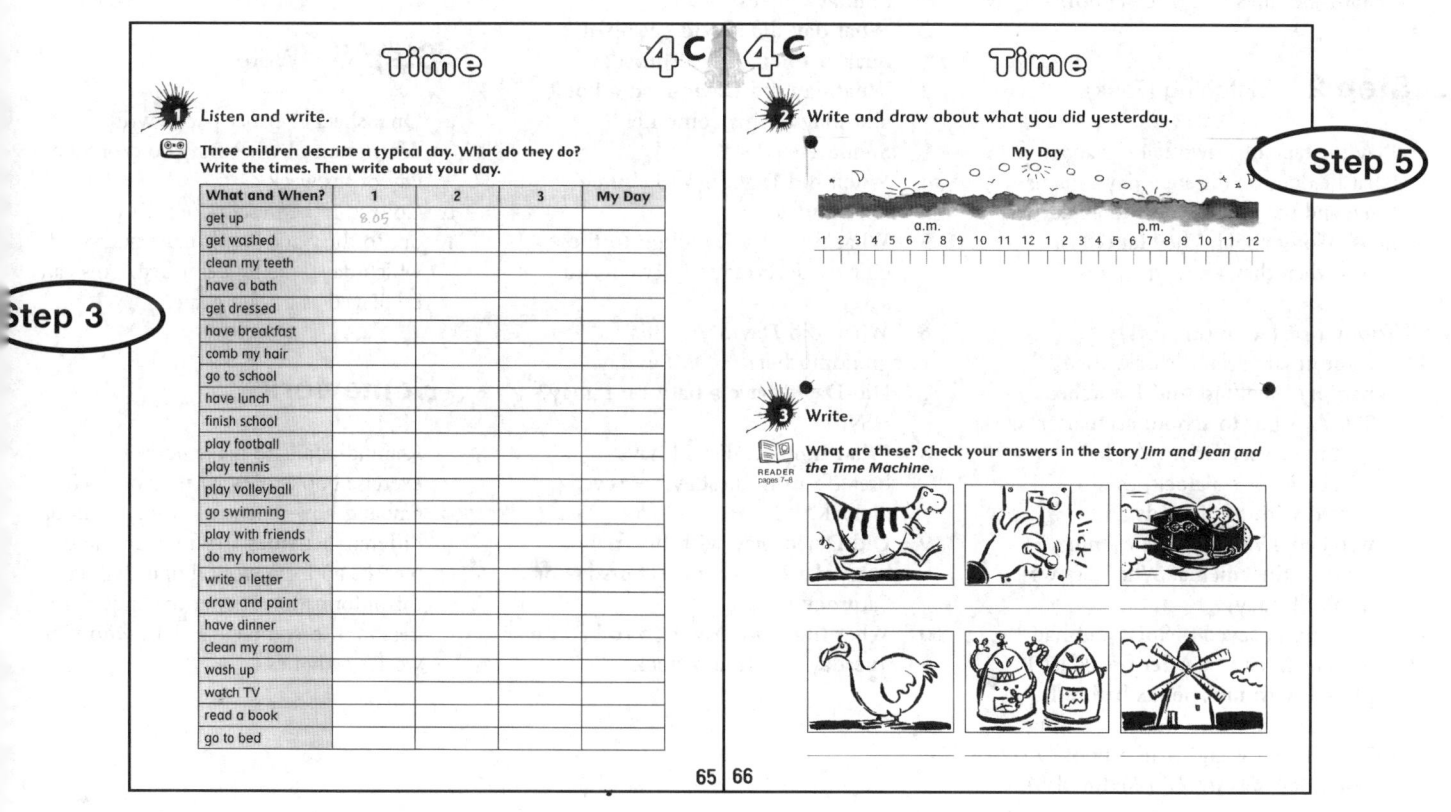

Time 4c

1. Listen and write.

Three children describe a typical day. What do they do? Write the times. Then write about your day.

What and When?	1	2	3	My Day
get up	8 05			
get washed				
clean my teeth				
have a bath				
get dressed				
have breakfast				
comb my hair				
go to school				
have lunch				
finish school				
play football				
play tennis				
play volleyball				
go swimming				
play with friends				
do my homework				
write a letter				
draw and paint				
have dinner				
clean my room				
wash up				
watch TV				
read a book				
go to bed				

65

4c Time

2. Write and draw about what you did yesterday.

My Day

a.m. 1 2 3 4 5 6 7 8 9 10 11 12 p.m. 1 2 3 4 5 6 7 8 9 10 11 12

3. Write.

What are these? Check your answers in the story *Jim and Jean and the Time Machine*.

READER pages 7–8

66

4c Lesson 2

Main Language Items		Resource File	Materials Needed
Simple past tense	breakfast	16	cassette/cassette player
What did you do?	lunch	26	
Did he ...?	dinner	39	
visited		49	

Step 1 Presentation

Say 'Open your Coursebook on page 52. Look at the chart at the bottom of the page.' Ask questions about the chart e.g.
What do the red squares mean?
What time did David get up on Monday?
What time does he usually get up?
What does he do after he gets up?
What time does he go to school?

Step 2 Listening (Task)

Play the tape of David talking about what he does on different days. Pupils listen and try to work out which day he is talking about. They raise their hands when they know the answer.

Tapescript (with answers):

1. I got up at seven o'clock, then I had my breakfast and I watched TV. // I got to school at quarter to nine. I was early. // I left school at four o'clock, then I played with my friends and watched TV. // In the evening I went to the cinema. What day was it? // (Friday)
2. I got up at seven o'clock and had my breakfast. // After breakfast I played with my friends before I went to school. // In the evening I watched TV and read a book. // What day was it? // (Wednesday)

Step 3 Quiz

a Divide the class into two teams. Coursebooks should be open on page 52.
b Play the tape. The first pupil to raise their hand and answer the question correctly wins a point for their team.

Tapescript:

1. Did David play with his friends on Sunday? ~ Yes.
2. What day did David get up at quarter to eight? ~ Thursday.
3. What day did David read a book and play on his computer? ~ Sunday.
4. When did David go to church? ~ On Sunday.
5. What time did David go to the cinema on Friday? ~ Twenty to seven.
6. When did David visit his grandmother? ~ On Sunday.
7. Did David have a bath on Friday? ~ No.
8. What time did David have breakfast on Tuesday? ~ Seven o'clock.
9. Did David play with his friends every day? ~ No, not Thursday or Saturday.
10. What time did David go to bed on Tuesday? ~ Nine o'clock.

Step 4 Game (pairs)

a Divide the class into pairs. P1 thinks of one of David's days. P2 asks 'yes'/'no' questions to find out which day P1 is thinking of. Demonstrate first with one pupil in front of the class. Ask questions, e.g. 'Did he get up at 8 o'clock?', 'Did he read a book?', 'Did he go to school?' etc.
b Pairs change roles and repeat.

Step 5 Write

a On a sheet of paper pupils write a description of what David did on one day of his week.
b Collect in the descriptions. Read them out to the class. Pupils must guess which day is being described. This can be played as a team game.

Homework

Remind pupils to make notes in their exercise books of what they do each day and how much time they spend on different activities. Try to keep these records up for a week. Pupils will use this information later at the end of 4E Lesson 3 to complete a chart with their week's activities.

Days and Weeks

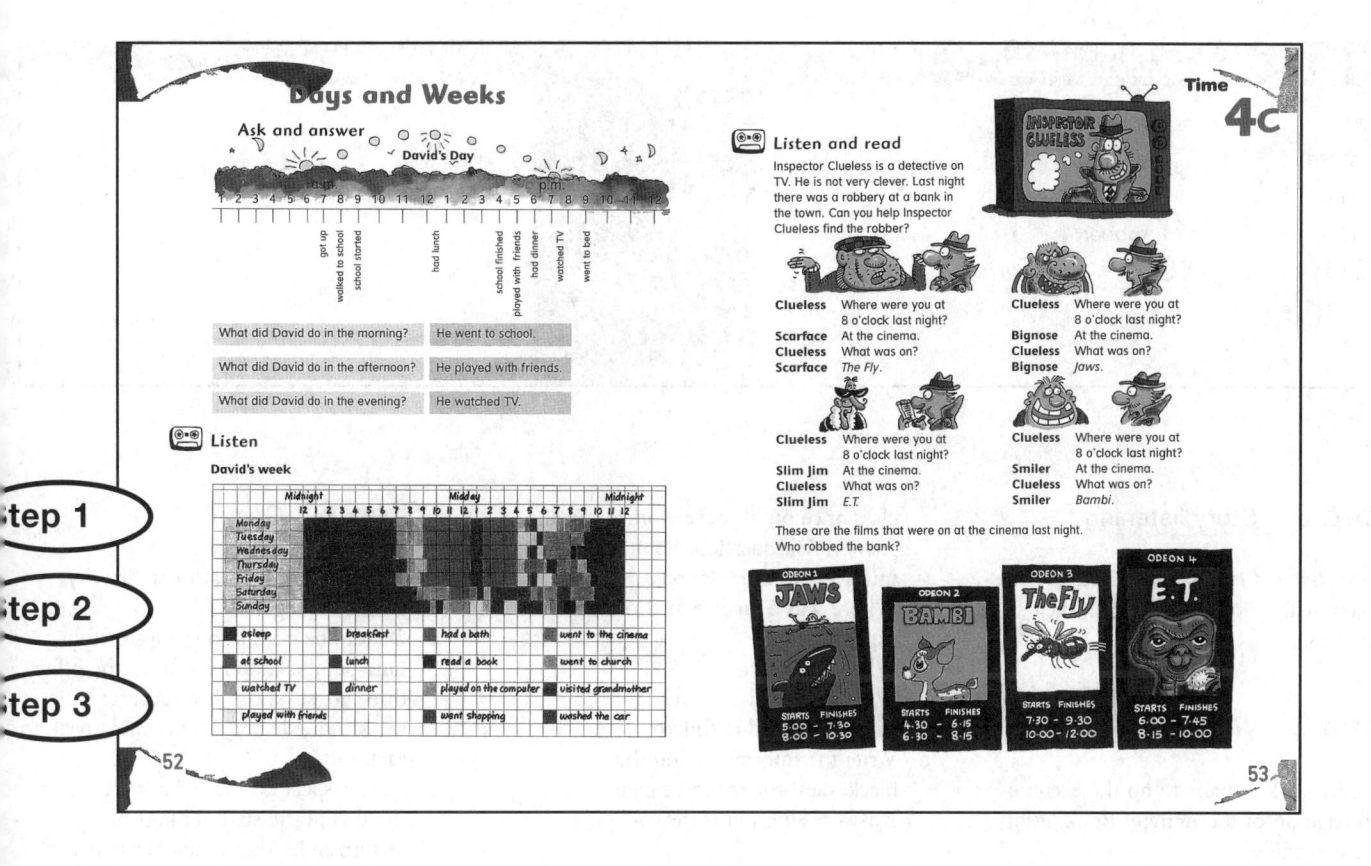

Ask and answer

David's Day

a.m. | p.m.
1 2 3 4 5 6 7 8 9 10 11 12 1 2 3 4 5 6 7 8 9 10 11 12

- got up
- walked to school
- school started
- had lunch
- school finished
- played with friends
- had dinner
- watched TV
- went to bed

What did David do in the morning?	He went to school.
What did David do in the afternoon?	He played with friends.
What did David do in the evening?	He watched TV.

Listen

David's week

	Midnight 12 1 2 3 4 5 6 7 8 9 10 11	Midday 12 1 2 3 4 5 6 7 8 9 10 11	Midnight 12
Monday			
Tuesday			
Wednesday			
Thursday			
Friday			
Saturday			
Sunday			

asleep	breakfast	had a bath	went to the cinema
at school	lunch	read a book	went to church
watched TV	dinner	played on the computer	visited grandmother
played with friends	went shopping	washed the car	

Time 4c

Listen and read

Inspector Clueless is a detective on TV. He is not very clever. Last night there was a robbery at a bank in the town. Can you help Inspector Clueless find the robber?

Clueless Where were you at 8 o'clock last night?
Scarface At the cinema.
Clueless What was on?
Scarface *The Fly*.

Clueless Where were you at 8 o'clock last night?
Bignose At the cinema.
Clueless What was on?
Bignose *Jaws*.

Clueless Where were you at 8 o'clock last night?
Slim Jim At the cinema.
Clueless What was on?
Slim Jim *E.T.*

Clueless Where were you at 8 o'clock last night?
Smiler At the cinema.
Clueless What was on?
Smiler *Bambi*.

These are the films that were on at the cinema last night. Who robbed the bank?

ODEON 1 — JAWS
STARTS FINISHES
5.00 – 7.30
8.00 – 10.30

ODEON 2 — BAMBI
STARTS FINISHES
4.30 – 6.15
6.30 – 8.15

ODEON 3 — The Fly
STARTS FINISHES
7.30 – 9.30
10.00 – 12.00

ODEON 4 — E.T.
STARTS FINISHES
6.00 – 7.45
8.15 – 10.00

Step 1
Step 2
Step 3

4c Lesson 3

Main Language Items		Resource File	Materials Needed
Story revision	rob(bed)		
Past simple tense	detective	36	Reader
Where were you?	bank	42	cassette/cassette player
What was on?	robber	49	
What time did … ?			
start(ed)			
finish(ed)			

Step 1 Story listening

Read *Jim and Jean and the Time Machine* again, with pupils following in their Readers.

Step 2 Write

Pupils work in pairs to do the exercise on page 66 of the Activity Book, using their Readers.
Solution: dinosaur; switch; Time Machine; dodo; robots; windmill

Step 3 Presentation

a   Say 'Open your Coursebook on page 53. Listen to the tape and read at the same time.'
b   Play the tape. Briefly ask questions to check comprehension:
How many men did Inspector Clueless talk to?
Who did he talk to first?
Which film did Bignose watch?
What was on at Odeon 1?
What time did *Jaws* start? etc.

Step 4 Reading (Task)

a   Three of the men are telling the truth, one is lying. Pupils read through the information on page 53 to find out who the robber is.
b   Go over the exercise with the whole class once pupils have worked out the answer. Ask questions about each interview to guide pupils:
Where was Scarface at 8 o'clock last night?
What was on?
What time did it start?
What time did it finish?
c   Write the information on the blackboard for reinforcement.
Answer: Slim Jim is the robber.

Step 5 Role play

a   Divide the class into groups of three. One pupil is Inspector Clueless and the other two are suspects.
b   The suspects decide who is going to be the robber. One of them must tell a lie about the films when the inspector interviews them.
c   Inspector Clueless interviews each of the suspects in turn. Use the questions on page 53 to help. The inspector must decide which suspect is lying, based upon what he is told and the information about the films on page 53.
d   Pupils change roles and repeat.
e   To make the exercise more challenging the pupils should try and memorise the information about the films and close their books. The suspects need only know about the film they say that they watched, but the inspector will need to know about all four films.

Step 6 Game

a   Tell pupils to look at their Activity Books on page 67.
b   Divide the class into groups of four. One pupil is a police officer, the other three are suspects. The suspects must work individually, they cannot speak to each other.
c   Each suspect decides what time he or she was in the six buildings in the picture and writes a number between five and ten on the signs outside each building (use pencils so that the game can be repeated). The police officer decides what time the bank was robbed but does not tell any of the suspects.
d   The police officer then interviews each of the suspects in turn to find out who was in the bank at the time it was robbed.
e   Pupils change roles and repeat the game.

Days and Weeks

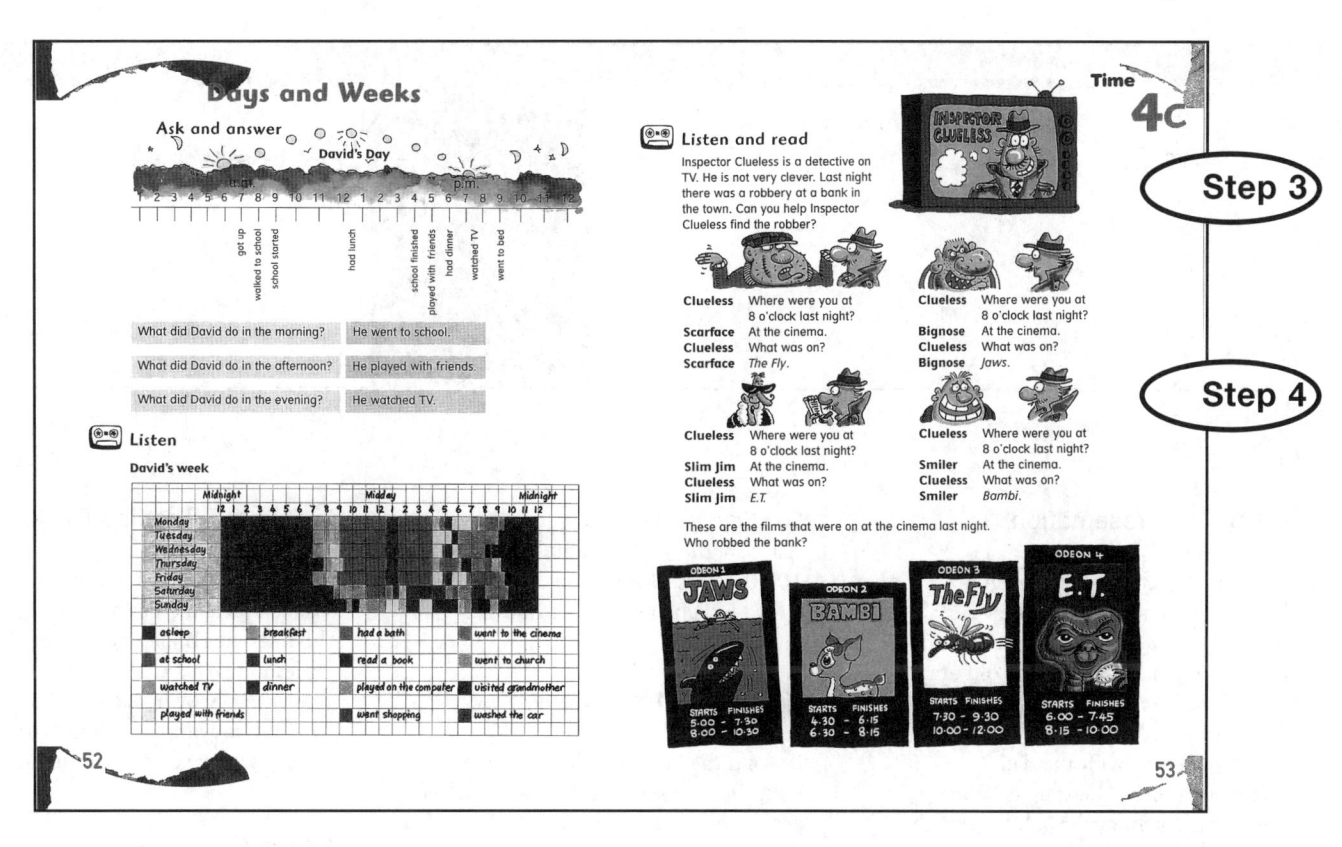

Ask and answer

David's Day

a.m. — p.m.
1 2 3 4 5 6 7 8 9 10 11 12 1 2 3 4 5 6 7 8 9 10 11 12

got up
walked to school
school started
had lunch
school finished
played with friends
had dinner
watched TV
went to bed

What did David do in the morning?	He went to school.
What did David do in the afternoon?	He played with friends.
What did David do in the evening?	He watched TV.

Listen

David's week

	Midnight 12 1 2 3 4 5 6 7 8 9 10 11	Midday 12 1 2 3 4 5 6 7 8 9 10 11	Midnight 12
Monday			
Tuesday			
Wednesday			
Thursday			
Friday			
Saturday			
Sunday			

- asleep
- at school
- watched TV
- played with friends
- breakfast
- lunch
- dinner
- went shopping
- had a bath
- read a book
- played on the computer
- went to the cinema
- went to church
- visited grandmother
- washed the car

52

Time 4c

Listen and read

Inspector Clueless is a detective on TV. He is not very clever. Last night there was a robbery at a bank in the town. Can you help Inspector Clueless find the robber?

Clueless Where were you at 8 o'clock last night?
Scarface At the cinema.
Clueless What was on?
Scarface *The Fly.*

Clueless Where were you at 8 o'clock last night?
Bignose At the cinema.
Clueless What was on?
Bignose *Jaws.*

Clueless Where were you at 8 o'clock last night?
Slim Jim At the cinema.
Clueless What was on?
Slim Jim *E.T.*

Clueless Where were you at 8 o'clock last night?
Smiler At the cinema.
Clueless What was on?
Smiler *Bambi.*

These are the films that were on at the cinema last night.
Who robbed the bank?

ODEON 1	ODEON 2	ODEON 3	ODEON 4
JAWS	BAMBI	The Fly	E.T.
STARTS FINISHES	STARTS FINISHES	STARTS FINISHES	STARTS FINISHES
5.00 – 7.30	4.30 – 6.15	7.30 – 9.30	6.00 – 7.45
8.00 – 10.30	6.30 – 8.15	10.00 – 12.00	8.15 – 10.00

53

4c Time

2 Write and draw about what you did yesterday.

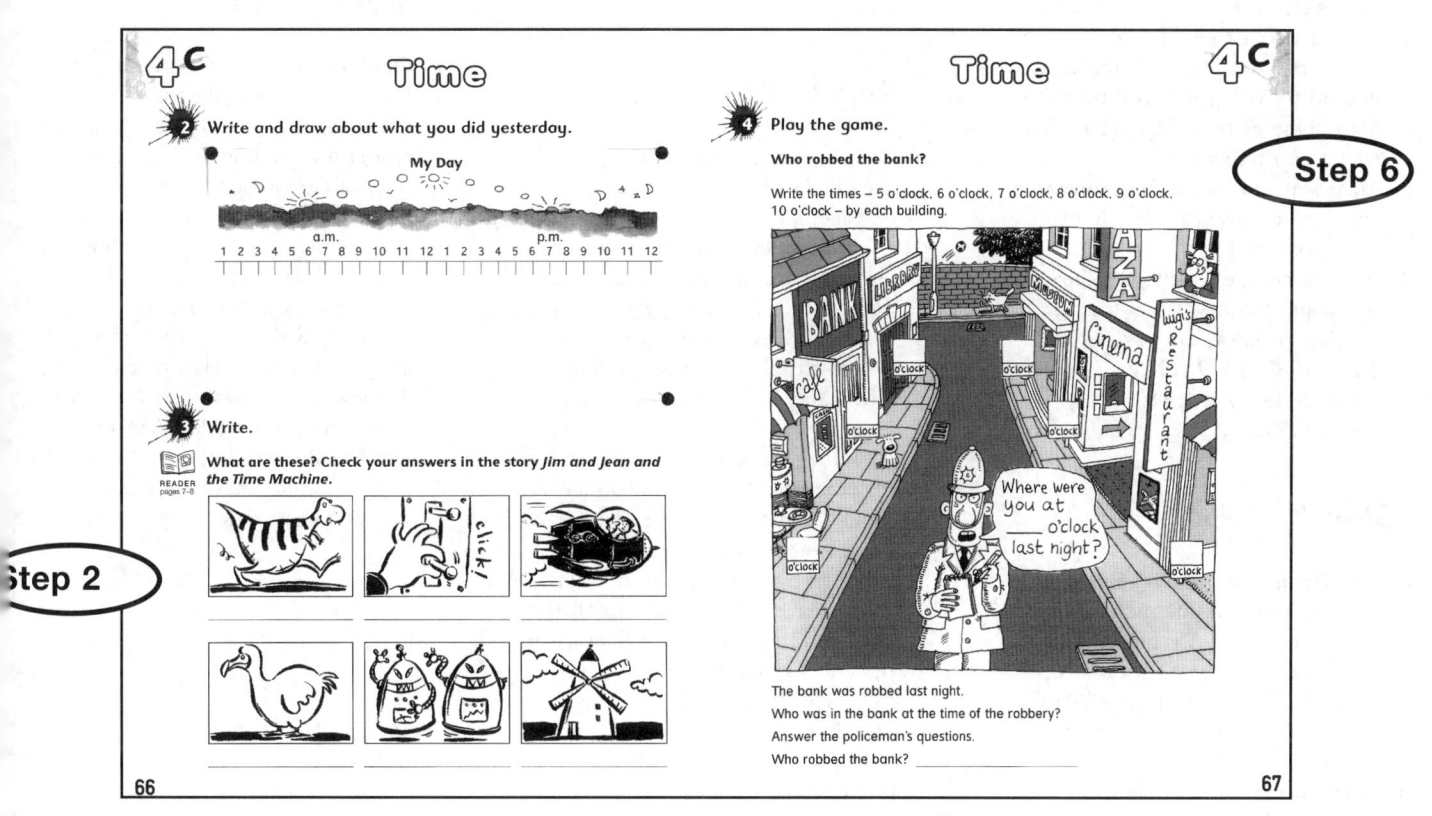

My Day

a.m. — p.m.
1 2 3 4 5 6 7 8 9 10 11 12 1 2 3 4 5 6 7 8 9 10 11 12

3 Write.

What are these? Check your answers in the story *Jim and Jean and the Time Machine*.
READER pages 7–8

66

Time 4c

4 Play the game.

Who robbed the bank?

Write the times – 5 o'clock, 6 o'clock, 7 o'clock, 8 o'clock, 9 o'clock, 10 o'clock – by each building.

Where were you at ___ o'clock last night?

The bank was robbed last night.
Who was in the bank at the time of the robbery?
Answer the policeman's questions.
Who robbed the bank? _____

67

4D Lesson 1

Main Language Items		Resource File	Materials Needed
Dates of the year What does this mean? When was … ?	past future 	present 17 52	cassette/cassette player

Step 1 Presentation

a Draw a long horizontal line on the blackboard. Put a cross at the midpoint. Write today's date under the cross. Ask some pupils '**How old are you? When was your last birthday?**' Mark their birthday on the line to the left of the cross, with the date underneath. Ask other pupils '**When is your next birthday?**' Mark these with a cross on the right of today's date.

b Draw a second line. Mark this year in the middle. Ask pupils '**When were you born? When will you be 18?**' Mark these years to the left and right of this year respectively.

c Then write the words **Past, Present** and **Future** above each line in the appropriate place.

d Write some dates on the blackboard. Ask pupils to say whether they are in the past or future, e.g. 23/2/2001, 13/6/1987, 25/2/1981, 27/4/2025, 1/1/1999, 25/12/1772.

Step 2 Puzzle

a Say '**Open your Activity Book on page 68. Look at the pictures at the top of the page.**' Ask pupils to identify each picture. Then ask '**Is it from the past or the future?**' Pupils individually write the appropriate date next to each picture.

b Round up with the whole class, ensuring all agree with the appropriate dates.

Solution: Penny farthing – 1900; space shuttle – 1984; dinosaur – 100,000,000 BC; moon colony – 2110; Egyptian statue – 2500 BC.

Step 3 Story listening

Rewind the tape and play the verse story *Jim and Jean and the Time Machine* again while pupils follow in their Readers.

Step 4 Quiz

a Divide the class into two teams. Pupils need to have their Coursebooks open on pages 54 and 55. Give the pupils a few minutes to look at the map. Ask a few questions to make sure that they understand the symbols, e.g.
What do the red lines mean?
Which city is nearest to London?
How can you get from London to Lisbon?
How long does it take by train?

b Play the tape. All the questions are about the map. Award one point for a correct answer. The quiz can be answered by individuals or in teams. (Note: Make sure pupils realise they can travel right to left as well as left to right i.e. the quickest way to travel from New York to Tokyo by plane would be to travel westwards (18 hours).
(See tapescript on page 178)

Step 5 Reading (Task)

a Pupils use the map in the Coursebook to complete the passage on page 68 of the Activity Book and answer the questions. This can be done individually or in pairs.

b Round up with the whole class. Clarify any disagreements about time or places.

Step 6 Write

a Pupils use the map to work out how long the journey at the top of page 69 in their Activity Book takes. They then answer the questions and write the story of the journey in their exercise books (i.e. **I went from _____ to _____ by _____ and it took _____ hours. Then …**). This can be done individually or in pairs.

b Round up with the whole class. Clarify any disagreements about time or places.
Answer: It took 448 hours (18½ days) to go around the world (New York to Lisbon – 8 hours, Lisbon to Cairo – 54 hours, Cairo to Tokyo – 12 hours, Tokyo to New York – 374 hours)

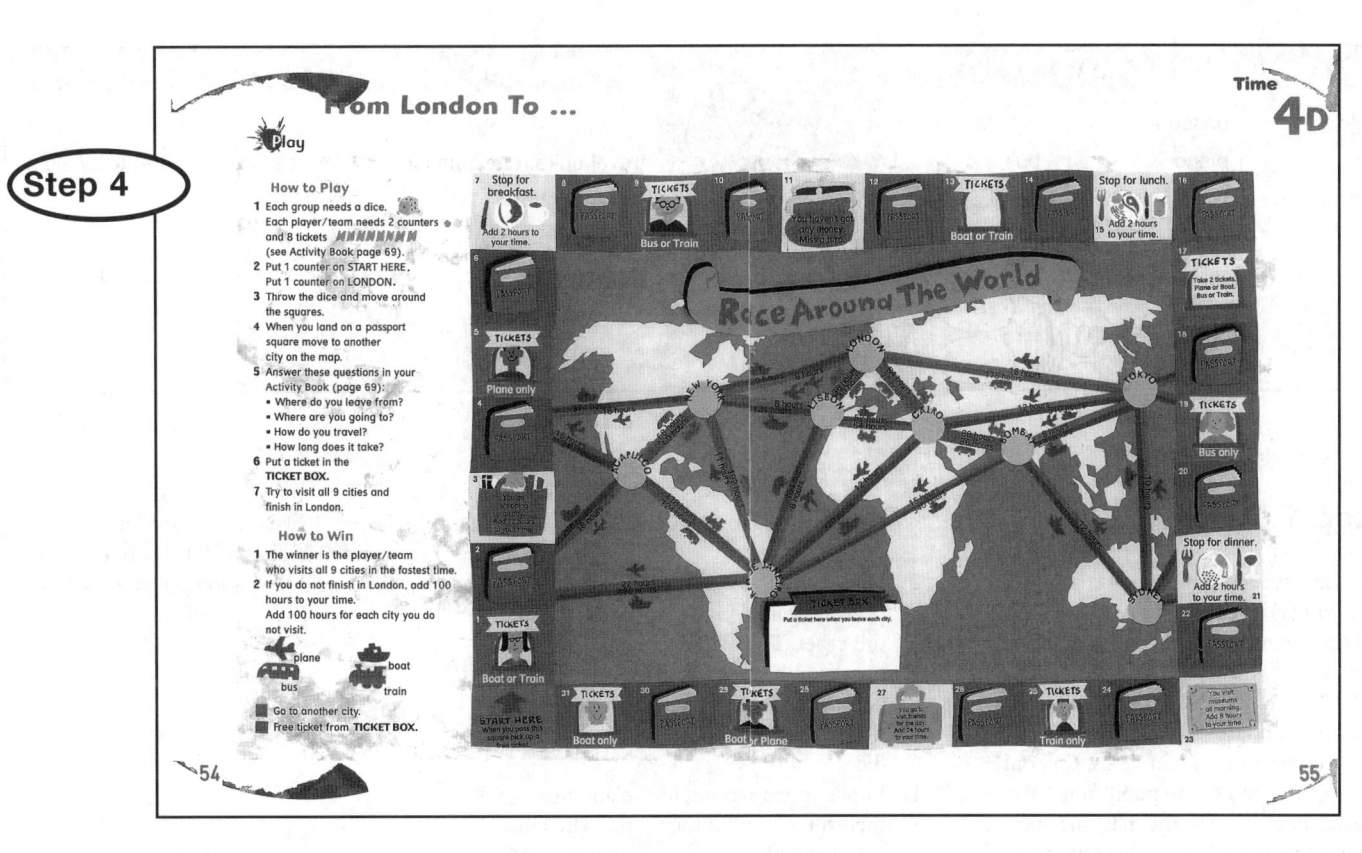

From London To ...

Step 4

Play

How to Play
1. Each group needs a dice. Each player/team needs 2 counters and 8 tickets (see Activity Book page 69).
2. Put 1 counter on START HERE. Put 1 counter on LONDON.
3. Throw the dice and move around the squares.
4. When you land on a passport square move to another city on the map.
5. Answer these questions in your Activity Book (page 69):
   - Where do you leave from?
   - Where are you going to?
   - How do you travel?
   - How long does it take?
6. Put a ticket in the TICKET BOX.
7. Try to visit all 9 cities and finish in London.

How to Win
1. The winner is the player/team who visits all 9 cities in the fastest time.
2. If you do not finish in London, add 100 hours to your time. Add 100 hours for each city you do not visit.

- plane
- boat
- bus
- train
- Go to another city.
- Free ticket from TICKET BOX.

Race Around The World

Time 4D

Step 2

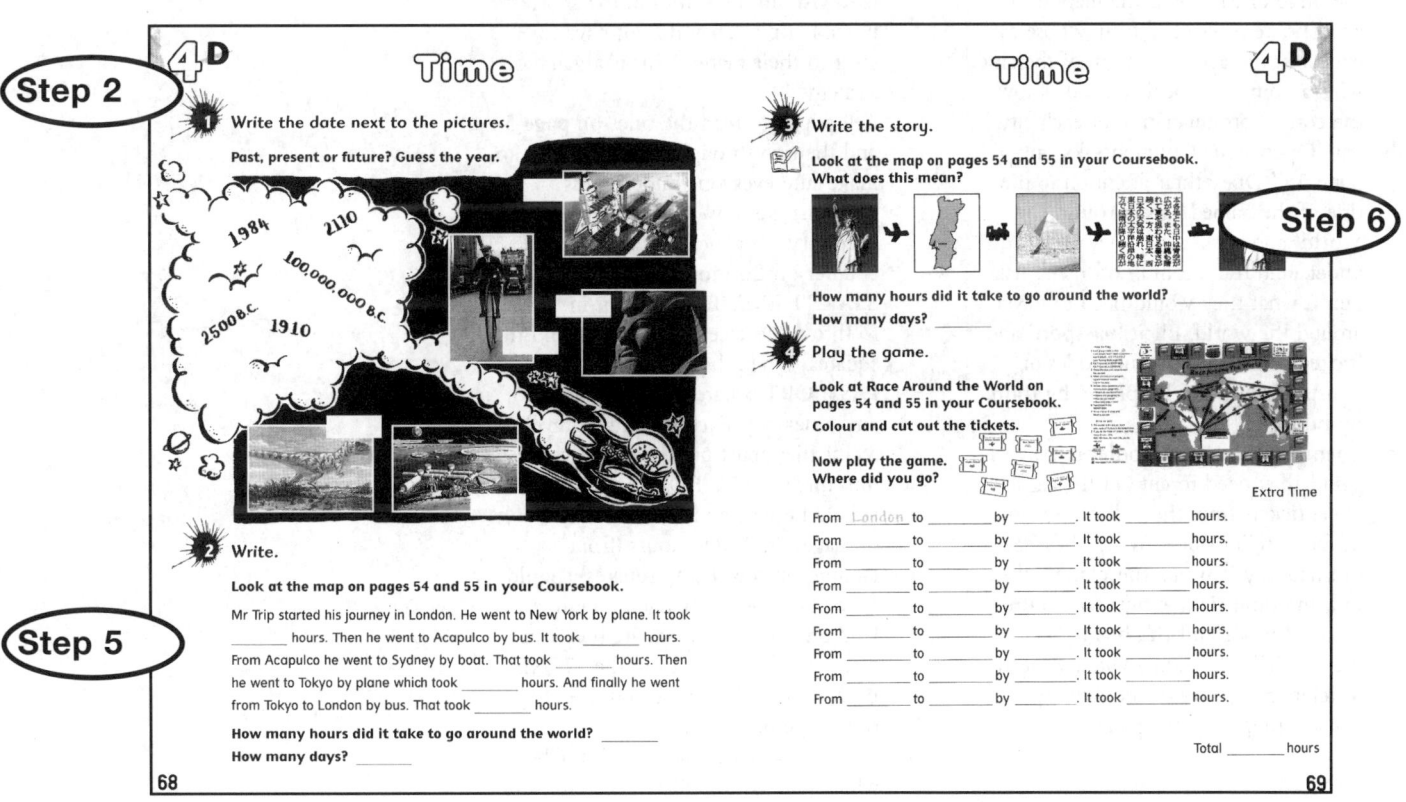

4D Time

1 Write the date next to the pictures.

Past, present or future? Guess the year.

1984   2110
100,000,000 B.C.
2500 B.C.   1910

Step 5

2 Write.

Look at the map on pages 54 and 55 in your Coursebook.

Mr Trip started his journey in London. He went to New York by plane. It took _____ hours. Then he went to Acapulco by bus. It took _____ hours. From Acapulco he went to Sydney by boat. That took _____ hours. Then he went to Tokyo by plane which took _____ hours. And finally he went from Tokyo to London by bus. That took _____ hours.

How many hours did it take to go around the world? _____
How many days? _____

Time 4D

3 Write the story.

Look at the map on pages 54 and 55 in your Coursebook.
What does this mean?

Step 6

How many hours did it take to go around the world? _____
How many days? _____

4 Play the game.

Look at Race Around the World on pages 54 and 55 in your Coursebook.
Colour and cut out the tickets.

Now play the game.
Where did you go?

Extra Time

From	to	by	It took	hours.
From London	to _____	by _____	It took _____	hours.
From _____	to _____	by _____	It took _____	hours.
From _____	to _____	by _____	It took _____	hours.
From _____	to _____	by _____	It took _____	hours.
From _____	to _____	by _____	It took _____	hours.
From _____	to _____	by _____	It took _____	hours.
From _____	to _____	by _____	It took _____	hours.
From _____	to _____	by _____	It took _____	hours.
From _____	to _____	by _____	It took _____	hours.

Total _____ hours

4D Lesson 2

Main Language Items			Resource File	Materials Needed
It takes/took …	passport	tickets	61	travel ticket cut-outs (see pull-out section of the Activity Book)
Miss a turn	plane	bus	62	dice/counters
I'm going to …	boat	train		coloured pencils
I went …				card/scissors

Step 1 Warm up

a If you have a world map available, you could play a team game as a warm up. Write the names of the cities in the game on two sets of cards. Put a piece of ®Blu-tack on the back of each card. Divide the class into two teams and give each team a set of cards. Call out one of the cities: one pupil from each team should run to the map and stick the piece of card onto the map in the appropriate place. The team whose card is nearest the actual location of the city, wins a point. Check that pupils know the correct pronunciation of each city.

b Say 'Open your Coursebooks on page 55.' Draw their attention to the title of the game 'Race Around the World' and ensure that they understand the meaning of 'race'. Ask pupils what they would need to travel around the world. Elicit 'passport' and 'ticket' and also different modes of transport: **by boat, by plane, by train, by bus.**

c Then tell them that in order to play the game, they need to cut out the eight travel tickets from the pull-out section of the Activity Book. When they have finished, say '**Colour the plane tickets red, the boat tickets blue, the train tickets brown and the bus tickets green.**' Tell pupils they will also need to refer to page 69 of the Activity Book throughout the game.

Step 2 Board game

a Divide the class into groups of four to play the game. One pair plays against the other. This will encourage co-operation between the partners. Each pair needs two counters and eight tickets. Each group of four needs a dice.

b Pupils spend ten minutes planning their route around the world. The aim is to visit all nine cities in the shortest possible time. They do not have to stick to their plans – this is a game of strategy.

c Tell pupils to read the rules on page 54 and then go through them as a class to make sure everyone understands. Demonstrate how to play the game if necessary. To play, each pair puts one counter on **London** and one on START HERE. Teams take it in turns to throw the dice and move around the squares. When they land on a PASSPORT square, they can move to any other city. Each time they travel to a city, they must put the used ticket into the TICKET BOX. Each move should be written in the Activity Book on page 69. Added hours (from landing on the yellow squares) should be written there too. Each time they land on a TICKETS square they can pick up a free ticket from the TICKET BOX (only if it is there and it is the right type of ticket).

d Allow all groups time to finish. Check which pair got round all nine cities the fastest. Pairs who do not finish in London should add 100 hours to their time. And they should add 100 hours for each city not visited.

From London To ...

Play

How to Play
1. Each group needs a dice. Each player/team needs 2 counters and 8 tickets (see Activity Book page 69).
2. Put 1 counter on START HERE. Put 1 counter on LONDON.
3. Throw the dice and move around the squares.
4. When you land on a passport square move to another city on the map.
5. Answer these questions in your Activity Book (page 69):
   - Where do you leave from?
   - Where are you going to?
   - How do you travel?
   - How long does it take?
6. Put a ticket in the TICKET BOX.
7. Try to visit all 9 cities and finish in London.

How to Win
1. The winner is the player/team who visits all 9 cities in the fastest time.
2. If you do not finish in London, add 100 hours to your time. Add 100 hours for each city you do not visit.

- plane
- boat
- bus
- train
- ■ Go to another city.
- ■ Free ticket from TICKET BOX.

Step 1
Step 2

Time — 4D

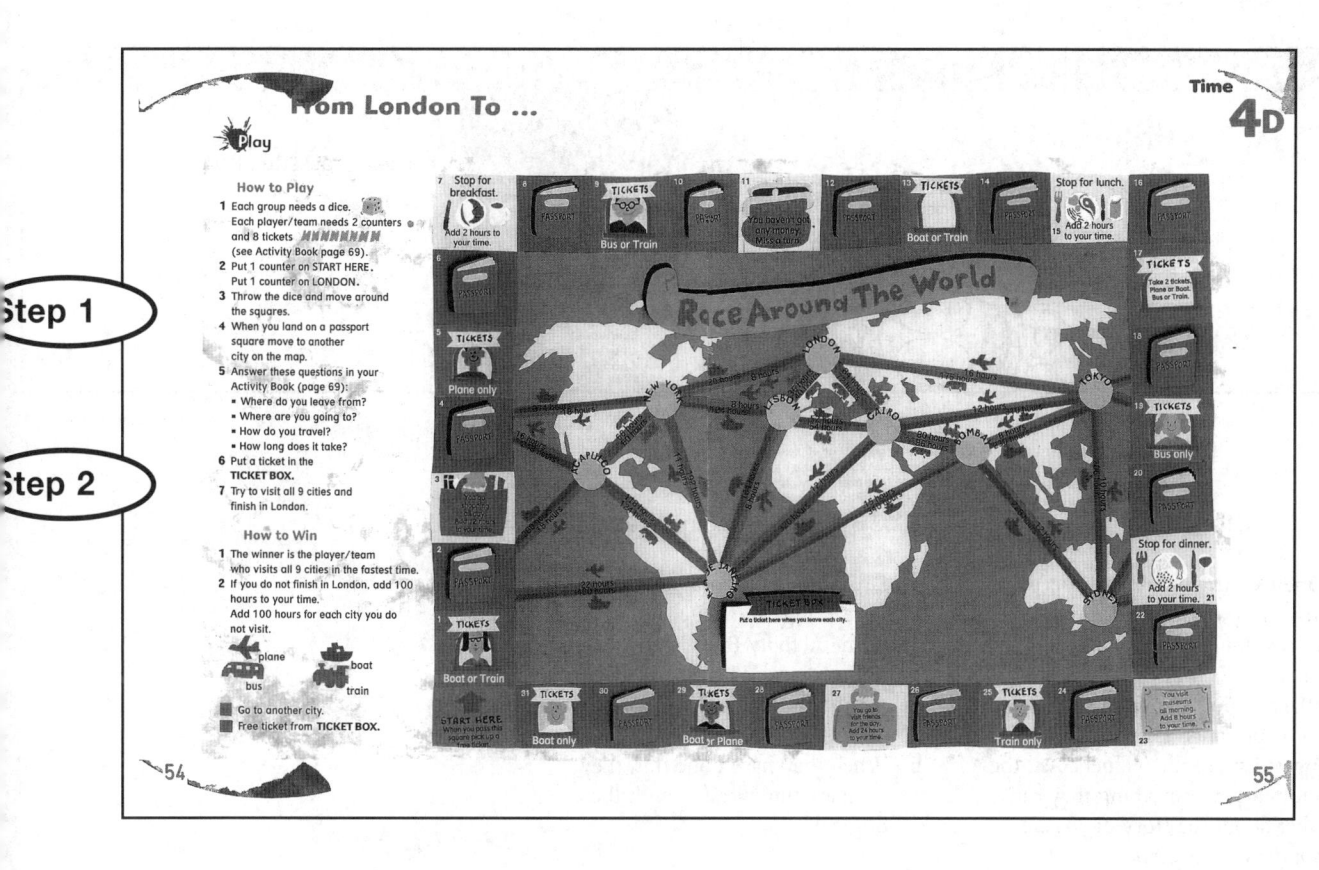

1. Write the date next to the pictures.

Past, present or future? Guess the year.

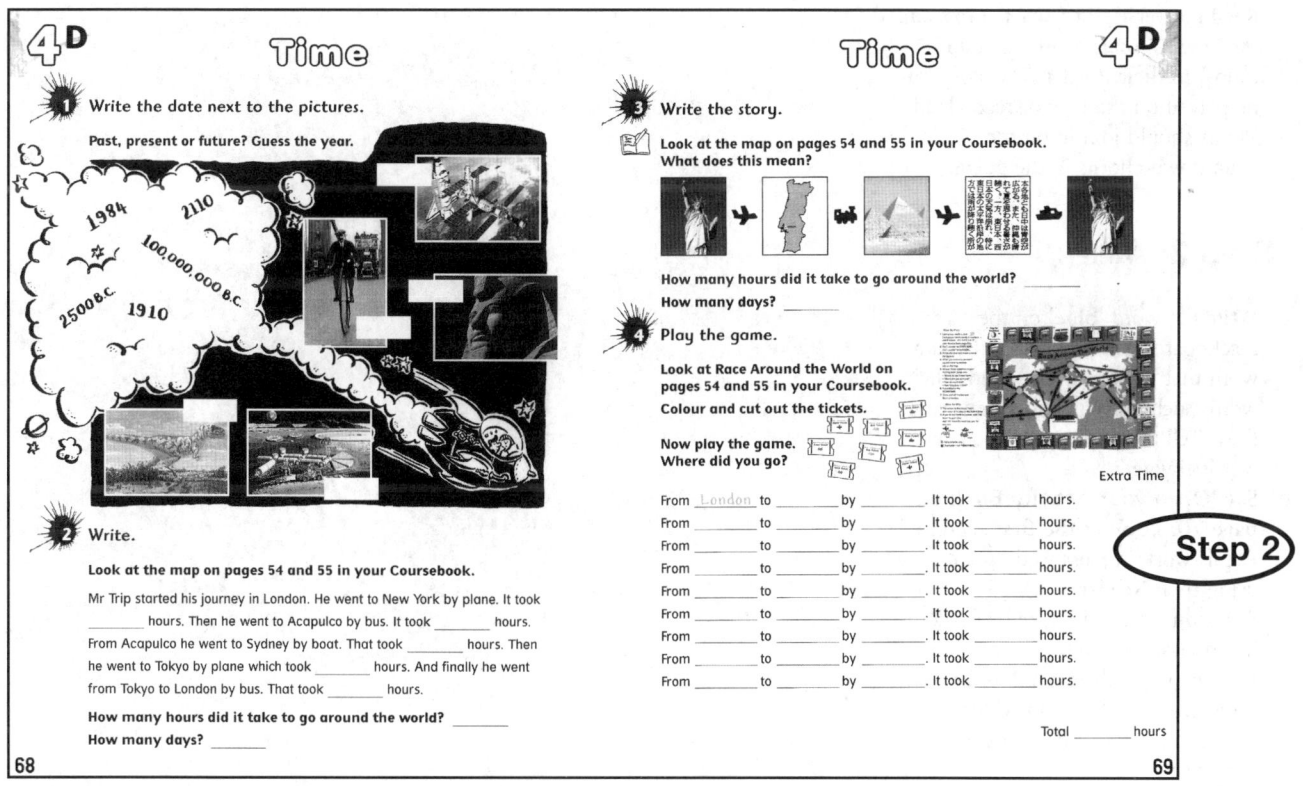

1984   2110
100,000,000 B.C.
2500 B.C.   1910

2. Write.

Look at the map on pages 54 and 55 in your Coursebook.

Mr Trip started his journey in London. He went to New York by plane. It took _____ hours. Then he went to Acapulco by bus. It took _____ hours. From Acapulco he went to Sydney by boat. That took _____ hours. Then he went to Tokyo by plane which took _____ hours. And finally he went from Tokyo to London by bus. That took _____ hours.

How many hours did it take to go around the world? _____
How many days? _____

3. Write the story.

Look at the map on pages 54 and 55 in your Coursebook. What does this mean?

How many hours did it take to go around the world? _____
How many days? _____

4. Play the game.

Look at Race Around the World on pages 54 and 55 in your Coursebook. Colour and cut out the tickets.

Now play the game. Where did you go?

Extra Time

From _London_ to _____ by _____. It took _____ hours.
From _____ to _____ by _____. It took _____ hours.
From _____ to _____ by _____. It took _____ hours.
From _____ to _____ by _____. It took _____ hours.
From _____ to _____ by _____. It took _____ hours.
From _____ to _____ by _____. It took _____ hours.
From _____ to _____ by _____. It took _____ hours.
From _____ to _____ by _____. It took _____ hours.
From _____ to _____ by _____. It took _____ hours.

Total _____ hours

Step 2

4D Lesson 3

Main Language Items	Resource File	Materials Needed
Simple past tense Where did … ?	24 41 47	cassette/cassette player Reader

Step 1   Story 'Join in'

a Say 'Open your Coursebook on page 46. Work in pairs.' Give pupils a time limit of two minutes to try and remember as much of the story vocabulary as possible, using the pictures as prompts. The pair which has the longest list are the winners. Ask the pupils to tell you everything they can remember about the story of *Jim and Jean and the Time Machine*.

b Read the verse story *Jim and Jean and the Time Machine*, while the pupils follow in their Reader. The story can be played on the tape or read aloud. Pupils should join in on the countdown chorus in the poem.

Step 2   Write

a Write the word '**blue**' on the blackboard. Ask pupils to tell you a word that has the same sound. Elicit words such as: **two, shoe, new, true, flew**. Tell the pupils that all these words rhyme.

b Say '**Open your Activity Book on page 70. Look at the first exercise.**' Pupils work in pairs to do the exercises using their Reader.
Solution: chips; door; red; afternoon; lunch; more; machine; inside

c Encourage pupils to think of as many other words as they can which also have the same sounds as the words in the story.

Step 3   Reading (Task)

a Divide the class into pairs. Pupils have to rearrange the sentences on page 70 of the Activity Book without referring to the poem. When they have agreed a version they should write it into their exercise books.

b When they have done this, they compare their version with the original.

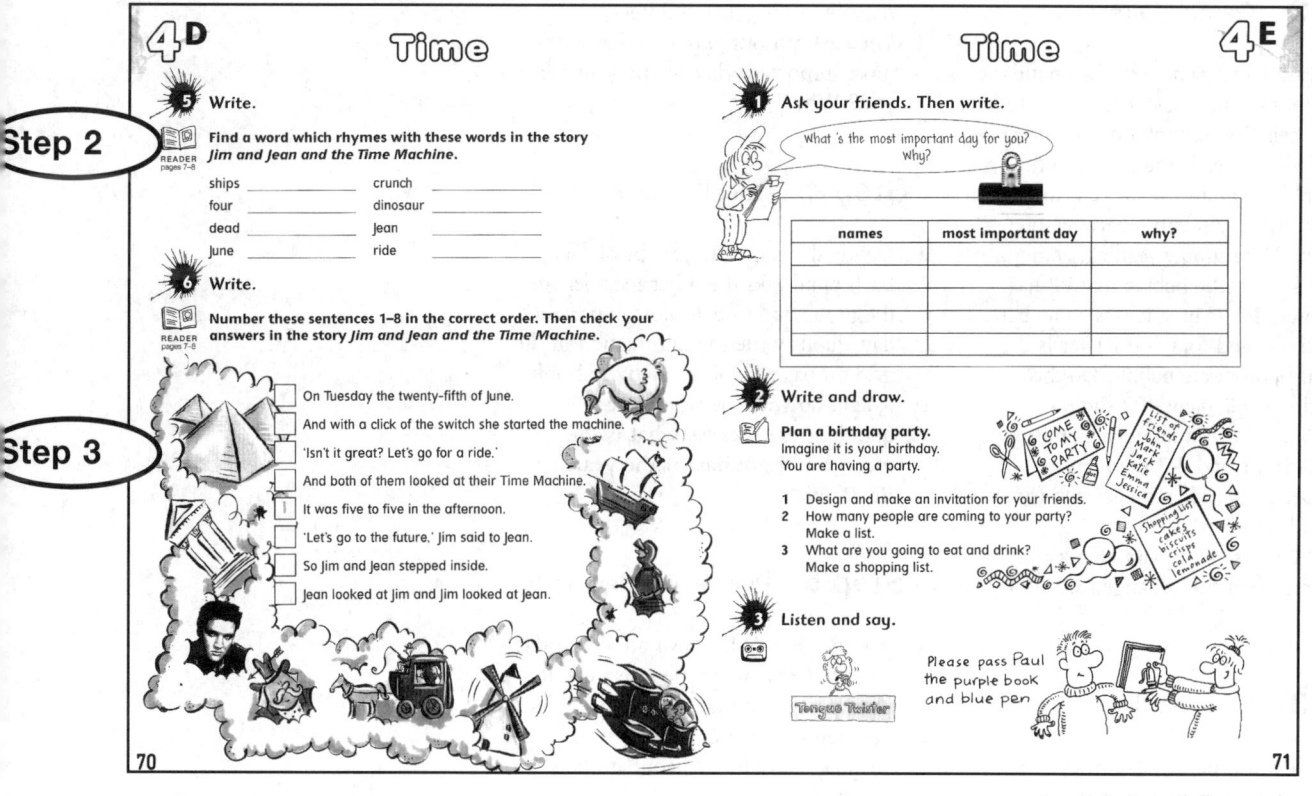

Step 1

4 Time

STORY

Jim and Jean and the Time Machine

4D Time

Step 2

5 Write.

Find a word which rhymes with these words in the story *Jim and Jean and the Time Machine*.

READER pages 7–8

ships _____   crunch _____
four _____   dinosaur _____
dead _____   Jean _____
June _____   ride _____

6 Write.

Number these sentences 1–8 in the correct order. Then check your answers in the story *Jim and Jean and the Time Machine*.

READER pages 7–8

Step 3

☐ On Tuesday the twenty-fifth of June.
☐ And with a click of the switch she started the machine.
☐ 'Isn't it great? Let's go for a ride.'
☐ And both of them looked at their Time Machine.
☐ It was five to five in the afternoon.
☐ 'Let's go to the future,' Jim said to Jean.
☐ So Jim and Jean stepped inside.
☐ Jean looked at Jim and Jim looked at Jean.

4E Time

1 Ask your friends. Then write.

What's the most important day for you? Why?

names	most important day	why?

2 Write and draw.

Plan a birthday party.
Imagine it is your birthday.
You are having a party.

1 Design and make an invitation for your friends.
2 How many people are coming to your party?
   Make a list.
3 What are you going to eat and drink?
   Make a shopping list.

3 Listen and say.

Tongue Twister

Please pass Paul
the purple book
and blue pen

153

4E Lesson 1

Main Language Items			Resource File	Materials Needed
Simple past tense	went	saw	5	cassette/cassette player
Where did … ?	ate	bought	24	Reader
What is the most important day …?	found	looked	49	coloured pencils
The most important day of the year …				paper for display
Why …?				card
Because …				

Step 1   Story reading

Read the verse story *Jim and Jean and the Time Machine*. Give pupils different parts to read e.g. one group reads the countdown, another group says 'whoosh'. One pupil reads Jim, another Jean. The teacher can be narrator. Experiment with different versions.

Step 2   Game (pairs)

a Demonstrate the game with two pupils at the front of the class first.
b P1 has their Coursebook open on pages 56 and 57. P1 reads the phrase in the first bubble: 'Jim and Jean went to … ' P2 then says any number between one and four. P1 continues reading, adding the words from the bubble that P2 has just chosen. P2 again chooses a number between one and four and P1 reads from the appropriate bubble. Do this across the whole game (P2 should choose a total of six numbers), until pairs reach the end. P2 then has to remember the whole sentence and try to say it back to P1.
c Divide the class into pairs. Pupils play the game. Then they change roles and repeat.

Step 3   Presentation

a In their L1, ask pupils what they think is the most important day of the year. Write down their answers on the board. Next ask them why these days are important for them and their families.
b Say '**Open your Coursebook on page 56. Listen to the tape and read what the children say.**' Play the tape twice.
c Ask some questions to check comprehension e.g.
**What is the most important day of the year for Kim?
Why?**
Ask about the other children.
d Then ask various pupils, '**What is the most important day of the year for you? Why?**'.

Step 4   Questionnaire

a Divide the class into groups of four. Each pupil asks the other members of the group about their most important day. Pupils write the information in the grid on page 71 of the Activity Book.
b Round up with the whole class. Ask questions like '*Maria*, **what is the most important day of the year for** *Tom*?' etc.

Step 5   Plan a birthday party

a Ask the class '**Who has had a birthday party?**', '**How many people were at your party?**', '**What did you eat?**' etc.
b Tell pupils they are going to organise a birthday party for someone in their group.
c Divide the class into small groups and direct them to the questions on page 71 of the Activity Book.
d All the planning should be in English. The lists for food and guests are to be written in English. Prompt pupils to think of English songs and games.

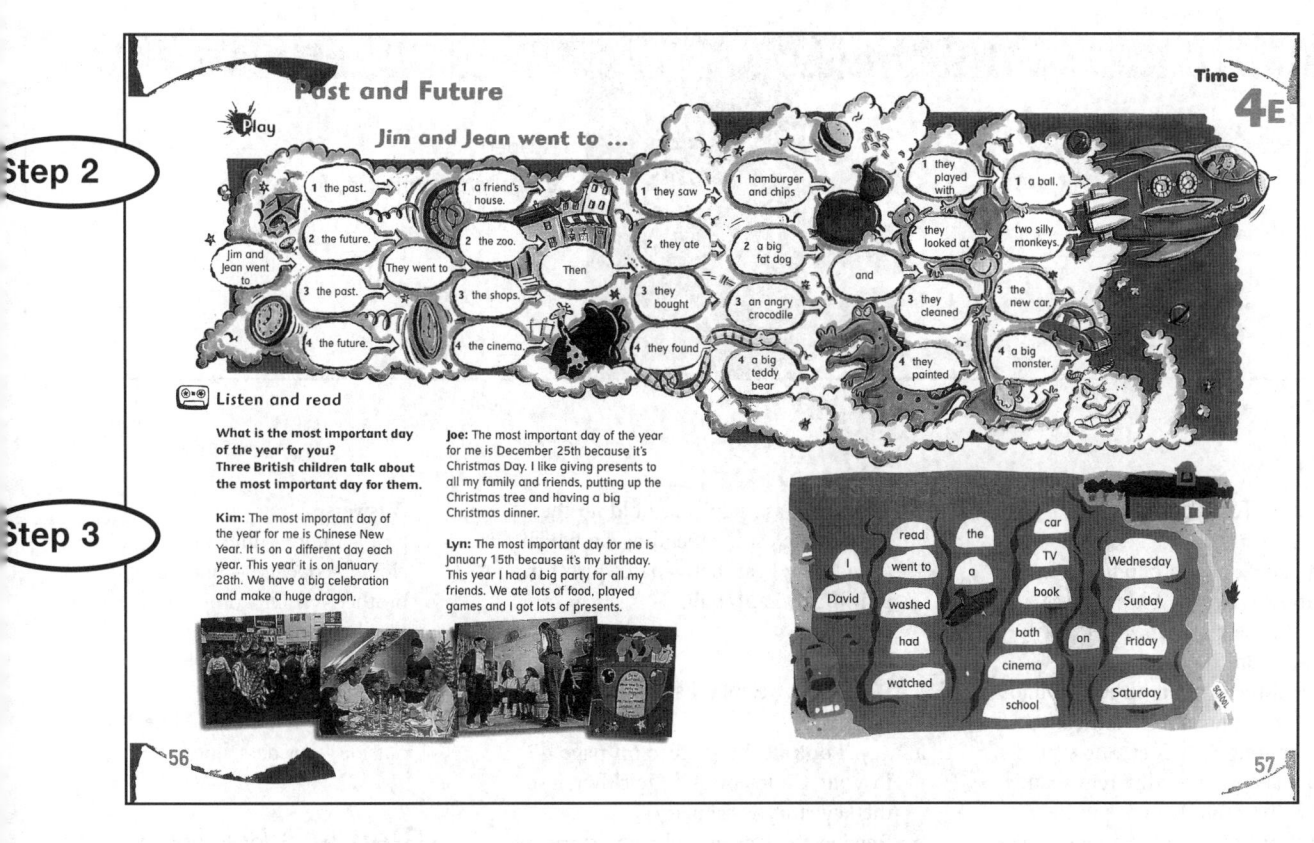

Past and Future

Time 4E

Play

Jim and Jean went to ...

Jim and Jean went to
1 the past.
2 the future.
3 the past.
4 the future.

They went to
1 a friend's house.
2 the zoo.
3 the shops.
4 the cinema.

Then
1 they saw
2 they ate
3 they bought
4 they found

1 hamburger and chips
2 a big fat dog
3 an angry crocodile
4 a big teddy bear

and
1 they played with
2 they looked at
3 they cleaned
4 they painted

1 a ball.
2 two silly monkeys.
3 the new car.
4 a big monster.

Listen and read

What is the most important day of the year for you?
Three British children talk about the most important day for them.

Kim: The most important day of the year for me is Chinese New Year. It is on a different day each year. This year it is on January 28th. We have a big celebration and make a huge dragon.

Joe: The most important day of the year for me is December 25th because it's Christmas Day. I like giving presents to all my family and friends, putting up the Christmas tree and having a big Christmas dinner.

Lyn: The most important day for me is January 15th because it's my birthday. This year I had a big party for all my friends. We ate lots of food, played games and I got lots of presents.

I / David / read / the / car / TV / Wednesday
went to / a / book / Sunday
washed / bath / on / Friday
had / cinema / Saturday
watched / school

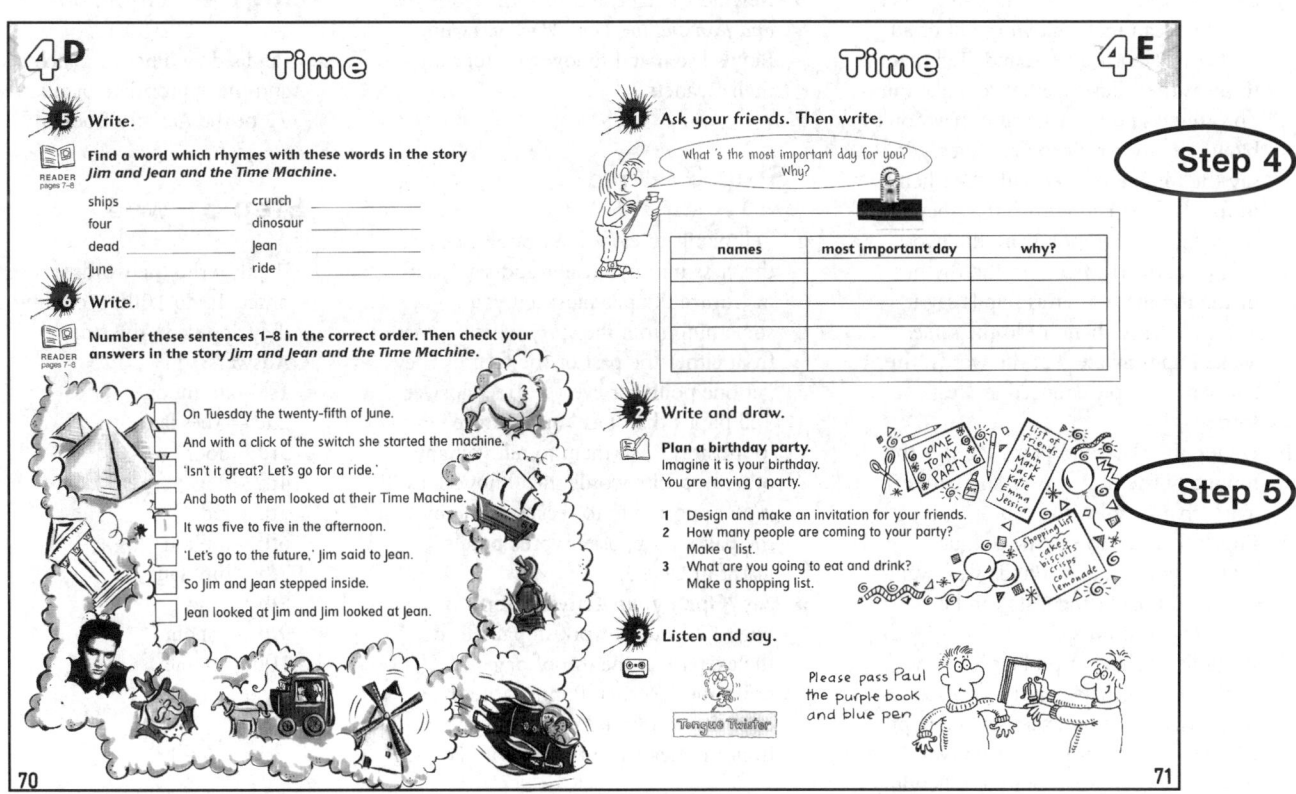

4D Time

5 Write.

Find a word which rhymes with these words in the story *Jim and Jean and the Time Machine*.

READER pages 7–8

ships _____   crunch _____
four _____   dinosaur _____
dead _____   Jean _____
June _____   ride _____

6 Write.

Number these sentences 1–8 in the correct order. Then check your answers in the story *Jim and Jean and the Time Machine*.

READER pages 7–8

☐ On Tuesday the twenty-fifth of June.
☐ And with a click of the switch she started the machine.
☐ 'Isn't it great? Let's go for a ride.'
☐ And both of them looked at their Time Machine.
☐ It was five to five in the afternoon.
☐ 'Let's go to the future,' Jim said to Jean.
☐ So Jim and Jean stepped inside.
☐ Jean looked at Jim and Jim looked at Jean.

Time 4E

1 Ask your friends. Then write.

What's the most important day for you? Why?

names	most important day	why?

2 Write and draw.

Plan a birthday party.
Imagine it is your birthday. You are having a party.

1 Design and make an invitation for your friends.
2 How many people are coming to your party? Make a list.
3 What are you going to eat and drink? Make a shopping list.

3 Listen and say.

Tongue Twister

Please pass Paul the purple book and blue pen

4E Lesson 2

Main Language Items	Resource File	Materials Needed
Story revision please pass	24 44 52	Reader cassette/cassette player

Step 1 Tongue twister

a Play the tape once so pupils can listen to the tongue twister. Play it twice more, with the class repeating. As usual, build up the tongue twister slowly and focus in on difficult sounds in isolation if pupils have difficulty saying the tongue twister. Show pupils how to make the two different sounds /p/ and /b/. Tell them to put their hand in front of their mouth and make sure they can feel a blowing out of air as they make the /p/ sound. Tell them to press their lips together to make the /b/ sound and to make sure they don't blow out any air. Encourage them to say the tongue twister with their hand in front of their mouth so that they can see if they are pronouncing the two sounds correctly. Beat out the rhythm of the tongue twister as pupils say it and encourage them to do the same. Make pupils aware that the words 'the' and 'and' are pronounced as weak forms.

b Divide the class into pairs. P1 says the tongue twister. P2 checks and corrects. They change roles and repeat.

c Pupils then try to say the tongue twister more quickly. Pupils who want to try in front of the class can be encouraged to do so.

d If pupils are having problems distinguishing between the two sounds, do a discrimination exercise. Tell pupils to write the letters **p** and **b** on two pieces of paper. Read out the following words and ask pupils to hold up the appropriate card, depending on which sound they hear: **bath/path, pin/bin, pair/bear, Paul/ball**.

Step 2 Story listening

a Say '**Look at the picture on page 47 in your Coursebook.**' Quickly revise the key story vocabulary.

b Rewind the tape and play the story *Jim and Jean and the Time Machine* again. Pupils listen and follow the story in their Readers.

Step 3 Write

a Tell pupils to close their books. Divide the class into two teams and say '**past**' or '**future**'. Pupils must tell you something from the story which comes from either the past or the future. They get one point for every correct answer. Tell pupils that '**past**' and '**future**' are '**opposites**'. Ask them to tell you any other opposite words they know. This is an opportunity to recycle some of the pairs of opposite words pupils learnt in Unit 3.

a Say '**Open your Activity Book on page 72.**' Pupils work in pairs to do the exercise at the top of page 72, using their Reader. Pupils write the opposite words and the line number from the Reader in the Activity Book.

Answers:
past – future – line 11
closed – opened – line 12
brother – sister – line 24
slowly – quickly – line 27
white – black – line 15
new – old – line 34
morning – afternoon – line 1
outside – inside – line 6

Step 4 Words and pictures

Pupils draw lines to match the words and the appropriate pictures on page 72 of the Activity Book.

Step 5 Write

Pupils write the words in exercise 6 in order, 1st to 10th, according to where they appear in the story.
Answers:
1st – afternoon
2nd – Tuesday
3rd – door
4th – dogs
5th – red
6th – million
7th – dinosaur
8th – Egypt
9th – armour
10th – home.

4 Time

STORY

Jim and Jean and the Time Machine

Step 2

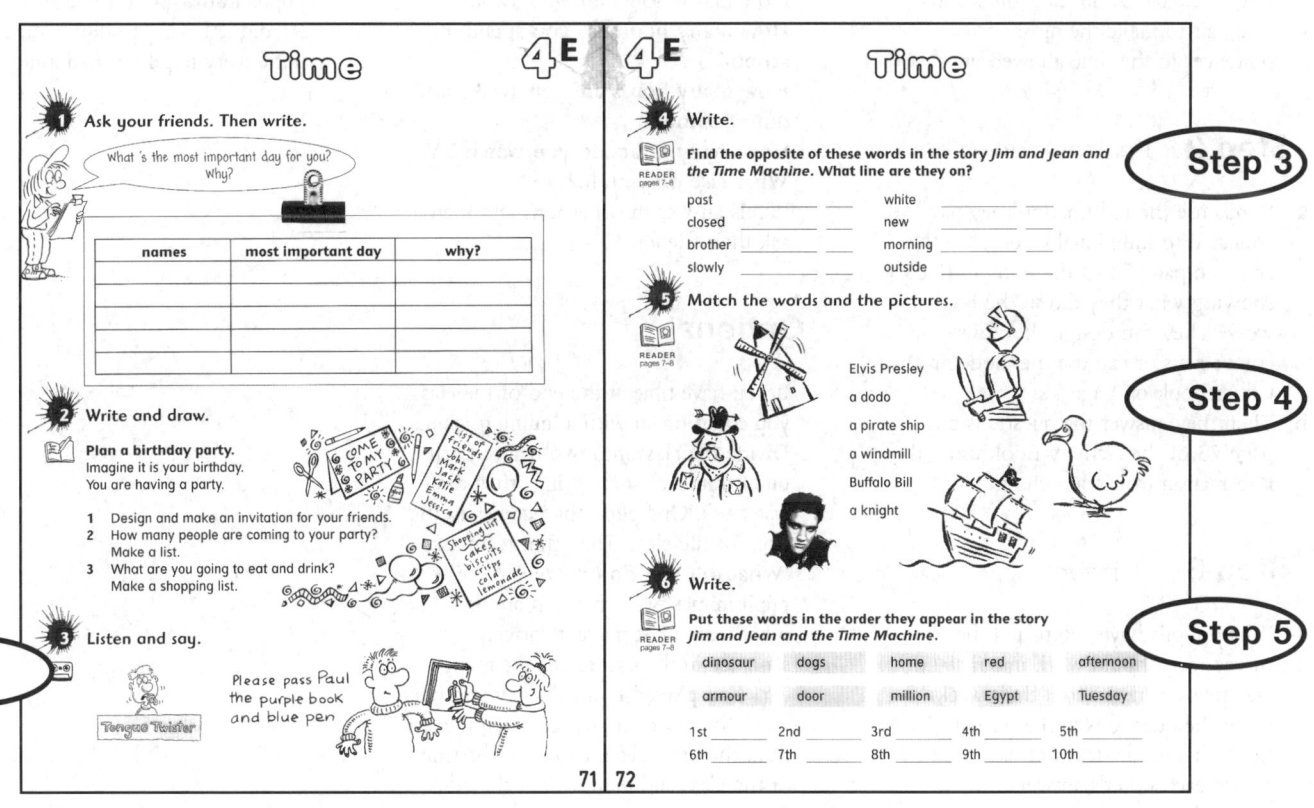

4E Time

1 Ask your friends. Then write.

What's the most important day for you? Why?

names	most important day	why?

2 Write and draw.

Plan a birthday party.
Imagine it is your birthday.
You are having a party.

1 Design and make an invitation for your friends.
2 How many people are coming to your party? Make a list.
3 What are you going to eat and drink? Make a shopping list.

3 Listen and say.

Tongue Twister

Please pass Paul the purple book and blue pen

Step 1

4E Time

4 Write.

Find the opposite of these words in the story *Jim and Jean and the Time Machine*. What line are they on?

past _____   white _____
closed _____   new _____
brother _____   morning _____
slowly _____   outside _____

Step 3

5 Match the words and the pictures.

Elvis Presley
a dodo
a pirate ship
a windmill
Buffalo Bill
a knight

Step 4

6 Write.

Put these words in the order they appear in the story *Jim and Jean and the Time Machine*.

| dinosaur | dogs | home | red | afternoon |
| armour | door | million | Egypt | Tuesday |

1st _____ 2nd _____ 3rd _____ 4th _____ 5th _____
6th _____ 7th _____ 8th _____ 9th _____ 10th _____

Step 5

4E Lesson 3

Main Language Items	Resource File	Materials Needed
Simple past tense	10 26 31	coloured pencils

Step 1 The Stepping Stones Game

a Divide the class into pairs. Pupils write as many sentences as they can in ten minutes from the words on the stones. Work from left to right and take one word from each column.
b The sentences must be both grammatically and factually correct, based on their own weeks and David's week on page 52 in the Coursebook.
c The pair to make the most correct sentences in the time allowed wins.

Step 2 Personal survey

a Pupils use the information they have collected to individually complete the chart on page 73 of the Activity Book showing what they did in the last week. They can design their own colour keys or can use the model in the Coursebook on page 52.
b Then they answer the questions on page 73 of the Activity Book using the information from their charts.

Step 3 Pairwork

a When pupils have completed the survey they should work in pairs and ask their partners about their week, using the questions in the Activity Book as a guide. It is not necessary to record each other's answers.

b Finish the exercise by asking pupils questions from the survey about themselves or their partners.

Step 4 Survey round-up

Write the following questions on the blackboard:
How many hours do you sleep each week?
How many hours are you awake?
How many hours do you spend at school?
How many hours are you awake and not at school?
How many hours do you watch TV?
What else do you do?
Pupils answer the questions and then ask their friends.

Optional

a If you have time at the end of the class, you could finish with a 'miming' game. Divide the class into two teams. Each pupil thinks of some things they did last week. One pupil then comes to the front of the class. The other team asks 'What did you do on *Monday*?' The pupil mimes what they did and the other team must make a correct sentence in the past about the mime. e.g. '**You played tennis.**' They win one point for a correct answer. Then a pupil from the other team comes to the front of the class and mimes what they did on a certain day. Continue until all the pupils in each team have had a go.
b Pupils can play a similar game in groups of three or four. One pupil (P1) thinks of something they did on a particular day last week. The other pupils have to try to guess what they did by asking questions such as '**Did you *play tennis*'**. P1 can only answer '**yes**' or '**no**'. A maximum of ten questions are allowed. If the other pupils in the group can't guess what P1 did, P1 wins a point. Continue until every pupil has had a go.

Past and Future

Play

Jim and Jean went to ...

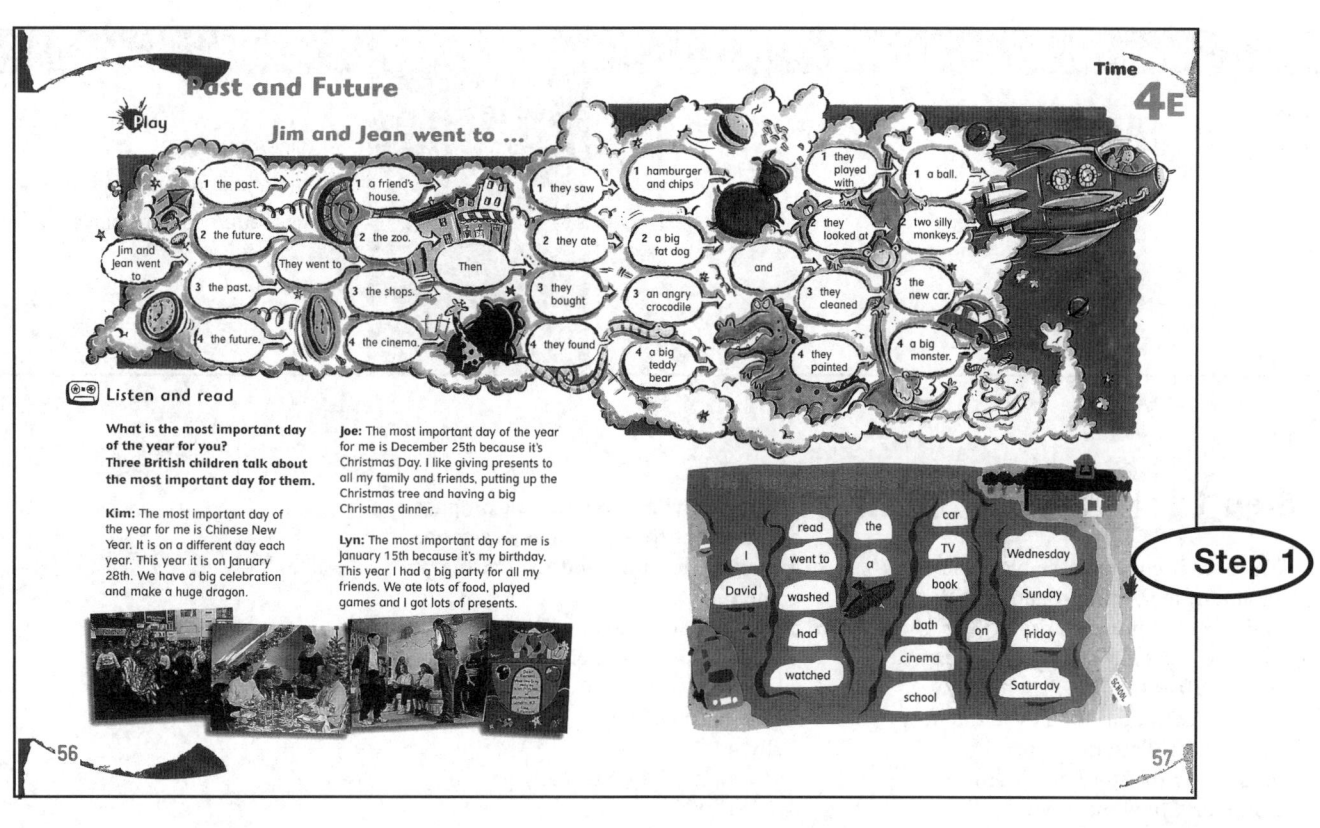

Jim and Jean went to
- 1 the past.
- 2 the future.
- 3 the past.
- 4 the future.

They went to
- 1 a friend's house.
- 2 the zoo.
- 3 the shops.
- 4 the cinema.

Then
- 1 they saw
- 2 they ate
- 3 they bought
- 4 they found

- 1 hamburger and chips
- 2 a big fat dog
- 3 an angry crocodile
- 4 a big teddy bear

- 1 they played with
- 2 they looked at
- 3 they cleaned
- 4 they painted

and
- 1 a ball.
- 2 two silly monkeys.
- 3 the new car.
- 4 a big monster.

Listen and read

What is the most important day of the year for you?
Three British children talk about the most important day for them.

Kim: The most important day of the year for me is Chinese New Year. It is on a different day each year. This year it is on January 28th. We have a big celebration and make a huge dragon.

Joe: The most important day of the year for me is December 25th because it's Christmas Day. I like giving presents to all my family and friends, putting up the Christmas tree and having a big Christmas dinner.

Lyn: The most important day for me is January 15th because it's my birthday. This year I had a big party for all my friends. We ate lots of food, played games and I got lots of presents.

Words: I, David, read, went to, washed, had, watched, the, a, book, cinema, school, car, TV, bath, on, Wednesday, Sunday, Friday, Saturday

Step 1

4E Time

4 Write.

Find the opposite of these words in the story *Jim and Jean and the Time Machine*. What line are they on?

READER pages 7–8

past _____ ___   white _____ ___
closed _____ ___   new _____ ___
brother _____ ___   morning _____ ___
slowly _____ ___   outside _____ ___

5 Match the words and the pictures.

READER pages 7–8

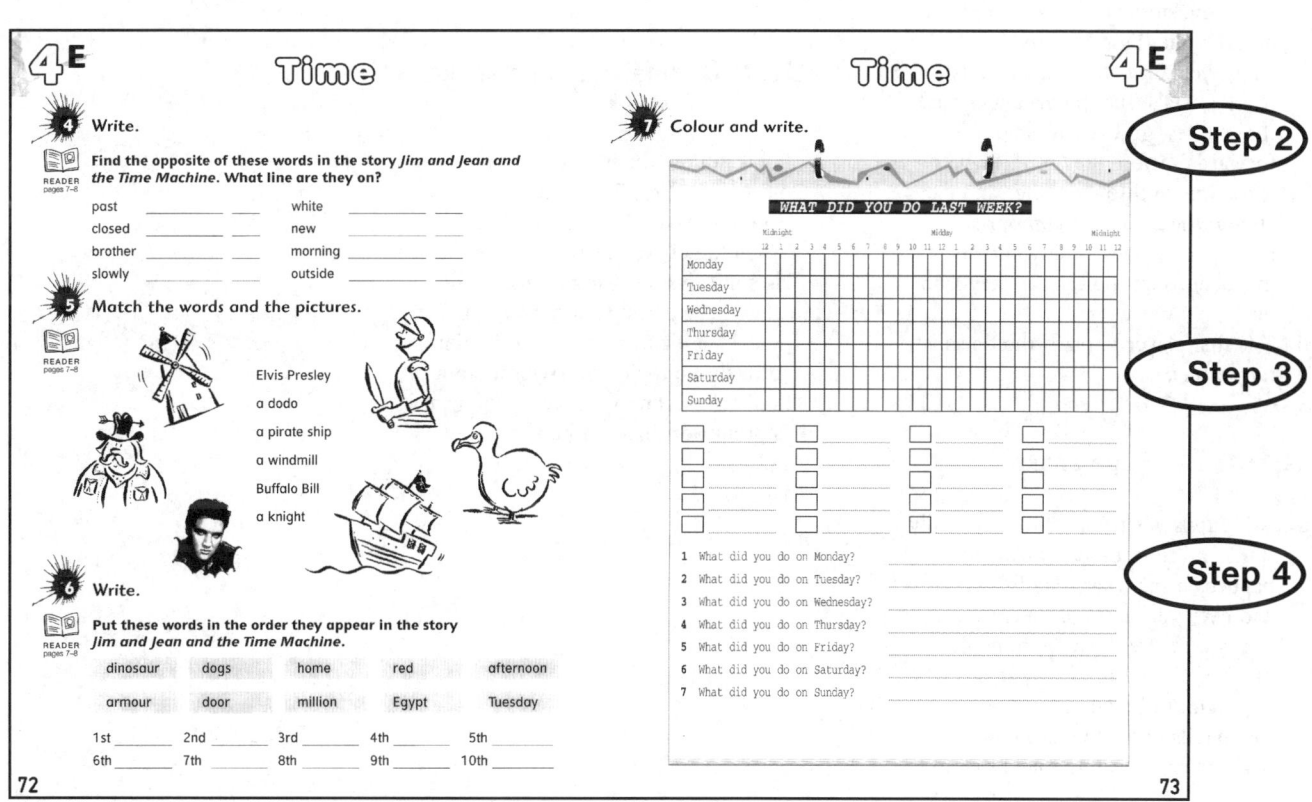

Elvis Presley
a dodo
a pirate ship
a windmill
Buffalo Bill
a knight

6 Write.

Put these words in the order they appear in the story *Jim and Jean and the Time Machine*.

READER pages 7–8

dinosaur   dogs   home   red   afternoon
armour   door   million   Egypt   Tuesday

1st _____ 2nd _____ 3rd _____ 4th _____ 5th _____
6th _____ 7th _____ 8th _____ 9th _____ 10th _____

Step 2

Time 4E

7 Colour and write.

WHAT DID YOU DO LAST WEEK?

	Midnight 12 1 2 3 4 5 6 7 8 9 10 11	Midday 12 1 2 3 4 5 6 7 8 9 10 11	Midnight 12
Monday			
Tuesday			
Wednesday			
Thursday			
Friday			
Saturday			
Sunday			

Step 3

1 What did you do on Monday? _____
2 What did you do on Tuesday? _____
3 What did you do on Wednesday? _____
4 What did you do on Thursday? _____
5 What did you do on Friday? _____
6 What did you do on Saturday? _____
7 What did you do on Sunday? _____

Step 4

4F Lesson 1

Main Language Items	Resource File	Materials Needed
Story revision	36	dice/counters
Days of the week	37	materials for making a clock
late	46	cassette/cassette player
lines		

Step 1 Story game

a This is a dice game to be played in groups of four, using counters, a dice and one book for each group.

b Quickly revise the story *Jim and Jean and the Time Machine*. Play the tape again or ask pupils to tell you the story. Look at the illustrations that accompany the story. Say '**Point to a dodo**' or '**Show me a windmill**' to revise the story vocabulary. Pupils can do the same thing in pairs.

c All players place their counters on START. Make sure pupils understand the phrases '**go back to**' and '**go forwards**' before they start. Players take turns to throw the dice and move around the board the appropriate number of squares, following any instructions on the squares they land on.

d The first player to reach the finish is the winner.

Step 2 Supersnake

a Ask pupils what time school normally starts and finishes. Ask them what happens if pupils are late for school and elicit various punishments (in L1 if necessary). Use this opportunity to make pupils aware of why it is important to be on time. Make sure that pupils know the meaning of '**writing lines**' before they listen to the story.

b Say '**Open your Coursebook on page 59. Look at the Supersnake cartoon. Listen to the story and read at the same time.**'

c Ask pupils some comprehension questions to check their understanding of the story:
Is the teacher happy?
Why not?
How many lines did Willy get on *Wednesday*?

Step 3 Make a Supersnake clock

a Pupils follow the instructions and pictures on page 74 in their Activity Book to make a Supersnake clock.

b When they have finished, divide the class into pairs. Each pair needs one Supersnake clock. Call out various times. The first pair to show the time correctly on their clock wins a point. Pupils then continue playing the game in groups of three or four.

Step 1

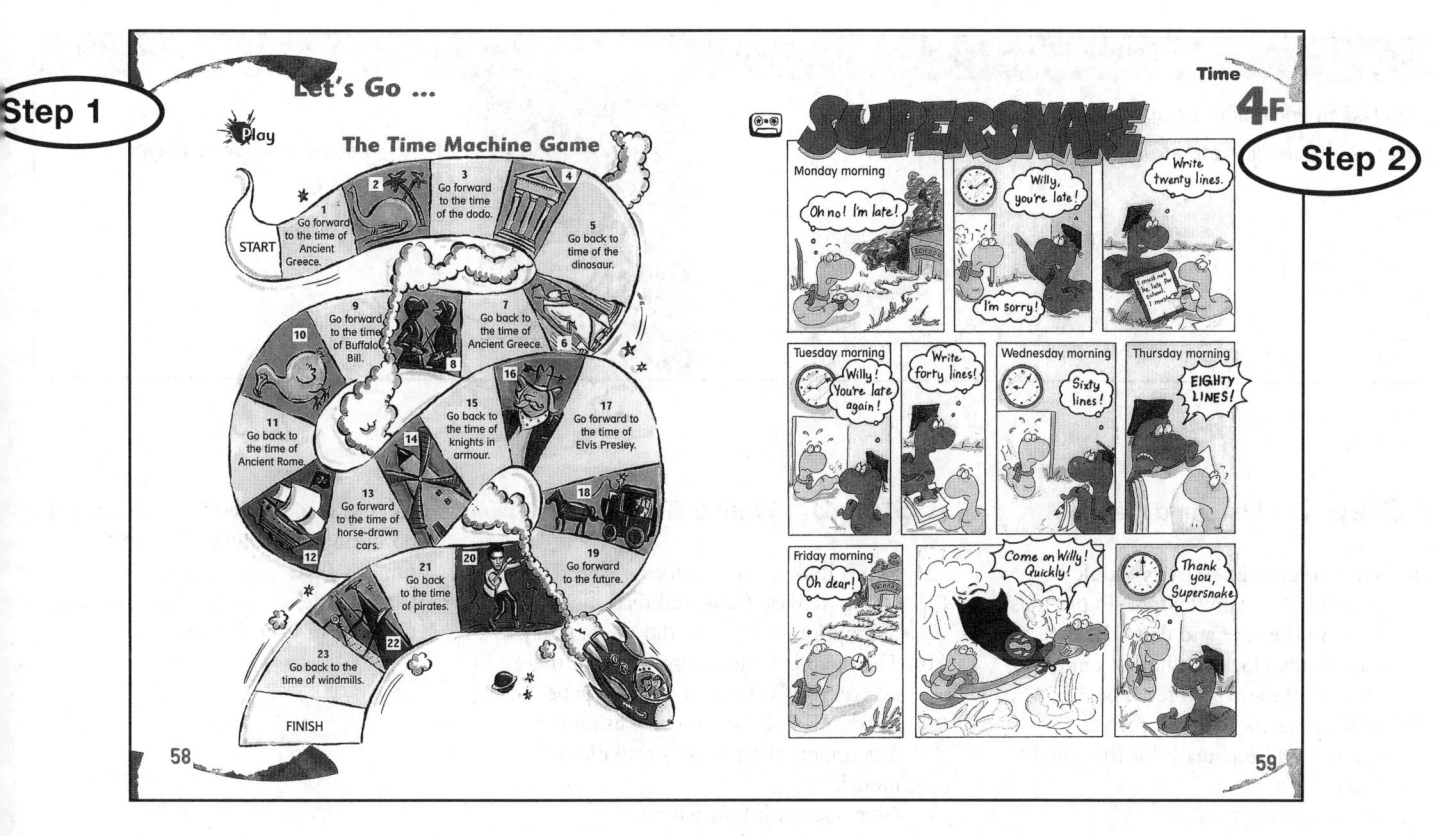

Let's Go ...

The Time Machine Game

START
1 Go forward to the time of Ancient Greece.
2
3 Go forward to the time of the dodo.
4
5 Go back to time of the dinosaur.
6
7 Go back to the time of Ancient Greece.
8
9 Go forward to the time of Buffalo Bill.
10
11 Go back to the time of Ancient Rome.
12
13 Go forward to the time of horse-drawn cars.
14
15 Go back to the time of knights in armour.
16
17 Go forward to the time of Elvis Presley.
18
19 Go forward to the future.
20
21 Go back to the time of pirates.
22
23 Go back to the time of windmills.
FINISH

Step 2

Supersnake

Time 4F

Monday morning — Oh no! I'm late!
Willy, you're late!
I'm sorry!
Write twenty lines.

Tuesday morning — Willy! You're late again!
Write forty lines.
Wednesday morning — Sixty lines!
Thursday morning — EIGHTY LINES!

Friday morning — Oh dear!
Come on Willy! Quickly!
Thank you, Supersnake.

Step 3

4F Time

1 Make — A Supersnake Clock

You need: a pencil, felt pens, card, a small paper plate, a compass, scissors, tape, a paper fastener

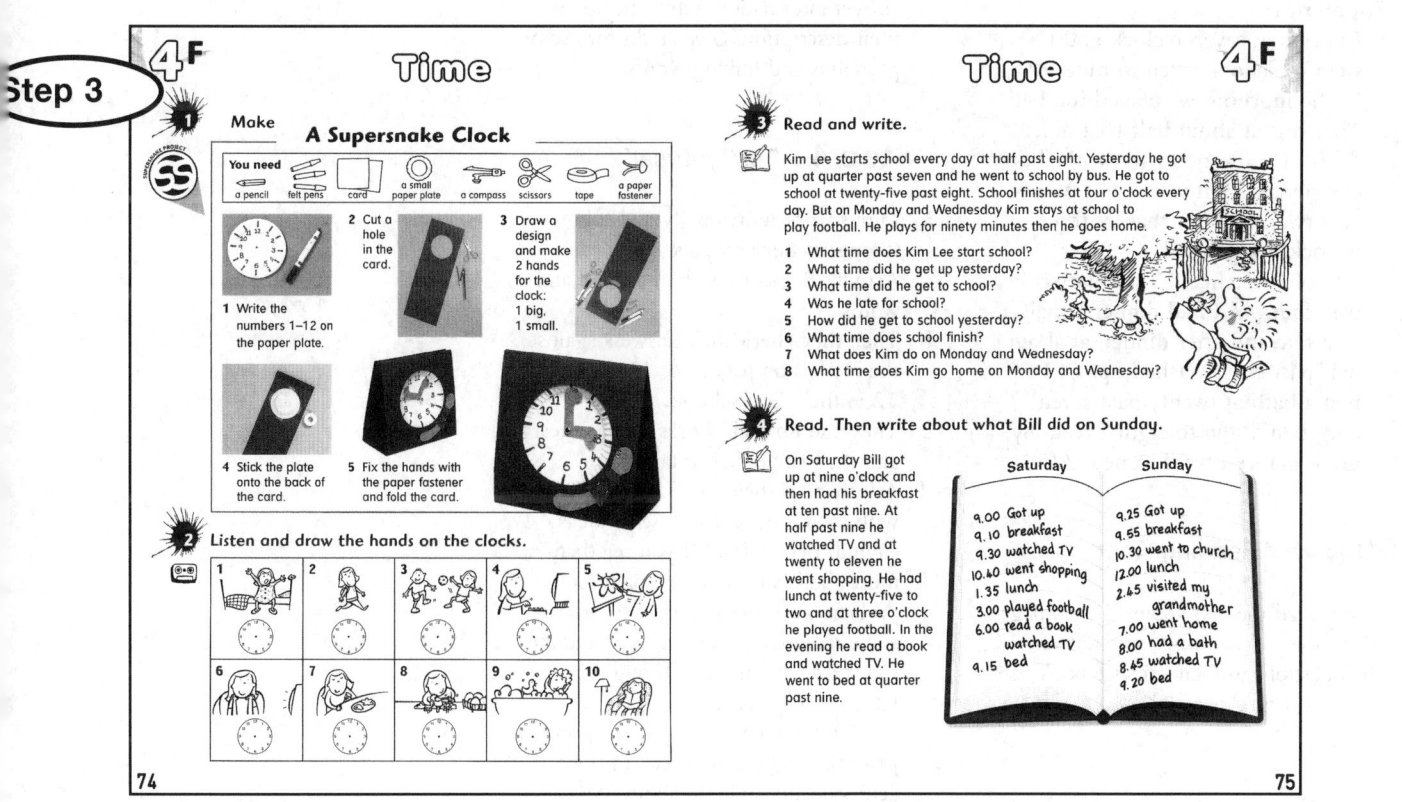

1 Write the numbers 1–12 on the paper plate.
2 Cut a hole in the card.
3 Draw a design and make 2 hands for the clock: 1 big, 1 small.
4 Stick the plate onto the back of the card.
5 Fix the hands with the paper fastener and fold the card.

2 Listen and draw the hands on the clocks.

Time 4F

3 Read and write.

Kim Lee starts school every day at half past eight. Yesterday he got up at quarter past seven and he went to school by bus. He got to school at twenty-five past eight. School finishes at four o'clock every day. But on Monday and Wednesday Kim stays at school to play football. He plays for ninety minutes then he goes home.

1 What time does Kim Lee start school?
2 What time did he get up yesterday?
3 What time did he get to school?
4 Was he late for school?
5 How did he get to school yesterday?
6 What time does school finish?
7 What does Kim do on Monday and Wednesday?
8 What time does Kim go home on Monday and Wednesday?

4 Read. Then write about what Bill did on Sunday.

On Saturday Bill got up at nine o'clock and then had his breakfast at ten past nine. At half past nine he watched TV and at twenty to eleven he went shopping. He had lunch at twenty-five to two and at three o'clock he played football. In the evening he read a book and watched TV. He went to bed at quarter past nine.

Saturday
9.00 Got up
9.10 breakfast
9.30 watched TV
10.40 went shopping
1.35 lunch
3.00 played football
6.00 read a book watched TV
9.15 bed

Sunday
9.25 Got up
9.55 breakfast
10.30 went to church
12.00 lunch
2.45 visited my grandmother
7.00 went home
8.00 had a bath
8.45 watched TV
9.20 bed

161

4F Lesson 2 – Evaluation

Main Language Items	Resource File	Materials Needed
Round-up lesson (including tests) *Revision of all vocabulary and structures*		cassette/cassette player Reader mirror(s)

Step 1   Listening (Test)

a   Say 'Open your Activity Book on page 74.' Explain the task. Pupils must listen to the tape and draw the time on each of the clocks at the bottom of the page. Play the tape three times.

b   Give one mark for each correct number, and one mark for the correct time.

Tapescript:
I got up at seven o'clock and I went to school at ten to nine. // In the morning we played football. That was at about half past nine. // In the afternoon we worked on computers. That was about twenty past two. // After that, at three o'clock, we painted. // After school I watched TV at quarter past four. // I had dinner at half past five and after dinner, at about half past six, I washed up. // I had a bath at twenty past seven and then at ten to eight I read my book before I went to bed. //

Step 2   Reading (Test)

Pupils read the text about Kim on page 75 of the Activity Book and answer the questions in their exercise books or on a sheet of paper.

Step 3   Writing (Test)

a   Pupils look at Bill's diary on page 75 of the Activity Book and read the description of what he did on Saturday.

b   Then pupils write a description in their exercise books or on a sheet of paper of what Bill did on Sunday, using the description of Saturday's activities as a model.

c   Give one mark for each piece of correct information pupils include in their description. Give credit for use of pronouns and linking words.

Step 4   Test yourself

a   Pupils work individually and follow the instructions on page 76 in their Activity Books to write the times and words.

b   Then they check their answers against the models on pages 36, 48, 49 and 52 in their Coursebook.

c   They add up their scores for each test and then circle their total score.

d   Ask them in their L1 if they are happy with their scores. If not, what areas should they review? If you see that most pupils still have one or several problem areas, make a note to prepare some reinforcement activities for these specific areas, and leaf through the Resource File for ideas.

e   Finally, comment on pupils' progress in general, congratulate them on their achievements and talk about the coming year. Suggest what they might do during the summer to keep their English alive.

f   Close the lesson with a favourite song or game, or a small party.

4F Time

1 Make — A Supersnake Clock

You need: a pencil, felt pens, card, a small paper plate, a compass, scissors, tape, a paper fastener

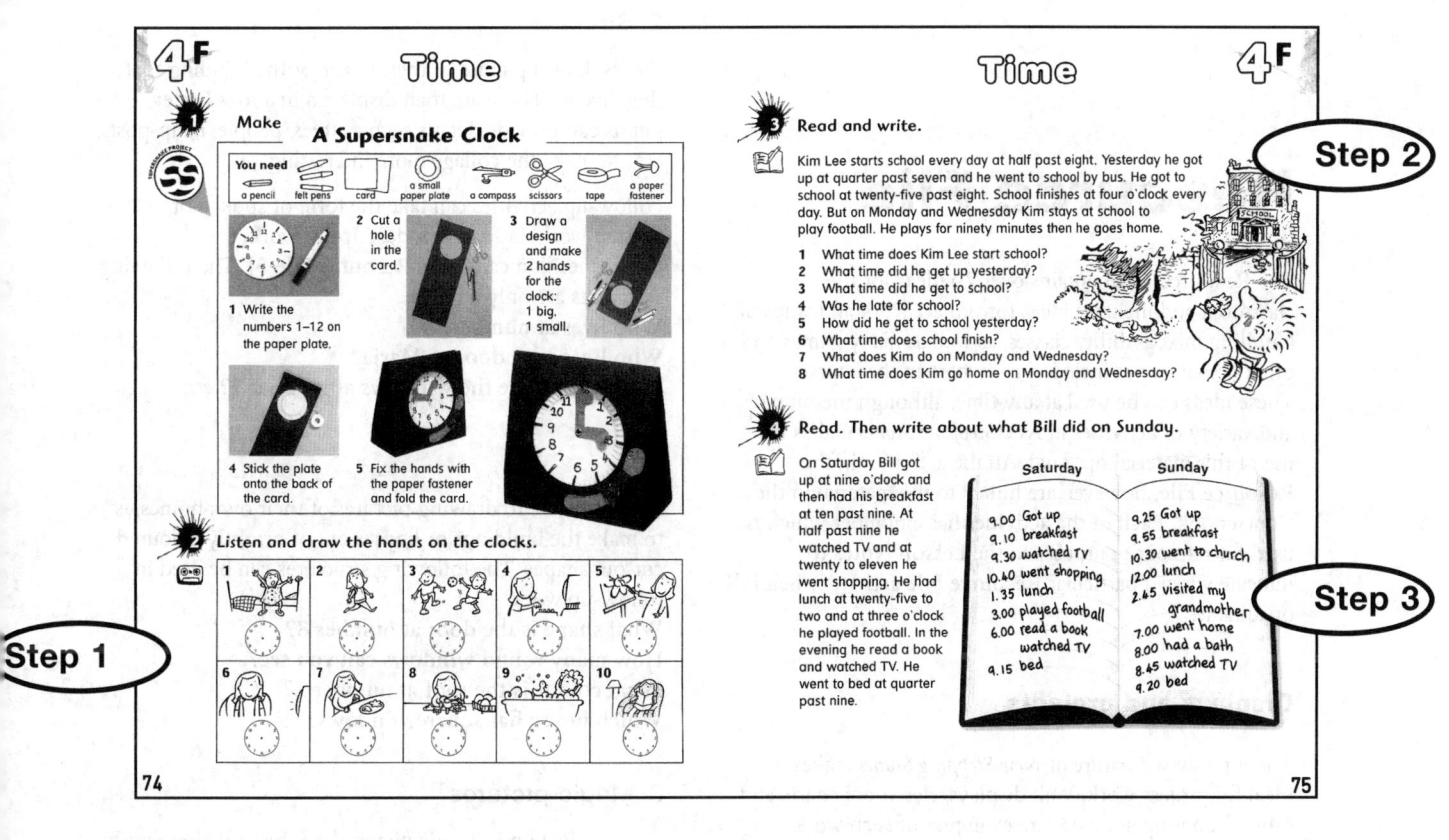

1 Write the numbers 1–12 on the paper plate.
2 Cut a hole in the card.
3 Draw a design and make 2 hands for the clock: 1 big, 1 small.
4 Stick the plate onto the back of the card.
5 Fix the hands with the paper fastener and fold the card.

2 Listen and draw the hands on the clocks.

4F Time

3 Read and write.

Kim Lee starts school every day at half past eight. Yesterday he got up at quarter past seven and he went to school by bus. He got to school at twenty-five past eight. School finishes at four o'clock every day. But on Monday and Wednesday Kim stays at school to play football. He plays for ninety minutes then he goes home.

1 What time does Kim Lee start school?
2 What time did he get up yesterday?
3 What time did he get to school?
4 Was he late for school?
5 How did he get to school yesterday?
6 What time does school finish?
7 What does Kim do on Monday and Wednesday?
8 What time does Kim go home on Monday and Wednesday?

4 Read. Then write about what Bill did on Sunday.

On Saturday Bill got up at nine o'clock and then had his breakfast at ten past nine. At half past nine he watched TV and at twenty to eleven he went shopping. He had lunch at twenty-five to two and at three o'clock he played football. In the evening he read a book and watched TV. He went to bed at quarter past nine.

Saturday
9.00 Got up
9.10 breakfast
9.30 watched TV
10.40 went shopping
1.35 lunch
3.00 played football
6.00 read a book watched TV
9.15 bed

Sunday
9.25 Got up
9.55 breakfast
10.30 went to church
12.00 lunch
2.45 visited my grandmother
7.00 went home
8.00 had a bath
8.45 watched TV
9.20 bed

4F Time

5 Test yourself.

TEST 1 ★ What's the time?

★ Check your answers on pages 48 and 49 in your Coursebook.
SCORE /6

TEST 2 ★ Write the days of the week.

M___ T___ W___
T___ F___ S___
S___

★ Check your answers on page 52 in your Coursebook.
SCORE /7

TEST 3 ★ Write the months of the year.

J___ F___ M___
A___ M___ J___
J___ A___ S___
O___ N___ D___

★ Check your answers on page 36 in your Coursebook.
SCORE /12

TOTAL /25

Circle your total score:
25 Excellent   24–22 Very good   21–16 Good
15–13 Quite good   12–0 Do it again!

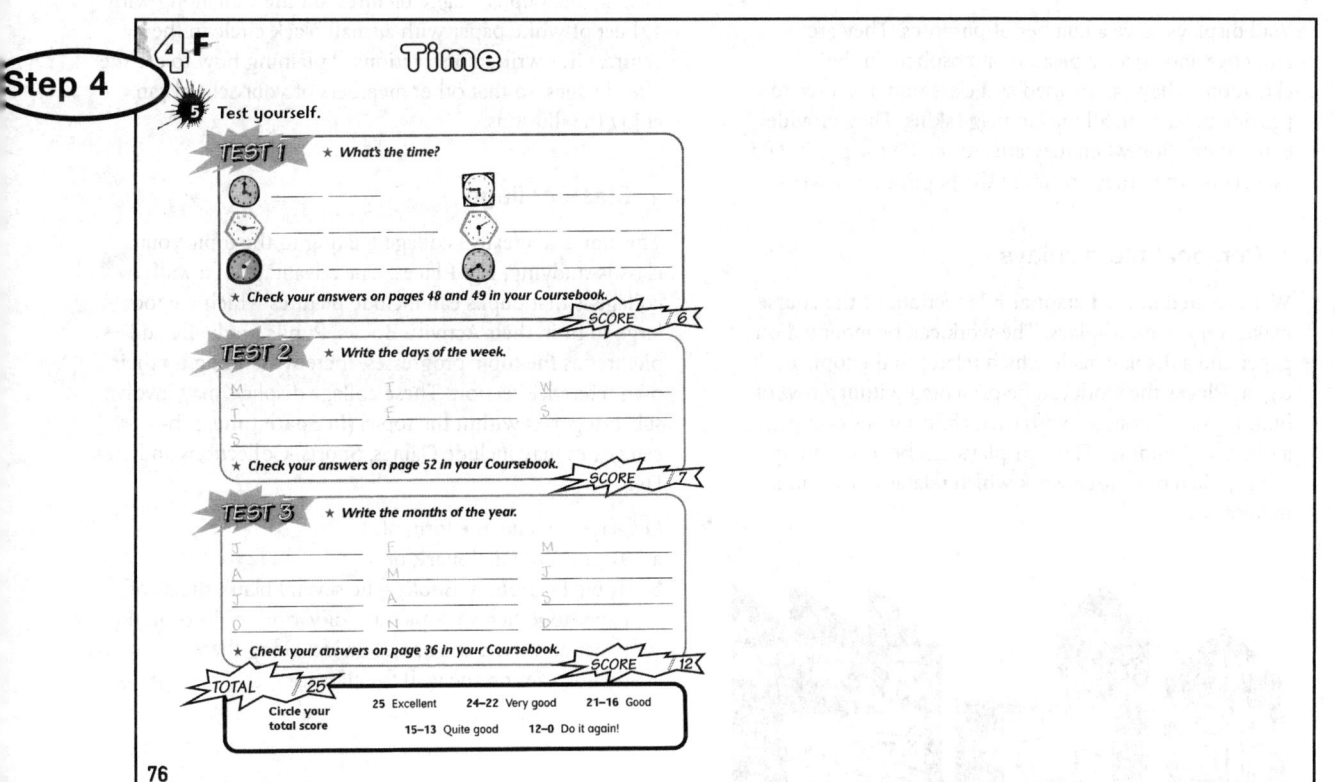

Resource File

The **Resource File** contains over 70 ideas for the classroom and includes ideas for project work and ways of handling mixed-ability classes, as well as many games and other activities not included elsewhere in the course. These ideas can be used at any time, although the range and variety of activities in *New Stepping Stones* makes the use of this material optional. All the activities in the **Resource File**, however, are linked to the material in the Coursebook. Each of the activities has a number which is used for reference purposes in the **Lesson Notes** to indicate when a particular **Resource File** activity is helpful or suitable.

Displays and projects

The topic-based nature of *New Stepping Stones* makes it ideal for project work. Wall displays, classroom charts and other follow-up activities are examples of such work.

Wall displays serve a number of purposes. They are attractive and create a pleasant atmosphere in the classroom. They can be used as a classroom resource to provide practice in all the language skills. They provide extra motivation when they are created by the pupils and especially when they are about the pupils themselves.

1 Personal file displays

Work created in the **Personal File** sections of the course makes very good displays. The work can be mounted on paper and a display made which relates to the topic itself, e.g. in **Places** the work can be presented within a row of buildings in silhouette, with each child's work occupying a different building. These displays can be followed up with spoken or written work which relates to the pupils themselves.

2 Street

Pupils draw a picture of their house or the building that they live in. These are then displayed in a row. Faster pupils can provide details such as trees, people, lamp-posts, etc., to make the collage more interesting.

Follow-up activities can take the form of spoken or written work, i.e. quizzes, descriptive work, comprehension cards (see **Resource File 5**). The following structures are only a guide:
Who lives at number 5?
Who lives next door to Maria?
What colour are the windows at number 7? etc.

2a

An alternative to drawing pictures of their own homes, is to make the buildings or houses out of brightly coloured cut-out shapes. The following structures can be used in follow-up work:
What shape is the door at number 8?
How many round windows can you see?
What colour is the roof at number 2?
Which house has square windows? etc.

3 Magic pictures

Display the pupils 'magic pictures' on the wall along with a sheet of white paper with a small black circle in the centre. Give written instructions explaining how to see the after-images, so that other members of your school can enjoy the illusions.

4 Class collage

The aim is to create a collage relating to the topic your class is studying, e.g. **Places**. The advantage of a wall collage is that pupils can include pictures which are too large to fit in their Activity Books. Pupils gradually add pictures as the topic progresses, thereby building up their own reference section. These collage displays may involve sub-categories within the topic. (In **Spare time**, sub-categories may include Games, Sports, Collections and Heroes.)

Displays can take the form of:
a Topic Wall Dictionary, or
b Topic Dictionary Books – tie several blank sheets of paper together, stick pictures of various objects on the paper and write the names inside. Hang these dictionaries on the wall for class use.

4a

A possible variation on the content of the collage displays is to use realia other than pictures cut from magazines, e.g.
Spare time – stamps, coins, etc.
Places – bus tickets, postcards, etc.
Opposites – pupils' heights and sizes, etc.
Times – clocks, watches, dates, etc.

5 Class surveys

The information gathered in **Surveys/Questionnaires** can be presented in wall charts, giving personal information in note form, e.g. in **Spare time**, at the start of the topic pin a chart to the wall.

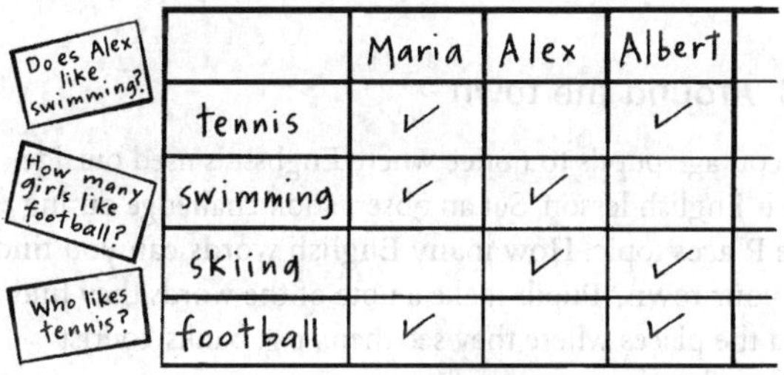

Gradually add the information to the chart as the topic progresses. Put questions around the display to add interest and focus attention on different aspects of the topic. Such displays can relate to any of the topics in *New Stepping Stones*:
Spare time – most popular hobby, differences between boys' and girls' hobbies.

Places – based upon pupils collecting information about their town rather than personal information, i.e. types of shops in the town, traffic survey on different streets.
Opposites – people with long hair or short hair, fair hair or dark hair, a class birthday chart.

6 Traffic survey

Extend the survey on page 34 of the Activity Book by dividing the class into small groups to study different aspects of local traffic e.g. colour, make, nationality, number of passengers, clean/dirty, number of wheels.

On returning to the classroom, all the information can be collated in graph form and provide a basis for further written work.

7 Where is it from?

Use a string and pin display on a world map. This can be a printed map or a large sketch. This is an ongoing display, using any items of realia pupils can bring to class which come from different countries. Stick the items around the map, label them and connect them to their country of origin.

The display can be topic-specific, e.g. using postage stamps (while working on Unit 1C in **Spare time**) or across all topics, e.g. using stamps, bus tickets, sweet wrappers, magazine pictures of tourist sites, postcards, etc.

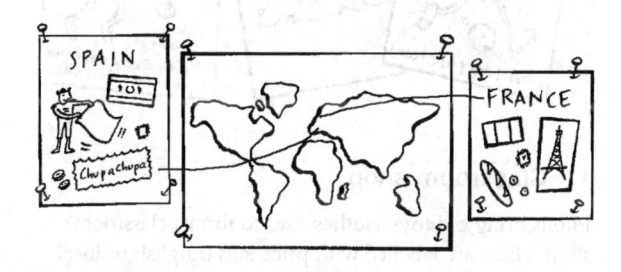

8 My country

Alternatively, in **Places**, pupils can make a string and pin display based around a map of their own country. Label various places, classify them into town, city and village, say where pupils come from, say which part of the country the town is in, list important buildings in the towns, etc. Postcards from different towns can be used as part of the display.

9 World map

If you are teaching a multi-national class, use the string and pin display technique to focus on countries. Use a map of the world and attach labels naming the countries. Pupils write their name and the name of their town under their country. Produce follow-up work, either guided (using question labels, writing questions on the blackboard, preparing workcards) or free (pupils can write as many true sentences as they can using the information in the visual).

10 Pupils' files

Pupils can be encouraged to keep a file of their own work, including work they do in their English lessons. This is more flexible than an exercise book since all work done on paper can be easily stored. Work from wall displays can then be kept in the files after the displays have been taken down. This can also add another dimension to the **Personal File** activities: work from these can form part of a pupil's file. Pupils can practise the drawing and writing in their Activity Books and after correction, display finished pieces of work in their file.

11 Classroom shop

Pupils bring old toys, clothes, etc., to form a classroom shop. These are labelled with price tags (English or local currency) and placed on a table at the front of the classroom, which becomes the shop. Prepare shopping workcards:

> You have 50 pence.
> Go to the shop and buy 3 things.
> ----
> a. What did you buy?
> b. How much did you spend?
> c. Do you have any change? How much?

Pupils carry out the task and answer the questions on paper. (The past tense form is passive. Pupils do not need to write their answers in sentence form.)

12 Shops

Divide the class into groups. Each group will require paper, scissors, glue, magazines or coloured pencils to make a shop. Pupils draw items and/or cut out pictures for the items in their shop. Each group discusses and marks the price of each of them, in English or local currency, and then the shops are displayed on the wall, either at random or in a row.

Prepare a set of shopping cards:

> Buy:
> 1 kilo of oranges _____
> 2 bottles of milk _____
> a T-shirt   _____
> a newspaper   _____
>   Total: _____

Having a variety of cards will enable all pupils to work at their own pace. Divide the class into four groups and give each group a different card, to avoid all pupils going to the same shop at once. The task is to read the shopping list, go to the shop and buy the item by making a note of the price. On completion, pupils bring their list to the teacher to be checked before receiving another list to complete.

13 Around the town

Encourage pupils to notice where English is used outside their English lesson. Set an observation challenge during the **Places** topic: **How many English words can you find in your town?** Pupils make a note of the words they find and the places where they see them, e.g. banks, tourist offices, hotels, shops.

14 Towns, cities and villages

Study your local area in more depth in the medium of English. Maps and tourist information will be very useful here. (Places such as libraries, tourist information offices, the British Council, etc., will probably be helpful).

a Look at the differences between towns, cities and villages by making a list of local places and classifying them under these three headings, i.e. **Is Seville a town, city, or village?**

b Draw a map of your county or area and mark places of interest, using the string and pin display technique to label the map with names, and write brief descriptions about size, places of interest, etc.

15 Collect a picture

This activity extends the collage activities of Levels 1 and 2. Instead of simply collecting thematically linked pictures and displaying them, pupils focus on subcategories within the topic. (E.g. in **Opposites**, examples of large/small objects can be juxtaposed as part of a wall display.)

Pupils stick pictures of relevant subjects on the display sheet and write simple captions or labels alongside as a continuing activity throughout a topic or unit.

16 Time surveys

The topic **Time** lends itself to class surveys and questionnaires. The following questions could each form the basis of a questionnaire:
When do most people go to bed?
How many hours of TV do pupils watch per day?
How long does it take to get to school?
Rather than the whole class doing the same survey, pupils can work in pairs on different aspects of time. They can write their own question(s) and then ask their classmates. The information gathered can be presented in wall charts.

17 Getting there

Set up a survey on methods of transport used by pupils and their families to get to school/work and how long it takes them to get there.

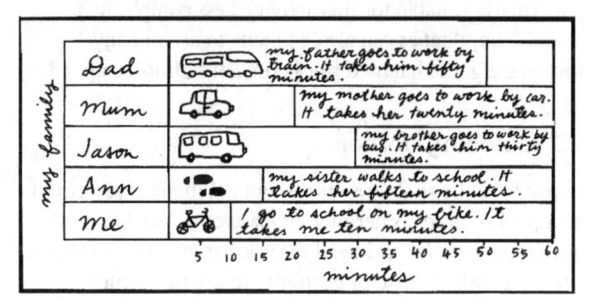

18 Top secret

This mystery quiz can continue throughout the work on spies in **Opposites**. You need a large envelope. Write **Top Secret** on the envelope. Set the scene by telling pupils that you've received some top secret information. Inside the envelope there is information telling of a dangerous spy lurking in your midst! (It could be one of the other teachers, if pupils know the staff.) Either have a full description of the person inside the envelope (colour of hair, eyes, height, weight, date of birth, etc.) or build up the mystery lesson by lesson, revealing one fact at a time. Stick each new message on a wall poster for pupils to refer to and eliminate suspects and/or guess the spy. Clues should be very general to start with and gradually become more detailed. Messages could be made from letters cut out of newspapers and magazines. Pupils can make a note of each new piece of information in their exercise books and keep their eyes open for the spy at all times! If you have parallel classes, each class can prepare clues for the other.

19 Venn diagrams

Venn diagrams can be used to focus on particular language points (e.g. **can/can't**, **like/don't like**), at the same time promoting free discussion.

Pupils work in groups of two or three. Each group needs a large sheet of paper. They draw two or three large intersecting circles on the paper, one per group member. If the topic is sports, pupils first decide which sports they like. Each person then writes the names of the sports they like in their own circle but sports liked by more than one pupil should be written where the appropriate circles intersect.

Work with the class to produce a list of structures/topic areas that can be treated in this way and let each group choose one. The displays will then be varied.

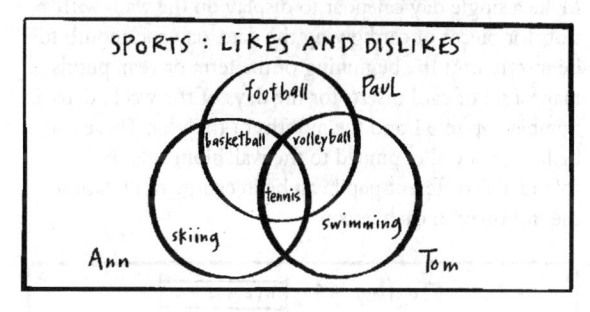

20 Times around town

Set an observation challenge during the **Time** topic. Tell pupils to look out for the opening and closing times of local shops and buildings. Pupils note down the times and then in class compile a list of their findings, e.g.
The bank opens at ten o'clock and closes at …
The Ritz Restaurant opens at …
Follow up this exercise with some prepared questions, e.g.
Which shop opens first?
What time do the banks open?

21 Class calendar

Make a large calendar at the beginning of the year for display on the wall. Pupils fill in important dates. These could be colour coded, e.g. blue for birthdays, red for holidays, grey for exams. A simplified version can list the months of the year in one column with a blank column alongside. Pupils sign their names next to their birth month.

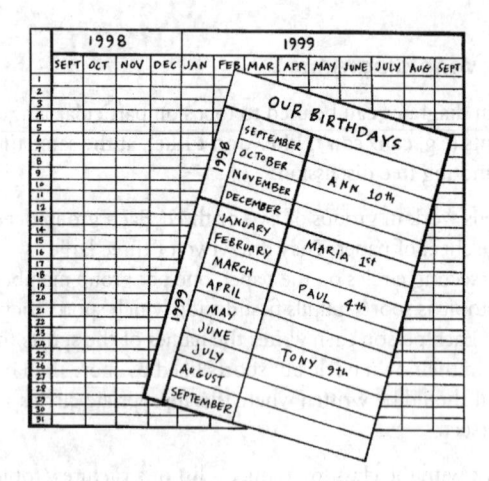

22 Changing displays

Make a single day calendar to display on the wall, with slots for pieces of card giving the date, day and month to be inserted. At the beginning of the term or year, pupils make a set of card inserts for the days of the week, dates in numbers up to 31 and the months of the year. These can be kept in a wallet pinned to the wall alongside the calendar. A different pupil can be in charge of updating the information each lesson.

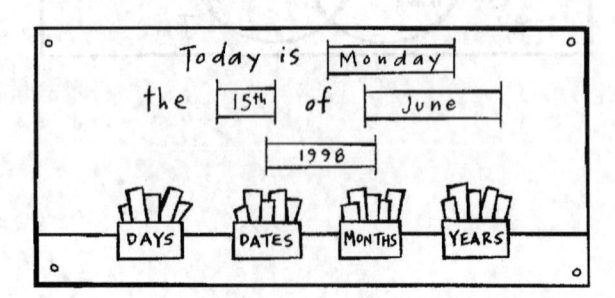

23 Alphabet word frieze

This vocabulary activity can continue throughout the term and is not topic specific. Cut out large alphabet letters from light-coloured paper. Mount these on the wall at such a height that pupils can write on them. Pupils then write any English words they like on the cut-outs, putting each word on the cut-out letter with which the word begins. Encourage pupils to look at the frieze from time to time to see what the others have written, and remind them to write their own words.

24 Sound effects

One way of livening up a story and encouraging pupils to listen several times is to let them record it with accompanying sound effects.

You will need a tape recorder with a microphone and blank cassette(s). This is best done as a group activity. For a shorter activity, allocate a few sounds or a section of the story to each group. Alternatively, let each group make their own complete version. Only one group can record at a time, unless you have access to lots of equipment. Make sure you have activities to occupy the rest of the class while each group is recording. Each group makes a list of possible sound effects and then works out how to produce each sound. Sounds can be made using voices or available props. Each group then records their story with effects. If no recording equipment is available, each group can perform their story for the rest of the class: one or two pupils read the story while the rest of the group create the effects in the background. The range of possible effects will be limited in this case.

The story of *Jim and Jean and the Time Machine* is particularly suitable for this activity. Less complicated 'sounds-only' tapes can also be made to accompany pictures, e.g. the haunted house on Coursebook page 38.

25 Listening corner

If you have the space, resources and equipment, you could set up a listening corner in your classroom. All you need are a tape recorder and headphones. Set up a rota to ensure that all pupils have an opportunity to use the corner.

Pupils can listen to the stories in *New Stepping Stones* for valuable extra listening practice.

The listening corner can also be used to advantage with mixed-ability classes, either giving faster pupils an opportunity to broaden their exposure to recorded English beyond the course materials or giving slower pupils a chance to consolidate their grasp of the recorded course materials.

26 Time line

This will describe pupils' everyday activities. Fix a long sheet of paper to the wall. Divide it into 24 sections, representing the hours in a day. Write the time or draw a clock showing the time in each section. As a continuing activity, pupils write about things they do every day on pieces of paper and stick them under the appropriate time on the time line.

A variation on the timeline would be to divide the line into days of the week. Pupils write about when they play particular sports or practise hobbies etc.

Games

In general, the games in this section are oral games though some involve reading and writing.

27 I-spy

The game can be played either in pairs, groups or as a whole-class activity, although initially it is only recommended as the latter. Referring either to objects in the classroom or pictures in the Coursebook, say **'I can see something beginning with "b".'** The class then try to guess the object. The pupil who guesses correctly thinks of the next object.

28 Battleships

Divide the class into pairs. Each pupil requires an identical grid to his or her partner.
There can be any number of sports or hobbies along the top of the grid. A total of about twenty squares is ideal.

Each pupil places ten ticks at random on their grid. Pupils must not look at one another's grid.
In **Spare Time**, the grid could look like this:

	SPARE TIME		
	Football	Tennis	Basketball
Monday		✓	✓
Tuesday	✓		
Wednesday	✓		✓
Thursday		✓	
Friday	✓		✓

Players take it in turns to ask questions to find the location of their opponent's ticks, e.g. **'Do you play football on Tuesdays?'**

The first player to find all their opponent's ticks is the winner. This type of exercise can be adapted to any topic, e.g. for **Places**:

	Mary	Tom	Ann	Fred
red car			✓	
white car				✓
yellow car	✓			
motorbike		✓		

For the above grid, use the question form **'Has Mary got a yellow car?'**

29 Playground game

You will need a large open space to play this game. Draw large shapes on the ground with chalk. (See below).
All pupils stand in the middle, **X**. The teacher then gives instructions, e.g. **'Walk into the circle slowly. Point to the square. Don't go into the triangle. Stand in the rectangle and turn around. Girls go to the circle. Boys go to the square.'** etc.

Direct individual pupils by name, or according to the colour of their hair, eyes or what they are wearing.

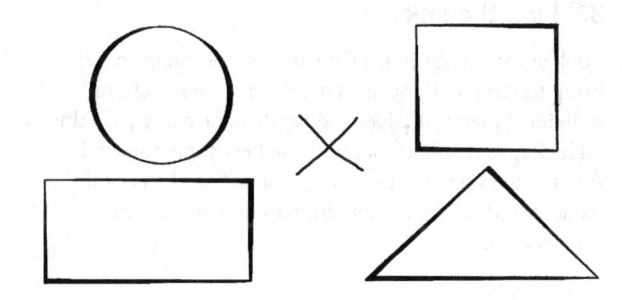

30 Observation

Pupils look carefully at their surroundings and notice the shapes around them. Ask pupils '**How many shapes can you see in the classroom?**' Ask them to write down the shapes, noting the name of the object, shape and colour:
Rectangle – blackboard, table, door, book, etc.
Square – windows, wall, etc.

Pupils can also count shapes in their homes or in the streets.

31 Mime

One pupil comes to the front of the class and mimes a sport or other activity. The first pupil to guess the sport or activity then takes over and mimes.

32 Horse racing

This dice game (to practise ordinal numbers) can be played alone, in pairs or in groups. Each player or group needs a dice and four different coloured counters. Draw a race-track as follows on a sheet of paper:

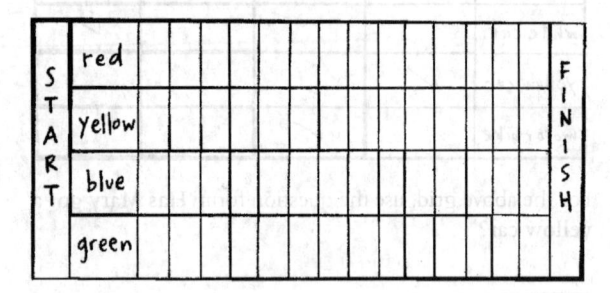

S T A R T	red							F I N I S H
	yellow							
	blue							
	green							

Place the counters at the start. Throw the dice in turn for each colour and move the horse the appropriate number of squares. Pupils note which horse is the winner, second etc. Encourage pupils to write out their results in full sentences, i.e. **The blue horse is first. The yellow horse is second.**
The exercise can be used for practising the past tense, '**was**', with pupils reporting back the results of their race to the whole class.

33 Find the link

Look at the stamps in the Coursebook (or stamps pupils bring to class with them). Write the numbers 1–21 on individual pieces of paper and lay them face down on the table. Pupils then pick out two numbers at random and find the relevant stamps in the picture. The object of the game is to think of as many similarities between the stamps as possible.

Pupils are awarded a point for each similarity they say, e.g.
They are from Italy.
Pictures of sport.
They are red.

34 Do you sell soap?

Write the names of different types of shop on the blackboard. One pupil thinks of a shop and the rest of the class have to ask questions to determine the shop he or she is thinking of, using only the question form, '**Do you sell soap?**' etc. This game can be played competitively in teams or simply as a whole-class exercise.

35 Have you got any cars?

This game is an extension of the exercise on page 29 of the Activity Book. (The game can of course be played using real objects or pictures cut out of magazines.)

When pupils have coloured and priced the toys in their shop, bring six pupils (or less, depending on class size) to the front of the class. Each pupil (shopkeeper) stands behind a desk (counter) with a sheet of card to hide his or her book. The rest of the class prepare their shopping lists and then queue up at the shops to buy the items on their list. Add a further element by encouraging the pupils to get the best deal, buying their toys at the cheapest price.

36 What's the time Mr Wolf?

This is a playground game and requires an open space. Pupils form a circle and one pupil (Mr Wolf) stands in the middle. As they circle the wolf, pupils chant '**What's the time Mr Wolf?**'. Each time, the wolf replies shouting a different time, e.g. '**One o'clock**' etc. The pupils take a step forward. This continues until the wolf answers '**Dinner time!**' Pupils must run away and the wolf tries to catch one of them. This pupil becomes the wolf and the game continues. Teach pupils the game in their English lesson and they can play it in the playground at break times.

37 Mr Wolf card game

This is a variation on the playground game above and can be played in small groups in the classroom. Divide the class into groups of four. Each group will need to prepare a set of twelve cards in advance. On each card, draw a clock (the cards should show the time on the hour from one to twelve o'clock). One pupil (Mr Wolf) takes the cards, shuffles them and lays them face down. The other pupils take it in turns to ask '**What's the time Mr Wolf?**' Each time the wolf turns over a card and says the time. If the clock is set at 12 o'clock then the wolf says '**Dinner Time!**' and 'eats' the pupil who has asked him the time. Pupils could start with five points and lose a point each time they are caught.

38 Memory sequences

Four pupils come to the front of the class. The teacher says a sequence of letters to each pupil in turn who has to repeat the exact sequence in the same order. Start with three letters and add one letter each round. If a pupil makes a mistake or can't remember the letters, he or she is out of the game. The winner is the last player remaining. Then bring four new pupils out to the front.

The game can be played competitively by dividing the class into two teams and selecting two players from each in turn and awarding points.

38a

The above game can also be played using cardinal or ordinal numbers, months of the year or any vocabulary set.

39 Memory chains

Pupils successively add to a sentence by repeating what previous pupils have said and then adding something themselves. It is a memory game that can be used for practising a wide range of structures and vocabulary, and is particularly useful for developing fluency.

You can ask a question to elicit the target structure, e.g.
'What time did you get up?'
P1 starts the chain: 'I got up at eight o'clock.'
P2 continues: 'I got up at ten to seven and he got up at eight o'clock.'
P3 continues: 'I got up at five past eight, she got up at ten to seven and he got up at eight o'clock.'
If a pupil forgets the sequence or makes a mistake, the next person in line starts a new sequence.

Other chain questions could include:
What did you do last night?
Where did you go on holiday?

Weaker students may find it useful to use playing cards as prompts. (These will need to be made in advance.) Pupils take turns, turning over cards and naming the sequence. Emphasis is then taken away from remembering the sequence to simply remembering the English names for things.

40 Spell it

This game practises the letters of the alphabet. The teacher spells out any word to the class, saying the letters in quick succession, i.e. '**D-O-G**'. The first pupil to say '**dog**' wins a point for their team. Pupils must not write the letters down. Start off with short words and gradually increase the level of difficulty.

41 Busy pictures

Many of the large full- or half-page pictures in the Coursebook can be used as the starting point for games. To practise vocabulary, pupils study the picture for one minute, close their books and see how many objects they can remember. Pupils can simply list items or add size, colour, location of object etc., depending on how complicated you want the task to be. Pupils can list the items orally or in writing.

41a

Use the pictures on pages 6, 18–19, 27 or 41 of the Coursebook. One pupil selects a person or animal in the picture and his or her partner or group members ask '**yes/no**' type questions to determine who it is, e.g.
Is it a man?
Is he wearing a hat?
Has he got black hair?
Is he standing in front of the chemist's? etc.

The game can be played competitively with points awarded for correct and incorrect guesses, or in small groups with pupils taking turns to ask questions.

41b

Pupils write a brief description of a person or object in one of the pictures, on a piece of paper. The teacher reads it to the class and pupils try to guess the object or person, using the picture to help e.g. on page 41 of the Coursebook: **She's wearing a blue skirt. She's drinking.**

42 Alibi

This is a simplified version of the detective game *Alibi* to practise asking simple questions in the past tense. The game is played in groups of four or six. Two players in each group are suspects and there are either two policemen working individually or two groups of two policemen. Write the following questions on the blackboard:
What three films did you see?
What days did you see the films?
What times did they start and finish?

Or prepare the following cards for suspects and policemen:

SUSPECTS
Last week you went to see 3 films.
1. What were the films?
2. What days did you see the films?
3. What time did they start? What time did they finish?

POLICE OFFICERS
Ask these questions. Write the answers.
1. What films did you see last week?
2. What day did you see...?
3. What time did... start? What time did... finish?

The suspects work together. They have two minutes to decide upon their answers to the questions (there are effectively nine questions to be answered, three questions about each of the three films). The suspects must agree on their answers about each film to make a perfect alibi. After the two minutes have passed, the policemen interview each suspect in turn and try to find a difference in their stories. If they find a difference, then they are the winners and the suspects are 'guilty', if not the suspects are 'innocent'. (The suspects may not make notes about their alibi, although the policemen can).

43 Password

A simple activity to bring the spy theme into the classroom. At the end of the previous lesson set a password. Choose any word – perhaps one which pupils have difficulty pronouncing or need to remember. The first pupil to come to class the next day has to say the password before they are allowed into class. This pupil then 'guards' the door and makes sure all other pupils say the password.

Extend the activity by making pupils spell the password as well as say it. This game does depend on you being the first one in the classroom!

43a

Pupils can make identity cards or passports for themselves, giving their name and personal information. These have to be shown in order to enter the classroom. Pupils can be required to answer questions based on the information on their ID cards.

44 Opposites tennis

Divide the class into two teams, A and B. Player 1 in Team A says a word and Player 1 in Team B must answer immediately with the opposite of that word. Player 1 in Team B then says a word for Player 2 in Team A. If a player cannot answer immediately then the other team scores a point. If a player answers wrongly, the point again goes to the other team. However, if a player says a word and the opposing player does not answer, then the first player must say the word they were thinking of. This prevents pupils giving words that have no opposite as well as ensuring that they know the answer themselves.

45 Time challenges

These simple games reinforce time and numbers while practising other language points. Tasks involve the maximum number of times pupils can do something within a given time limit. Pupils work in pairs to monitor one another, but all time challenges are individual. It is useful to have a stopwatch or watch with a second hand, although counting the seconds can add to the excitement. e.g.

How many times can you say the alphabet in two minutes?
How many times can you throw a six in one minute? (Each player needs a dice).
How many seven-letter words can you say in two minutes?
How many times can you stand up and sit down in forty-five seconds?

46 Time race

Divide the class into two teams. Draw two large clocks on the blackboard. Say a time, e.g. **'twenty to eight'**. P1 from each team races to the board and draws the hands in the correct position on their clock. The first one to do so wins a point. Continue until all players have had at least one turn. Vary the way you give the time if pupils can cope with it, e.g. **'ten fifteen'**, **'quarter past ten'**.

47 Finger writing

This is a simple vocabulary reinforcement game. Pupils work in pairs. P1 traces a word on P2's back using their forefinger. P2 tries to guess the word. Each pair counts how many they can get right in five minutes.

48 Whispers

This simple game can be used to practise any structure or grammar point. The whole class stands in a circle. Whisper a sentence in the ear of the pupil to your left. They then pass the sentence on to the pupil on their left. But will it be the same sentence when it gets back to you? You could write down the original sentence and get the last pupil in the circle to give their version first and then read out the original.

49 Bingo

Bingo is not often used in *New Stepping Stones 3*, but it can be helpful for practising the different forms of key verbs, especially irregular verbs. Elicit verbs from pupils and write them on the blackboard. Pupils draw a large nine-square grid. They write a verb from the list in the present tense in each square. While pupils are making their Bingo cards, prepare a set of call cards, one for each verb. To play the game, pick out a call card at random and give the past tense of the verb. Pupils cross out the verbs on their Bingo cards as they are called. The first player to eliminate all their nine words and shout '**Bingo!**' is the winner. That player can then take the role of Bingo caller. The same game can be played the other way round with the past tense on the Bingo cards and present tense forms on the call cards.

49a Mime bingo

The teacher requires a set of call cards with a verb written on each one. Prepare these while pupils are making their Bingo cards. To play the game, pick out a call card and mime the verb. The first player to eliminate all their words and shout '**Bingo!**' is the winner. Pupils can then take the role of miming the bingo words.

49b Alphabet bingo

Each pupil draws a twelve-square grid on a piece of paper and writes a letter of the alphabet in each square. The bingo caller (teacher or pupil) writes the alphabet on a piece of paper and calls out the letters in random sequence, crossing them out as she does so. Pupils cross out the letters on their Bingo card as they are called out. The first player to eliminate all their letters and shout '**Bingo!**' is the winner. Then play the game in small groups.

50 If …

Write the following sentences on the blackboard:
If I were a colour, I would be …
If I were an animal, I would be a …

Other examples include **town, car, country** – elicit ideas from the class. Pupils copy the sentences and complete them with their own preferences. Then pupils go round the class and guess what their friends have written, e.g. '**If you were a colour, I think you would be yellow.**'

51 Spycatcher

Elect one pupil to be the spycatcher. This pupil leaves the room. Elect another pupil to be the spy. They hide a secret tape or other clue about their person. The spycatcher comes back in and asks pupils questions with '**yes/no**' answers to find out who the spy is, e.g.
Is it a boy?
Is he wearing a blue jumper?
Has he got black hair?
Is he sitting near the window?

When the spy is caught, another pair is chosen. The game can be played competitively by awarding points for correct/incorrect guesses or by timing the spycatcher.

52 Spot the mistakes

This reading and listening activity can be used to reinforce students' grasp of any of the stories in *New Stepping Stones 3*. It also encourages speed reading.

Read the story to the class. Pupils listen and follow in their Readers at the same time. Change some of the words or make deliberate mistakes as you go. Pupils must shout '**Stop!**' every time they hear a mistake and try to correct the error.

53 Puzzle box

Pupils make their own word puzzles. Get pupils to copy the best ones onto card. Make them into a lasting resource by covering them with clear adhesive plastic. Store them in a puzzle box (a shoe box is ideal). They can then be used by other pupils and classes.

The puzzle box is a very useful time filler for faster pupils. They can either do some of the existing puzzles or make up their own to add to the box.

54 Change the sentence

This activity practises opposites and can be done either as oral or written work. Give pupils some simple sentences, e.g. '**He was tall and thin.**' The task is for pupils to substitute opposite adjectives. So they would write '**He was short and fat.**' Pupils work in pairs. Give each pair three different sentences to change. When they have finished, they swap their version with another pair. They change each other's sentences. This should bring them back to the original versions. Circulate and supervise the swapping.

55 Magic mirror

This is a follow up activity to *The Magic Mirror* in the Reader. Pupils draw and describe other things they think Arnold might have seen through the mirror. This provides reading and writing practice.

> **The Magic Mirror**
> In Bob's house the phone was enormous but the table was tiny.
>
> **The Magic Mirror**
> In the park the flowers were taller than the trees.

56 Shape pictures

Pupils make pictures out of coloured shapes following written instructions. Write the instructions on the blackboard or prepare workcards in advance, e.g. '**Use a square, a rectangle and two circles. Make a picture of a car.**'

Alternatively, allow pupils to use any shapes they choose to make pictures. Then write a description alongside the picture, e.g. '**This car is made from a blue rectangle, a green square and two red circles.**'

57 Word steps

This is a written version of the game 'Word tennis'. Divide the class into pairs or small groups. Each pupil writes a word at the top of a piece of paper then passes the paper to his or her partner (or the person on the left). Pupils build up word steps by adding words beginning with the last letter of the preceding word, e.g.

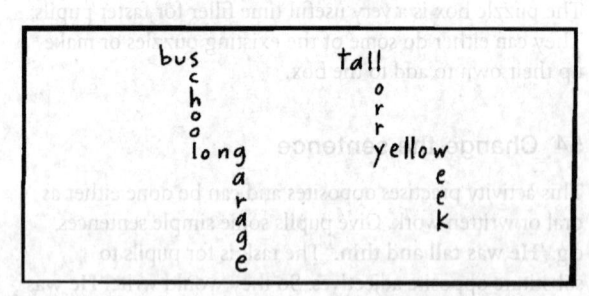

```
bus            tall
 c              o
 h              r
 o              r
 o              yellow
 long            e
    a            e
    r            k
    a
    g
    e
```

If it is impossible to add another word, pupils start a new set of steps.

58 Word wall

If space is available, a large scale, ongoing version of **Word steps** can be created. Stick a very large sheet of paper on the wall and start a **Word step**. The ultimate aim is to fill the whole sheet with words. When you reach the end of the paper, turn around by adding words that end in the same letter as the previous word.

59 Alphabetical order

This is a remedial exercise to practise alphabetising. Pupils write words on separate pieces of paper and arrange them in alphabetical order manually.

60 Number plates

For homework, instruct pupils to collect car registration numbers, making a note of the colour, size and make of the car. Ask a few questions, such as:
How many did you collect?
Where does the car come from?

The main purpose of this task is that pupils will have made their own alphabet and number dictation sequences, and can dictate them to their partners.

61 Speed writing

Instruct pupils to write a set of words:
Write five words beginning with 'r'.
Write the names of four vegetables.
Write eight colours.
Write the alphabet.
Write ten things you find in a house. etc.

The first pupil to finish shouts '**Stop!**' and everyone must put their pens down while the words are checked. If correct, award a point and give the next instruction. If wrong, the race continues.

62 Crosswords

Write a word vertically on the blackboard, e.g. **ATHENS**. Pupils must quickly write one word beginning with each of the letters that make up the word, e.g.
Animal
Toy
Happy
Everybody
Newspaper
Seven
Demonstrate the game on the blackboard. The game can then be played co-operatively in small groups, pairs or with pupils working alone.

174

The game can also be played competitively by stopping the activity when the first pupil finishes, checking the words and allocating points.

63 Drawing dictation

Each pupil needs a piece of paper and coloured pencils. Pupils build up a picture following instructions. Either prepare the instructions in advance and read them to the class, or have one pupil at a time give an instruction, e.g.
P1 – **Draw a small circle.**
P2 – **Colour the circle red.**
P3 – **Draw a cat by the circle.**
P4 – **Draw a triangle under the cat.**
P5 – **Write 'Hello' in the triangle.** etc.

64 Hieroglyphics

This is a whole class activity and involves cracking a code to work out the meaning of hidden messages. The code could be as follows:

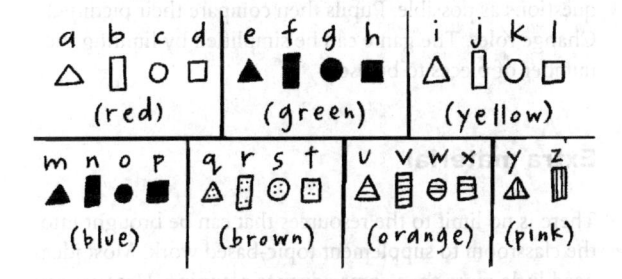

[code chart showing symbols for letters a–z grouped in colours: red (a–d), green (e–h), yellow (i–l), blue (m–p), brown (q–t), orange (u–x), pink (y–z)]

Copy out each hieroglyphic with the letter it represents onto a separate piece of paper. Give each pupil one of the pieces of paper (or more than one if there are less than 26 pupils in your class). Write some coded messages on the board, e.g.

1. (What's your name?)
2. (Have you got a brother?)

Pupils copy down the messages and then try to crack the code as quickly as possible by asking other class members what their symbols mean.

65 Rubbings

Pupils make rubbings of plaques or man-hole covers by placing a piece of paper over the plaque, taping the edges down, then rubbing the surface with a soft pencil or crayon. These can be displayed in the classroom with an accompanying note of the building or place where it was made.

66 Optician's chart

Make an optician's eye chart to practise the letters of the alphabet. Cut different-sized letters out of a newspaper or magazine and stick them in rows. Alternatively, write the letters neatly.
The eye chart can then be used as part of a role play. One pupil is the optician. Another pupil plays the receptionist and makes appointments. The rest of the group are patients. For each appointment, the optician points to letters and asks patients questions such as, '**What letter is this?**' and '**Can you read this row?**'

67 Instructions

Use the cut-out town pieces from the centre pull-out section of the Activity Book. Either make flashcards or get pupils to write instructions on paper, e.g. **There's a hotel opposite the park.** Working in pairs or using the flashcards in a whole class activity, pupils read the instructions and put the pieces in the appropriate place on their baseboard.

'Making' activities

Although **Making activities** are time-consuming, some teachers choose to expand topics into other areas of the curriculum or simply feel that there is sufficient scope to extend a particular theme further. Constructing three-dimensional displays or making things which can be used as a focus for extra language practice are two ways of doing this. Such activities are also fun. However, it is more rewarding if these activities are not simply an end in themselves but are a means to an end or part of a larger activity.

Therefore, there should be a linguistic purpose either in the task itself or as a follow-up to, or extension of, the **Making activity**. This can take the form of a guided reading task, prepared in advance or written on the blackboard. Alternatively, objects made by the pupils can be used in role plays or as the basis for written descriptions, surveys, questionnaires, etc.

68 Making money

Pupils make coins out of silver paper or notes from paper or card. These can be used in role plays.

69 On screen

Make a large cardboard cut-out of a TV screen from an old box. This can be used in a variety of TV role plays; presenting news broadcasts, advertisements, puppet shows, etc.

70 Make a TV

Make a TV set using a small box, knitting needles and a long strip of paper. Pupils draw a sequence of pictures (and words) on the paper, wrap the paper around the needles then turn the needles around to present each picture on screen as they narrate their story.

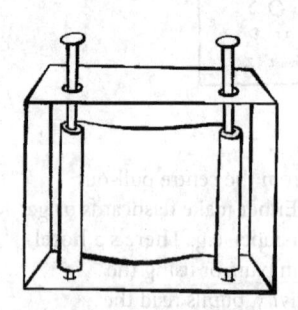

71 Menus

Pupils make their own menu cards, including typical national and regional foods and local currency. These can be used in role plays.

72 Animation

Use the corner of an exercise book or staple two pieces of paper together. Draw a similar figure on each piece of paper but slightly change the body position on the second sheet. Then roll the top sheet around a pencil. Move the pencil quickly backwards and forwards to create the illusion of movement. Pupils can move around the class and try out their classmates' pictures. Talk to the pupils about their picture, e.g.
Anna, have you drawn a boy or a girl?
What's he/she doing?

73 Flick books

More complex animations can be created by drawing several figures on successive pages, each performing a different stage of an action. Flick the pages quickly and watch the figure move.

74 Twenty questions

Pupils work in pairs using the town pieces and baseboard. P1 makes a picture. P2 asks **yes/no** type questions and tries to create an identical picture, e.g.
Is there a bank in your town?
Is the bank by the library?

P2 may ask a maximum of twenty questions. The object is to work out his or her partner's picture by asking as few questions as possible. Pupils then compare their pictures. Change roles. The game can be simplified by limiting the number of pieces to be used.

Extra material

There is no limit to the resources that can be brought into the classroom to supplement topic-based work. Most ideas need little more than some advance planning. Here are just a few ideas.

75 Thirty days

A collection of English nursery rhymes is a useful teaching resource. Modern rhymes, particularly, where the vocabulary and meaning are less obscure, can be effective vehicles for reinforcing language points or presenting language items in a new context.

This traditional English rhyme, for example, can be used to reinforce the names of the months of the year:
Thirty days has September,
April, June and November.
All the rest have thirty-one.
Except February alone,
Which has but twenty-eight days clear
And twenty-nine each leap year.

Pupils could write the rhyme out on a large sheet of paper and use it as part of a wall display or scene-setter for the topic.

176

76 Realia

All teachers use realia in the classroom even if it is just picking up everyday objects and asking pupils to identify them. There are many exercises in *New Stepping Stones* in which the use of everyday objects will add an element of realism to the language practice. The following are only suggestions – you can probably think of many more.

76a English newspapers

Many countries have a newspaper for their English-speaking community, e.g. the *Athens News* in Greece. Their TV guides can prove very useful as they present authentic English within the context of the pupils' own community. (It is often highly amusing to see the foreign translation of a programme title, too.)

76b Food packets

To make role plays more realistic in the **Places** topic, bring empty packets of food items into the classroom.

76c Toy cars

Toy cars can be raced to physically demonstrate ordinal numbers.

Organising your classroom

77 Storing materials

In terms of classroom management, there are advantages in keeping each pupil's cut-outs in the classroom to avoid them being lost or forgotten. The sheets can be cut out and stored one at a time, either the first time a particular set is used, or alternatively a lesson can be set aside early on in the course to prepare them all at once. (The cut-outs should be returned to pupils at the end of term.) The logistics of storing these materials will be influenced by the availability of space, class size, and the number of classes you teach. The ideas below are intended only as suggestions.

1 **If space is limited:**
a Give each pupil a large envelope. Tell them to write their name and class clearly on the envelope. Put the sheets of cut-outs inside. Collect the envelopes and store in a folder.
b When cut-outs are used for the first time, hand out the envelopes. Pupils cut out their own pieces. Give each pupil an elastic band or a small envelope for storing the pieces after use. (The cutting-out can, of course, be done in advance.) Always return individual envelopes to the class folder for storage.

2 **If there is more space available**, the individual packs can be stored in separate folders.
a Store the original sheets as suggested in 1a above.
b Use a separate folder for each pack. You will need four small envelopes for each class member. Instead of returning all cut-out material to the large envelope, put it into small envelopes and store in separate folders. It is useful to colour code the folders according to the topics in the Coursebook. Use either coloured folders or attach coloured stickers to the folder.

Encourage pupils to take care of the materials. To avoid the problem of misplaced items, it is useful to get pupils to count the pieces before putting them away. This activity is also useful for practising counting aloud in English.

Tapescripts

Starter Lesson 1
(continued from page 14)

Tapescript (with answers):
1. What colours are the pens? // (Red and purple)
2. How many legs has the monster got? // (Five)
3. What letters are in the picture? // (A and F)
4. How many carrots are there in the picture? // (Three)
5. What colour's the plane? // (White and yellow)
6. What colour are the monster's teeth? // (Yellow)
7. Is the pencil brown or blue? // (Brown)
8. How many different vegetables are there? // (Four)
9. What's the girl wearing? // (A sweatshirt and a skirt)
10. What colour's the sofa? // (Pink)

4ᶜ Lesson 1
(continued from page 142)

Tapescript

1
I get up at five past eight, then I get washed and clean my teeth at about ten past eight. // I get dressed at quarter past eight and then have my breakfast at about twenty-five past eight. // Breakfast takes about twenty minutes. Then I comb my hair and go to school at ten to nine. // I have lunch at quarter past twelve every day and finish school at half past three. // After school, I usually play with my friends at about four o'clock. I do my homework at about five o'clock and have dinner at about quarter to six. // After dinner, at about seven o'clock, I wash up and then read my book at about eight o'clock // and go to bed at about nine o'clock.

2
Let me see, what did I do yesterday? I got up at nine o'clock and I got washed at about five past nine. // I had breakfast at about twenty-five past nine and went to school at about quarter to ten. // I had lunch at ten past one and I finished school at twenty past four. // After school, I played football - that was about half past four - and then I went home. // I did my homework at about quarter to six and then I wrote a letter to my penfriend at about half past six. // We had dinner at about quarter past seven and at eight o'clock I watched TV. I went to bed at twenty past nine.

3
I usually get up at half past seven and every morning I have a bath at about quarter to eight. // Then I get dressed at about eight and have my breakfast at about ten past eight. // Breakfast takes about twenty-five minutes. // I usually go to school at a quarter to nine. // I have lunch at school at five past twelve every day and I finish school at twenty-five past three. // After school, I usually play volleyball from about half past three to half past four . // After volleyball I go swimming at five o'clock and then I go home. // We have dinner at about seven and I always go to bed quite early, at about quarter past eight.

4ᴰ Lesson 1
(continued from page 148)

Tapescript:
1. How long does it take to get from Sydney to Bombay by boat? ~ 228 hours.
2. How long does it take to get from London to Lisbon by train? ~ 36 hours.
3. How long does it take to get from Tokyo to Sydney by plane? ~ 10 hours.
4. How long does it take to get from New York to Tokyo by boat? ~ 374 hours.
5. How long does it take to get from Acapulco to New York by bus? ~ 68 hours.
6. How long does it take to get from Lisbon to Cairo by boat? ~ 52 hours.
7. How long does it take to get from Rio to Sydney to plane? ~ 22 hours.
8. How long does it take to get from Tokyo to London by bus? ~ 175 hours.
9. How long does it take to get from Bombay to Cairo by train? ~ 80 hours.
10. How long does it take to get from Cairo to Rio by plane? ~ 12 hours.
11. How long does it take to get from London to Tokyo by boat? ~ 494 hours.
12. How long does it take to go round the world from London to London by plane? ~ 42 hours.

Wordlist

This wordlist contains all the words presented in *New Stepping Stones*, Level 2, and gives the pages upon which they first appear. The letters AB indicate that the words are in the Activity Book and the letter R indicates that the words are in the Reader. The words in **bold type** are used actively in production and the pupils should know these words. Pupils may have an active knowledge of other words, though it is not a requirement of the course that they are able to produce them.

Word	Page	Word	Page	Word	Page	Word	Page
add	54	**boat AB**	51	clown AB	2	Dutch	11
address	21	**body AB**	53	**coins**	10	each	54
advertise	45	born AB	61	**collect**	11	earth R	7
advertisement	45	both R	7	collection	11	earthworm	17
aeroplane AB	51	bottle AB	31	**comb**	13	east	20
after R	2	bought R	1	come on R	5	edge	49
again	AB	brave	15	**comic**	14	Egypt R	8
all	54	**bread**	24	compass AB	74	eighty	59
along	49	**breakfast**	50	costs	14	**elephant**	7
alphabet AB	48	Britain	10	could R	6	**empty**	40
always	34	British	11	count	3	engine	27
American AB	21	brush	51	counter	54	**England**	21
ancient R	8	building	15	countries	10	**English AB**	8
angry	57	burger R	3	cross	28	enormous R	5
another	54	burn	27	crunch R	8	European Union	17
answer AB	41	bus	26	cry	34	**evening**	52
April	36	but R	5	cut out AB	11	every AB	75
art	14	**butcher's**	24	**dance**	8	everyone	36
asleep	50	**buy**	24	danger	28	excellent AB	22
ate	57	by	23	**dark**	40	excited R	8
August	36	cafe	23	darkest AB	55	exercise book AB	30
Australia AB	20	calendar AB	45	**date**	49	eye	2
autograph	10	capital	39	daylight R	2	face	13
awful R	7	**car park**	23	dead R	7	family AB	11
back AB	6	**card AB**	30	December	36	fast	15
backwards R	6	**cartoon**	14	describe	37	**faster**	26
badge	10	celebration	57	design AB	71	**fat**	35
baker's	24	changed R	6	detective	53	**father AB**	41
bank	30	check AB	22	diary AB	59	**favourite**	7
bar of chocolate	24	cheeseburger AB	30	dice	54	**February**	36
basketball	6	**chemist's**	24	dig	20	feet	7
be careful	31	children AB	8	dinosaur R	8	felt pen AB	74
beautiful	15	chimp	15	**dirty**	40	fetch	27
because	42	Chinese	57	divide AB	61	few R	8
behind	38	Christmas	57	dodo R	8	field R	7
between AB	26	**church**	23	**doll**	11	fill	34
bicycle R	3	**cinema**	23	dragon	57	**film**	15
bigger	26	circle AB	2	**draw**	12	finally AB	68
biggest AB	26	**clean**	12	dress AB	30	find	2
bird R	1	**cleaned**	50	**drink**	12	finish	9
birthday AB	11	clever	34	drive	28	fix	34
blackboard AB	26	click R	7	driver AB	34	**flag**	17

179

flew R	1	homework	12	lots	57	opened R	7
floor	7	hop R	1	**love AB**	41	**opposite**	23
fold AB	38	hope	51	lunch	50	order AB AB	46
foot AB	8	hopped R	1	machine R	7	other side R	4
football	6	**horse**	8	magazine	14	outside AB	72
forty	59	horse-drawn car R	8	magic R	4	packet	24
forwards AB	54	**hospital**	23	make AB	71	**paint**	12
found	57	hotel	23	Malta	28	**painted**	57
France	10	hour	48	map	54	paper	3
free	54	**how many ...? AB**	2	**March**	36	paper clip AB	38
Friday	52	huge R	6	match AB	46	paper fastener AB	74
friend AB	4	human R	3	**May**	36	**park**	23
full	40	hundred AB	8	measure	36	parrot	20
furniture	24	hurry up R	8	**medicine**	24	party	57
future R	7	image R	6	met R	8	**pass AB**	71
garage	30	imagine AB	71	midday	52	passport AB	52
gave R	8	important	57	midnight	52	**past**	48
get dressed	50	**in front of**	38	million	29	**pen AB**	30
get up	50	inside R	7	**minute**	48	pence	24
get washed	50	island	20	mirror R	4	pencil sharpener AB	30
ghost	38	Italian	11	**Monday**	52	people	10
giant R	6	**Italy**	10	**month**	36	person	36
give	57	**January**	36	**morning**	13	**pet shop**	4
glass	40	Japan AB	20	most	56	**piano**	8
goal AB	6	**Japanese**	11	mother R	5	picture AB	4
gold	17	journey AB	68	**motorbike**	26	piece	3
good at AB	19	**July**	36	**mountain**	20	pig	14
goodbye R	6	jumped R	1	moustache AB	21	pirate	20
got dressed	50	**June**	36	move	54	**play**	6
got up	50	knight in armour R	8	**museum**	23	**played**	52
grandmother	52	large	24	myself	51	player AB	6
great R	7	**last**	7	name AB	8	pointed R	5
Greece AB	20	laughed R	5	**near**	23	**Poland**	10
greedy AB	42	leap year AB	61	never	34	policeman R	2
group	36	leave	54	New Year	57	popular	10
guess AB AB	46	left R	3	New Zealand AB	20	population	29
guitar	8	left-hand side	28	**new**	35	**postcard**	10
had	50	let's R	5	newsagent's	24	poster	45
hairy R	2	**library**	23	newspaper	24	**pound AB**	30
half	48	**light**	40	next R	6	pour	27
happen	39	lightest AB	55	ninety AB	75	present	57
happy	35	line AB AB	46	**north**	20	programme AB	17
hate AB	41	list AB	71	**November**	36	put	7
have a bath	12	listen R	3	number AB	21	puzzle AB	7
have a nice time	31	longer	36	nurse R	2	**quarter**	48
height AB	52	look for	20	**o'clock**	13	**question AB**	41
here AB	41	**look like**	42	**October**	36	quickly AB	4
hero	15	look out R	8	of course R	5	raining	9
himself R	4	looked	AB	oh dear	59	ran R	1
hobby	10	70		**old**	35	**read**	8
hole AB	74	**lorry**	26	oldest	37	ready, steady, go! AB	61

180

rectangle AB	2	smallest AB	44	**telephone number AB**		walked R	8
ride	8	smiled R	4		25	wanted R	1
right AB	41	smoke	28	tennis	6	**wash**	13
right-hand side	28	so R	1	the UK AB	20	**wash up**	12
river	20	**soap**	24	the USA	10	**washed**	52
road	28	someone AB	11	their R	7	**watch**	12
roared R	6	**something**	2	then AB	68	watch out	31
robbed	53	sometimes AB	26	**there AB**	41	**watched**	50
robber	53	song AB	8	**thick**	40	wave	51
robbery	53	sorry	59	**thin**	35	waved R	6
robot	15	**south**	20	**thing**	2	**Wednesday**	52
round AB	11	space	34	**third**	7	week	48
roundabout	28	**Spain AB**	11	thought R	8	weight AB	52
run R	1	**Spanish**	11	thousand R	8	went R	5
Russia	21	**spell**	21	throw	54	were	53
sad	35	**sports**	11	thud R	8	**west**	20
safety pin AB	11	**spy**	2	**Thursday**	52	**wheel**	26
said R	4	**square AB**	2	**ticket AB**	51	who	53
sail AB	53	**stamp**	10	**time**	48	wild	28
same	37	stand	34	tiny R	5	windmill R	8
Saturday	52	start	9	tired R	8	winner	54
saw R	5	started R	7	together	34	**woman**	35
say	34	**station**	23	tomorrow AB	63	work R	3
school R	2	stay AB	75	too R	4	world	10
scissors AB	38	step	51	**toothpaste**	24	**write**	12
score AB	22	stepped R	7	top	34	**year**	36
scream R	3	stick AB	74	total AB	22	yesterday AB	59
second	7	stopped R	8	touch	7	**young**	35
second	48	stopwatch AB	59	touched R	4	youngest	37
secret AB	49	story	14	town R	2		
select	37	strange R	2	traffic lights	28		
September	36	street R	2	**train AB**	51		
shape	3	stretch	51	transport AB	34		
ship R	8	string	36	travel	54		
shocked R	7	strong	15	treasure	20		
shopping list AB	29	studio	45	tree	15		
shortest	36	stupid	34	**triangle AB**	2		
shouted R	5	suddenly R	4	triangular AB	11		
silly	57	**Sunday**	52	**trousers AB**	2		
silver	26	supermarket	23	**Tuesday**	52		
sing	8	surprised R	7	turn	2		
sit	34	swam R	1	twenty	59		
sixty	59	swimming pool AB	6	two-thirds	50		
skate	8	switch R	7	understand R	4		
ski	6	take	54	upside down	39		
skip	8	talk	15	**van**	26		
sky R	7	tallest AB	28	**Vietnam**	10		
sleep	12	tape AB	11	visit	54		
slept R	1	taxi AB	34	visited	52		
slow	35	team AB	19	**volleyball**	6		
slowly R	6	**teddy bear**	57	waiter R	2		

181

New Stepping Stones

SURVEY OF CONTENTS

Level 1

Topics

Colours and numbers
Pets
School
Families
The Body
Festivals:
    Christmas
    Easter

Main language items

Hello.
Hi.
I'm ...
What's your name?
Who's this?
What's this?
This is ...
What's that?
Is it a ...?
Is this ...?
Where's the ...?

What colour is ...?
Prepositions: in, on, under
I've got ...
My brother is called ...
His/Her name is ...
Possessive –'s
How old are you?
Is Julie tall?
How tall is she?
She's got long hair.
How many legs has the monster got?

Level 2

Topics

The alphabet
Clothes
Food
Animals
Homes
Festivals:
    Hallowe'en

Main language items

What's this?
What are these?
Whose is this?
What are you wearing?
Is she wearing a coat?
I'm wearing ..., She's wearing ...
I like ..., I don't like ...
Does he like ...?
Yes, he does. No, he doesn't.
My favourite colour is ...
can/can't

Can tigers swim?
What do lions eat?
Do lions eat meat?
They eat ..., They don't eat ...
Prepositions: next to, between
Where do they live?
Does Julie live in a flat?
What's the biggest room in her house?
What's on the table?
There's ..., There are ...

Level 3

Topics

Shapes
Spare time:
   Collecting things
   Comics and heroes
Places:
   Towns
   Buildings
   Shops
   Transport
Opposites
Time:
   Measuring time
   Past and future

Main language items

What's he/she doing?
What are they doing?
He's playing tennis.
They're playing volleyball.
first, second, third, last
Are they Spanish? No, they're …
My favourite comic is …
My hero is …
Where does she live? Where do they live?
What's her address?
How do you spell …?
Prepositions: at, behind, by, in front of, opposite
Where can I buy a …?

It's bigger/faster than …
I'm taller/older than …
Elephants are bigger than …
How old are you?
When's your birthday?
It looks like a …
What's the time?
four o'clock, quarter past/to …
half past …
ten past six, twenty to five, *etc.*
What time did she …?
What did he do in the morning/afternoon?
Where were you at 8 o'clock?
Days of the week
Months of the year

Level 4

Topics

Senses:
   Sight
   Hearing
   Touch
   Taste and smell
Nature:
   The animal world
   Animals of the past
   Animals in danger
   Animals of Britain
Space:
   The solar system
   Robots
   Aliens
   Life in the future
My autobiography:
   Who am I?
   Family, firned and school
   Likes and dislikes
   My future

Main language items

It looks/smells/tastes like …
It feels rough.
I can see/hear a …
I think it's a …
I don't think it's a …
Does he look happy?
I think he looks sad.
What kind of animal is a penguin *etc.*?
It's a bird/fish *etc.*
They are killed for sport.
They are collected as pets.
What's the weather like?
It's hot/cold/snowing *etc.*
Have you seen a …?

Which planet is nearest the sun?
Which planet is between …?
Future will
Are you good at drawing *etc.*?
Would you like to …?
Do you think that …?
I was born on …
I want to be a doctor/teacher/*etc.*
When I was five, I wanted to be a …
When I grow up, I will be …
uncle, aunt, cousin, *etc.*
How many brothers/sisters have you got?
I'm scared of …

183

Addison Wesley Longman Limited,
*Edinburgh Gate, Harlow,
Essex CM20 2JE, England
and Associated Companies throughout the world.*

© Julie Ashworth and John Clark, Addison Wesley Longman Ltd. 1998

"The right of Julie Ashworth and John Clark to be identified as authors of this Work has been asserted by them in accordance with the Copyright, Designs and Patents Act 1988."

All rights reserved; no part of this publication may be reproduced, stored in a retrieval system, or transmitted in any form or by any means, electronic, mechanical, photocopying, recording or otherwise, without the prior written permission of the Publishers.

First published in this edition 1998

ISBN 0 582 31133 0

Set in 3.5mm Columbus

Printed in Spain by Graficas Estella

Cover illustration by Chris Mould

Illustrated by: Bernice Lum, Trevor Dunton, Julie Ashworth, David Le Jars, Chris Mould, Emma Holt, Neil Layton, Lisa Smith, Uwe Mayer, Tanya Hurt-Newton, Julian Mosedale, Sue Twekesbury David Lewis.

Acknowledgements

Thanks to the following people who helped in the development of *New Stepping Stones*:

In Argentina: María Mónica Marinakis, Myriam Raquel Pardo Herrero.

In France: Christiane Fatien, Catherine Quantrell-Park, Jean-Pierre Top.

In Poland: Magdalena Dziob, Ilona Kubrakiewicz, Urszula Mizeracka.

In Spain: Ana Baranda, Mercé Barroetabeña, Maribel Cequier, Marisa Colomina Puy, Paloma Garcia Consuegra, Susana Garralda, Jordi Gonzalez, María Antonieta Millán Gómez, Immaculado Minguez, Mady Musiol, María Elena Pérez Márquez, María Angeles Ponce de León, Antonio Tejero.

In the UK: Viv Lambert, Sally McGugan.

and to those who contributed so much to the original edition:

Janet Ashworth, Sylvia Bakapoulou, Kathleen Chiacchio, Lety Dominguez, Marijke Dreyer, Peta Harloulakou, Gilbert Horobin, Mrs Ioannou, Anita Lycouri, Lucy McCullagh, John Oakley, Mr Proudfoot, Lorena Rosas, Gordon Slaven, Ray Tongue, Jo Walker.